Totteridge

P. Mfs's Esqr

M. Da Cfha Esq.

Whetstone

P   A   R   I   S   H

Button Hole

Frith

Green

Alms Hawse

Cold Harbour

Wood Side

C   o   m   m   o   n

Fryan-Barnet

VIII

Wood House

Colney

Hatch

Veather Street

Grass
Farm
Finchley

F   I   N   C   H   L   E   Y

Lane

Ballards

Ba llards

VIII

B   A   R   N   E   T

VIII

Dutchseller's
Lane

Place Lane Lane

Short
Lane

Brown Well

Church

Long

Ackobbler

Wroted Cw

VII

Copts
Farm

East

End

Hog Marki

Finchley

Park
Gate

Forty Green

Hanson Bridge

Muswell Hill

MILL HILL

To Peter

We walked Mill Hill together
60 years ago

Best Wishes

[signature]
Aug 1984.

The end papers of this book are a section from the
map, 'A Topographical Map of the County of
Middlesex' by John Rocque, published in 1754.

MILL HILL

A HISTORY OF MILL HILL
IN ITS ENVIRONMENT

BERNARD H OAK

THE PENTLAND PRESS LTD
Edinburgh, Cambridge, Durham.

First published in 1994 by
The Pentland Press
Hutton Close
South Church
Durham

© Bernard H Oak 1994

ISBN 1 85821 202 2

Illustrations by John Martindale MCSD
(except where indicated by typeset captions)

Printed in Great Britain by Bookcraft (Bath) Ltd

This book is dedicated
to
Sheila

ACKNOWLEDGEMENTS

First of all I thank Sheila Faruk for making me believe that there really is more to life after retirement than household chores, who convinced me that there is a need for this book and that I should write it. My appreciation also to the members of my family, and our close friends, for their patience and all the encouragement they gave during the revisiting of places long forgotten, and subsequent writing and editing. To those who bothered to answer my letters I can only say that I could not have written the book without you.

My thanks also to Dr David Bosworth for reading and editing the chapter on Geology and Geography, to the librarian of the Royal Society for providing me with reference biographies of the Fellows who lived or worked in Mill Hill, to Arthur Ingram (who knows more about trains and buses than I will ever know) for checking the chapters on road and rail transport, to Patricia Austin the librarian of the British Transport Museum, to Jim Rea of the London Borough of Barnet Parks Dept who without hesitation pointed me in the right direction and gave me a piece of his valuable time. Last, but certainly not least my thanks to my son Peter (Ned) who spent so many hours getting to grips with the new computer and software.

My appreciation to the total strangers who were prepared without introduction to answer my questions and to those people who found the time to read through the chapters that concerned them. Finally my gratitude to Lewis Brooks BA, and my son Christopher who both read the entire script looking for over-duplication and anomolies, even though Mill Hill is almost foreign territory to them.

FOREWORD

L ocal history and other green and environmental issues have been popular topics for some time and any library or bookshop reflects this interest. No doubt the fact that these subjects are now taught in our schools is a contributing factor but there are other reasons and there seems to be a genuine desire to know what is happening on our planet and what happened in the past. I was delighted to be asked by Bernard Oak to write a foreword to his book. After 50 years when not a single author thought that Mill Hill was worthy of a study there have now been three in the last four years but all very different. There is certainly room for another volume.

The difference between this book and the others is the scope and the depth. The author does not assume that the reader has an extensive background knowledge of people in history, or any other aspect of the past, but goes to great lengths to fit the local events into a broader national perspective. All features of social and local history have been documented and where necessary expanded. The chapters are presented in a logical sequence that makes the reading easy, but nevertheless totally absorbing. In most cases the chapters are self contained which means that there is no need for the frustrating process of cross reference just when the reader is getting interested.

Occasionally the author brings in small references that relate to his own experiences at the time. These help to tie the event to a personality, but they are not overdone. The history of the name Mill Hill, its geology and geography, the people and transport, and much more are all dealt with in a well documented way. The story of Mill Hill's gas works and why it took so long for the Hendon area to be connected to an electricity supply is almost worth a book on its own, and the same could be said for many other items in the book. Most of the chapters are broadly based and in addition some items of a more general historical nature have been included to show where Mill Hill fits into the overall picture. Examples of these are education, the railways, and the history of health care.

Much of Mill Hill is still relatively unspoilt and I am sure that most of the people who live in the area would like to keep it that way. This book should certainly encourage an active interest. It is a book of considerable diversity and offers a fascinating insight into this little bit of north London to anyone who wants to know something about the place in which they live.

Martyn Kempson.
Controller of Libraries and Arts, London Borough of Barnet.

INTRODUCTION

A s a child I knew Mill Hill nearly as well as I knew my own back yard. I lived in Finchley, but on the borders of Mill Hill so there was not a single footpath I hadn't walked, or stream I hadn't dammed, and as a family we knew all the best places to gather blackberries or sloes or crab-apples. And when a few years later to walk was to escape from prying eyes then the best place for a kiss and cuddle became suddenly important, the fields of Mill Hill had a new attraction.

I have lived in Hertfordshire now for 35 years, so it is quite a long time since Mill Hill was my personal stamping ground. To be honest, for many years I hardly ever gave it a thought except as a cut to avoid the traffic when the A1 or the road through Finchley and Barnet were particularly badly blocked.

Then it was suggested to me by a Mill Hill librarian that maybe I would like to write a history of Mill Hill, 'Because after all you know the area well'. I protested that my knowledge was really quite sparse, definitely out of date and certainly not as good as people still living there who would not buy a book about their area written by a 'foreigner'; and it was years since I had set foot on the roads and footpaths. In short I did not think that I was competent to write the book.

But persistence paid off. I borrowed every book that I could find that made any mention of Mill Hill (it is surprising how many do and how they contradict each other), searched through my own large collection of books, and started to read. Fine so far, but the next step was to walk the roads and lanes and footpaths again and take notes and photographs. This was the hard part. Slowly I became hooked on the project.

Finally it is certainly true that more people than ever are becoming interested in environmental issues and local history. This is partly the reason that I was asked to write this book in the first place. Unfortunately individual mobility is a mixed blessing: on the one hand we can visit places of our choice when we want to quickly and easily and learn to appreciate them, on the other hand the irresponsible people amongst us use their cars as a means of disposing of unwanted junk and deposit it in hedgerows and public places everywhere. As I walked Mill Hill I was made aware of this rubbish in every place that I visited that was accessible to wheeled traffic. Probably the worst places of all are the verges and hedges on either side of the A1 between Apex Corner and Stirling Corner and most of this rubbish is unlikely to have been dropped by the residents of Mill Hill. In some places there were even whole lorry loads dumped by 'fly tippers' and the filthy mess left behind when some of the so called 'travelling people' had moved on. This was the only aspect of writing this book that saddened me, and this sort of behaviour certainly did not happen 50 years ago when far fewer people owned cars.

When Macauley wrote, 'An acre in Middlesex is better than a principality in Utopia' we do not know whether he was writing about a particular location. It would be nice to think that he had the Mill Hill area in mind, but even if not it is reassuring that he made such a statement about Middlesex rather than one of the more well recognised pretty places. Much of Middlesex is delightful, and Mill Hill is certainly no exception; it has hills and valleys, old buildings, pleasant walks, and much else, of interest both to the new arrival or established resident, and the casual visitor to seek out.

To remind us that there is indeed much in Mill Hill worthy of a visit, and of preservation too there are places that are blessed with a London Borough of Barnet Blue Plaque, and rather more that are buildings listed by the Department of the Environment as being of historical or architectural interest. All these are listed at the end of the chapter of notable buildings.

As we all know, officially Middlesex is no more, killed off in the great reorganisation of 1965. Yes it was a small county (only Rutland was smaller, and that was swallowed up too), but as an administrative area it

was very ancient. It may be officially dead but it refuses to lie down and to its credit the Post Office seems determined to perpetuate the name, and the Middlesex Cricket Club certainly has no intention of going out of existence or even changing its name. A number of places still have Middlesex as part of the address, Mill Hill alas does not, having long ago been relegated to 'London NW7'. But is there a ray of hope? Of late official looking signs have appeared on some roadsides which display MIDDLESEX and the old coat of arms.

Mill Hill has a very long history, and later chapters will tell more of this. The earliest maps show Mill Hill, and the first guide books have entries, in some cases quite extensive. Strangely enough many of the older guides have much more to say than those of today. For instance *The Handbook to the Environs of London* by James Thorne published in 1876 said of Mill Hill:

'*MILL HILL, Middlesex, a hamlet and eccl district of Hendon, from which it is about two miles north. The Mill Hill station of the Great Northern Railway (Edgware and Highgate line) is three-quarter mile SE of the village. The Midland Railway station is 1 ½ miles west. Population of the eccl district 1,335. Inn 'The King's Head'. The village is an irregular, disjointed collection of houses stretching for a mile along the summit of a hill away from any main line of road. From every clear spot wide views are obtained, and on all sides is a pleasant open green country. Mill Hill is consequently a favourite place of abode, and many good seats with well stocked grounds occur and fine large elms line both sides of the way'.*

The entry then goes on to describe many of the important buildings of the time in over 1,000 words. By comparison the guide books of today have much less to say and often dwell on the trivial aspects, whilst *Bartholomew's Gazetteer of Britain* published in 1977 being an alphabetical list musters a few words, viz:

MILL HILL. London dist in borough of Barnet 9ml/14km NW of Charing Cross'.

This would lead the reader to believe that Mill Hill is about to vanish completely, or at least lose its identity. It is after all now part of a very large London borough. Fortunately this is not likely to happen; people like to have an address with a meaning and the maintenance of the Green Belt will help to prevent Mill Hill from vanishing into a jungle of concrete and red brick. After all we still talk of Bloomsbury, Belgravia and Pimlico and their official identity vanished years ago and when there was a proposal to drop the name Chelsea from all official documents there was such a strong protest that the new borough was named The Royal Borough of Kensington and Chelsea.

But what of Mill Hill today? Fortunately much of the old part has withstood the passage of time very well, a number of buildings are now protected by Preservation Orders so ensuring that they cannot be interfered with or demolished without permission from the Department of the Environment. Even the somewhat unexciting council estate on the southern edge has mellowed with the years. And no doubt as more and more people purchase these houses and thereby gain the right to alter the appearance (the first change is usually a new front door followed by modern windows, both usually totally unsuitable for the style of house) the mellowing process will accelerate.

It would be possible to write a book with page upon page of facts and figures and there is plenty of archive material to make this possible. Most people would prefer, I believe, to have a book for reading as well as a book of reference and that is the way that I have tried to write it, with each chapter as far as possible self-contained. The biggest problem is what to omit and how much to include and the right amount of space for each entry. After all a book of this kind is a very personal thing and can only be a sort of anthology of that which appeals to the writer. For those readers who may feel that the balance is awry I hope that they will appreciate why the text is the way that it is. Spellings, particularly of some family names are another kind of problem: there are in some instances a number of different versions and whilst the most simple in each case has been used in the text the alternatives have been been given as well where they are relevant.

In Potters Bar (where I have lived for many years) much hot air has been generated in recent months about a proposed Tesco development. If the results of rather crude customer surveys are accepted the majority of local people are against it, would not use the Tesco superstore if it is built, and prefer to do their shopping in the old traditional small shops. Which shops? Where are they?

In this book mention is made of the shops of Mill Hill, mainly those in The Broadway, with a passing reference to The Ridgeway and elsewhere. The writing of Mill Hill is now finished and just as all is ready for the Publisher's verdict, Dewhurst's the country's biggest butchers chain, has announced that 600 of their shops will be closed with a loss of 1,000 jobs. Once nearly every town had its Dewhurst's. The directors say that they are hoping some shop managers will purchase their stores which seems rather optimistic.

There are still some small privately owned butchers, and one of these is Vincett's Quality Butcher at the top of Hammers Lane, a one-shop business of 152 years standing, and recently cited in the Daily Telegraph as being at the opposite end of the butcher's chain to Dewhurst's. The current proprietor, Bernie Longhurst, admits that to keep going against the supermarket chains is a struggle. There is no denying that the majority prefer to make all of their purchases under one roof in spite of protestations to the contrary. No doubt many of Mr Longhurst's clientele come from the better-off parts of Mill Hill and are not distressed by the sight of raw meat in a butcher's shop, and appreciate the guidance that a professional can give. The labels on a supermarket shelf are no help.

Nevertheless people prefer to buy bloodless, anonymous meat wrapped in clear plastic. Or worse still, pre-cooked, and almost pre-masticated food that requires no knowledge of cooking or nutrition at all. The volume of advertising for convenience foods that we see on television is an indication of the demand for these foods.

One other point; it is not realistic to write only of Mill Hill as if it is an island. In the early years it was a part of the Manor of Hendon and to this day remains tied to Hendon in many ways. The history of Mill Hill has had to be written with its neighbours very much in mind.

Bernard H Oak. 1994

A HISTORY OF MILL HILL

CONTENTS

CHAPTER I

THE GEOGRAPHY AND THE GEOLOGY

In the years before 1965 Mill Hill was a part of the Borough of Hendon: a large borough approximately 11km long and 5km wide on the north-western edge of Greater London in the county of Middlesex and pushing hard against the Green Belt to the north. In the great boundary realignments and county reorganisations of 1965 Hendon was combined with its neighbour Finchley and the Barnets to create the London Borough of Barnet. A huge administrative area of 8,953ha (22,123 acres or a little under 35 square miles) and a population at the time of around 316,000.

The Mill Hill at which we shall be looking is really two quite distinct places one within the other, or rather one specific place the original Mill Hill Village - and the London NW7 postal district, a part of the London Borough of Barnet now labelled Mill Hill.

Geographically Mill Hill is situated between $51^038'6''$ and $51^038'33''$ N Lat and $0^0.11'40''$ and $0^0.15'50''$ W Long. The Medical Research Centre on The Ridgeway is probably as near to the centre of Mill Hill as makes no odds, (it is also the most prominent building) and its map reference is Pathfinder 1140 (TQ29\39) 233925. The area of Mill Hill is approximately 1,400ha (3,460 acres).

WHY WE ARE HERE

The late Dr C E M Joad when asked a question would always answer, 'It all depends upon what you mean', and then proceed to give a qualified reply. If we pose questions about the geology of any place we must be sure that we know the time scale about which we are referring.

By normal standards Mill Hill is contained within an area of geological stability. That is to say we are not usually subject to violent upheavals (such as earthquakes) and we do not expect that this situation will change. Certainly not within the historical times covered by this book. But we are really only talking here about some 2,000 years, hardly a speck in time compared with the age of the earth. If there had not been progressive changes in past ages and indeed at times violent ones then the shape of Mill Hill, its hills and valleys, its streams and lakes, and the type of soil would be quite different from what they are today.

If we agree that in the short term the only changes taking place are those caused by *Homo Sapiens* that is only true insofar as we refer to what we can see from day to day. Nevertheless small subtle changes are taking place all the time: streams are continually eroding their banks as they meander, and as they erode away in one place they deposit silt and pebbles elsewhere. Sometimes there is a bigger change, for instance when we experience a long spell of particularly wet or dry weather and a stream either overflows its banks and changes course, or a pond dries up for ever. Sometimes these changes are inconvenient to land owners and official bodies, then the streams are culverted and lost.

Are we in a stable environment? In the short term probably yes, in the long term definitely no. Firstly there are the changes caused by our own carelessness or selfishness: acid rain which if unchecked will eventually kill all of our trees, the greenhouse effect which could raise the World's ambient temperature and may already be causing all sorts of changes to the weather, the destruction of the ozone layer which would expose us to undesirable levels of ultra-violet light with high risk of skin cancers, and the dumping of toxic waste including untreated sewage sludge, and over application of nitrogen fertilizers which may well poison our water supplies and worse. All these factors affect Mill Hill as much as anywhere else. It is no use putting signs on lamp-posts saying 'Acid-rain free Zone' like some towns and boroughs put 'Nuclear-free Zone': it will not keep the problem away. As long ago as the 17th Century John Donne wrote 'No man is an island entire of itself....And therefore never send to know for whom the bell tolls: It tolls for thee', and in those days the environment was not at risk. The problem is that we do not know when we have gone too far, if indeed we have not already done so. The changes are progressive and may not be noticed in a single life time. Nevertheless we must not think that they are really something that we cannot influence, neither should we say that in any case the effects will probably not be felt during out lifetime so they are someone else's problem.

Natural changes are different. They are nearly always long term and therefore may not seem relevant to us here. True, but they are interesting none the less because they tell us why our environment is as it is. Leaving aside the early evolution of the Earth, first there is the Ice Ages. 'Is' rather than 'was' because each Ice Age in the past has been followed by a period of temperate climate when the ice and glaciation retreated to the polar regions. We do not know whether the last Ice Age was truly the last or whether we are just in one of the temperate spells. We do know that Ice Ages that are past have left their influence. Secondly there is the progressive tilting of our island: roughly speaking the land south of a line drawn from The Wash to the Bristol Channel is sinking and the land to the north is rising. Fortunately we are too far from the sea and too high above sea level for this to affect us in Mill Hill directly.

Some natural changes take place very quickly, and although the effects are only short term on a geographical basis they are very important to us. They can be dramatic too, and the ravages of the recent plague of Dutch Elm Disease are certainly proof of this. In the space of less than five years all of our old elms, so much a part of the English landscape shrivelled and died. It could be centuries before these majestic trees once again grace the skyline. (What would a Constable or Gainsborough landscape be without elms?).

Then of course there was the terrific storm of October 1987 (which is always referred to as the 'hurricane' although meteorologically just a very vigorous depression) when in five hours (not five years this time) millions of mature trees in south east England were either smashed or flattened and Mill Hill being in the main high and very exposed certainly did not escape. Since then we have had a series of severe storms, particularly at the beginning of 1990, and this time because there were no leaves on the deciduous trees the main casualties were evergreens, and scots pines and cedars suffered very badly with many losses. Nevertheless other trees were destroyed too, for instance a magnificent beech on The Ridgeway known to be about 300 years was blown over. Of course there is nothing really peculiar about this: germination, growth, death, and decay are all a part of the natural order and will always be so.

In Rudyard Kipling's poem *The River's Tale* (which for those who are not familiar with it is about the River Thames) are the lines:

> *'But I'll have you know that these waters of mine,*
> *Were once a branch of the River Rhine,*
> *When hundreds of miles to the east I went*
> *And England was joined to the Continent'*

Geologically the time referred to in this poem is only yesterday because there was a land bridge to the continent only 7,000 years ago. A study of geological maps of the area around our island shows that it has gone through a series of changes. The 'land' has been very hot and very cold, very humid and completely arid and sometimes even pleasantly temperate. In addition 'land' in one period has been under the sea at another, in fact the sea to land and back sequence has occurred many times. Perhaps the most graphic illustration of this is a coalfield in the north of England where there were 18 seams one above the other, so this area was submerged 18 times.

Any local gardener will confirm that the natural sub-soil of Mill Hill is clay, an orange coloured colloidal sticky substance which is only workable in the spring and autumn but a gluey mass in the winter, and often sunbaked with cracks you could nearly fall down in the summer. But this only applies to the clay near the surface: deep down it is slate-grey in colour, highly compressed and therefore much harder. The surface clay obtains its colour from the oxidation of particles in the clay which contain iron.

The London clay in the Finchley, Hendon, Mill Hill area is of considerable thickness, in places up to 70m. At some of the highest points there is a capping of sand, and between the sand and the clay is a sandy loam of varying thickness. On the sides of the River Brent valley there are in places considerable deposits of a river gravel, which indicate that a much greater river flowed through this valley in the distant past. The valleys through which the small streams such as the Dollis Brook run today once contained rivers large and vigorous enough to gouge out these valleys. The Dollis Brook and River Brent have another peculiarity, that is banks of rounded pebbles are continually being deposited as these streams twist and turn which would not be expected as the flow is over clay. The origin of the pebbles is not known, although no doubt geologists have their theories about them.

The main interests to geologists are the layers of clay, chalk and gravel. In the early periods of the Earth's formation, from Silurian, Devonian etc to Cretaceous the area that is now the south east of England was more often under water than dry land, and during this period the underlying chalk beds of the Thames Valley were formed.

Throughout the Eocene epoch a huge river delta lay across southern England over the old and by now eroded chalk bed. From time to time the sea flooded from the east. In the frequently (by geological standards) changing conditions of delta, brackish lagoons and flooded shore-line the great variety of sands, pebble and gravel beds, and of course the London Clay were laid down.

In the Oligocene Period which followed, the area was once again flooded and in some places thin layers of marl and limestone were laid down. During the Miocene Period the sea retreated once again and almost all of what is now the British Isles became dry land, the first time for millions of years and no further deposition took place.

From this it will be seen that the hills and valleys that make up the Mill Hill of today are not as a result of a piling of sediments but rather the eroding away by rains and rivers of what was once a high flat plateau.

To obtain an accurate picture of the stratigraphic layers beneath our feet we have to rely on the analysis of cores from drilling. These normally have a commercial purpose but are very informative for a geologist as

4

well. An earlier writer (E T Evans) reported on a 19th Century deep well in Kentish Town of 397m (1302ft) and listed nine different layers beneath the London clay: various sands, flints, chalk and conglomerates, and surmised that the same layers are probably present elsewhere in the area. Most of our main sewers were also laid down 100 years or more ago, long before the ground had been disturbed to any depth, and these excavations uncovered many interesting finds. There were reports of a great variety of fossilised remains of prehistoric animal and plant life. An article of the time likened many of the fossils to plants that are to be found in sub-tropical areas today. Proof that where we now stand was once much warmer than it is today or rather that this country was once in a much warmer latitude than it is now.

Unfortunately no complete geological survey of the area that includes Mill Hill has been carried out for many years and it is unlikely that this will be done in the foreseeable future. Indeed because these *Ordnance Survey* maps are prepared on a purely commercial basis and the demand is very small there are no plans to even reprint the last edition. No copies of the last printing are available.

Although there are no great heights around London the altitude varies considerably and the gradients are quite steep. There is a ring of hills with the Chilterns in the north and the Downs in the south, and within this ring are other hills and ridges. The London Basin, with its surrounding hills is all a part of the fold system that formed the Alps, the Pyrenees, the Weald and the South Downs, and even the centre ridge in the Isle of Wight ending at the Needles. To the north and west of London, the area that concerns us here, is a series of prominent ridges. Nearest to central London is a ridge which contains Crouch Hill, Hampstead Heath, Highgate Hill, and Muswell Hill. Outside this is a more complicated series of heights separated from the central range by the valley of the River Brent.

There is a long ridge running from High Barnet through Arkley, Barnet Gate, and Elstree to Stanmore. The highest point on this road is at Barnet Gate and is 141m (it is just outside the Mill Hill boundary). From this ridge two transverse ridges extend southwards starting at Barnet Gate, one to form Totteridge Common and the other Highwood Hill and the ridge which contains Mill Hill Village.

Totteridge Lane for this stretch is on an almost level ridge with a spot height of 126m about 300m east of the junction with Hendon Wood Lane. Ellern Mede is contained within a 125m contour which borders the biggest of the Totteridge Long Ponds. (Ellern Mede is an interesting building, it is now a private nursing home but was originally built as a country residence and is in red brick, the favourite building material of the architect, Norman Shaw). The land on either side of Totteridge Lane falls away quite sharply, with the drop from Ellern Mede to the brook (a tributary of the Dollis Brook) of about 50m. Going towards Whetstone, after the War Memorial the land eastwards slopes away again down towards the main part of the Dollis Brook.

Highwood Hill is the southern extremity of the first part of the other ridge mentioned above with a spot height of 137m. Between this point and Barnet Gate the highest contour is 145m at Mote End Farm. At the foot of Highwood Hill there is a spot height of 112m so the descent is 25m in 600m. From here there is another steep rise to The Ridgeway which is almost level at around 120m. From The Ridgeway there are sharp drops on all sides and all roads leading from here have steep gradients: Hammers Lane, Bittacy Hill, Milespit Hill and Holcombe Hill. The altitudes of some other places in Mill Hill are: Mill Hill East and Mill Hill Broadway stations 70m, Northway Circus 82m, National Institute for Medical Research 120m, St Joseph's RC College 105m. Other places of significance in the vicinity are: High Barnet Church 125m, Hendon Parish Church 87m, Hampstead Heath (highest point) 80m, Brockley Hill Stanmore 143m.

Because the highest points of Mill Hill are higher than many other local hills the views are extensive and a considerable distance can be observed, always providing of course that the weather is suitable. Probably the farthest is Leith Hill near Dorking which can be seen from the high point on Mote End Farm. The Round Tower of Windsor Castle can also be seen from this spot and it is also visible from The Ridgeway. The heights of Harrow block the view to the south-west but looking more westwards the hills around Beaconsfield can be made out. The high ground of Totteridge prevents any view to the north, although a short distance outside Mill Hill is Brockley Hill, Stanmore, and from the top of this hill St Albans Abbey can be seen at little more than middle distance.

STREAMS, RIVERS AND LAKES

Mill Hill is watered by two main streams, and within the bounds of Mill Hill are a number of ponds and lakes of various sizes. Some of these are isolated from surface running water, but most either drain into the Dollis Brook to the east or Deans Brook to the west. There are two ponds on The Ridgeway that are important to the Village, the Village Pond, or Angel Pond at the top of Milespit Hill and Sheepwash Pond on the other side of The Ridgeway about 200m north. These must be of considerable geological antiquity. Because of their altitude they have to be spring fed, even so in long dry summers such as those of 1989 and 1990 they both shrank to a fraction of their normal size. Sheepwash Pond is a reminder of earlier days and recalls the period when sheep farming supplemented the staple industry of Mill Hill; growing grass for hay production.

Dollis Brook runs into the River Brent, taking this name at the confluence of the Dollis Brook and the Mutton Brook (by the junction of the A1 and A406 North Circular Road). The Deans Brook joins with the Edgware Brook at Deansbrook Road, Edgware and is called the Silk Stream from this confluence. Both the River Brent and the Silk Stream flow into the Welsh Harp, otherwise known as the Brent Reservoir or in the 19th Century, Kingsbury Reservoir.

The source of the Dollis Brook (and therefore of the River Brent) is a small pond at map reference TQ217946 to the north of Moat Mount Open Space and at an altitude of 110m. From here the flow follows the

plants of the genus Fritillaria

fall in the terrain east or northeast parallel with the ridge which carries Totteridge Lane and on the northern side. At Barnet Underhill the flow turns southwards having dropped to 75m. The general southerly direction is maintained until Woodside Park when a considerable tributary, the Folly Brook, joins from

a westerly direction. This stream rises at the foot of Highwood Hill in Holcombe Dale and follows the valley between Totteridge and Mill Hill until map reference TQ244933 when the stream runs into an area of marsh and lake set in trees which are mainly broad leafed types known as Darlands Lake or Totteridge Ornamental Waters. This is a valuable site because it is on the flight path of some migratory birds. There are also a number of plants of the genus *Fritillaria* for which the area is noted. From here the stream follows a general south-easterly course for about 1.5km to join with the main part of the Dollis Brook. For much of the next 7km or so there are public footpaths and open spaces on one or both sides of the Brook and it forms the boundary between Finchley and Mill Hill until the middle of Holders Hill Road.

The Dean's Brook has its source at the Leg of Mutton Pond in Moat Mount Open Space. A stream from here runs under the A1 to the

Stoney Wood Lake in the Mill Hill Golf Course. Almost immediately it dives under the M1 Motorway and the Midland Railway and then runs into the lake in Stoneyfields Park. It then goes under the A41, runs down the western side of the grounds of John Groom's Crippleage and enters Edgware. For much of the way it is in heavily built up areas of residential property, surfacing occasionally in a park or recreational ground. A writer towards the end of the 19th Century claimed to have seen a kingfisher somewhere around here, today there is more likely to be a discarded supermarket trolley

After the confluence with the Edgware Brook at Deansbrook Road, the combined flow (the Silk Stream), runs down the rear of Edgware General Hospital grounds beside the Northern Line *Underground* on to Burnt Oak and Colindale, under Colindeep Lane and through The Hyde to join the Welsh Harp.

In the years preceding the building of the Watling Estate there was no bridge where the Deans Brook crosses Hale Lane, there was a ford known as the Water Splash which was finally culverted in 1926. Mill Hill was surrounded at one time by fords like this which tended to isolate the communities of Mill Hill from the surrounding area in really bad weather.

The River Brent leaves from the southern extremity of the Reservoir and eventually joins the River Thames at Brentford. Much of the flow is syphoned off at Hanwell into the Grand Union Canal.

FLORA AND FAUNA

Mill Hill was once buried deeply in the large ancient forest that covered the greater part of Middlesex, Hertfordshire and Essex. Very little of this remains local to Mill Hill, just isolated pockets here and there. The largest wooded areas are Scratch Wood, Nut Wood, and Barnet Gate Wood. There are a number of smaller areas of wooded land but there is no way of knowing whether these are really the remains of ancient forests or replantings at a much later date. Farther afield, but still a part of ancient forests are Hadley Woods and Epping Forest, but even these are always under intense pressure from developers and road builders.

The hedgerows of Mill Hill have lost their elms but it is good to see that here and there the old roots are sprouting new growth. We can only hope that there will be insufficient to re-attract the dreaded beetle that is the vector for Dutch Elm Disease. Even without this disease elms are notorious for becoming dangerous as they age because they tend to rot from the centre. There used to be an avenue of elms facing Mill Hill School on The Ridgeway that had been there for over 200 years and after one of these collapsed in a severe storm in 1917 the whole avenue was cut down as a safety measure. A certain amount of replanting of mixed broad leaved trees would not go amiss to replace those killed by Dutch Elm Disease and destroyed by the recent severe storms.

No-one ever expected the motorways (and a section of the M1 runs through Mill Hill) to become a haven for wild life, but that is exactly what has happened. Because the grassy banks are forbidden to ramblers and are not sprayed with insecticides and herbicides they have an advantage over other grassy areas in that (the noise of the traffic apart) they are undisturbed. It is surprising how quickly the wild life learnt to avoid the carriageways: witness the crows that strut up and down the hard shoulders (picking up insects that have been stunned or killed by the traffic) but rarely walk past the edge of the hard shoulder and on to the carriageway and get themselves killed.

Many small wild animals, butterflies, moths, and other insects, plus of course the plants upon which they live and feed, are multiplying on the motorway verges. They are becoming a ribbon eco-system, able to spread plants and small animals quickly and into areas where they may not normally be found. In a few years time it will be well worthwhile carrying out a study of the wild life of the motorways. The smaller birds of prey, particularly kestrels have already made their study and are frequently to be seen hovering over the embankments.

In general the open land of Mill Hill has traditionally been kept for grass and the percentage sown in cereal crops is much less than in the fields a little farther north. During World War II many fields in the Hendon area (and some of these were in Mill Hill) were turned over to cereal crops and yielded a very worthwhile harvest. The fields of Copt Hall were sown in wheat. More surprising than this were the fields sown with flax in Mill Hill Park. Such a beautiful blue when in bloom but a dreadful crop to harvest, all hand work because the complete plant is used even the roots. And the dreadful smell when the plants have been left to decompose in dams (ponds) to get them ready for drying and processing at the flax mill. For many years flax was not grown anywhere in the British Isles, even Irish linen has been made from imported flax. However, because of the need to diversify (and to replace some of the hectares of unwanted wheat) flax is now being grown in considerable quantities in Cambridgeshire, Lincolnshire and Northamptonshire.

Mill Hill has fortunately so far been spared the sickening smell and garish yellow of oilseed rape flowers in the spring. It is regrettable however that there are few true meadows any more. They do not really fit in with the planned farming of today. This means that it is much harder to find anything like the variety of wild flowers, butterflies, and other insects that flourished in these fields in days gone by, however all is not lost because there are a number of open spaces owned by Barnet Borough Council that are left as natural grasslands. Because Mill Hill's fields have not all been turned over to grain production many of the old hedgerows remain so there is something left for the local wildlife.

It would not be possible here to list all of the different types of trees, plants, grasses, fungi (and other flowerless plants) to be found in Mill Hill. The mixture of fields and woods, farms and hedgerows, not to mention ponds and well fertilized gardens, and a nature reserve gives scope for a huge variety of plant types. A search for fungi alone would lead to the discovery of enough species to fill a sizable book, indeed while researching for this chapter a large bright yellow toadstool was seen on a verge in Hammers Lane which came as a very pleasant surprise. The study of the natural history of Mill Hill is worth the attention of an expert and is diverse enough to warrant a volume of its own. For those who are interested the Hertfordshire and Middlesex Wildlife Association welcomes new members, and they have species lists.

A hundred years ago the local ornithological society would have been able to list upwards of 75 species of birds that were to be seen regularly in the local district, and as a bonus there were peacocks at Copt Hall and their screeching could be heard for a long, long way. This number of species could not be achieved today, but nevertheless there is still a considerable variety. There are some notable changes among the more conspicuous types, for instance there are fewer rooks (at one time there was a large rookery in the lower part of Lawrence Street, now Mill Hill Broadway) but far more magpies, fewer jackdaws and jays, probably fewer song birds thanks to magpies and the domestic cat (and it would be a miracle to hear a nightingale or nightjar) and fewer owls of all types. There are still various kinds of water fowl (Mill Hill and district has plenty of ponds and lakes) and the occasional visiting heron finds the attraction of well stocked garden ponds irresistible. The early rising gardener may well have the dubious pleasure of seeing his expensive collection of fish removed almost in the blink of an eye. Probably the biggest variety of small birds in a small area is to be found in the graveyard of St Paul's Church on The Ridgeway.

There is nothing like the variety of wild mammals that were reported by earlier writers. No doubt there are still plenty of rats, (some say as many as there are people) *Rattus norvegicus* and the common house mouse *Mus musculus* but those we can do without and there are certainly voles and shrews around Darland's Lake. On warm summer evenings some bats can still be seen. The grey squirrel is a plentiful pest everywhere and comes right into built-up areas to take cold chips and old apple cores from litter bins as readily as acorns from an oak tree. They will survive because they have adapted to the ways of man. Foxes are also on the increase and in recent years have become much bolder, perhaps they realise that they are in fact safer in town away from the farmer. They are also prepared to rob litter bins. There are still a good number in open areas too and on a recent winter walk around the Darlands Lake the fresh spoor of a large fox could be clearly seen in the soft clay and was easy to follow for a considerable distance.

The flora and fauna of Mill Hill is really what is to be expected today of an area on the edge of London that is half built up and half almost completely rural and all surrounded by main roads. Nothing exotic but worth close examination, and for the knowledgeable some quite unusual wild flowers to be discovered. Plenty too for the artist and photographer, and the keen naturalist and bird-watcher will always find enough to make a walk worthwhile in any weather or at any time of year.

CHAPTER II

THE STORY OF THE NAME

I n many ways the siting of the original hamlet, now Mill Hill Village, was in an obvious place, with the whole of the land to the north of London (Middlesex and much of Hertfordshire) covered with dense and hostile forest a village on a high ridge (some 120m above sea level) would have been well protected. The land falls away quite steeply on both sides giving fine views to the other heights around the north of London, and indeed on clear days much farther afield too.

It is a fair assumption that Mill Hill was so named because it was the hamlet that grew in the vicinity of a mill, and as will be seen there is strong evidence to support this. It should be noted however that the first windmill made its appearance in Britain in the late 12th Century and there was a hamlet on The Ridgeway before that time. To the north of the village is the Mill Field which is reputed to be the site of the original mill of the fourteenth century. There is certainly no mention of a mill in the Domesday Book, but as will be shown windmills had not been invented at the time.

The Mill occurs in the Manorial Accounts for the Abbey in 1373, and Stephen Nicholl the first recorded member of this the oldest Hendon family, is designated as the miller. Stephen Nicholl figures in the *Black Survey* of Hendon dated 1321 and is listed as the owner of a farm on le Regway (The Ridgeway).

However it is hard to believe that this was the mill for the whole of the manor, so evidence will be produced to prove that this was so; even today with good roads it would be a considerable trek from one side of the manor, (i.e. Hendon), to the other. It may be that the Lord of the Manor had an arrangement with an adjacent manor and some corn was milled elsewhere. Mill Hill is nowhere near the centre of the manor. As for the name of the hamlet before the mill was built, that we know because in 1320 a garden was prepared behind the Church (St Mary's) in a north-easterly direction. The work was carried out by three men from Lotharlei which was the old name for Mill Hill, and no doubt the two names were used simultaneously just to add to the confusion.

In February 1932 the Hon. Secretary of the Mill Hill Historical Society, D G Denoon wrote two papers for publication in the Hendon Times & Guardian headed *'How Mill Hill got its Name'*, and very carefully examined the options and the facts that were available. Denoon started with a warning that will be familiar to anyone who has ever engaged in any kind of historical research: quite simply nothing is straightforward, so check all 'facts', and the obvious meaning of anything, particularly names, must be treated with extreme caution.

Major N G Brett-James published his book *'The Story of Mill Hill Village'* in 1907 and we have made references to this elsewhere. In his book Brett-James stated that no claim of the origins of the name Mill Hill can be made with any degree of certainty, but too much has been discovered in the last 80 years for this to be still true. In the first place the documents on the Manor of Hendon that are held in the archives of Westminster Abbey and the library of All Souls College, Oxford have revealed a considerable amount of information and they have never been fully researched. A great deal of work was carried out by Eleanor Lloyd BA over 30 years ago. The old documents in Westminster Abbey are in Medieval Latin so translation was difficult, in addition there are the usual spelling aberrations and the scribes have used many abbreviations which like a stenographers short forms today are only obvious to the person who wrote them. More important even than these was the finding in 1931 of the original manuscript of the *Black Survey*. This discovery answered some questions although (of course) it asked some new ones. The Survey says 'There is a windmill there worth by the year XIIs' (twelve shillings), but does not say where in the Manor the mill was located. But let us return to the beginning and Denoon's analysis.

In Sir Montague Sharp's book, *'Middlesex in British, Roman and Saxon Times'* there is a reference to the remains of a small Roman building which was found in the vicinity of Moat Mount. This led another author to suggest that perhaps a sentry or even a centurion was posted on the high ground in this district as a kind of outpost. If we follow normal development (you cannot stand still, you either go up or down) it is possible to assume that this outpost developed in importance to the point where the commander's successor had advanced to the rank of military knight which in Roman times was known as Miles. This is a possible origin of Miles Hill which can be given some credence by the Roman ruins at Moat Mount mentioned above.

The transition from Miles Hill to Mill Hill is not at all far-fetched in terms of name development. There have been references to fields called knights near to the Totteridge boundary but these are low lying near to the Folly Brook and any connection with Roman knights or miles is doubtful. Whilst nothing can be proved neither can it be totally disproved but it is still worth remembering that in the period in question there were few fields and almost the whole area was dense forest. Furthermore no architectural remains to indicate Roman occupation have ever been discovered in the Mill Hill Village area. We must therefore look elsewhere for the likely origin of Mill Hill.

To refer again to Brett-James' book in which he said 'Local tradition mentions a windmill in the field opposite Belmont which bears the name the Old Mill Field, but there is no written record of any mill. . . . but the old inhabitants will not readily allow the tradition of the old mill to die'. But this was written a long time ago so it is worthwhile considering all the evidence that we now have, and at the end you will probably agree that the obvious conclusion is the one that we are looking for; Mill Hill is a village where there was a mill on a hill.

When the jurors acting on behalf of the *Domesday Book* compilers visited a manor they always asked whether there were any mills. In feudal times mills were of considerable economic importance and a valuable part of manorial administration and management. It must be remembered that the mills were water mills because the first windmill did not appear in Europe, and that was in England, until 1191, which was after *Domesday*. Therefore William the Conqueror's commissioners were enquiring about water mills which could only be on streams of some size. Denoon in his paper mentioned a number of known mills not far outside the Manor of Hendon but there was no mention of a mill in the Domesday entry for Hendon.

The Lord of the Manor would always have a mill in the manor if this were possible. In a feudal manor this was owned by the Lord and all the inhabitants were bound to have their corn ground at the home mill. This was the source of a good profit for the owner.

THE OLD MILL FIELD

At the beginning of this chapter it was remarked that a windmill, if there was one, would normally be near the centre of the village for the sake of convenience. But there is no record of a mill being anywhere near the Parish Church or the Manor House which between them would have been the centre of Manorial existence. We now know that at a later date there was definitely a windmill at the Old Mill Field near to Holcombe Hill and therefore it is fairly safe to assume that the mill of 1321 was on the now traditional site.

The early windmills were not the solid structures with which we are familiar. They were post mills. In other words they consisted of a post on which was fixed all the machinery in a box structure together with the sails. The pole was let into the ground and then suitably braced to stand the strains. A long pole protruded from the back and this was used to turn the structure manually to ensure that the sails were always in position to catch the wind. Being made of nothing but wood the time would come

when the entire structure would have decayed to the point of collapse. So the remains of the original are hardly likely to exist today.

Two centuries later and there is a deed in All Souls College dated May 2 1544 referring to 'Wood sales at Myll Hylles to Richard Shepard'. We are going to assume that this is intended to represent the place known today as Mill Hill which means that the name was already in use in the reign of Henry VIII and what is more it strength-

a windmill at the Old Mill Field...

ens our conviction that the 1321 windmill was at Mill Hill in the Mill Field. It is of course significant also that this mention of Myll Hylles is the very first written mention of Mill Hill. A few years later and there is another record of wood sales to Richard Shepard also on a deed at All Souls (May 1 1533), therefore Myll Hylles had a definite meaning as a locality by that time.

MANORIAL SURVEYS

Sir Edward Herbert commissioned a survey in 1574 of the Manor of Hendon, it mentions Mill Hill and proves beyond any doubt that it was by then a recognised and listed place. We read in this survey that among the responsible freeholders who provided information were Richard Nicoll and Robert Marsh of Myll Hylles. (We are going to hear a lot about these families in later chapters).

A copy of a *Court Roll* dated 1593 mentions 'Longcroft at Mylhill' along with various other places. This is the same year that Norden published his *'Speculum Brittanniae'* in which both Hendon and Mill Hill are mentioned. (This is also referred to later on). Here we have the first printed mention of Mill Hill.

Local wills can also be a reliable source of information regarding localities and we have a will of John Marsh of Myles-pitt (Milespit Hill) in 1612 which contains a reference to William Marsh of Mill Hill.

During the years 1632-35 another survey was carried out and in this we read of Robert Crane who held 'a cottage, two crofts and a mill with appurtenances and by estimacionn 2½ acres'. This property was described as being adjacent to Hocomb Hill. The crofts would probably have been in the Old Mill Field which gives us the first reference to the mill associated with property and provides us with the name of the miller.

In 1679 John Seller's map of Middlesex was published and this not only shows Mill Hill in the Hendon part of the map but also below that of Holcombe Hill is the symbol for a windmill, furthermore no other indication of any kind of mill is shown within the bounds of Hendon.

The miller's property is mentioned again in a survey of 1685-87 with the detail the same as above but now owned by Robert Crane's heirs. We know that the mill was still in existence at the end of 17th Century and is shown in early 18th Century maps.

THE END OF THE WINDMILL

We find the existence of a windmill at Mill Hill proven. It came into being sometime before 1321 and was either removed or simply decayed and finally fell down between 1710 and 1754. Messeder's *Field Book* published in 1754 which gives a most detailed account of the Manor does not mention anything about a mill, so by 1754 it had disappeared. No doubt in due course all the documents mentioned earlier will be fully researched and more facts will be revealed but even without any extra information we know how the name by which the Village has been known for 400 years came about.

CHAPTER III
THE EARLY YEARS

U ntil fairly recent times there was little in the way of remains of a definitive nature to suggest that the Neolithic peoples, or for that matter Bronze Age or Iron Age Britons developed any permanent encampments in the Hendon area. The heavy clay soils and dense, damp, oak forests would have been very uninviting compared with the chalkier, drier ground to the north and west. These lands have much evidence of prehistoric occupation. This situation was changed somewhat when a member of the Hendon & District Archaeological Society discovered flints both Mesolithic and Neolithic, and a Bronze Age arrowhead at Brockley Hill, Stanmore in 1987 and 1988. HADAS were excavating on this site at the time looking for Celtic and Roman remains. From the nature and distribution of the finds it was apparent that early man had visited the

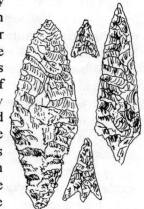

area many times before the Romans came and built their camp, and kilns for making pottery.

In September 1988 a silver coin, subsequently identified by the British Museum as Belgic from the reign of Cunobelinus, was picked up in a field on Brockley Hill. This king (of the *Catuvellauni)* reigned for over 40 years and died about AD40 just before the invasion by Claudius in AD43. Because Celtic coinage was allowed to circulate with Roman coinage until the Boudican revolt in AD61 this find does not prove the existence of a Celtic settlement in this area. It is nevertheless of considerable interest even if only because it suggests this possibility. At the same time and location another very worn coin was found which was attributed to the Emperor Domitian (AD81-96). The finder was also a member of HADAS.

UP TO ROMAN TIMES

To what extent the Romans established permanent camps in the Hendon area is a matter of conjecture. In the Roman invasion of BC55, led by Julius Caesar many historians consider that Brentford was the most likely place for the crossing of the River Thames to have taken place. For many reasons Caesar did not pursue the fleeing Britons after the crossing. Trade links had probably been established before the Romans came and these visitors would have been the first people to use the ford at Brentford. Here the river is comparatively narrow and even at that time would have had firm banks on both sides. The river to the east by contrast wound its way through numerous marshes so that any crossing would have been difficult and dangerous. There is now strong evidence that in the invasion of BC55 Caesar crossed the Thames around Tilbury and encountered a different British tribe in what is now Essex.

Nearly 100 years were to pass before a later emperor, Claudius, with his general Aulus Plautius passed through the places which were to become Middlesex. After the Roman invasion of AD43 Londinium quickly became the centre of Roman administration and it was necessary to have a permanent crossing. A bridge was constructed roughly where London Bridge stands today to provide this. In Roman times this part of the Thames was not tidal, this facilitated the bridge building and made dock construction much simpler. Today the Thames is of course tidal as far west as Teddington Weir.

There is some evidence of a minor Roman encampment to the south-west of Hendon in Kingsbury although this may have been little more than a temporary halt, but Stanmore Hill which rises over 150m has a stronger claim. The name Stanmore is in fact derived from stony mere (or pool) which is supposed to have been dug by the Romans to provide water for a military camp. Two miles to the east there certainly was an important Romano-British village on Brockley Hill, called *Sulloniacae,* which contained a posting house and pottery making facilities. A Roman pavement is still to be seen here and coins (both base metal and gold) and urns have been discovered close by. The whole area sits within the Thames basin so that more than adequate supplies of pottery clay were always readily available, and there was plenty of water, and wood for firing.

Pottery making was an important business at *Sulloniacae* from about AD70 until at least the end of the second century, possibly later. Some of the items made there were peculiar to this facility and consisted of various lidded bowls and jars as well as flagons of many types. One particular item was made in large quantities, mortaria, which were the Roman cooks' mixing and grinding bowls, and these carried the name on the rim of the potter responsible. This stamp enables us to trace the distribution of *Sulloniacae* products to towns and camps all over Roman Britain. In fact we know that potteries of the area supplied about half of all the mortaria used in the kitchens of the Province. It is generally assumed that the Romans took the more direct route where they subsequently built Watling Street, and followed by the Edgware Road today, when they headed northwards for their battle with the Cassivellaunus for their capital *Verulam*. It is possible nevertheless that some of the soldiers on the flanks penetrated the woods and took the alternative route which would have taken them along the ridge where Mill Hill village is today.

In 1769 some Roman coins and a lamp were found in Mill Hill, and the historian Sir Montague Sharp has quoted examples of a few Roman remains found within Mill Hill, and many more from the surrounding area. At various times in the 16th, 17th and 18th Centuries Roman objects were found in the vicinity, mainly coin, jewellery, and pottery ware. Other Roman remains have been found at The Burroughs in Hendon including fragments of pavement. A number of the lanes of Mill Hill are very ancient and are considered by some to be of possible Roman origin (See also the chapter on Roads). This would seem possible since the track of a Roman road was found in Copthall fields.

During the Roman festival of Ambarvalia it was a part of the rituals for the inhabitants to 'Beat the Bounds', which like so many pagan customs was eventually taken over by Christianity. At intervals on the boundary line the 'beaters' would blaze the side of an oak (Burnt Oak is almost certainly the site of one of these) and chapels were erected. These being superseded at a later date by parish churches built on the same foundations. Arkley, Finchley, Hendon, Stanmore and Totteridge are local examples of Roman *Compitalia*, or boundary chapels.

The Hale probably dates back to Roman times but under a different name: Hale comes from the Old English *healh* meaning an angle or corner of land. When the bounds were beaten in early Christian times a prayer was recited at stopping places and The Hale was one of these points on the Parish boundary. Some say that The Hale was so named because the prayer used was the Hail Mary, however the Angelic Salutation was not used until the 11th Century and the first record we have of The Hale is in 1216. In addition the Romans placed surveying stones, equivalent to the *Ordnance Survey* bench marks of today, and these were at Stoneyfield, Stone Grove and Whetstone; the first of these is within the boundary of Mill Hill.

As time passed the Romans developed Verulam into the much larger Roman town of *Verulamium*, (near to today's St. Albans), which was described by Tacitus at the time as a *Municipium* (chartered town) in the strict and legal sense. With *Londinium* (London) rapidly becoming the starting point for so many Roman roads, a situation that remains to the present day, and so much evidence of the Roman occupation close at hand it is hard to believe that the Romans just visited the Hendon area without actually building. The problem for archaeologists is that any Roman remains and artifacts are by now likely to be buried quite deeply and under built-up or at least much disturbed land making discovery difficult.

The Manor of Hendon as originally defined consisted of 10 hamlets, of which Mill Hill was one. There would certainly have been a manor house but unfortunately we do not know where it was sited. The most likely place is somewhere near Hendon Parish Church in The Burroughs. Much later it was relocated in Parson Street and called The Rectory, then at Hendon Place which was renamed Tenterden Hall in the 19th Century.

SAXON TIMES

In the first mention of Hendon it was spelt *Heandun* which almost certainly meant 'high hill', however Mill Hill apart the rest of Hendon is not particularly high. It is spelt *Handone* or *Hendun* in early Saxon records which is near in meaning to 'the town on the hill' and is acceptable. Needless to say apart from these different spellings there are also various other versions of the actual meaning of the name. The most likely derivation of these is from two Saxon words meaning high-down and because of the elevated situation of part of the Manor this makes some sense. In the *Domesday Book, Handone* is used and the historian Norden says that this is derived from *Highendone* (although other sources give the origin as *Heandune*) which means high wood and was so named because of the ample amounts of wooded land particularly on the hills. Another historian, Taylor, prefers a completely different meaning and states that the word comes from the Anglo-Saxon *hean* meaning poor, and this refers to the poor soil. James Thorne in his *Environs of London* pours scorn on this because as he points out the soil in most of the Manor is not poor. It is always possible however that by giving the place a name meaning poor the dues payable would be assessed at a lower rate. What all this does mean is that we have no way of knowing the true origin and can only guess.

Although the name is Saxon, Hendon would at one time have been under Danelaw. In AD878 Alfred the Great defeated the Danes and in the Treaty of Wedmore the Country was divided between Danes and Saxons and even though Hendon had been part of Alfred's kingdom it was transferred to the Danes, the boundary being Watling Street.

Widmore, who was one of the first historians to study the origins of

Westminster Abbey dismisses much of what had been written earlier as myth. However he did believe that two Saxon charters were genuine. One dated 785 is a charter of King Offa, and this conferred various lands upon the monastery at Thorney where Westminster Abbey was later to be built. Hendon is not mentioned by name in this charter, however we know that by this time King Offa was in virtual control of all lands south of the Humber, so would be able to dispose of lands and property as he thought fit. (Offa was king from 757 to 796). After Offa's death England was overrun by Danish invaders so that the infant religious community at Thorney was almost certainly destroyed and the monks dispersed.

The origin of the name Westminster is simple; the West Minster to distinguish it from the Eastern Cathedral, St Paul's. The site chosen was a solitary, sandy island, choked with thorny thickets, surrounded by running streams, and liable to flood at any time: 'Thorney Island'. It was outside the walls of London proper, quite in the country, and eminently suitable for meditation. Some of the monks called it a venerable place, others less complimentary, terrible. The exact year when the first Benedictine monk set foot on Thorney is not known. Some chroniclers stretched their imagination to 178, and claimed that the first church on the site was built over the foundations of a pagan temple during the reign of the British King Lucius, but this is just one of many legends.

Another Westminster charter (of 790) states that half of the Manor of Hendon was given to the Abbot of Westminster, and half to the Abbot of St. Alban's. If this is genuine, by the time of Dunstan's charter of 959 the earlier one had lapsed, or more likely the earlier document was a fake. As a matter of interest the diocesan boundary runs between South Mimms (which was in Middlesex before 1965) and North Mymms which from the earliest days has been in the Diocese of St. Albans.

Later during the reign of King Edgar, St. Dunstan, who restored the Benedictine order in England, founded a new order in Thorney and obtained a charter which conferred various lands and privileges upon the monastery. This was in 960. But here again there is uncertainty because two charters of the same period are at variance: one known as *The Great Charter of King Edgar* says (referring to various locations): *'quas tamen venerabilis Dunstanus a me, una cum predicto loco, emerat'*, or translated 'which nevertheless the venerable Dunstan, together with the aforesaid places obtained from me by service'. In other words there was no payment. However the Dunstan donative charter lists various buildings actually purchased from King Edgar (not in exchange for services rendered) and the prices paid. Amongst them is, *'ITEM, I have purchased from the venerable Ethelwold, Bishop of Winchester, ten houses, and ten*

*which belonged to Wolnoth the knight for eighty pieces of good silver,
and which are in the same domain at the place called Hendun* (Hendon):
I have added these to the monastery'. This charter is dated 959, and
carries Dunstan's seal. By 979 the Manor of Hendon and its Benefices
had become part of the property and lands under the control of the Abbey
of St. Peter at Westminster. This situation was confirmed by Royal
Charter of Edward the Confessor in 1047 and reaffirmed on New Year's
Day 1066.

It must be said that Widmore, who was at one time the Abbey
librarian, cast doubts upon the authenticity of all these documents and for
good reason. Other historians feel that they are genuine but that the
scribes got some of their facts wrong or just the dates muddled. Another
explanation is that the monks did not feel that an earlier charter was
specific enough in that manors were not mentioned by name. They
rewrote the texts actually mentioning the names of the manors involved,
and this included Hendon. We will never know for sure, what we do know
however is that Hendon did exist at that time and probably therefore the
hamlet of Lotharlei where Mill Hill Village is today.

It may seem a long way from Westminster to Hendon and a
difficult journey 1200 or more years ago and therefore unlikely that the
Abbot of Westminster would be involved in individual houses of such a
remote and small place. This was necessary however because the Abbot
obtained his living income from very manor in the diocese.

CHAPTER IV

THE MANOR : RISE AND FALL
FROM THE NORMANS TO THE 17TH CENTURY

A mong the *Domesday Book's* gifts to the historian are two very important sets of facts, a list of every place worthy of note and details of population. It is true to say that there are very few place names on the map today that are not in *Domesday* (the spelling will probably have changed) and which were possibly already centuries old when the *Domesday* enquiry was made. The population figures in the entries for each place enable us to estimate with a fair degree of accuracy not only the total population but also each person's level in the society. This information is not available for any other nation or locality. Hendon appears in Domesday.

The *Domesday Book*, being really a glorified national tax assessment, has an entry for the Manor of Hendon which accepts that the Abbey of St Peter at Westminster was the owner and details all the lands within the Manor, their areas and values so that the new bureaucracy could collect taxes.

The full text in *Domesday* relating to Hendon is:

MIDDLESEX

In hundredo de Gare Manerium, HANDONE, tenet abbas SANCTI PETRI pro xx, hidis se defendebat. Terra xvi. corucate. Ad dominium pertinet x. hidis et sibi sunt iii carucae. Villani habent viii. carucas et quinque adhunc possent fieri. Ibi presbyter habet i virgatum et iii villani quisque dimidiam virgatem et xii bordarii qui tenent dimidiam hidam et vi cotarii et i. servus. Pratum ii. bovum. Silva mille porcis et x. solidos. In totis valentiis valet viii libris. Quando receptum similiter. Tempore Regis Edwardii xii libris. Hoc Manerium jacuit et jacet in dominio ecclesie SANCTI PETRI.

When this is translated it means:

MIDDLESEX

In the Hundred of Gare (Gore) MANOR. The Abbot of St Peter's holds Handone (Hendon). It was assessed for twenty hides. The (arable) land is sixteen carucates. Ten hides belong to the demesne, and there are three ploughs there. The villanes have eight ploughs and five more could be made. A priest there has one virgate, three villanes each have half a hide, seven villanes each have one virgate, sixteen villanes each have half a virgate. Twelve bordmen hold half a hide, six cottages and one serf. There is meadow for two oxen, wood for a thousand pigs and ten shillings (rents). With all profits it is worth eight pounds; the same when received. In the time of King Edward its value was twelve pounds. This manor lay and lies in the demense of the church of St Peter.

Many of these words are not used today, and in any case even at the time of writing had imprecise meanings. Some guidelines would therefore not go amiss:

BORDLAND Part of the demesne reserved by the lord for furnishing his own table.

BORDMEN or BORDERS Tenants of that land who were bound by the conditions of the holding to supply the lord with provisions.

DEMESNE Manorial lands not let out to tenants.

HIDE A measurement of land that could be anything from 60 to 120 acres. It is taken to mean meadow or untilled land, enough for a household.

VIRGATE Another measure of land, commonly 30 acres.

CARUCATE As much land as one team of oxen could plough in a season, and said to be about 100 acres.

It is also worth noting that there were woods for 1,000 pigs which confirms that a large part of the Manor was forest. Pannage (feeding on common land) for this many pigs would need a considerable area. Because we know that the Manor of Hendon contained 10 small hamlets, we can guess at the value and extent of Mill Hill at that time.

Another interesting fact is that the value of the Manor had dropped from £12 during the reign of Edward the Confessor to £8. This is probably because William I had laid to waste large areas of Middlesex and the values of many manors had suffered accordingly. In addition the Normans were essentially soldiers and hunters, not farmers and husbandmen so that the amount of land actually under cultivation was allowed to decline.

Hendon's next door neighbour, the Manor of Edgware, does not feature in *Domesday* and at that time was probably a part of *Stanmer* (Stanmore). There is a mention in a deed of 978 of *Aegces* Wer, the weir or fishing pool belonging to *Aegces* (a man's name).

The Manor of Hendon remained as a possession of Westminster

Abbey until about 1150 when the abbot, Gervase de Blois, a bastard son of King Stephen, granted it to Gilbert Fitz-Gunter. The rent was £40. It seems that this abbot signed away most of the property of the Monastery in this way. According to Widmore much of the lands which were disposed of (to various of the abbot's friends and relatives) remained in fee-farm down to the time of the Dissolution.

Stephen's reign brought disaster to the Abbey and the lands and property. The King forced the monks to elect Gervase de Blois to the high post of abbot, but there was nothing saintly in his behaviour. Gervase wasted the wealth of the monastery on his own entertainments, lavish hospitality, and immoral living. Other property besides Hendon was disposed of, for instance Chelchethe (Chelsea) was given to his mother Dalmeta. Gervase then confiscated the altar jewels and relics, but when he tried to lay his hands on the regalia the monks rebelled and petitioned the

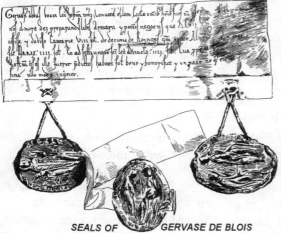

SEALS OF GERVASE DE BLOIS

Pope (Innocent II) who admonished him. This had little effect and he continued his profligate life-style for another 19 years, when he was deposed. His successor inherited an empty treasury, even the abbot's house was devoid of furniture and fittings.

Gilbert Fitz-Gunter appears to have relinquished his interest in Hendon, and he assigned the Manor to another family, le Rous. This family retained ownership for a considerable period (it is considered likely that they actually resided in the Manor). In 1268 Galfridus de Rous, the sheriff of Bedfordshire and Buckinghamshire petitioned the King for compensation of £60 for houses and corn that been destroyed by fire during a raid, and £32 6s 8d (£32.33) for various other items. The raid appears to have been carried out by rebel barons led by John d'Eyville who also took £22 10s (£22.50) belonging to the King.

The country at this time was in a state of upheaval with barons led by Simon de Montfort the Earl of Leicester in open revolt against the King. This internecine struggle had only been resolved the previous year at the Battle of Evesham, decisively won by the King's men.

Whether de Rous had earned the wrath of d'Eyville and the raid was retaliation or whether it was just a general raid with Hendon the unfortunate target we do no know. The former seems likely because the King's most successful commander and his relatives were land holders of some importance in the area.

The Manor of Hendon had been restored to the Abbey by 1321 when the *Black Survey* was made. The Survey was in many ways like a *Domesday Book* in miniature. A jury was assembled of 12 local farmers and they were required to list all the tenants by name together with their holdings, with areas and the rents they paid in money, kind, and in labour.

The Survey court consisted of three monks of the Abbey and as the Survey was taken five years after the Abbey had taken control it can be assumed that it was to enforce the Abbot's policies. The produce was not sold, as hitherto, but was delivered to Westminster to feed the monks and their servants, plus workmen and visitors.

> *I have fed purely upon ale;*
> *I have eat my ale, drank my ale,*
> *and I always sleep upon ale.*

George Farquar (1678-1707)

In Medieval times, and for a long time afterwards, the brewing of ale was very important (it was safer to drink than the frequently polluted water) so much so that the head of catering at the Abbey was the cellarer.

It was normal for the Lord of the Manor to reserve the right to enforce the assize of ale, that is to see that it was up to strength and quality. In Chester in 1086 the penalty for brewing bad ale was the cucking stool. (To be tied in a seat in front of their own door and be pelted by the mob). Cuck was an OE word meaning to defecate, so no prizes for guessing what was probably thrown!

Presumably those who had drunk well did not notice the poor quality of the food. Second to the cellarer was the granger who was responsible for the granary and farmhouse and other buildings. After Michaelmas each year the granger appointed a farm manager to oversee farm work and forestry and to collect the rents in cash and kind. Initially the manager was accompanied by a man from the Abbey (known as a *serviens*) to make the accounts but as the people became more trustworthy a capable farmer was appointed as assistant (called *prepositus* or first among equals).

In 1378 on May 9th Abbot Nicholas executed a charter which apparently gave to the prior and convent certain houses and markets in Hendon at a rent of 30 oak trunks to be cut in the woods of Hendon by the brothers of the monastery. Previously this had all belonged personally to the abbot. The timber was to be used in building the new abbey and the smaller branches for kindling and firewood.

In the Peasants' Revolt of 1381 led by Watt Tyler two Hendon men played prominent parts; John-in-the-Hale, and John Child of Childs Hill. Unlike their leader both were ultimately pardoned. Tyler was beheaded and his head displayed on London Bridge. With the death of Tyler the rising in London was over but the malaise of revolt had spread and much of England was in turmoil. Many villages around London were plundered and burnt, including Hendon and Harrow.

The most notable Hendon families in the Middle Ages were the Mortimers, Rous and Scropes. Hendon also has its royal associations, a part of the Manor having been given to the Abbey on two separate occasions to provide Masses for the souls of deceased queens: Eleanor the beloved wife of Edward I and Anne of Bohemia the devoted wife of Richard II.

The next time there is a record of the Manor of Hendon is in 1448 from an entry in the *Memorandum Roll,* and concerns a claim by the Abbot of Westminster *'to divers issues and amerciaments arising out of certain tenements, messuages and lands of the same Abbot, by pretext of a charter thereof, made by King Richard III'.* This probably deals with parts of the Manor leased by a previous abbot, (quite likely Gervais de Blois). The claim refers to the lands of John Breynt and also of William Nicoll of Heywood (Highwood) and William Page. This is significant because not only is it the first mention of the important families of Nicoll, Page and Breynt (Brent) on one document, but also the first time that we can positively identify what is now Mill Hill except that at that time Heywood was a separate hamlet.

We have now come to the reign of Edward IV. During the first year of his reign in 1461 a new document makes its appearance, the *Court Rolls,* and straightway we are introduced to Nicoll and other names that are part of the history of Hendon: Marsh, Downer, Page, Parsons, Gybbes (Gibbs Green was a district near The Hale), and others. Most of them have been perpetuated in road names.

All these held lands as tenants of the Manor at the time of the Dissolution, up to that time the Abbots of Westminster were the land lords. At the Dissolution, Hendon, with their other properties were given to Bishop Thirleby. Thirleby was a poor manager and once again the property was dispersed and therefore reduced to a deanery. Later it became the property of Sir William Herbert, brother-in-law to Henry VIII.

There is no evidence of Queen Elizabeth I having any particular interest in Mill Hill except that she passed through the area on numerous occasions on route to her lands at Shenley in Hertfordshire. Elizabeth did however make numerous visits to Hendon Place which had once been the property of the Abbot of Westminster, and was now the residence of the Herberts. Elizabeth's Lord High Steward was Sir William Herbert, Earl of Pembroke, father of Sir Edward. Elizabeth paid another visit to Hendon Place after Sir Edward had let the house to Sir John Fortescue.

In 1603 Sir John had another royal visit. Queen Elizabeth had died and in the year of his accession James I stayed at Hendon Place. Whilst he was there he knighted two gentlemen, William Fleetwood of Buckingham and Thomas Hesketh of Lancashire.

THE HENDON CHARTER

The early history of the Manor of Hendon is dominated by the various charters that affected the ownership of the Manor and therefore of Mill Hill too. A number of these have already been mentioned. In some cases it has been pointed out that it is necessary to regard these documents with caution; their authenticity cannot be determined with any degree of reliability. Indeed because they sometimes contradict each other it is essential to outline the possibilities that each one illustrates rather than take them as a statement of historical fact.

Some charters are however apparently irrefutable, and the *Hendon Charter*, which dates back to the year of the Norman conquest is in many ways the most important. E T Evans in his book *'The History and Topography of the Parish of Hendon Middlesex (1890)* quotes an abstract of this in detail. Because of its importance to the people of Hendon, to their history, and the long time that its provisions held good a full summary is included.

According to Evans, at the time of writing his book the Charter still applied. This would be of little relevance today except as a piece of history because the provisions do not apply at this time. Since Hendon is no longer a borough, let alone a manor, and is a part of the London Borough of Barnet the Charter could not apply, in any case the provisions of the Charter lapsed in the 19th Century.

For eight centuries the inhabitants of Hendon, whether actual tenants of the Manor or not, enjoyed an immunity from tolls that was shared by few places in the realm. The origin goes back to Dunstan: it seems that in the first grants of Hendon to the Abbey at Westminster the King at Dunstan's instigation exempted the people of Hendon from all taxes (imposts) except contributions for military expeditions, and for the construction of bridges and fortresses. Edward the Confessor confirmed the Charter and the existing exemptions and also freed the inhabitants from all regal and episcopal taxes as well. These exemptions were subsequently reaffirmed by succeeding sovereigns up to the time of William and Mary.

CHARTER

(Granted to the Inhabitants of Hendon)

'Edward, King of England, by his Charter bearing date the ninth Calends of January in the Year of Our Lord 1066, did give unto the Church of St Peter's at Westminster divers Lands in Hendon and freed the inhabitants from all Toll, both by Land and Water.

'Henry the 3rd, King of England, by his Charter bearing date at Woodstock the fourth day of July in the ninth year of his reign confirmed the said Charter and freed the inhabitants of Hendon from all Tolls and Fairs and Markets and from all Street Tolls for carrying of Things, Wares, or the like and Toll for Cattle.

'Richard the 2nd, King of England, by his Charter bearing date at Westminster the eighteenth day of December in the 17th year of his reign confirmed the aforesaid Charter and freed the Inhabitants of Hendon from all Tolls whatsoever in every Fair and Market and over every Bridge and in every way and Water and also by Sea for themselves and Wares''.

'Henry the 8th, King of England, by his Charter bearing date at Westminster the twentieth day of May in the 2nd year of his reign confirmed the aforesaid Charter'.

'William Lord Abbot of Westminster and the Convents and Monks there by their Deed enrolled in the Chancery bearing date tenth day of January in the thirty-first year of Henry the 8th granted their Monastery with the Lordship of Hendon and Rectory or Parsonage thereof to the said King for ever and which was confirmed by Act of Parliament upon the Dissolution of all Religious Houses'.

'And the said King by Letters Patent bearing date at Hampton Court the twentieth day of January in the thirty-first year of his reign gave both to Thomas, Bishop of Westminster, the said Lordship and Parsonage of Hendon and all the Freedoms and Privileges thereof and acquitted the Inhabitants of and from all Tolls in Fairs and Markets.

'And the said Thomas, Bishop of Westminster, by Deed bearing date the twentieth day of March in the 4th year of King Edward the 6th and enrolled in Chancery, granted to the King the Lordship and Parsonage of Hendon for ever.

'And the said King Edward by Letters Patent under the Great Seal bearing date at Greenwich the ninth day of April in the 4th year of his reign gave the said Manor and the Church and Parsonage thereof to William Lord Herbert Earl of Pembroke and his Heirs for ever with all their Privileges and Freedoms and acquitted the Tenants and Inhabitants of all Tolls in all Fairs and Markets or elsewhere.

'King James by Letters Patent dated at Westminster under the Great Seal the eighteenth day of May in the 7th year of his reign over England confirmed the said grant to William Herbert, Knight, the Owner of the said Manor and Lordship and expressly charged all Officers whatsoever that all the Tenants and Inhabitants of Hendon may freely enjoy their liberties and Privileges of the aforesaid Freedoms from Tolls and such like payments according to the Charter and Grants aforesaid without any hindrance or denial in anywise whatsoever.

'William and Mary by their Letters Patent dated at Westminster the seventh day of September in the 5th year of their reign did give grant and confirm unto Sir William Rawlinson, Knight and Sergeant-at-Law, the aforesaid Charter and all the Privileges above mentioned and thereby did free the Inhabitants of Hendon aforesaid of and from Tolls in all Fairs and Markets and of and from all Street Tolls and every other Toll whatsoever in every Fair and every Market and every Bridge and every Way and Water and also by Sea for themselves and their Wares for ever'.

E T Evans obtained the extract from a Mr William Matthew Hearn who held a copy inscribed on ancient parchment. It was believed at that time that all people claiming the benefits of the Charter held a copy of this extract. The Hearns settled in Hendon in 1805. The Charter cannot now be traced and the location of any copies, if they exist, is not known either.

It is exceptional and most unusual for any charter to be reaffirmed as late as during the reign of William and Mary, although this sort of privilege was quite common in earlier times. The last Patent was apparently not enrolled, however by a decision of the Court of Common Council given at Guildhall on October 27 1796 the Charter was held to exempt from tolls within the City of London and the rights that it gave were still exercised well into the 19th Century by farmers and tradesmen.

THE CIVIL WAR AND BEYOND

The 17th Century is dominated by the events leading up to and during the Civil War and Commonwealth. The Herberts were supporters of the Crown cause, but Hendon, partly because it was near to London inclined towards supporting Parliament. The Powis castle in Montgomeryshire was stormed by the Parliamentary forces in 1644 and Lord Powis was despatched a prisoner to London but was paroled to live in his own home. The Manor of Hendon had been sequestered by Parliament because Sir Percy Herbert, the Lord of the Manor had given support to the King.

Sir Percy was lucky to escape with his life because among his 'crimes' were raising armed bands in Montgomery for defence of the castle and collecting money for the King's cause. He was arrested in 1641 and summoned to attend a Parliamentary committee where he was forced to swear allegiance to Parliament. He was released on bail but in 1650 a heavy fine was imposed and all his estates were sold, which included Hendon.

The Parliamentary Commissioners had control of the Manor of Hendon during the Commonwealth years and were responsible for lettings. By some means the Manor was let to relatives of Percy's wife, Elizabeth Craven, and in 1649 John Craven and William Gibson are listed as Lords of the Manor. The following year Sir William Craven was a tenant.

In 1660 the monarchy was restored and Hendon was returned to the Herberts. The new Lord of the Manor was William who was elevated to marquis, and later Duke of Powis by James II. In 1680 the Manor was let for £400pa to a Mr Samuel Turner. William, Duke of Powis was a staunch supporter of James II.

The historians of today are not totally in agreement about James' policies or his ambitions. He is accused of planning to return to Catholicism and many of his actions would seem to prove this. More likely he wanted to introduce a degree of religious toleration, which meant all shades of religion from Quakers to Catholics. Whatever his intentions it was not to be, he failed to persuade the Anglicans to accept even limited freedom of expression for Catholics.

The time was ripe for the end of James and a new era. King William's invasion from Holland, a couple of skirmishes which never amounted to a battle and the Glorious Revolution (sic!) saw the end of James II. He fled to France and with him went his supporter William Duke of Powis.

For this grave transgression the Duke was declared an outlaw and all his lands and titles were forfeited to the Crown. His son Lord Montgomery did not travel with him and he made some kind of peace with the new sovereign. His father's estates were not however handed over to him automatically and the Crown agents continued to receive revenues from the Manor of Hendon.

A few years later in 1693 Lord Montgomery felt that the return of the Manor to him and his family was due and he petitioned to have all the estates leased to him. The proposed rent was £770pa. There were objections to this request, one of the Middlesex Receivers (they were commissioned by the Treasury to investigate the application) maintained that the Crown would lose out at this rent and existing tenants could well be insecure. In addition it was considered to be unwise to hand over an estate to someone whose loyalties were in doubt when these lands were so

Garrick built himself a new house.: Hendon Hall

near to London. Another report saw no valid objection and stated that any problems could be overcome before the title was changed.

With two reports that were totally at variance in their findings the Treasury avoided making a decision and as a consequence the Manor was passed to the Earl of Rochford in 1696. This act incensed Lord Montgomery even more and he made a new protest and restated his case. At this time he was able to prove that before the Duke had been outlawed he had settled the Manor on his wife. With this new evidence the Manor was restored to the Duchess and subsequently to Lord Montgomery.

The greatest change in the history of the Manor was shortly to take place. William the last Marquis of Powis died without issue in 1748. In 1756 the executors of the late Marquis directed that the Manor be sold by auction. The successful bidder was a Mr Clutterbuck who made the purchase on behalf of the great actor, man about town and raconteur David Garrick (qv) and he paid the (by our standards) trivial sum of £13,381 for the Manor and Lordship and the rights of the Benefice of St Mary's, the Parish Church in The Burroughs. Garrick is said to have regretted the purchase later although he admitted that it gave him status.

Garrick built himself a new house, Hendon Hall (this is now Hendon Hall Hotel) and he is reputed to have lived there in the style befitting the Lord of the Manor until 1778. There is however no hard evidence that he did actually take up residence. The great columns of the portico of this house are supposed to have come originally from the great mansion of Canon's Park which belonged to James Brydges, Duke of Buckingham and Chandos. This mansion was demolished in 1747. After Garrick's purchase the Demesne lands were sold to various buyers for a total sum of £40,580.

THE END OF THE MANOR

With the sale of the Manor and Benefice of Hendon to David Garrick this was the end of the old style land ownership for the Manor. The Medieval structure based upon feudal authority and dues was gone for ever. In effect it disappeared with the Dissolution of the Monasteries, but took a long time to die. With the beginning of the 18th Century a new era had arrived, the age of the private property owner.

Mill Hill was still a rather unimportant part of the Hendon Parish. In 1754 the most important hamlets in the north of the Parish (and they did not amount to much) were The Hale, Lower Hale, and Highwood. Lower Hale consisted of just six houses the biggest being Hale Grove Farmhouse whose 18th Century frontage survived into the present century. The hamlet of The Hale included the *Green Man* public house.

Upon Garrick's death the property was held in trust for his nephew Carrington Garrick (he died in 1787). The manor was next sold in 1790 to John Bond Esq who was the last complete owner. Before the end of the 18th Century the Manor was resold several times and then broken up and the various parts sold piecemeal. The Manor of Hendon as a governing entity was no more. As a name the Manor staggered on for over 100 more years. In fact the last entry in the Vestry Minute Books was not until 1913 and the final Court of the Manor of Hendon was held in 1916. Right to the end tradition was maintained in that the Court was held in the White Bear in Hendon. The year 1922 saw the abolition of Copyhold Tenure and therefore the end of *Manorial Courts*, even so the last actual entry in the Court Ledger was dated August 8 1934.

Later on we have the formation of the Hendon Urban District followed by the Borough of Hendon. Mill Hill was just a ward in both of these. The most recent change was in 1965 when the new London Borough of Barnet was formed and both Hendon and Mill Hill became just parts of this very large new borough.

CHAPTER V

MILL HILL IN THE WARS

T he works manager of Mill Hill Gas Works, F J Pierce, writing in the staff magazine in 1948 related how he had stood in the darkness outside the blacksmith's shop and watched a Zeppelin crash during World War I. It had been shot down by a fighter aircraft and crashed at Cuffley. This was just about all there was as far as Mill Hill's direct experience of that war. Their men were far away, dying in places like the Somme battlefield.

Within an hour of the Declaration of War on September 3 1939 the sirens sounded in earnest for the first time. An unidentified plane had crossed the coast, it was a false alarm but the War had begun. When World War II broke out no-one knew quite what to expect. Coming just 20 years after the end of World War I there were still plenty of people who remembered the horrors of bombings and shellings, but most of all poisonous gas. Everybody had been issued with a gas mask but for how long could we tolerate wearing one? Fortunately of all the suffering that followed this was spared us.

It was inevitable that Mill Hill would suffer from the visits of the Luftwaffe during the war and sustain damage to property, even injury and death. It is near to central London and contained the barracks on Bittacy Hill as well as the WRNS training depot in the recently completed (1939) building for the Medical Research Council on The Ridgeway. There was also the aerodrome, which although not in use as an operational fighter base certainly did have an emergency role to play, and there were a number of factories on the Edgware Road and beyond that were producing war materials.

EARLY DAYS AND THE BLITZ

The school holidays were drawing to a close when war was declared in 1939, but few schools reopened on the appointed day. Many were turned into first aid or civil defence posts. This time no-one believed that the War would be over by Christmas as they had done 25 years before. Everyone knew that it could be a long job. Nevertheless schools could not stay shut for ever, children had to be educated, and in any case it was most undesirable that they would be wandering the streets.

After a while children gathered in houses for a few hours each week to be taught by peripatetic teachers. Then any convenient hall was opened, usually those belonging to churches, and most children attended for four or five half days per week. It must have been a year or more before many children returned to anything like full-time education, by which time the bombing had begun and it was then a case of in and out of the air raid shelters and a quick dash home when the all clear had been sounded.

Some American press man coined the phrase *phoney war* for the period of apparent inactivity that followed the Declaration of War. All sorts of stories circulated during this time about what would happen but most were imagination and nonsense. The phoney times ended abruptly when the German army invaded Belgium, France and The Netherlands in May 1940, and these countries capitulated so quickly that an invasion of Britain became a distinct possibility.

After the long battles of World War I the dramatic end to the war in France came as a complete surprise and shock. The only partial success was the evacuation from Dunkirk which was proclaimed as a victory. Now another wait began, but this was to be a short one. In August the battle for air supremacy over Britain began in earnest with the Luftwaffe using every effort to destroy all Channel shipping and to put all fighter airfields out of action. In this they failed, but only just. The German High Command over-estimated British losses and underestimated the production of our aircraft factories and the will of the British people. When they thought that we would have nothing left their bombers were still met by formidable opposition.

In the two weeks between August 24 and September 6 British losses were 295 fighters destroyed with 171 severely damaged. We could not go on at that rate for very long. But then a mistake was made, on a raid intended for Rochester and Chatham a plane got lost and dropped its bomb load on central London. This led to an immediate reprisal raid and 80 British bombers paid a visit to Berlin the following night. The war of attrition had begun and Hendon along with all the other London boroughs was in the front line.

In the period that came to be known as the Battle of Britain, which was only from July to the end of October 1940 the Germans lost 1,733 aircraft, nothing like the 2,698 claimed by our anti-aircraft gunners and fighter pilots, and we lost 915 fighters compared with the 3,058 that the Germans gave out in their news broadcasts.

We were never to enjoy the same success against night bombers. The bombing of our major cities and industrial areas went on for much longer and was much more devastating.

Children were not too worried about the progress of the War, unless they were actually 'bombed out'. They quickly adapted to the disturbed nights and disrupted school lessons and it has been said that many were healthier than they had ever been because a greater effort was made than ever before to see that the necessary amount of nutrition and vitamins were made available.

Children (and adults) did find that aerial dog-fights were exciting, and daily visits to the parks and golf courses looking for anti-aircraft shell splinters or the thin strips of foil (dropped by enemy aircraft to upset the British radar) was more interesting than school. These souvenirs were greatly treasured particularly if a complete shell nose-cap was found. More macabre was the search for bomb splinters, the fins from burnt out incendiary bombs, or pieces from the parachutes of parachute mines. These finds were more 'valuable'.

Clearly there were parts of London and the South-east that sustained much more destruction from air raids than Hendon, nevertheless there was considerable damage to Hendon property. Taking the War as a whole 579 high explosive bombs came down in Hendon (of which approximately 100 landed in Mill Hill). In addition there were 70 unexploded bombs. There were 261 incendiary bomb concentrations, (40 of these were in Mill Hill), to which must be added 39 oil bombs and five phosphorus bombs. Some of our high explosive went astray and 77 anti-aircraft and rocket shells added to the damage. In addition 196 returned to earth that fortunately failed to explode. Particularly nasty were the 10 parachute mines, because they came down relatively slowly so made hardly any crater and nearly all of the blast went sideways.

In the whole course of the War , including attacks by V1s and V2s , 18,740 houses were damaged or totally destroyed, 275 food shops and their stocks were destroyed, and 509 other buildings were damaged or destroyed. The services took a pounding too: 92 gas mains were severed (some of these were quite spectacular) 77 water mains and 76 electricity cables were cut, and 83 main sewers were damaged, many seriously.

In all this destruction 242 people died and another 505 were seriously injured. Less serious injuries totalled 809 and many suffered mentally for a long time.

A look at a map showing were the bombs landed in Mill Hill is interesting. As would be expected the building now occupied by the National Institute for Medical Research which was used as a training depot for the WRNS was a target and 16 high explosive bombs fell quite near. The Mill Hill Barracks seems to have been the target for 22 HE bombs, but 19 of these fell on open ground well to the north. Three landed within the perimeter fence (two on a playing field) and there were three incendiary bomb concentrations. One stick of 14 bombs came down in a straight line across Edgwarebury Open Space which was a bad miss or a pilot decided to jettison his load. A much better aim, but fortunately just off target was a stick of six that exploded very close together just north of the opening of the Elstree railway tunnel and in line with the direction of the rails.

There were no bombs on or even very near the gas works. Because Mill Hill includes a considerable amount of open space: parks, large gardens, Moat Mount, and the Totteridge Vale, a high proportion of all bombs fell away from property.

THE 'V' WEAPONS

The night of June 13 1944 was fine and warm. The allied landings in Northern France were one week old and seemed to be going favourably. There had been no serious air raids for a long time and most people felt that this aspect of the War was finished. Over the last week or so there had been a couple of unexplained explosions in the London area causing death and damage but no-one was particularly worried.

Sometime after midnight the sirens sounded, most people stayed in bed or just looked out of the window. They were in for a shock. All members of the ARP Service had to report to the nearest post. Suddenly all hell was let loose, and a small plane which seemed to be on fire appeared below the cloud cover. The anti-aircraft gunners thought that they had scored a hit and fired all the harder. The plane was blown to pieces and these were scattered over a wide area of Finchley.

The plane was one of the first of the V1s, later to be nicknamed *Doodle Bugs*, and it was not on fire when hit, the flame was from its reaction propulsion unit. The German military command had wanted to delay the launch of the first 'V' weapon until June 16/17 and start with a massive barrage but had been pressed to bring the date forward by Hitler. The first V1 was a warning of the thousands that were to follow.

The Government was not at all surprised that this happened. Aerial reconnaissance as early as January 1943 had revealed extensive activity at the German experimental station at Peenemunde with regard to both pilotless planes (V1s) and ballistic rockets (V2s). The Germans had in fact been experimenting with rockets since 1932. The V1 had been given the highest priority in June 1942.

The construction of launch sites had begun early in 1943 in the area between the Pas de Calais and Cherbourg for both V1s and V2s. Unfortunately British intelligence failed to realise the magnitude of the threat and heavy bombing of the launch pads was not begun in earnest until after the weapons had started to arrive. The Allied Command did not want to dilute the air offensive of Germany at the time. In the event it was not long (a few months) before most of the sites were overrun, but even so an enormous amount of damage was done, mainly in the London area. When the launch sites (for V1s) had all been captured a few were launched from aircraft.

Over the next few months the people of the South East of England became all too familiar with the V1s: their flight pattern and the distinctive sound that they made is something never forgotten. They were supposed to have been driven into the ground but owing to a design fault the engine cut out when the final dive began - so everyone knew when to duck. The author ducked many times, on one occasion in Nether Street Finchley when the V1 came down at the back of Brent Way next to Dollis Brook and caused a great deal of damage. Earlier in the War on two occasions large HE bombs had come down near to this same spot.

V1 FLYING BOMB IMMEDIATELY BEFORE IMPACT

As far as V1s were concerned Hendon escaped comparatively lightly. The Home Office plan of V1 incidents in the London area shows 13 in Hendon (two of these in Mill Hill: at Mill Hill Circus and in the fields to the west of Bittacy Hill). Compare this figure with Penge in south-east London where 18 were reported, and Penge is only one eleventh of the size of Hendon.

At the time that the V1 exploded at Mill Hill Circus two astronomers of the University of London Observatory on the Watford Way were making good use of the blackout for some research work. From their log, and the somewhat laconic report we know precisely when the bomb came down. To quote from the Wilson Observing Log for August 3 1944:

'Started exposure at 21h 44m GMT. Flying bomb exploded very close and shifted star in declination out of the field. Star recovered and exposure restarted at 21h 47m GMT. Just after starting the second time, a second flying bomb

exploded. This was more distant and though it shifted image from the (spectrograph) slit, star did not go out of field and was quickly recovered. Exposure ended 22h 07m GMT'.

The German plan was for the V1s to fall in central London where they would cause the greatest disruption to business, services, and government. By the use of double agents the German High Command was told that the bombs were over-shooting their target, they adjusted the range and south London took the brunt of the attacks.

Altogether 10,000 V1s were launched, of which 25% went astray, leaving 7,400 that were actually seen at the English coast. Once the defences got the measure of them 80% were destroyed (in August 1944): in all 1,846 were destroyed by fighter aircraft and 1,878 by anti-aircraft fire. The V1s were faster than almost all of our piston engined aircraft and only the recently introduced Gloucester Meteor, the first British operational jet aircraft, could match them for speed in level flight.

The V2 was very different. It was a rocket and was launched nearly vertically. The launch weight was 12tons with a warhead of approximately 1ton. The rocket attained a speed of Mach 5.5, which meant that they could be heard coming only after they had arrived. The explosion was the first intimation that the rocket had been launched, except for those who were unfortunate enough to be close to the point of impact in which case they probably knew nothing.

The V2 rocket was very expensive to produce (six times the cost of a German bomber aircraft) but nevertheless 1,070 were launched and most of these landed within the London Civil Defence area. Only two landed within the borders of Hendon (according to Home Office records).

WAR'S MEMORIALS

This chapter has been mainly about damage to property, but the greater destruction was to bodies and minds. Wars are about death, and its glorification is a way of making the sufferings acceptable. It suited the Government and national fund raisers to depict the ordinary soldier as invariably cheerful, someone who enjoyed the excitement of war. Who looked forward to the next chance to beat the Bosche, which he surely would, and was pleased to be doing his bit for King and Country. Censorship of soldiers' mail helped to maintain this image.

It's a Long Way to Tipperary was written shortly before World War I and its tone is a long way from that of the poems and songs written later. After around 850,000 soldiers had perished these lines were more to the point:

What passing bells for those who die as cattle?
Only the monstrous anger of the guns,
Only the stuttering rifle's rapid rattle
Can patter out their hasty orisons.

(*Anthem for Doomed Youth*) Wilfred Owen

Owen was a World War I poet who died shortly before the Armistice was signed.

Mill Hill suffered its bereavements too. Standing on The Ridgeway opposite to the Sheepwash Pond is the Mill Hill War Memorial, and there is little to distinguish it from thousands of others up and down the Country. It is a great sadness that no town or village, no matter how small is without its reminder of man's inhumanity to man.

Annual Armistice Day Parades are still held at the Mill Hill Memorial but because fewer and fewer people can remember a world war many feel that it is no longer relevant. Between the two world wars everything came to a halt nationwide for two minutes, not just around the Cenotaph in Whitehall and similar assemblies, but everywhere. And as far as possible this took place on November 11, not the nearest Sunday. We have moved it for convenience, to have any significance it should be inconvenient!

One hundred years earlier and the names on the Memorial would probably have been quite different. Not one of the names associated with old Mill Hill; Nicoll, Brent, Wise, Marsh, etc. is represented in the list of inscribed names.

The Memorial does not carry any identification of the designer, but at this time just about every stone-mason in the country had to construct at least one of these memorials. Apart from the rather special designs many were almost 'off the peg'. The memorial in Mill Hill was erected sooner than most and was unveiled at an Armistice Service at 3pm in the afternoon of Sunday November 14 1920. Apparently there was an apology from the foundry because the bronze tablet was not delivered in time for the Service. The official ceremony was performed by Lieut. General Sir George MacDonogh KCB KCMG the Adjutant General.

Some lines from the poem *For the Fallen*, (written by Laurence Binyon before the War was three months old) became the best known lines of the 1920s and 1930s and have been recited at The Cenotaph, and war memorials around the Country, at the annual services ever since. They are still a poignant reminder of the losses that involved every family and community in the land:

They shall not grow old, as we that are left grow old:
Age shall not weary them, nor the years condemn
At the going down of the sun and in the morning
We will remember them.

To those old enough to remember, World War II is still like yesterday (and know doubt so is World War I to some 90 year olds). Each person who has lived through a major war has his or her own private reminiscences quite apart from those things that affected everyone. There was the blackout, rationing, nights in air-raid shelters, etc. for those at home, and for the serving long periods of boredom and waiting, followed by action, injury and even the death of ones friends. Fortunately we are able to push the unpleasantness to the back of our minds and remember the funny events, the laughs, and the camaraderie best of all.

The author was living in Finchley all through World War II (having refused to be evacuated abroad like many of his friends were) and can record many things that whilst not significant to the progress of the War as a whole were nevertheless important on a personal and family level. Exciting things like watching an enemy bomber in a cone of searchlights trying in vain to escape into the comparative safety of the surrounding darkness, or standing on a hillock watching an aerial battle oblivious of the danger. And later on seeing the *Doodle Bugs* coming from the east and taking bets as to when the engine would cut out. There were little things too: what do bananas taste like and will sweets ever be free of rationing again?

BASE HUMOUR

One school day the air-raid siren sounded in the middle of the morning (it often did). When lunch time came and all was quiet a decision was taken by the teachers to let the children go home under escort. This meant walking in small groups with members of the school staff for about two-thirds of the way and then running alone for the remainder. But always ready to lie flat if an aeroplane should appear.

It was a rainy day with very low cloud. Without any warning a plane came below the clouds and released three bombs, the first came down on the Northern Line south of West Finchley station, the second flattened a house in Lansdowne Road and the last landed in allotment gardens almost under the viaduct that carries the *Underground* to Mill Hill East. To the author the risk of trouble at home for ruining clothes by lying in the gutter or the lesser risk of injury left no real choice, so just a low crouch was in order. Unfortunately the teacher in charge of the group, a Mr James, did not appreciate this logic, particularly as he was covered in muck.

The bomb that landed in the allotments caused some wry and rather wicked humour. There was a policeman at the time who seemed to win every award at local shows for the quality of his vegetables, and this was the source of considerable envy. His allotment was changed by the bomb into a crater 10m deep, and it must be said that many people were amused.

CHAPTER VI

THE DEVELOPMENT OF
MAPS AND GUIDE BOOKS

E ven early peoples were concerned with the place in which they lived: the immediate environment and who controlled it, the fertile land, the rivers and surface contours, and the tracks that connected with the outside world. The art of cartography has been practised in a simple form for as long as there has been any civilisation, the earliest 'chart' in existence is a Babylonian clay tablet drawn about 4,300 years ago. There are also maps of parts of Egypt that were found in the tombs and these are nearly as old. It is safe to assume therefore that some form of maps must have been in use even before those that we are fortunate enough to have in our museums.

Among the peoples of the ancient world, the Greeks were probably the most accomplished at cartographical surveying. They were always seeking to expand because Greece was short of arable land, and this led to their exploration of the Mediterranean countries. They recorded where they went and what they saw. The most important figure in this early period was Ptolemy, who was really the first person to elevate geography and map making to a science. His influence remained well into the Middle Ages. His one great mistake was to grossly underestimate the size of the Earth, so that when Columbus sailed the Atlantic he really did believe that he would reach India after a few days sailing.

The next people on the map making scene were the Romans and although under the influence of the Greeks their maps were simpler and more basic. They concentrated less on mathematical geography and more on the practicalities of military logistics such as their roads and administrative areas.

A Roman general Marcus Vipsanius Agrippa commissioned a map of the known world based upon the already extensive system of Roman roads. Watling Street runs through Hendon, adjacent to Mill Hill, so even in these early times Mill Hill was virtually 'on the map', and this is over 1,500 years ago.

The end of the Roman Empire led to a void in map making (and to a void in much else besides). The importance of trunk roads declined and the Roman roads fell into decay. As far as we know no maps worthy of the name were produced which gave any detail of the British Isles for hundreds of years. In any case invasions by Norsemen, Saxons, and finally the Normans meant that there were no long periods of stability and the country was divided. There was no one authority that could have ordered that maps be produced.

THE BEGINNINGS OF PROPER MAPS

Mention has been made in an earlier chapter about the entry for Hendon in the *Domesday Book* so we know that during the reign of Norman the Conqueror Hendon and its hamlets was recorded. The first actual mention of Mill Hill by name was in Norden's *Speculum Brittanniae* which was published in 1593. There was a considerable mention of Hendon, which is not surprising because Norden is believed to have been living there at the time. Mill Hill was only given a bare mention, as were Dalis (Dollis), Hendon House, Brent Street and Drivers' Hill (now Bittacy Hill). In previous pages attention has been drawn to the likely origin of Mill Hill and because there was no actual mill before the 14th Century nothing by way of a record could have been written much before Norden. In the map of Middlesex which was published by him and improved and edited by Speed in 1610 Mill Hill is just a dot, as are the other places mentioned above. In these early maps no indication of the size is given.

Even in these far off times the small settlements and hamlets were connected by a pattern of paths and tracks. The first map of any part of the Mill Hill area (which is the property of All Souls College) is dated 1597. It shows the fields and groves of 'Olders Hilles' (Holders Hill Road) which lay between Ashley Lane and 'The Waye from Parson Street to Dallis'.

The map makers of the Renaissance and after were more concerned with display than geographical accuracy. In every piece of available space their maps and charts were covered with monsters, lions, and flowing initials with swash lines and decorations. The cartographers of the 18th Century were more interested in proper scientific detail and reliable information for administrators and surveyors. Chronometers, theodolites and telescopes were now available so that a higher degree of accuracy with surveys was possible and the proper calculation of degrees of latitude and longitude.

An attempt was made even on ancient maps to give some accuracy to the planimetric detail; shorelines, rivers and streams, and later roads. It was not possible to give any real illustration of contour, and until recent times this was really left to the ingenuity of the cartographer. A 17th Century map of Middlesex (spelt Middle-Sexia) shows the Hundreds (administrative areas) and most of the villages and hamlets reasonably well. We can recognise many of the names without difficulty although the spelling had not been standardized: Totteridge is Tatteridg, Dollis is Dilis, the Barnets are spelt Bernet, Brockley Hill is Brokeley Hills, Bushey is Bushye, and Mill Hill is in one word. The position of the River Brent is hopelessly wrong and according to this map would have been flowing uphill for much of the way. With no contours as such the hills and ridges of north London and Middlesex are drawn as individual peaks in ranges and even these are in the wrong places.

The map *'Middlesex by Robt Morden at the Atlas in Cornhill'* (Robert Morden 1650-1703) was an improvement on all that had been published before. It was included in *The New Description and State of England* published in 1701 with a second edition in 1704. Later in 1708, the atlas was republished as *'Fifty-six new and Accurate maps of Great Britain, Ireland and Wales'* with amendments by Herman Moll. He added a compass indicator and made some alterations to the actual cartographic detail. In 1730 the map appeared again in *'A Compleat History of Middlesex'* printed by E and R Nutt which was sold by T Cox. *The map of*

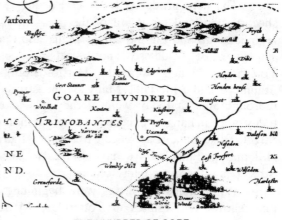

THE HUNDRED OF GORE

Middlesex by John Seller, published in 1679 is very important to us. In the Hendon part of this map Mill Hill is shown and also below that of Holcombe Hill a symbol to represent a windmill. This was the first map that indicated the windmill of Mill Hill, and of equal significance was the fact that no other mill, (water-mill or windmill), is shown anywhere else in Hendon or the immediately surrounding districts. Early 18th Century maps also show the mill of Mill Hill.

In Morden's map, roads are shown and it is possible to identify Watling Street, Holders Hill, Bittacy Hill and The Ridgeway, part of Totteridge Lane and Barnet Lane, and of course the main route from London through High Barnet to the northwest. North of High Barnet is indicated to Holy Head which must have been many days travel in the early 18th Century. The map in *'A Complete History of Middlesex'* gives a table of the Hundreds and a list of place names with their actual locations indicated by a system of letters and numbers. A scale of latitudes is included in the left margin and there is no extraneous decoration. Longitude is shown 'A Longitude in Minutes of a Degree from London' and a scale of 10 miles (in three inches) is indicated in the right margin.

Although land enclosure had been taking place in a modest way throughout the 16th Century, mainly as a way to secure large pasture lands, this had not had any great effect upon the counties around London. The 18th Century led to a big change in much of the Country and during this period (up to 1800) most of the corn growing lands of the east, north-east, and east Midlands for instance were enclosed. This did not affect the Hendon area to any great degree, most of the land was already reserved for pasture and the hay crop.

The map produced by John Rocque in 1754 (of Middlesex in four sheets) shows all the detail of the previous maps but by now all the land is divided up and the individual fields and their boundaries are illustrated. The map of Middlesex north-east covers most of the Barnets and Totteridge (which were in Hertfordshire) plus Hendon, Kingsbury, Stanmore and Mill Hill. Many of the streets and lanes that are still the thoroughfares of today were already in existence and most of the names today are unchanged except for a few minor differences in spelling. Page Street, Wise Lane, Lawrence Street, and Highwood Hill are shown in Mill Hill and in Finchley we have Ballards Lane and Neather Street (Nether Street), and there are many others.

With enclosure, farms were beginning to be named and Rocque's map shows two estates in Totteridge: M da Costa Esqr. who lived in Copped Hall (now Darlands and not to be confused with the Nicoll mansion, Copt Hall) and P Miass Esqr. (a misspelling of P Meyer) who lived in Pointer's Grove.

John Rocque was a Frenchman who had settled in England and between the years 1734 and 1762 he produced a great number of maps and charts. Although there are no flamboyant touches on the map surface Rocque's cartouche is a huge affair stating 'To Her Royal Highness the Princess Dowager of Wales, this Actual Survey of Middlesex is Most Humbly Inscribed. To Her Highness's Most Dutiful and Most Obedient Servant John Rocque Chorographer to Their Royal Highness's the Late and Present Prince of Wales 1754'. Phew! The map title was really sufficient without all this verbiage, *'A Topographical Map of the County of Middlesex by John Rocque 1754 by Act of Parliament.*

In 1754 Isaac Messeder published his *Field Book* which gives a most detailed account of the Manor of Hendon and the property within it. The cottage shown in earlier references as belonging to the miller is still indicated. By this time however there is no mention of the mill, but all the fields have names: Great Mill Field, Little Mill Field, Pear Tree Field, Saffron Field, etc.

In 1792 John Cooke, who described himself as 'Engraver at Mill Hill', produced a map of the 'Roads from London to Mill Hill & Barnet' which clearly shows most of the main roads of the district that are still with us today. Cooke had moved to live in Mill Hill and the map was to show his friends and business associates how to get to his new address. He was in no doubt that Mill Hill was a distinct location as the acknowledgement on his map indicates: 'J Cooke returns his sincere and grateful acknowledgements to his friends and the public in general for past favours. He has taken this method to inform them that he has removed from London to Mill Hill'.

ORDNANCE SURVEY MAPS

By the middle of the 18th Century power conscious European states had become increasingly aware of the need for accurate and reliable maps. This activity was well beyond the scope and ability of private cartographers. Originally these maps were prepared by the military for military purposes but as time went by the national survey organisations were taken over by civilian authorities. Typical of these are the *Institut Geographique National* of France, *Landestopographic* of Switzerland, and of course our own *Ordnance Survey*.

The first OS map of Middlesex (the map was named London) was published on Aug. 1 1822 with the survey having been completed between 1804 and 1813, some local amendments were accepted almost right up to publication day. The survey was executed at a scale of 2ins to 1 mile by Royal Military surveyors, probably assisted by local technicians specially hired for the task. From the field drawings a final draft was presented to the engraver at a scale of 1in to the mile.

Apart from the arterial roads of the 20th Century these maps are quite outstandingly complete when compared with those of today (those that are to the same scale). There were a few spelling aberrations. To avoid confusion (there being much other detail) field boundaries and spot heights were omitted although both of these had been included on the surveyors' drawings. This map was reprinted throughout the 19th Century until 1891 when the railways were added. This also necessitated some minor amendments to road alignment and the addition of some bridges. An attempt at contour indication was made, however not with contour lines like we find on our maps today but with line hatching. At least The

Ridgeway was no longer drawn as a range of mountain peaks but rather the ridge that it is.

A look at the map shelf of any book shop today will confirm that other map making did not cease when official cartography was introduced by OS. In 1828 a new map was published by Francis Wishaw and in this a new important feature has been added, the Finchley Road. This road (see also Roads, Paths and Tracks) was established by *Act of Parliament* in 1826.

In 1862-3 a new survey was carried out for a series of OS maps to a much larger scale. These were at 1:4340 (or about 15ins to 1 mile. Maps were now available of sufficient accuracy for builders and developers. Although contour lines were still not included there are frequent spot heights, fields are all numbered and the areas indicated, and even the flow direction of open drains and streams is shown. Property was beginning to spread along the main thoroughfares, such as Holders Hill Road, and individual houses were included and named. There was still no development on Bittacy Hill. Bittacy House was at the top of the hill on the western side (where Watchtower House now stands) and Bittacy Farm became Mill Hill Barracks. The farm house and out-buildings were at the foot of the hill.

GAZETTEERS AND GUIDE BOOKS

Ninety years on from Isaac Messeder's *Field Book*, and people were on the move, even though the railways and quick travel had not yet arrived. And they wanted to know a little about the places that they were about to visit. In 1842 Lewis's *Topographical Dictionary of England* was published with potted biographies of just about anywhere worth a mention. Hendon has an entry and in it there are a few words about Mill Hill: 'A church was erected on Mill Mill in the later English style, at the expense of the late William Wilberforce Esq.'. Note that it says 'on' rather than 'at' Mill Hill which implies that it still had not been recognised by everyone as a named village, only a location. The entry also mentions the Nicoll Almshouses and the Protestant Dissenters' Grammar School, now Mill Hill School (founded in 1807).

The first *Kelly Directory* for Hendon and Finchley was published in 1887. But this was certainly not the first guide. Since Messeder's book in 1754 there had been *Cooke's Survey* in 1796 and *Wishaw's Guide* in 1828. Even at this comparatively late stage Mill Hill was still not given (by them) a location as a village, but merely as a hill, and the name The Ridgeway is not mentioned at all. This is a strange omission because we know that le Regway (The Ridgeway) was mentioned in the *Black Survey* 550 years before, so it must have been known by this name for a very long time. In the Mill Hill street directory published in 1898-9 the old families do not get a mention, they had already died out. However some of the people detailed in the chapter on notable people are shown.

TODAY'S MAPS AND GUIDES

By now the new railways were spreading throughout the land and people were able to travel far quicker, easier, and safer than ever before. Guide books started to make their appearance and one of these was mentioned in the *Introduction* to this book. Many famous people had taken up residence in Mill Hill and it had become the place to visit. Mill Hill was now on the map in every sense.

From this point on the range of maps available proliferated. In the early 1960s a young Frenchman came to work in London, a friend of the author. He asked if it would be easy to obtain a map showing the location of the building in which his employer was situated. He was asked the purpose for which it was required and told that he could have 4 miles to 1in, 1in to 1 mile, 2½in to 1 mile, 6in to 1 mile, 25in to 1 mile, and 50in to 1 mile: he thought this was just a joke. He just could not believe that all these scales were available, they were because the British Isles is probably the most mapped country in the World. And this is not the full picture by a long way, there are many other map publishers besides OS. Needless to say all the scales that our Frenchman discovered are still available except that they are now metric: 2½ins to 1 mile is 1:25,000 etc. Such are the changes to our environment that a 50 year old map is virtually useless today except as an historical document. OS map Sheet 160 NW London dated 1930 with later amendments and reprinted 1945 has none of the all important post World War II major roads but shows lots of now non-existent railways. Even the Quarter-Inch Map of 1970 is not much better although it does show a bit of M1 and A1(M). All these old maps were on thick paper or even canvas, but this would be pointless today because changes take place quicker than the time taken to wear out the maps.

Readers will need no introduction to the maps of today, there are plenty available for every purpose in any reliable book shop. For those who really mean to walk Mill Hill and rediscover the interesting places for themselves perhaps the best map is the OS Pathfinder series 1:25,000 of the area, or if real detail is required OS sheet TQ29 SW which is at a scale of 1:10,000. Enough detail here for every purpose.

Small scale maps (up to 1:25,000) are available from any reputable bookshops, 1:10,000 and larger can be obtained from a main dealer in maps such as Edward Stanford of Long Acre, London WC2. The old (19th Century) OS maps have been reprinted and are now available from David and Charles, Brunel House, Newton Abbot, Devon. Reprints of most of the the other maps, including those by Norden, Morden and Rocque are available from local public libraries at a modest price.

At this point it is worth mentioning some of the books that have been published in the last 100 years or so, either about Hendon at large or Mill Hill in particular. Needless to say they vary considerably both in scope and accuracy. The most scholarly and therefore the best is *The History and Topography of the Parish of Hendon Middlesex* by Edward T Evans published in 1890. His research is thorough although obviously limited to the documents that were known at that time. As a record, particularly of social history, this book is more comprehensive than any other.

Unfortunately a number of errors of fact appear in the writings of Norman G Brett-James, particularly his biography of Peter Collinson. In addition he seems to have taken some persistent legends about Mill Hill and quoted them as facts, casting doubt upon the remainder of the texts. Many other books and pamphlets have obviously taken Brett-James as a reference and his suppositions are repeated many times. His book *'The Story of Mill Hill Village'* is better, chatty and easy to read and and tells a good story well, but beware of the legends! He wrote this book before the *Black Survey* was discovered so it is not his fault that he did not know about the mill of Mill Hill. One sentence in his book epitomises the biggest change that Mill Hill has suffered, viz roads: (referring to the Catholic Church at Mill Hill Broadway):

'Cardinal Bourne dedicated the church in 1924, and like the churches of other denominations it is situated at the corner of Lawrence Street (now Mill Hill Broadway) and Flower Lane, near to the point where the new trunk road to Watford is planned to pass'.

Various other guide books, notably those about London's environment, mention Mill Hill, usually limiting their quotation to describing one or two buildings. Unfortunately the books by Evans and Brett-James are now almost impossible to obtain but some of the old books on London have been reprinted in recent years. The most recent publication is *The Story of Mill Hill*, a slim volume published by the Mill Hill History Society in 1990.

CHAPTER VII

ROADS, LANES, PATHS AND TRACKS

T hroughout history right up to the 19th Century, Mill Hill was an isolated backwater, a hamlet on the edge of a manor which was itself off the beaten track. The nearest south-north route, the Roman Watling Street ran on the western side and no route of any kind was constructed nearby on the eastern side until the 17th Century. This isolation did not prevent the development of local lanes and by-ways. Many have been in existence for hundreds of years. The Ridgeway was almost certainly walked by pre-historic man and some other lanes are possibly Roman in origin. The Roman roads were made for the transportation of men and stores so they are as straight as possible, the lanes of Mill Hill were trodden by the people so they twist and turn to avoid obstacles long since gone.

MAIN ROAD ROUTES AND TRUNK ROADS

When the Romans built Watling Street on its way to *Verulamium* (near St Albans) and the north-west they also built the more distant (to Mill Hill) Ermine Street to the east in the Lea Valley. These two roads were the only important transport routes northwards in the area for hundreds of years, but long before the Normans came in 1066 the actual roads had long since fallen into decay and were no longer visible.

In Medieval times a somewhat circuitous route was developed by usage, rather nearer to Mill Hill, on the eastern side, from London to St Albans via Finchley, Barnet and South Mimms. Much of this road followed existing farm tracks. Although Edgware was on the old Watling Street the route through Barnet became the more important and it was therefore Barnet that developed into a town, and even today it is possible to see how important it was by the number of old coaching inns.

In the 17th Century came the Great North Road, a straighter and more direct route that went through Potters Bar, and in the early 19th Century a vastly better road which became the original A1. Although this road also followed some existing farm tracks it was a new road practically throughout the whole of its length. The road was made (following an Act of Parliament in 1826) and was intended to be an outlet from George IV's new park (Regents Park) northwards. This was always designed to be a trunk road and little expense was spared in the construction, however being a turnpike the users had to pay a toll and Finchley residents fought

51

in vain against this imposition. A part of the Edgware Road was also a turnpike road with tolls. The turnpike was situated at the junction of Deansbrook Road and Edgware Road until 1872 and is indicated by a Blue Plaque high up on the wall.

By the early 18th Century many of the roads with which we are now familiar were already in existence and named. Indeed they have in many cases kept the same name or a similar one from these times.

But now a quiet revolution was taking place because transport between main towns by road was becoming more important. It was sometimes necessary to shift the military from place to place in a hurry, but of more significance were the requirements of commerce which were steadily becoming more demanding.

Up to 1555 all roads were the responsibility of the manor through which they ran. An Act of Parliament transferred this authority to the parish councils and they retained this until the 19th century. Under this Act the parish had to appoint a Surveyor of Highways from the parishioners, often more than one, and Hendon was divided into two wards for this purpose. The position of Surveyor was not a popular one (so the post was not retained by one person) because all the tools, cartage, and labour necessary had to be provided free by the parishioners. The Surveyor rendered an account to the local JPs and they authorized the raising of a Highways Rate to cover the cost of materials. In Hendon most of these were gathered locally and much of the gravel was quarried in Mill Hill.

From 1691 the appointment of the Highways Surveyor was confirmed at special highways sessions by local JPs. The accounts of Hendon Surveyors began in 1703.

In 1888 the *County Courts Act*, in an attempt to improve main roads and introduce an improved standard of construction and maintenance gave the county councils the responsibility for all these roads. A further act, the *Local Government Act* of 1894 made the District Councils responsible for some classes of local road, ensuring at last that roads were no longer just pot-holed mud. The man who revolutionised the building of roads, John McAdam, was born in Scotland in 1756. After much experimenting at his own expense he arrived at a formula for construction that would produce roads that would last, and his methods were adopted officially after a Parliamentary enquiry in 1823. Without his specifications, Acts of Parliament to determine responsibility would have been futile.

Throughout all these times Watling Street as a route remained virtually unchanged. There was no need for realignment because being a

Roman road it was straight and had been well made, although obviously by now nothing visible remained to show how it was built. In fact over 350 years ago no trace could be found of the actual Roman road.

By the beginning of the 1930s it had become obvious that the line of the A1 through Finchley, Barnet and Hatfield must be changed. The original A1 was downgraded to A1000 when the Barnet by-Pass was built. The by-pass became the A1 of today and runs through Mill Hill. This most important of roads, is now dual carriageway from the southern border of the London Borough of Barnet to Newcastle.

This new road was without doubt an essential development, but of course in recent years has become dangerously overcrowded at certain times of the day, particularly the evening rush hours. Traffic through Mill Hill is frequently at a crawl or standstill. Unfortunately this road does virtually bisect the area, separating east from west, particularly during busy periods. One of Mill Hill's oldest roads, Lawrence Street, was cut in half by Mill Hill Circus and the southern part renamed Mill Hill Broadway.

Much more dramatic in its effect was the extending of the M1 Motorway from its original southern terminal to Staples Corner on the North Circular Road. This runs parallel with and adjacent to the British Rail Midland line and necessitated a rather gloomy bridge over the southern end of Mill Hill Broadway. A slip road to the M1 was built using one of the arches of the bridge that carries the A1 over Bunns Lane. This is now disused for the second time, having originally been used to carry the line of the Edgware LNER (GNR Highgate-Edgware Line) on route between Mill Hill East and Mill Hill for The Hale. (See also Railways). The site of this motorway spur on the western side of the A1/A41 has now been redeveloped into a super-store area. The motorway spurs are now at Fiveways Junction right on the edge of Mill Hill giving access to and from the A1.

It is worth noting that John Laing plc, the construction company that won the contract for the first four sections of the M1 which were opened to traffic in the spring of 1959, has its headquarters in Mill Hill, one building occupying a large site on the western side of Page Street near to where the railway line to Edgware mentioned above used to run.

MILESTONES

When the Romans constructed their main roads they added distance markers at 1,000 pace intervals (which would be about 1,400m or 1,620 yds). These were the forerunners of our milestones, although no other authority bothered with such refinements for centuries: they did not even build decent roads. Unfortunately the Romans were frequently guilty of sycophancy and these markers eventually became plaques for the adulation of the emperor with the real and original purpose taking a secondary role.

Milestones as we know them today were introduced on main roads after the *General Turnpike Act* was passed in 1773. They were an aid to charging, which was calculated on the distance travelled. Since that time the only marker posts as such have been on our railways, and of course in the last three decades or so to mark motorway junctions.

There is a route into Mill Hill where milestones can still be seen, from Hampstead to The Ridgeway. It is not a continuous road, certainly not a main route to anywhere. It is a rambling way between two points that have no obvious connection and it is hard to see why they were ever erected. The line ends at the top of Highwood Hill. The milestones are short and rectangular in section and are unevenly placed over 11 miles. Peter Collinson described them in 1752 as newly erected and commented on the tenth which was opposite the sheep wash on The Ridgeway. Today this stone does not look much like a milestone at all. It is small, (about 300mm high) and any inscription is either obscured or has weathered away.

LANES ANCIENT AND MODERN

It is a little surprising that the Nicoll family, so important in the Hendon, Mill Hill area for hundreds of years was never perpetuated in a road name unlike so many other people associated with the locality. Perhaps their house was of such importance that a road by the name was considered unnecessary, except that the house Copt Hall is no more.

Many of the lanes of Mill Hill are very old indeed, much older than the names given to them now, and have been locally important routes for centuries and may even date back to pre-Roman times. These lanes of Mill Hill always seem to be going nowhere in particular. They wind this way and that as if there was never any hurry to arrive, even if you knew where you were going. Perhaps by confusing the visitor they kept Mill Hill to itself, and if you arrived from outside you were unlikely to find your way out.

Needless to say it is not possible to mention all the roads and lanes of Mill Hill by name, so we have confined ourselves to those that are historic or that have historic connections either in the road or because of the buildings that are in them. There is no Lakeside Avenue or Sea View but almost as silly is Vineyard Avenue backing on to Mill Hill Gas Works, and Woodland Way (which runs parallel and next to the M1) that needed no forestry destruction for its creation. Indeed there have been no forests around here for a very long time.

Long before the lanes had any proper or regular names (although they all no doubt had names by common parlance) the places that they connected had names which always gave some information about the place. Not many miles from Mill Hill we have such names: Brockley - the field of the badger, Boreham Wood - the home of the wild boar, Elstree - the hill of the elder trees, Chipping Barnet - Barnet of the cheap (or market), Friern Barnet - the town of the friars, Monken Hadleigh - the locality where the monks lived, Finchley - the place of the finches, etc.

Bittacy Hill

No matter how the original Mill Hill Village is approached a long uphill pull is unavoidable. Before motor transport Bittacy Hill must have been quite a trial. This road was originally known as Drivers' Hill and is shown on John Rocques map of 1754. The high land to the south of The Ridgeway is however still shown on the OS map (1:10,000) as Drivers Hill. On the 1898 OS Map the name is Bittacy Hill with Bittacy House at the top, Bittacy Cottages a little lower down, and Bittacy Farm by the junction of Sanders Lane on the opposite side.

Milespit Hill

The gentler way to The Ridgeway is via Milespit Hill and must have been the favourite alternative. Rocque calls this Dold Street although in the 1in OS map of 1822 this name appears to be against the lane now known as Hammers Lane. On later maps only the section south of Wise Lane is named differently, but Dole Street, not Dold Street was by Wise Lane. The name Dole Street was unacceptable to its new residents of the early 1930s, the Dole (unemployment pay) being too familiar in these times. The origin of the name Milespit is uncertain and there are three suggested possibilities.

There is of course the tradition of the the mill of Hill Hill so perhaps an earlier spelling is a corruption of this. The hill may have been named after an early landowner and to help substantiate this there was a Milespit Farm in 1475 and an area at the top of the hill on the western side is named Myles Down on the 1898 OS Map of Mill Hill Village. Perhaps the most likely origin is that the name is a different corruption and refers to the fact that the hill is one mile long. The evolution of the spelling of the name does not really help or confirm anything having been variously spelt Milespit in 1475, Milspit in 1563, Myles Pytt in 1574, and Milles Pitt in 1588: four versions in just over 100 years! It is really a case of take your pick.

From a historical point of view probably the most important buildings on Milespit Hill are the six almshouses that were erected on the orders of Stephen Nicoll in 1696. The houses were repaired by a Mr Pinder Simpson in 1893 and modernised by the Constitutional Club and others in 1923. There are also some rather pleasant weather-boarded cottages that are quite old and a group of modern cottages similarly clad in a successful effort to conform in design.

Almshouses erected in 1696

It makes sense to mention the High Street at this point because it is really an upper extension of Milespit Hill. One thing is certain, it is only 'high' in altitude, definitely not in importance. Along its 100m or so there are some rather pretty 18th Century cottages on one side, but the other is filled with ultra modern town houses which are no doubt very comfortably appointed internally but from the outside look like luxury byres. The antique shop at the end of the road only opens by appointment so there is no chance of a browse here. The rather nice private house called Blenheim Steps was once the school tuck shop for Mill Hill School.

The Ridgeway

This is the main road of the old Village. Being more or less level and on average 122m above sea level it is an obvious route, and indeed has been used as such by Romans, Saxons, Danes, Normans, and every age since then. In all probability the Celts walked The Ridgeway too before all these people. It is still the centre of the Village and many of the important buildings are on The Ridgeway or close at hand.

The Ridgeway and beyond (Highwood Hill and Totteridge Common) were the first parts of the area to show any real tendency to development. In the 18th and 19th Centuries many eminent people came and built fine houses here, some of these still exist although as is to be expected there have been many alterations and some additional building work over the years.

The Village of Mill Hill, (as opposed to the district) is really The Ridgeway and surrounds. It is the oldest part by far, certainly the most picturesque and the place where the gentry came to escape the hurly burly of working in the City and to bring up their families, whilst at the same time being close enough to London to commute to their place of business. One of the most prominent buildings is Mill Hill School, but historically just as important are various cottages, two unusual churches, and for that matter two ponds, Sheepwash Pond and Angel Pond. The whole road and surrounding area has been declared a conservation area.

As Bittacy Hill becomes The Ridgeway there is a row of well maintained 1930s houses, each sporting its own burglar alarm (are they all real?). Opposite the top of Wills Grove there stands an ancient timber framed cottage which had been re-duced to just the frames and the chimney stacks. This is Rosebank, a 17th Century building now com-pletely refurbished and once the home of the Society of Friends, or Quakers, of Mill Hill. This was  *Sheepwash Pond....* originally a one-storey building, but a second floor was added when the building was converted into a private residence.

The Ridgeway also contains some buildings that are important because of their function. Watchtower House, the headquarters of the Jehovah's Witnesses in the UK is one of these and stands on the site once occupied by Bittacy House. This building would be unlikely to win a Prince Charles award, it is however well concealed behind sturdy walls and the abundance of mature trees in the grounds has been maintained.

Unlike many modern designs the National Institute for Medical Research building does give the appearance of being finished. In spite of its vast size the design is quite pleasing and although already 50 years old it does not appear to be and carries its age well.

As a complete contrast, next door to the NIMR, and almost completely hidden behind fences and trees is Fir Island: a rather splendid Victorian house on the triangular plot formed by the two arms where Burtonhole Lane joins The Ridgeway.

Lawrence Street

The route of Lawrence Street is considered by some historians to date from Roman times, it is certainly of great age. Indeed much of the lane follows almost exactly the route of a much older lane called Tommy Cook's Lane. Some documents refer to this road as Gladwyn Street. It is shown and named on Rocques map with today's spelling although in 1680 there was Larance Street Farm.

Originally the road ran from the foot of Highwood Hill to the junction of Hale Lane and Bunns Lane. When Mill Hill Station was built on the Midland Railway the southern section of Lawrence Street was renamed Station Road. Later still it was changed again to Mill Hill Broadway, which is its name today. The Midland Railway station was changed at the same time to Mill Hill Broadway.

When the A1 Barnet by-Pass was constructed between the wars it would have cut Lawrence Street in half anyway and it would then have become illogical to have one name for the two parts. Although the western side of Lawrence Street is almost completely built up (apart from a small patch occupied by allotment gardens) the other side is grass for most of the way with good views of the tower of St Joseph's Missionary College between the trees. A fine specimen of a native species of oak, Durmast Oak (*Quercus petraea*) stands in the grounds. according to some writers this tree was used by Oliver Goldsmith as shelter and resting point on his walks around the district.

Page Street

Page Street is another very old lane, and many consider this route to be of Roman origins. As a Roman road ran through the grounds of Copt Hall this is quite possible. The name almost certainly refers to the Page family who lived in the area from the late 13th Century.

Burtonhole Lane

In the latest OS maps the lane from Partingdale Lane which loops round from Frith Manor to rejoin The Ridgeway just south of the Medical Research Centre is all named Burtonhole Lane. Forty years ago the first part from Frith Manor was known locally as Dirty Dick's Lane and because it really is two quite distinct lanes there is no real reason for one name from end to end. However it must be said that 18th Century maps do show this as one complete loop without any other sections of lane adjoining. In earlier maps the name was Buttonhole Lane.

The 'Dirty Dick's' end of the Lane is actually the boundary of Mill

Hill and in really wet winter weather that is just about all it was, a muddy boundary between two hedgerows and certainly not worthy of the name 'lane' at all, just a rather poor bridle path. In recent years it has been somewhat improved, apparently for the benefit of the large number of equestrian folk who use it. E T Evans, in his book lists this lane as a public footpath and describes it as 'The green lane from the Frith Manor to Burton Hole Farm'. The farm, another of Mill Hill's weatherboarded houses was built in the 18th Century.

The lane appears to have links with a 15th Century family and has been called Burtonhole or Button Hole Lane for over 200 years. It has

managed to retain an essentially rural character throughout its length and the houses are well scattered. At the western end is the large mansion 'Oakfields' which has recently been completely refurbished and boasts a rather elegant pair of initialled ornamental gates. It is now divided into luxury apartments. Round the corner is a rather square

Oakfields . . . recently refurbished

ancillary building which is part of the NIMR, the Medical Research Council Collaborative Centre.

Daws Lane

This is now one of the least lane-like of the old Mill Hill thoroughfares. It runs in a straight line from the foot of Hammers Lane to Mill Hill Circus and is completely urbanised with fortunately some variation in the styles of houses. The southern side for most of its length is taken up by the edge of Mill Hill Park.

Mill Hill Broadway

If the The Ridgeway is the centre of old Mill Hill, then Mill Hill Broadway is certainly the centre of the new. The bulk of the residential area is within 15 minutes walk of these shops and the railway and bus stations.

The Broadway has followed the trend that we find everywhere today, where local shopping streets are concerned: the number of actual shops (butchers, bakers, green-grocers, stationers, ironmongers, fishmongers etc.) is ever decreasing and fast food shops, building society offices and other service outlets is increasing.

In some respects The Broadway has fared rather better than many similar suburb or town centres in that there are still a good number of actual provision shops. At the last check two more butchers have shut up shop leaving just one, part of the 20 that close nationwide every month. There are now only half of the number of butchers shops that there were just 20 years ago, few shopping centres have any wet fish shops at all, and greengrocers are vanishing fast. The super-market with its bloodless,

One of Mill Hills oldest roads, (circa 1920)

pre-packed, convenience produce reigns supreme, fine providing that you don't mind the price penalty.

A visitor arriving at Mill Hill today could well come to the conclusion that the people of Mill Hill rarely cook but either eat out or survive on take-away food, there are so many eating places in The Broadway. Unfortunately fast food shops mean an appreciable increase in litter.

If nothing else The Broadway is a good place for churches. When St Paul's Church was built on The Ridgeway its main function was to make life easier for the people in the Village: they no longer needed to travel to St Mary's at The Burroughs Hendon. When the area around the railway station developed St Paul's in its turn became too far for the people in new Mill Hill and St Michael and all Angels was built. In addition we have the United Reformed Church on the roundabout and the Roman Catholic Church of the Sacred Heart on the junction of The

Broadway and Flower Lane, all three being in the space of 200m or so.

At the southern end of the Broadway are the bus and railway stations. The only virtue of having the bus depot under the motorway is that passengers are protected from the weather but it is very depressing.

Wills Grove

A motorist could be excused for thinking that Wills Grove is a quick route from Mill Hill Broadway to The Ridgeway, it certainly appears to be on the map. It is however a wide thoroughfare going no-where: there is a barrier in the middle because the road is a private road. This effectively preserves the road in the 19th Century, virtually traffic and noise free. On both sides is much land belonging to Mill Hill

..... *smart picket fence*

School. The are also one or two pleasant buildings including a rather nice weather-boarded house complete with smart picket fence.

Bunns Lane

Bunns Lane is a winding lane of great antiquity, and possibly the oldest lane of the parish. Unlike many others it seems to have kept to the same spelling over the centuries. Rocque's map shows this road quite clearly, (but without a name), with surrounding properties including Bone Farm just about in the middle. Another map of the Manor and Parish of Hendon published in the same period by James Crow gives the name and indicates a number of field names including Bunns Mead to the west and Bunns Hill to the east. There was also a field called Bunn's Bushes.

Running from Page Street to Hale Lane with no straight stretches makes Bunns Lane one of the longest and most interesting of the ancient ways. Unfortunately the eastern end, the part from Page Street to Flower Lane, particularly under the A1/A41 bridge, is now a bit of a mess.

Little is known of the Bunn family except that they were wealthy farmers in the 18th Century. Before that, in the 15th Century Bunns Farm appears to have been occupied by Simon Bunde. Mrs Jane Bunn, the wife of Thomas Bunn, who died on November 17 1795 is buried in the churchyard of St Mary's at Hendon.

Hale Lane

The first mention of Hale, perpetuated in Hale Lane, is Ralph in the Hale in 1294. Sixteen years later there was a John in the Hale who as mentioned earlier played an important part in the Peasants' Revolt of 1381. In 1525 the district had become just Hale and Netherhale in 1588. Although the lane appears in early maps the name does not appear to have been added until much later. The line of the lane has remained virtually as it was when first shown on a map of 1597. This is probably the lane for which Richard Nicoll left 20 shillings for maintenance in 1498.

By the time the railways were built The Hale was an established part of the district and there was a station on the old GN Railway originally named The Halt at The Hale later changed to Mill Hill the Hale.

Marsh Lane

The Marsh family is well documented and is certainly of long standing in the area. During the reign of Edward IV John Marsh took title to some land at The Hale. By the end of the 17th Century the Marsh family was large, well known in the Mill Hill area, and evidently prosperous. For a more complete story of this family see the chapter on notable people and families.

Marsh Lane runs from the *Rising Sun* inn at the top of Highwood Hill to Northway Circus, dropping steeply for most of the way. There is nothing of particular architectural merit or great age, however the upper part nonetheless has some fine houses on both sides of the road. This changes to rather more ordinary suburbia as the hill is descended.

Highwood Hill

One common factor about many of the names is the variations in the spellings, and the fact that there seems to have been more changes in the 16th Century than any other. It seems that everyone had their own version and their own favourite spelling, Highwood is another of these. The name is really self-explanatory and refers to the high wood. By the time that we get to the principle map makers of the 18th Century the name has already standardised at today's spelling. In 1523 however it was Hiwode, Highwode Hyll in 1543, Heiwoodhill in 1563, and Hyewoodhill in 1568.

By the beginning of the 19th Century Highwood Hill had reached the peak of its importance as a desirable place in which to live. It had (and has) magnificent views, there were quite extensive woods in the area, and it was close enough to London to make the journey in and out of the capital by horse drawn carriage relatively quick and easy.

Brent Street

Strictly speaking Brent Street has no place here because it is well outside the boundary of Mill Hill. It is worth a mention however because of a dispute over origins. The map maker Norden surmised that the River Brent and later Brent Street were named after the family of Brent (there were various spellings, Braint Breynt, etc.). Another historian, Dr Fuller, writing in 1662 (*Worthies of Middlesex*) says that this is preposterous and that the family took its name from the river. Fuller maintains that the family name was Falcatus or Fulke of Brent. Fulke was apparently a courtier of King John.

Wise Lane

The family of Nicholas Wise was living in Mill Hill in 1584. They were mentioned frequently in *Court Rolls* from 1633 listing various positions of authority held by them. Wise Lane had been named after them by the middle of the 18th Century. There is no evidence of the family in Mill Hill after this time.

Until the end of the 1930s Wise Lane still maintained a very rural appearance. This has changed somewhat but it is still a very desirable road in which to live. For a third of the length of the Lane there is green on both sides, Mill Hill Park to the west and School Park to the east. The rest of the Lane has houses on both sides, not mainly of any great age but substantial and sited well back off the road. It is a pity that money is not available to erect some decorative iron railings along the line of Mill Hill Park instead of the rather tatty chestnut paling fence.

Goldbeaters Grove

Goldbeaters Farm was situated to the west of Bunns Lane south of the Great Northern Railway line between Mill Hill The Hale and Edgware stations. Although Goldbeaters Grove is no doubt named after this family the road is a modern one and part of a between-the-wars estate. It is in fact not in Mill Hill but just over the border in Edgware. The name dates back to John le Goldbetere of 1321.

Gibb's Green

Gibbs Green is another road with ancient connections, although there is little to give this impression today. John Gybbe lived in the area in the early 16th Century and in *Cooke's Survey* of 1796 Gibb's is already shown as a continuation of Hankins Lane and Selvage Lane (which is more or less where it still runs today). There are details of lands in Gibb's Green in *Cooke's Survey.*

Maxwelton Avenue

Maxwelton Breas are bonny
Where early falls the dew
And t'was there that Annie Laurie
Gid me her promise true.
Gid me her promise true
That ne'er forgot will be
And were not for Annie Laurie
I'd lay me doon and dee.

Maxwelton Avenue and Maxwelton Close were named after a house that was in the vicinity in the 19th Century. The original Maxwelton House is in Dumfries in Scotland. A family called Hutchin came from there and it was probably them who named the house in Mill Hill. Maxwelton House was the home of Annie Laurie (1682-1764) who was immortalised by a rejected suitor William Douglas in the well known love song that was written about 1700.

Nan Clark's Lane and Hankin's Lane

Although these two lanes are quite separate and a fair distance apart they are considered together and for good reason.

When Moat Mount House was erected by Abel Browne in 1828 the whole estate was 60ha. Up to this time the lane leading up to the house was called Nan Clark's Lane but was subsequently renamed Moat Mount Lane. It was certainly called Nan Clark's Lane in the late 18th Century. In *Cooke's Survey* (1796) there is a reference to "The Property of Richard Jackson Esq., Nan Clark's Lane, Highwood Hill, a dwelling house with pleasure grounds, gardens etc. and a yard with the farmhouse etc., the whole formerly called the Moat Mount. A Freehold demesne of la 2r 20p" (0.7ha approx)". Some time ago the lane reverted to the original name although there is no record of when this second change actually took place.

On old maps there is some confusion about this road. John Rocque (1754) shows a lane that is clearly Nan Clark's Lane but as a complete loop rejoining Marsh Lane apparently where Hankin's Lane is today. Other cartographers have also drawn this, for instance John Cooke *(A Map of the Roads from London to Mill Hill and Barnet*, 1792) and *Cooke's*

Survey of 1796 so we must assume that the two roads were linked.

The story of Nan Clark is a local legend. There is some evidence that a woman of that name lived in the Highwood Hill area at the beginning of the 18th Century, and she was either the licensee or a barmaid of the *Three Crowns* Inn which was at the corner of the lane. By all accounts she was married and had two daughters. Local people claim that the ghost of Nan Clark can still be seen and although an investigation by psychic researchers failed to find any real evidence another medium claimed to have felt a definite 'presence'.

According to the legend Nan Clark is supposed to have been drowned in a local pond whilst out walking late one night or killed in the lane which bears her name, depending upon which version of the story you prefer. According to various local writers she was murdered either by her husband or lover. In other references she is said to have drowned as the result of an accident. A Mr F Hitchen Kemp wrote to the *Hendon & Finchley Times* in 1934 stating that an ale house once stood here and in 1696 Ann Clark the victualler had her licence revoked, although this seems a poor reason for haunting the place. Perhaps there are bits of the truth in all these stories. The last 'definite' sighting of the ghost seems to have been nearly 50 years ago by a sentry during World War II.

Today Nan Clark's Lane is a rather pretty road full of elegant houses, some very large but all with well manicured gardens. On a sunny summer's day this lane is just as worthy of a visit as many better known lanes. It is a cul-de-sac and there is certainly no way through to Hankins Lane even by footpath. Unfortunately being pretty brings its own problems, curious visitors, which has led to a proliferation of PRIVATE signs. Such a pity because they shouldn't really be necessary.

Hankin's Lane has also been in existence for a very long time and we would half expect to find references of a family with this name. Sadly there were none.

In Rocque's map he gives the name Hanging Wood Lane to the lane now known as Hankin's Lane. The name was obviously abandoned not long after this because in *Cooke's Survey* there are various entries for someone named Dollman (no first name or gender are given) who owned "The five acres near Hankin Lane". The similarity of the names would suggest that Hanging Wood was corrupted to Hankin's. As many lanes of this time were unnamed this title would appear to have some significance: perhaps someone was hanged there. It is unlikely that there was a gallows or gibbet here, they were usually placed on a cross roads as a warning to others.

The part of the lane that joined the two parts of Hankin's Lane and

Nan Clark's Lane would have been where the boundary of Highwood Park and White Lodge is today. Usually it is possible to trace these old lanes if not at ground level then certainly from the air. In this case this is not possible because Moat Mount School (the original name of this school) sits astride where the lane ran as do the playing fields and the land has been much levelled thus destroying any trace.

Ashley Lane

Nowadays Ashley Lane, which was formerly called Cardinal's Lane, is unimportant and for most of its length only a footpath running between the Mill Hill Golf Course (established 1903) and Hendon Cemetery and Crematorium (opened 1899). In earlier times this lane had more local significance, probably equal to Holders Hill Road and it is almost certainly older.

Cardinal Wolsey used Ashley Lane as part of his route when he travelled from London to York in 1530. Wolsey had been the Dean of York since 1513 and was appointed archbishop in 1514 upon the sudden death of Cardinal Christopher Bainbridge in rather suspicious circumstances. Bainbridge had been in Rome for five years acting as the King's (Henry VIII) agent at the Papal Court. He was assisted by Cardinals Gigli and Hadrian who had been appointed bishops of Worcester and Bath & Wells (although neither had ever been here) to improve English interests in Rome. Bainbridge died in July and it was suspected that a chaplain was guilty of poisoning him. He was tortured and confessed but later committed suicide to avoid further suffering. After an investigation his name was cleared and he was exonerated.

Although Wolsey was elevated to Cardinal Archbishop of York in 1514 he was never in the diocese even though unlike Gigli and Hadrian he was in England most of the time. The only time that he might have been in York was when he travelled to Scotland on a diplomatic mission for Henry VII in 1508.

In 1529 Wolsey was in disgrace and he never regained his power and influence. Various important people were scheming against him. He had moved from Esher to Richmond Palace which was considered by his adversaries to be too near to the Court. The Duke of Norfolk and Anne Boleyn particularly wanted him out of the way, (obviously he knew too much, and could still be regarded by some as influential) and finally the king told him that he had to take up his duties at York as archbishop. Wolsey tried hard to prevent this and claimed that in any case he did not have the money to permit him to travel in proper style. In fact the King paid him £1,000 in secret so that he could travel in a manner befitting a man of his rank.

Wolsey was renowned for the luxurious clothes that he wore (he also encouraged his clergy to wear silk and velvet). The journey north took place in Passion Week, just before Easter. The route would have taken him from Richmond to the Palace of the Abbot of St Peter's at Westminster, at Hendon. This was Abbots Grange later to be called Hendon Place, and later still Tenterden Hall. His route would then have taken him along what is now Tenterden Grove, into Ashley Lane, then northwards, probably along The Ridgeway, up Highwood Hill, across the grass track in the grounds of Highwood House to Moat Mount.

The second night was spent at the house of Lady Parr (Rye House), the third at Royston Monastery, and the fourth at Huntingdon Abbey. On the fifth day, which was Palm Sunday, Wolsey arrived at Peterborough Abbey and stayed there for several days. Finally he crossed the River Trent and entered the Diocese of York at Newark. He stayed at Southwell, the nearest that he could be to London, and yet comply with the King's order to reside in the diocese. Not many months were to pass before he was charged with high treason, but he defeated the executioner's axe by dying on the way back to London.

Holders Hill Road

The line of Holders Hill Road is shown clearly on Robert Morden's map of 1701 and John Rocque's map of 1754 but not named. Indeed there is no mention of anything to do with Holders Hill. A map dated 1597 which details the property of All Souls College shows the 'Fields and grove of Olders Hilles lying between Ashley Lane and the Waye from Parsons Streete to Dallys'.

Olders Hilles sounds like some awful pun of Old as Hills and there does not seem to be any record of a family with the name Olders. Early OS maps indicate Olders Hill 300m east of the Dollis Brook beside Hendon Lane.

At the end of Holders Hill Road is the roundabout known locally as Kelly's Corner although this name does not appear on maps (except some London Buses route maps). Kelly's was once the name of the garage on this roundabout which was presumably the name of the original proprietor. Holders Hill is shown on the first 1in OS map published in 1822 as a district and even the 1:2,500 OS map of 1896 (Second Edition) shows Holders Hill House and the road but does not name it.

Hammers Lane

This is another of the steep hills that lead up to The Ridgeway. In earlier times this lane was known as Ratcliffe Lane and today bears little resemblance to the road of those far off days.

The Lane drops fairly steeply from The Ridgeway to the junction with Wills Grove, Wise Lane and Daws Lane. At the top there are a few interesting old shops and cottages, in particular Murray House (formerly Sunnyside) which was once the home of Dr James Murray (qv) and his family. This is opposite to the *Three Hammers* public house. Below these is a rather pretty house, White Lodge, with a cottage attached.

Hammers Lane has collected a number of retirement homes, most of which are now getting on a bit like the occupants. Unlike those of more recent times the cottages are neatly laid out with pretty gardens. These are the Drapers' Cottage Homes or Marshall Estate. This is a mini estate of red brick bungalows on parade in neat avenues, each one named after a famous London department store. The estate was built in 1927. Below these again and on the other side of the road is a much larger and earlier (1897) building, the Marshall Hall with broad steps up from the pavement and imposing front garden. The building illustrates the indulgence permitted to architects and builders before these enlightened times, even for buildings designed for charitable purposes. The surrounding estate was extended in 1961.

The homes were founded in 1898 by William Marshall, of the store Marshall & Snellgrove and were designed by George Hornblower. They were intended for retired workpeople from the drapery trade. Both single persons and married couples are accommodated but in different types of residences. There is also a nursing home for those people who because of either senility or infirmity cannot be expected to live independently.

The lower half of the western side is the edge of Poets' Corner', an estate of straight roads and right angles built just after the turn of the Century, (See also the chapter *'The History of Private Property'*). The style of these houses tells us immediately when they were built.

Frith Lane

The Old English word frith or frythe has various meanings: a kind of weir for catching fish, a small woody place or field taken out of a common, a lake formed by the widening of a river, and others. Frith of Frith Lane and Frith Manor would appear to refer to the woody place. Although Folly Brook widens out to form Darland's Lake this was artificially created and Folly Brook is hardly worth calling a river. The actual origin of the name has to be a guess. Frith or Fryth Common (both spellings have been used simultaneously) has been shown since the earliest maps and Frith Lane certainly existed before the 18th Century. On 19th Century maps Frith Lane is shown as a complete loop rejoining Bittacy Hill just south of Burtonhole Lane, with the section which runs west from Frith Manor called Frith Lane North. Today this piece of the road is called Partingdale Lane.

Flower Lane

Belmont, the fine house on The Ridgeway built by Robert Adam in the middle of the 18th Century and now the junior house of Mill Hill School was once owned and occupied by Sir Charles Flower Bart (qv) a local landowner and one time Lord Mayor of London. Flower Lane was named after him.

Today Flower Lane is a bit of this and a bit of that. The houses are a mixture and some are quite imposing. There are some striking Victorian and Edwardian houses of individual design with more than ample gardens. In the main they have been maintained well and many look well set for the 21st Century, however the recent dry summers have taken their toll and some quite severe subsidence problems are in evidence which will be expensive to correct. On one double fronted house that has arched stone lintels the key-stones have dropped some 150cm.

Because the large houses are too big for most people today and too expensive to maintain many have been subdivided into flats. Needless to say the odd patch of redevelopment has also taken place but even here there is nothing objectionable. One of the more recent additions are the large mock Georgian houses which were very popular with builders a few years ago. Along one side for much of the road's length is the edge of Mill Hill Park which was cut in two when the Watford Way was built. At the junction with Bunns Lane is the Mill Hill Industrial Estate.

Partingdale Lane

In old references this lane is called Pattingdale and would appear to mean 'the path in the dale'. There is little of any great merit in this lane and there is no record of any important family ever living there. The interesting house Partingdale Manor is more or less dead centre. On the southern side of the lane is the boundary fence of Mill Hill Barracks and with some form of redevelopment expected here the rural aspect of this lane may well be under pressure.

THE FOOTPATHS OF MILL HILL

There is nothing new about thoughtless farmers or careless ramblers. *Plus ça change, plus c'est la meme chose*! (Alphonse Karr 1849). The Footpath Committee of the local Ratepayers' Association at the end of the 19th Century asked its members to keep a close eye on farmers and landowners because of the increasing number of incidents of footpaths being either re-routed or destroyed completely. They maintained however that if walkers gave due consideration to closing gates and avoiding all kinds of damage to property then they could expect more sympathy and less interference.

At the end of the last century 43 footpaths were listed in the Parish of Hendon of which 25 were all or partly in Mill Hill. Today the number is rather less. Some have fallen into disuse or have been incorporated into housing estates and are now merely short cuts. These footpaths are known as twittens in some parts of the country. Where new roads have followed old rights-of-way the line of the ancient footpaths is often preserved. In addition, permission has been given in some cases for farmers and land owners to partly re-route old rights-of-way.

With the new found emphasis on leisure time there is a new and more insidious attack upon our footpaths. The planning authorities are being bombarded with applications for golf courses to be laid out in the Vale of Totteridge and other places in Mill Hill. Whilst there is obviously no lack of support for these facilities and they prevent the likely development of the land for other uses they are frequently accompanied by other sporting activities that require additional buildings and these are usually big and ugly. Golf courses would also undoubtedly affect the nature and appearance of the whole area and be a considerable danger to walkers on the many footpaths that crisscross the Valley.

Fortunately there are also a few new paths where by frequent usage the track has been accepted as a path. The most interesting of these is a place where children have played ever since the development of the housing from Nether Street Finchley to the Dollis Brook and the southern extremity of the Woodside Park Estate in the 1930s. This is through the rough land that runs along beside the Dollis Brook on the western side then crosses Lovers' Walk and into what was the gardens of Nether Court and Rocklands. Much of this land was previously owned by the Finchley Golf Club. This footpath now runs all the way to the railway viaduct.

In spite of much construction of roads and buildings many of the old footpaths have also managed to survive although not all are easy to follow. One of these started at the north end of the churchyard of St

Mary's Hendon and followed a line almost due north to Page Street. This is now almost entirely in public land and runs through Sunny Hill Park and the grounds of Copthall Sports Centre.

A number of footpaths start on Totteridge Lane and follow a course either due south or south-west. Two of these meet at Folly Farm, one starts at St Andrew's Church and the other on the Common near the Long Ponds. This path continues southwards to Burton Hole Farm. The other runs diagonally across the sports fields to St Vincent's grounds on The Ridgeway. The last part has been redirected and is rather difficult to follow and extremely unpleasant where it passes St Vincent's Stables. It appears that when the stable yard is swept the footpath gets its share.

Other paths from Totteridge Lane start from west of Ellern Mede Farm and run to St Paul's School and to Holcombe Dale at the foot of Highwood Hill.

The only other important footpath in this area just starts in Mill Hill in the right angle formed by Burton Hole Lane and the lane referred to earlier as Dirty Dick's Lane. This path runs east and north-east to Laurel Farm.

Unfortunately as mentioned earlier there is no way through Nan Clark's Lane, although on earlier maps there was always a right-of-way. However the lane which branches off northwards to Mote End Farm leads to Moat Mount Open Space and divides by a guide post into three well defined paths that can be easily followed: past Barnet Gate Wood to Hendon Wood Lane, to the Hyver Hall gate on the Barnet Road, or westwards to the Shrubbery and camping site and thence to the A1. From these paths there are (on clear days) excellent views to Harrow and beyond.

Because of the area occupied by the Mill Hill School grounds it is no surprise that many old paths cross the sports fields etc. One of these worth a mention gives a view of the front of Mill Hill School (the rear faces The Ridgeway) and this path runs from Wills Grove to Hammers Lane. Its continuation is Milton Road (in Poets' Corner) and then on to Lawrence Street.

The footpath that starts at the slight bend in Wills Grove also runs through Mill Hill School grounds. The first part is easy to follow between hedges, thereafter the path passes beside the School cricket field and on to Wise Lane opposite the top of Page Street. A turn to the left in the middle of this walk and a path goes across Arrandene Open Space to the gates near Milespit Hill.

To protect the local environment from development the Hendon Urban District Council and later the Hendon Borough Council purchased any large areas of land that came on the market to be preserved as open spaces. Because Hendon was already largely built up much of these purchases were of land in Mill Hill. A number of old footpaths run

.... front of Mill Hill School

through these open spaces. Because the land is public property the actual line of the paths is rather academic but nevertheless there are usually paths in the parks which correspond to the old rights-of-way. The fact that the old paths are still identifiable is something that we should applaud.

Last of all is the straight and well defined footpath that runs from Ballards Lane Finchley to Frith Lane known as Lovers' Walk. Who were the lovers that gave the name to Lovers' Walk or is it just a walk for all lovers? It is quite old and they couldn't have been escaping from the built up Finchley because even up to 1930 at the top of this path (in Ballards Lane) there were a few old cottages and no roads at all between here and Nether Street (which is very old). Lovers' Walk between Ballards Lane and Nether Street is walled in on both sides and seems to be used mainly for exercising dogs!

Between Nether Street and Frith Lane is the more interesting part of the Walk. On Nether Street there is a white picket fence and the first part slopes gently down to the Dollis Brook between the gardens of Finchley Way and Landsdowne Road. It still looks much the same as it did 50 years ago. The wooden bridge over the Brook has been replaced. An easy climb follows up to Frith Lane which is much more overgrown than it used to be, probably because there are nowhere near as many ramblers or families just out walking as there were 50 or so years ago and certainly less children 'exploring'. It is far too dangerous to let them out on their own.

The part of Mill Hill west of the A1 is now completely built up and has been for years. Any paths that were in this area running on into Burnt Oak and Edgware have long since been built over, obliterated and lost.

CHAPTER VIII

PUBLIC ROAD TRANSPORT:
THEN AND NOW

T he introduction to this book makes it clear why Mill Hill cannot be considered in isolation, as if it is an island surrounded by water. In fact some things that did not happen in Mill Hill (but did occur elsewhere) are just as important to the history of Mill Hill as the things that did. The public transport of Mill Hill is all about where it comes from and where it goes to. People of influence, mainly politicians and merchants, started to come to Mill Hill to live in the 18th Century, and needed a reliable form of transport to get them to London. Certainly some had their own carriages but not everyone could afford this luxury as an everyday convenience, or even wanted to.

HORSES FOR COURSES

A timetable of London's omnibuses published in 1851 listed every regular route into London. Some of these brought passengers from a considerable distance. One of these early routes started in Totteridge and ran to Bishopsgate Street. The journey of 23km was via Highwood Hill (this must have been tricky without efficient brakes), Mill Hill, Hendon, Brent Street, Golders Green, Hampstead, Haverstock Hill, Camden Town, and Holborn. The run was scheduled to take about 2 hours and the full distance fare was 2/- (10p) or 1/6 (7½p) from Mill Hill.

A little later there was also a regular daily service from the *Angel & Crown* (now demolished) on The Ridgeway to the Bank, via Brent Street, Hampstead, and Tottenham Court Road. The fare was 2/- (10p) for a seat inside or 1/6 (7½p) outside. The upper deck was of course open to the elements and the expressions 'inside' and 'outside' continued to be used long after all buses had enclosed upper decks.

In the 1870s it was still possible to travel on a regular horse-drawn omnibus service from Hendon to the Central Post Office in London, but time was running out, the railways had arrived. Two services, Mr Woolley's coach and Mr Sutton's team, and another operator who ran from Hendon to Cricklewood and on to Oxford Street were to become the victims of progress. At this time there were also parcels carriers over the same routes.

The homeward journey had various starting points. The horse omnibus could be boarded at the *Elder Wine House* in Broad Street, St

Giles' Circus, or *The Bell* in High Holborn, and the homeward journey was via Camden Town, Hampstead Heath, Golders Green and Hendon.

When the Midland Railway from Leicester and Bedford was extended southwards in 1868 to Mill Hill (now Mill Hill Broadway) and then through to Moorgate Street it was obvious to the owners of the horse buses that they would lose out completely. They tried to stay in business by running services from the Village to the railway station and survived until the motor buses arrived.

Over London as a whole, particularly central London, the horse buses carried on for some years after the railways were built and even when motor buses were running. In 1900 the London General Omnibus Company had 16,790 horses and an average of 1,348 buses in service at any one time. During the year, LGOC buses travelled over 50m km and carried almost 200m passengers. This was part of a continuous development.

The number of passengers had been increasing steadily since the days of the first regular service. In 1856 28m passengers were carried by buses that travelled 14m km. By 1910 these had risen to 300.6m passengers and 62.4m km, and by the start of World War II 2,222m passengers and 459m km. In 1901 the number of horse buses increased slightly over 1900, but thereafter they declined. Probably the last regular service was operated by Fred Newman in 1914 although some horse buses were returned to service when the motor buses were sent to France for troop carrying.

Over the period from 1901 to 1911 the population of the City of London dropped quite dramatically but during the same period the population of the suburbs increased by about 35%, therefore a reliable commuter service was becoming increasingly necessary. Although the figures for buses in operation over these years seem remarkably consistent it must be remembered that one motor bus was equal (in carrying capacity) to two horse buses, and in some cases one replaced three. The buses licenced in Greater London over the years 1908 to 1912 were :

YEAR	HORSE-BUS	MOTOR-BUS	TOTAL
1908	2153	1133	3286
1909	1771	1180	2951
1910	1103	1200	2303
1911	786	1962	2748
1912	376	2908	3284

THE COMING OF THE MOTOR BUS

Shortly after the turn of the Century the first motor buses made their appearance; a bit ramshackle, slow and very uncomfortable (of necessity they had very stiff springs), and not always reliable. They had to be built very strongly because of the vibration, and that meant that they were heavy. As a proportion of the total weight, the vehicle represented much more than it does with today's buses. But they were able to provide a direct service against which the railways could not compete for many journeys and still cannot.

The very first buses were little different in design from the horse buses they replaced, and they still had steel tyres. One of these, the Fischer petrol-electric bus was tried out in 1903 but was returned to the maker after a few months. The driver sat high up as if on a stage coach, and it is impossible to believe that this vehicle could negotiate corners satisfactorily even at a walking pace.

It was not until 1905 that the tyre companies could supply solid rubber tyres that would give a reasonable mileage, the first ones that were made often had to replaced after less than 300km. In September 1904 the Milnes-Daimler double-decker entered service with Thomas Tilling. This was the first bus that did not look like a horse bus without the horse.

The Midland Railway and the *Underground* were built as radial routes and therefore ideal for travel from a suburb into central London. Bus routes are more flexible and can be frequently modified to link up urban areas, as and when places of education, work, and leisure are built or change their locations. An early route included Mill Hill, Golders Green and Harrow, a journey that would be very long and awkward by train. Rail and road transport have remained complimentary systems to this day.

The first motor bus routes in London, were limited to the City and West End. The routes then steadily extended outwards to the suburbs. In March 1911 when the LGOC published its first bus map it showed 23 routes and almost all of these terminated in the outskirts of London. Three are of interest to us: No1 Tower Bridge to Dollis Hill, No2 Childs Hill to Ebery Bridge, and No13 Childs Hill to London Bridge Station.

Although Mill Hill did not feature on the first destination boards other routes developed and Hendon was soon included. Two served Hendon by 1912, these were the 83 from Golders Green to Station Road Hendon, and the 13 which had been extended and ran from *The Bell*.

The onset of the Great War (World War I) had an immediate and dramatic effect on bus schedules however, they were suspended. Forty members from one garage alone were called up for military service.

REGULATIONS AND DEVELOPMENTS

Omnibus owners were very reluctant to change to pneumatic tyres when they became available and stuck with solids when many commercial vehicle operators had already converted to pneumatics. The Michelin Tyre Co. capitalized on this and when a pig breeder converted his trucks to pneumatics, published an advertisement showing a lorry full of grinning pigs passing a bus with the hapless passengers bumping along on solids. The caption read:

'Pigs comfortable on pneumatic tyres
You on solids!'

When the bus operators were prepared to change to pneumatic tyres they were prevented from doing so by police regulations. It was not until 1925 that London buses fitted pneumatics, and even then only on single-deckers. It was another three years before they were permitted on double-deckers. The regulations of the time imposed a maximum overall width of 7ft 2in when pneumatics were fitted, which was exceeded when they were fitted to the existing vehicles.

Eventually the police increased the limit slightly to 7ft 5in, but only on routes where there were no trams. So it became possible for a bus to operate locally, but impossible on almost any main thoroughfare. This made journey and route planning extremely difficult.

Eventually, in 1929, a public outcry lead to a further relaxation to 7ft 6in, and brought London in line with the rest of the Country. Journey times were now improved because the motor buses on pneumatics could travel at speeds up to 20mph, whereas those on solids could not exceed 12mph. Imagine a journey from Hendon to London Bridge at an average of 12 mph in 1929. This is as good as we can manage today with all our modern equipment!

The evolution of buses in London from the early years was the usual story of supply and demand. Initially no-one could see the need for a local bus service, people of substance used their own horse drawn vehicles of various types and the remainder just had to walk. In July 1829 George Shillibeer introduced a regular route between Paddington Green and the Bank, the first service that plied for hire in the streets and stopped to pick up passengers as and where they presented themselves.

The idea of fixed stopping places was not introduced until nearly a century later. When some of the local 'shoppers' buses were introduced during the last decade or so that have no fixed stops many people thought that this idea was something new.

Of course there had to be regulations and the first buses came under the control of the Commissioners of Stamps, a department whose main function was the collection of taxes. Plying for hire received legal authority with the *Stage Carriage Act* of 1832 and buses were now licensed and taxed on carrying capacity and mileage covered.

By 1837 there were already 400 or so two-horse buses operating in London. Another act (of 1838) required each bus to display visibly a license plate showing that the bus was a Metropolitan Stage Carriage and the number of passengers that it was permitted to carry. Drivers were also required to have personal licences with numbered badges. In 1842 the *Stage Carriage and Railway Passengers' Duty Act* regulated some features of bus operation and included a minimum seat space per person.

In 1853 the vehicle licensing was transferred to the control of the Metropolitan Police, and it was their duty to satisfy themselves that the vehicle was suitable, and safe to carry passengers.

The most important dates in London Bus History are:

1856 to 1900	'Knifeboard'	The regular route horse bus
1887 to 1914	'Garden Seat'	A later horse bus
1910 to 1927	'B' Type	The first reliable motor bus
1919 to 1932	'K' Type	
1923 to 1937	'NS' Type	Covered tops and pneumatic tyres introduced
1933 to 1954	'STL' Type	Diesel engines and fluid transmission introduced
1939	'RT' Bus	
1956	'RM' Bus	Probably the best known of all London's buses

'B' Type –
The first reliable motor bus

In 1928 various operators started to run express limited-stop coaches to bring in passengers to central London from the surrounding towns. These were up to 70km or so from Marble Arch. The LGOC quickly realised the potential and entered this market too, with the launch of Green Line Coaches Ltd (a

77

wholly owned subsidiary) on July 9 1930. The first route was between Charing Cross and Guildford, which increased in four years to 28 routes, many of which went right across London. At least two went through Hendon and Mill Hill.

The coaches were better appointed than the buses on the ordinary routes. Apart from journeys into London the Green Line was also a very convenient means of travel to places of interest outside London, such as Whipsnade Zoo or Windsor Castle. It was often possible to travel to these destinations without the inevitable changes when a combination of mainline and *Underground* trains was used.

When Gladstone made his famous remark 'The best way to see London is from the top of a bus' he was of course referring to an open-top horse bus. Nevertheless there is still some truth in this statement today, particularly now that smoking is forbidden and the upper deck is no longer as smoky as a four-ale bar.

THE AGE OF THE TRAMCAR

The LCC was rather slow in converting its horse-tram routes to electric operation. When they did they adopted the underground conduit system which created financial problems later on, and necessitated even greater disruption to the roads. Most operators in other cities preferred the overhead trolley system.

The first trams were south of the River but none ran north of the Thames in the central area until about the middle of 1905. This was due to the lords. The House of Lords refused to permit any trams to run across the Thames bridges or along the Embankment and they maintained this embargo until 1906.

The City and West End remained in the 19th Century until 1905, there were no electric trams or motor buses. The only public vehicles to be seen in the principal London streets were horse buses that could average about 4mph. It was said that to travel from electrified Liverpool or Manchester to the capital was to travel back in time half a century to an earlier world. When the first motor-buses made their appearance in 1905 the number of horse buses quickly declined and although the running costs on the motor buses were much higher than trams their virtual monopoly in central London and versatility ensured that they were a success.

The Metropolitan Tramways & Omnibus Company Ltd was set up in 1894 for the express purpose of building and operating a tramways network in north and north-west London. These were of course horse trams. In 1901 the company adopted a new name, the Metropolitan Electric Tramways Ltd, and the change to electric operation of existing routes and the building of new ones was negotiated with the County Council.

Although construction work was started in 1902 it was not until 1904 that a route extended into the boundaries of Hendon. The route that had terminated at Cricklewood was extended along the Edgware Road. Trams were not the first regular services along this thoroughfare, they merely followed the route taken by horse-drawn buses. For horse buses and trams this must be the ideal road: straight and wide with modest gradients. This tram route connected Cricklewood with Church Lane in Edgware and in 1907 Edgware was linked with Canons Park. Two years later tracks were laid from Finchley to Golders Green and from there to Hampstead.

Development continued all round London for 20 years or so and the 1920s became the golden years of electric tram operation. This situation was not destined to last and in 1936 the whole of the network in north and north-west London, except for routes to Highgate and Manor House, was converted to trolleybuses. After a quarter of a century of operation the cost of replacing the worn tracks and other equipment was too high.

No trams came to Mill Hill Broadway, and neither did their successor the trolleybus. As far as Mill Hill Village is concerned the approach roads are far too steep for either of these vehicles even if a route incorporating the Village had been commercially viable. Trams did however negotiate some quite steep hills. Both Denmark Hill in Camberwell and the hill to Barnet Church were parts of tram routes.

DEPOTS AND GARAGES

Most of the garages that accommodate the buses that go to or through Mill Hill are quite old. Over the years almost every garage in north and north west London, and even farther afield, has been involved with Hendon buses or trams at some time or another. Some facts about the most important have been included here.

CRICKLEWOOD GARAGE was originally known as Dollis Hill and was the first motorized depot used by the LGOC. Buses were first housed here in 1904 and the unit operated officially from 1905.

HENDON GARAGE was opened on March 3 1913 and a big programme of modernisation was begun in 1972. It has now been demolished and the land relegated to that of an open market.

FINCHLEY DEPOT is another old garage. It was built for the

Metropolitan Electric Tramways as the North Finchley Depot and was opened for maintenance work in 1905. The conversion to trolleybus depot took place in 1936/38. In 1961 it was converted to a bus garage and reopened in January 1962.

COLINDALE DEPOT was formerly the Hendon garage of the Metropolitan Electric Tramways and was built in 1904 and was closed in February 1914. The first trolleybus experiments in London were carried out from here on 1909. The depot was rebuilt for trolleybus operation in July 1936 and closed down when the trolleybuses were withdrawn from service in January 1962.

EDGWARE GARAGE was the last of the 'local' garages to be built. It was originally opened in April 1925. Just prior to World War II a new garage was built alongside with a considerable extension to the working area and greater space for open-air parking.

BUS ROUTES THAT HAVE SERVED MILL HILL

In 1925 a brochure on the attractions of Mill Hill said that the most convenient way to London's West End was by bus, service 104 or 104a to Golders Green and then by *Underground* for the rest of the journey. Route 104 ran from Edgware via the *Green Man* and The Ridgeway to Golders Green. This service was inaugurated on Nov. 26 1924 and ran until Oct. 1934 when it was replaced by Route 240.

The recommended alternative was to take the bus in the opposite direction to Edgware and from there an electric tramcar could be taken to Cricklewood, Wembley or Willesden. The trams vanished years ago, but in any case none of these journeys would be considered desirable today, they would all take far too long.

For many years after the introduction of motor buses only single-deck vehicles could manage the hills that lead up to The Ridgeway, but modern double-deckers take Hammers Lane and Bittacy Hill in their stride.

In 1935 a review of the garages was carried out, many of which needed extensive modernisation. The decision to convert the network to trolleybuses had already been made because the tram tracks were badly worn. Investment on a considerable scale was needed to put things right. Because of the decision to convert the routes to trolleybus operation the garages had to be completely refurbished.

In any case it is hard to imagine trams running on our main roads today with the volume of traffic in all our big cities. Although it must be said that many overseas municipalities still run tram services very successfully (and they also still use their canals!). Nevertheless boarding and alighting from a tram running in the middle of the road would be dangerous for passengers, and the rigidity of tramways would hold up other vehicles.

The change to trolleybuses obviously affected the work that had to be done at the garages and staff had to be retrained. Much new equipment was also needed.

Initially the trolleybuses came as a bit of a shock. Compared with the petrol buses of the day the acceleration took some getting used to. Many of the routes were long, for instance Route 645 North Finchley (extended to High Barnet) to Canons Park. They were also much larger than the vehicles they replaced and accommodated 70 passengers. It was almost impossible for the conductor to collect fares from this number, particularly in inner city areas and shopping centres where passengers travelled short distances.

We are now witnessing a measure of competition in London Transport. The actual name has changed many times in the last few years and there are now two separate companies, London Buses Ltd and London Underground Ltd. London Buses no longer enjoys an absolute monopoly. In addition companies such as Grey-Green have been awarded routes or in some cases they have been contracted out to them. In the early days it was every man for himself operating with much overlapping and in a very cut-throat manner. Whilst there is nothing wrong with competition we would not want to revert to this.

The old single-decker buses that have gone through so many different designs over the years are now looking more like overgrown mini-buses and have adopted a variety of names like Mini, Midi, Hoppa and Skipper. They are faster and more spacious than the single-deckers that they replaced, with easier access. The first minibus service (around Winchmore Hill) was commenced in 1972. In some cases they have taken over from double-deckers where these were under used.

Unfortunately these modern buses are not very kind to the old and infirm. Not only are there many more old people but they travel farther and more often than they used to. Additionally like the trolley-buses these new vehicles have much greater powers of acceleration and deceleration than the buses of even two decades ago so it is far more difficult for passengers that have just boarded the bus, or who are about to alight to keep their balance.

Over the years a great number of different routes have served Mill Hill and the surrounding area, some of these routes were very short lived, others have been running since the beginning of London's motor buses. It is not possible here to list every change to the routes, or indeed every route that has run into the area but the following will give some idea of the continuing development. It takes a bus enthusiast to document every change that has taken place and even with 'official' records it is not possible to be absolutely certain.

ROUTE 1 This bus was shown as running from Station Road Hendon to Tooley Street Tower Bridge in 1912. The route was via Cricklewood, Tottenham Court Road, Charing Cross, and Waterloo Bridge, If the weather was fine on Sundays the route was extended to Edgware and passengers were advised to alight at Colindale Avenue for the 'flying ground' (Hendon Aerodrome).

ROUTE 13 This route was originally from the West End to Childs Hill. Within a year or so it was extended and became London Bridge Station to Hendon The Bell and ran via Cannon Street, Fleet Street, Piccadilly Circus, Baker Street, and Finchley Road. There were no changes until after World War II. Today Route 13 is completely different and runs from North Finchley to Oxford Circus and Aldwych.

ROUTE 32 Introduced in 1970, this route runs from Edgware to Kilburn Park via Mill Hill Broadway.

ROUTE 52 This first ran in 1925 from Ladbroke Grove to Victoria. In 1932 it was extended to Mill Hill. A supplementary service was added, No 52a, Colindale to Boreham Wood in 1955.

ROUTE 83 This was from Golders Green Underground (the station was opened in 1907) to Station Road Hendon via Golders Green Road, Brent Street, Church Road, and The Burroughs. This route also had an extension to the 'flying ground' from December 31 1912 and the route was extended to Edgware (Sundays only) from March 19 1913. Today this route runs from Golders Green Station to Southall.

ROUTE 107 This semi-country route skirts the northern boundary of Mill Hill on its way from New Barnet Station to Queensbury. It goes via Stirling Corner, Boreham Wood, and Edgware.

ROUTE 102 This short lived route was created out of an older route, No 58, and ran from Trafalgar Square to Stanmore via Harrow, Cricklewood, Hendon, Edgware, and Canons Park. It last ran on September 21 1913.

ROUTE 104 This route was scheduled to run from Golders Green to Mill Hill from 1922. In 1925 the route was extended to Edgware and 104a ran to Mill Hill only. From 1924 104b ran from Edgware to Harrow. The service to Harrow was withdrawn in 1939 and the 104 route was then renumbered 240. The service to Edgware was ended in 1951 and the route extended to Mill Hill East Station as 240a.

ROUTE 105 This route ran from Kilburn to Watford via Cricklewood, West Hendon, Edgware, Canons Park, and Bushey. The service was withdrawn on March 28 1914 and the route was altered and renumbered 142.

ROUTE 113 The original with this number was on the other side of London, Kingston to Banstead. LGOC took over Birch Bros Route 214c and renumbered it 113. In 1939 the service was from Oxford Circus to Canons Park but was later contracted (in 1949) to Edgware Station. The full route is only operated Monday to Friday (since January 1976) and Brent Cross Shopping Centre is included during shopping hours.

ROUTE 114 This is a very old route and has been in existence since 1908. At that time the route was South Harrow to Mill Hill, later extended to Ruislip Station. In 1949 the route was extended in the north to Edgware and in the south to Rayners Lane. After a further revision in 1970 the route became Edgware to Harrow on the Hill via Stanmore. The route now terminates at Mill Hill East Station.

ROUTE 121 This route was withdrawn at the beginning of World War II. It ran from Hendon Garage to Peckham Rye on weekdays and from Mill Hill Broadway on Sundays.

ROUTE 125 This route has been altered many times. During the late 1940s the route ran from Winchmore Hill to North Finchley but in 1951 it was extended to Golders Green via Frith Lane, Holders Hill Road, and Parson Street. Later when the 221 service took in part of the same route the service from North Finchley was withdrawn. The route has now been contracted out to another company and terminates at Finchley Central Station.

ROUTE 140 This route no longer runs in this area. In its short lifetime in the district it was revised many times. Originally it ran from Colindale to Northolt but was amended to Stanmore to South Harrow in 1920. In 1924 it was extended at both ends and ran from Edgware to Pinner Green. A further alteration in 1932 made the route Hendon to Northolt and in 1936 the last revision was made taking in Mill Hill.

ROUTE 186 This route links the important shopping centres of Brent Cross and Harrow (it terminates at Northwick Park Hospital). The route runs via Watford Way and Edgware.

ROUTE 221 The original route in 1925 ran from North Harrow to Pinner and had been renumbered from Route 353. This remained the same until after World War II. Today the route is completely different and the full distance is from Edgware to Holborn Circus via Mill Hill Broadway, Mill Hill East, North Finchley, Wood Green, Turnpike Lane, Holloway, and Kings Cross. The full distance is not run at all times and the service is split part time with overlaps: Edgware to Turnpike Lane and North Finchley to Holborn .

ROUTE 240 See Route 104.

ROUTE 251 This route was originally Route 551, Burnt Oak to Edmonton. It was split into Route 604 Arnos Grove to Edmonton, and Route 251 Arnos Grove to Edgware. It was later extended to Stanmore.

ROUTE 292 A short local route from Boreham Wood to Edgware or Colindale, via Barnet Way, Selvage Lane, and Deans Lane.

ROUTE 797 This is part of an old Green Line route now run from Stevenage Bus Garage by Luton and District Buses. The route is from Cambridge to Victoria, and although the buses go through Mill Hill they do not stop. The nearest boarding places are at Apex Corner and Hendon Central.

ROUTE N59 This night bus runs from Trafalgar Square to Stanmore via West Hampstead, Golders Green, Mill Hill East, Mill Hill Broadway, and Edgware.

WHAT THE FUTURE HOLDS

For many years bus services were losing a great deal of money. Better vehicles and organization and a more commercial approach to route planning have helped to rectify his position. Few people today regard the bus as ideal long distance commuter transport, preferring the various railway networks. The advantages of buses are still as they have always been, the ability to pick up passengers at the street corner or shopping centre. For most of this century Londoners have used buses mainly for short distance travel and for this purpose they have been, and will remain the only transport for many people.

Today Mill Hill Broadway Station is an important North London terminus. Additionally there are other routes that go through The Broadway and others that serve Mill Hill but not The Broadway. The Mill Hill buses are essential to school children, shoppers, and the working people who are employed fairly locally.

Because of traffic congestion, and its effect upon timetables many routes have been shortened in recent years. Route 52, Mill Hill Broadway to Victoria which has been in operation since 1932 is in this respect something of a relic. Route 114, Mill Hill Broadway to Ruislip Station is completely different, and one of the routes that does a job that no railway could compete with. It connects a number of shopping centres.

Three of the four buses that run through The Broadway are all typical London peripheral routes; part built-up suburbia, part rural. The 221 from Edgware to Turnpike Lane takes in Frith Lane, 240 Golders Green never really gets far away from light suburbia, and 251 includes Lawrence Street, Highwood Hill, and Totteridge Lane and you cannot get more rural than that. Bus 32 is the odd one out, running from Edgware Station to Kilburn Park Station through entirely built-up areas.

Route 113, Edgware Station to Oxford Circus via Mill Hill Circus is another surviving long distance radial route. Not many people would want to travel all of the way, unless they have time on their hands and suffer from claustrophobia and cannot use the *Underground*. Another route that skirts The Broadway is No 180, Brent Cross to Northwick Park.

Mill Hill has had its buses since 1851. They were important to Mill Hill then and still are today. More alterations will be made as the demand changes because no public service can stand still. It will not be long before we can celebrate 150 years of buses in Mill Hill.

Somehow the World seemed a less violent place and safer for children before World War II. They were allowed to be more adventurous and travelled farther afield. The *Travel Cards* of today have their origins in the prewar days. The *All-Day Tickets* priced 6d (2½p) for children permitted a full day's travel on any bus, tram, or trolleybus north of the River Thames and another 6d would extend this facility south of the River. As a child the author remembers this well and visited Epping Forest, Hampton Court Palace, the most important of London's museums, and a host of other places. A sandwich pack, with a flask of tea and 6d and the World was yours.

CHAPTER IX

TRANSPORT BY WATER AND RAIL

Before the construction of the canals and then the railways in the 18th and 19th Centuries the transportation of goods and materials around the Country was difficult, expensive, and hazardous, and of course extremely slow. There were no roads of any quality and vehicles were primitive. For these reasons, heavy items (for instance stone for building) were transported as far as possible by sea and then up the navigable rivers, leaving the minimum distance at the delivery end for road transportation. Many of the small ports around the English coast had their heyday during these times and then declined in importance when internal transport became a practical proposition. Although people did travel over land this was always dangerous, the footpad or highwayman always had the advantage. With the natural cover he was always able to appear suddenly and just as quickly vanish.

CANALS

In 1750 a map of England and Wales showing navigable waterways was really a map of the principal rivers. By 1850 this position had changed completely and the countryside was covered with a network of canals. The majority of this vast system was finished by 1830 leaving few large towns more than 10 miles from navigable water. This was particularly astonishing considering that canals were largely a new technology. Most of the work was done manually and involved a great number of tunnels, bridges, aqueducts and locks. The difference in elevation between different parts of the same waterway can be considerable, for instance there are 16 locks in the Aylesbury Arm of the Grand Union Canal in the space of 9.5km.

Needless to say the building of the canals had little or no direct effect upon Mill Hill or its residents. Hendon did however make its modest contribution because the waters of the River Brent were needed to maintain an adequate water level in the southern section of the Grand Union Canal and the Paddington arm. The river flow was too variable to be reliable, therefore a reservoir was needed and this was built at West Hendon. The Welsh Harp was enlarged to form the Brent Reservoir. Perhaps because the Dollis Brook, the source of the Brent, flows through Mill Hill and the Silk Stream flows directly into the Welsh Harp we can claim a minor association. The Aldenham Reservoir near Elstree is also a feeder for the Grand Union Canal.

Although canals remained a picturesque and useful means of heavy goods transport right up to World War II and in a modest way on some stretches since then, the arrival of the railways in the middle of the 19th Century started the decline in their importance. Happily many of the once derelict canals have been given a new lease of life in the last few decades, not for commercial applications but as an extension to the facilities on offer to holidaymakers. Many of the canals are through extremely beautiful countryside and the slow pace of canal narrow boats is a restful way of spending the odd week or so, particularly if the weather is favourable. The latest waterways to be reopened, the Thames-Avon and Basingstoke-Woking Canals represent the successful conclusion to a 40 year battle.

Ironically when we were allowing our canals to deteriorate and silt up other European countries were still developing theirs, and still do. After all with non-perishable goods transit times do not matter: if barges leave every day from a certain place they arrive at daily intervals providing that there are sufficient in the system.

RAILWAYS

Unlike the canals and the Roman roads before them the railways did not ignore Mill Hill and two lines were to be built that would bring Mill Hill firmly into Greater London. At the time it was hard to see how one of these railways, the Great Northern, could ever be economically viable (in fact it never was). The populations of Finchley and Barnet were both very small by the standards of today, Edgware at the turn of the century was around 800 and Mill Hill was even smaller. The Midland Railway was built as a main line and therefore always had potential even if Mill Hill had not developed.

The first steam railway to carry passengers was opened between Stockton and Darlington in 1825. In the next 75 years the railways were constructed at such a rate that the whole country was covered. In other words a repeat performance of the canal expansion of a century earlier and all this without any of the heavy construction equipment that would be used on such a project today. Every size of village and town was brought into the ever increasing railway network. The tunnel and bridge building was necessary all over again, the difference being that this time the engineers had a previous experience to call upon. The network was to remain almost unaltered until the rationalisation programme of the 1960s when a great number of the minor rural routes were torn up.

At first there were numerous railway companies, each one controlling a particular line and many very small. Before long, mergers were arranged and many of the original romantic sounding names vanished. At the time of nationalisation in 1948 there were just four left, these were LNER (London & North Eastern Railway), GWR (Great Western Railway), LMS (London Midland & Scottish), and SR (Southern Railway). In recent years some of the old names have been revived; the electric train services from Kings Cross and Moorgate to Welwyn Garden City and Royston are now the Great Northern Line.

Needless to say London had its share of small lines with the shortest being the Muswell Hill Railway. This ran from Finsbury Park, and its prime purpose was to serve the Alexandra Palace which was at that time being built. This little line always had problems, with the service having been opened and suspended seven times between 1875 and 1898. Before that it had been closed for two years because the newly completed Alexandra Palace had burnt down in June 1873 and the railway had to wait for it to be rebuilt.

More interesting to us is the line that was opened in 1867 from Finsbury Park via Finchley and Mill Hill to Edgware, called the Edgware, Highgate and London Railway. This later became a part of the Great Northern Railway and ultimately the LNER.

THE MIDLAND RAILWAY

But more important from the point of view of Mill Hill was the Midland Railway's London extension to St Pancras. This was altogether a much more ambitious project both in its scope and as an engineering entity. Although the Great Northern line was opened first by one year we will start with the Midland Railway line.

The construction of this section of the line was something of a masterpiece for its time. The Elstree Tunnel is 1km long which is followed by a long cutting at The Hale. The Brent Valley had to be crossed by a viaduct and then on the lead into St Pancras Station is the Belsize Tunnel which is just over 1.5km.

The Midland Railway London extension was opened for goods and coal traffic to Brent and St Pancras early in September 1867. The station buildings and approaches were very near completion in December 1867 but on the night of the 14th there was a serious fire involving the buildings at Hendon which sustained considerable damage. After a lot of effort and hard work the buildings were restored and by March 1868 Hendon and Mill Hill were ready to handle local goods traffic. Passenger train services started in October 1868 with nine trains per day direct to Moorgate Street.

The arrival of a service direct to the City had an immediate and permanent effect on Mill Hill. No longer was Mill Hill just a convenient place for a country seat, whilst still a bit remote from the Capital. It was a place for commuters, with the travel time measured in minutes instead of hours. Of course housing development did not start at once, and because the station was a fair way from the proper Mill Hill on The Ridgeway the Village was not really affected by the railway for a little while.

Quite soon housing began to appear near to the station, first to accommodate the railway staff and then shops to serve them followed by the usual spread of buildings of all types that went with the arrival of the railways.

In E T Evans' book of 1890, he is a little sour about the arrival of the railways, and bemoans the amount of land that they were already absorbing. According to him the Midland Railway 'is continually widening its borders'. This railway had already acquired (some three or four years previously) sufficient land to lay an extra double set of lines, and within the Parish of Hendon had purchased 10.5ha for goods sidings. Although the two railway lines to Hendon had been in operation for over 20 years when Evans wrote his book he dismissed them in a couple of paragraphs and failed to appreciate the effect that their arrival would have on the communities, for both good and evil, except to say that 'A small rural village has been converted into a suburb of London'. Of course he was right in many ways, nevertheless the 'Village' of Mill Hill has managed to retain some of its rural character.

Although the actual line of the Midland has changed little since it was laid down some 120 years ago its appearance has altered considerably. It is now in all respects a main line with extra rails for slower commuter traffic. The last thing that gave the Midland through Mill Hill the country look was the station, which was demolished in July 1967. It was built in the style of hundreds up and down the country complete with pitched slate roof, ornate chimneys, serrated drop-edge canopies and real fires in the waiting rooms. The new station of Mill Hill Broadway is of the style that we see everywhere on the BR network today: clean lines, unfussy decor, functional and modern.

THE CINDERELLA LINE

But what about the Great Northern Line? This developed in a rather different way, if develop is the right word. It was always going to be under the shadow of the Midland, a Cinderella line, and for good reason. Initially it was intended to continue this line to Watford but this plan was quickly abandoned.

In the early days the station in Finchley was called Finchley and Hendon, which was a little optimistic considering the distance from any part of Hendon. The name was later changed to Finchley Church End and is now Finchley Central and has been since the introduction of *Underground* trains on this line in 1940.

Five years after the building of the Edgware line a branch line was opened to High Barnet in 1872. It is difficult to believe that at that time the line to Edgware was considered to have more potential than the track to Barnet and more worthy of a direct line to London Kings Cross. For trains to stations to Barnet it was necessary to change at Finchley Church End. This situation was to be reversed very quickly with priority being transferred to the Barnet Branch. As already mentioned the other railway, the Midland had already opened a line in 1868 which offered a much more direct route from Mill Hill to central London.

13 arch viaduct ... a landmark in the area

The station buildings at Finchley Central are very old: the station was originally opened in 1867. The building is mainly of light coloured bricks and the platform canopies are of the serated drop-edge type, much favoured with early railways. The old footpath across the line looks its age. The area that was once a large goods yard and sidings is now a car park. Only the booking hall has been completely modernised and refurbished. The 'temporary' waiting room on the down line which was put in position when building work was supposed to commence in 1939 was still there half a century later and has only recently been demolished.

The line from Finchley to Mill Hill presented problems, there is a deep valley with the Dollis Brook at the bottom. The drop is some 40m and necessitated the building of a long embankment with a steep incline for over 1km followed by a 13 arch viaduct. Even today this is a landmark and quite an attraction in the area, but it is hard to believe that anyone expected that the cost of this structure and its maintenance could ever have been paid for out of earnings.

After the viaduct the line continues along an embankment, crosses Frith Lane and the bottom of Bittacy Hill to enter Mill Hill East station. (named just Mill Hill until February 1928). The track was double from Finchley Church End to Mill Hill East.

Mill Hill station was opened in 1867 and today is largely as it was then; there is only one platform, which is made of wood and the station even lacks the refinement of a canopy to protect the passengers. There is a waiting room which like the rest of the station looks rather neglected and decrepit, and of course the real fire has long since been replaced by a gas appliance. The whole station is in poor condition with junk everywhere and seems to lack the pride that went with wayside stations in the early days.

From this station onwards the line curved in a series of arcs to Mill Hill for the Hale, passed under the line of the Midland Railway and on to Edgware. In the pre World War I *Bradshaw's Railway Guide* Mill Hill for the Hale was referred to as The Halt at the Hale, the name being changed on March 1 1928 at the same time as Mill Hill to Mill Hill East. All this was through completely open country. The line was never double track beyond Mill Hill East and always had the appearance of a real remote country line until the 1930s when housing developments meant that the ends of private gardens formed the view for some of the route. The railway was also a convenient boundary between Mill Hill and Hendon and for part of the way the track of the old railway still is.

The trains from Edgware dropped their passengers at Finchley Church End for a connection from the Barnet Branch, then the engine was unhooked, run into a siding of the Barnet branch and reconnected to the other end of the carriages ready to start the short 10 to 15 minute trip back to Edgware.

For much of the line, Kings Cross to Edgware and Barnet (the Northern Heights lines as it was known), it was tough going for the engines of the day. Kings Cross to Finsbury Park is a hard pull and the next 2½miles even worse, in fact on the main line it climbs all the way from Kings Cross to Potters Bar. With housing developments in Muswell Hill, Highgate and Hampstead the trains were crowded morning and evening. There were big changes in the population of Barnet too, which had grown from 3,375 in 1871 to 11,335 in 1911. This trend had not been repeated by Edgware: its population in 1911 was still less than 1,000.

In the years prior to World War I the services to Edgware and Barnet were surprisingly good. Passengers in 1872 had a choice of 23 departures from Barnet and 15 from Edgware (on weekdays). Nearly all the Edgware trains terminated at Finchley. Thirty years later there were 51 trains each day from Barnet, but of the 23 departures from Edgware all but three terminated at Finchley. Although the line was a part of the LNER some LMS trains ran and terminated their journeys at Broad Street. The LMS trains were in a distinctive maroon colour easily identified from the dark green livery of the LNER rolling stock.

The author can remember the two types very well. The child's fare for one station (Finchley Church End to West Finchley) was 1d, and this coin was carried in case it was raining hard when it was time to leave school. Sometimes this penny was not needed for weeks, but such a fuss if it had been spent when it was needed. For the journey to school (again, only if it was raining) there were two trains that were suitable, the 8.36 LMS train or 8.43 LNER.

From 1920 up to the beginning of World War II development for housing gathered pace along the line of the Great North Road and for some distance either side throughout Finchley, Totteridge and Barnet. Hendon became completely linked to Finchley with only the Dollis Brook to show where one ended and the other began. One area remained stubbornly rural during this period and much is still comparatively rural today: this is the triangle containing Totteridge, Arkley, Mill Hill and Edgware. In spite of increasing demand elsewhere the service to Edgware was actually reduced. Off-peak trains to Moorgate and Broad Street were discontinued in 1915. It was all very encouraging for the new electric trams and later for the trolley buses and *Underground,* and of course the Midland Railway.

In 1926 the Edgware goods yard was enlarged to cater for the enormous increase in domestic fuels, roadmaking, and house building materials that were needed for the suburban growth that had followed in the wake of the new *Underground* line to Edgware. The *Underground* extension also convinced the LCC to go ahead with the Watling Estate. The materials for this development were conveyed over the LNER line from Finchley into sidings that had been specially constructed in 1926 at The Hale to service the temporary site railways that had been built by the contractor.

In the 1930s, freight traffic on the Finchley-Edgware line remained relatively buoyant and eight trains per day were shared between the Barnet and Edgware lines. Towards the end of this period however the movement to Edgware of building materials tailed off as housing development in the

Burnt Oak area passed its peak.

As already mentioned west of Mill Hill East the LNER line was single track and somewhat primitive. Signals were almost non-existent and were limited to a fixed distant some way short of Edgware and a tall post actually on the platform to prevent drivers from crashing through the buffers on dark nights. It had never been very important commercially and was really no longer a viable route to central London. It was more direct and obviously quicker by the Midland Railway from Mill Hill Broadway or the *Underground* from Edgware or Hendon.

There were occasions when the line enjoyed brief spells of importance, in particular during the Hendon Air Display, an annual event held at Hendon Aerodrome. During the display the bridge at Bunns Lane became something of a vantage point. At one of these displays (on June 25 1932) trains were leaving Kings Cross from 1.30pm every few minutes for The Hale so that the line was solid with trains for 1½ miles waiting for the return journeys to begin at 5.24pm. Flagmen were present to control this movement, which for obvious reasons proceeded at a very low speed. It need hardly be said that the normal modest service was suspended for the day.

To get to The Hale and Edgware now required a change at Finchley except on the days when a special service was running and for this purpose one engine was maintained at Finchley in steam. In 1938 there was only one direct train in the morning from Edgware to Kings Cross and there was not even a corresponding return train in the evening.

LONDON GETS THE *UNDERGROUND*

By the early 1930s the passenger steam service, which had severe problems with reliability in winter, was at saturation point and the LNER lacked the capital and the will to put things right. In a plan of 1935 the whole of the service north of Highgate, the Northern Heights lines, was to be handed over to London Transport and converted to electric operation.

At this point something needs to be said about the development of London's Underground railway system. On the one hand the *Underground* lines were developed to cater for the existing needs of travelling Londoners, but almost equally the line owners anticipated demand by building new lines where they thought future urban development was inevitable. In this respect they made few mistakes.

In the early days the London *Underground* network was no different from the surface lines that preceded it. It was not an integrated system but rather a collection of individually owned and operated lines.

Each one having its own specifications and style of architecture. We are now well into the second century of the *Underground*, the first was opened in 1863, but it was a long time before it had any bearing on the lives of the people of Mill Hill.

The first two railways to be constructed were sub-surface, the trains run just under the surface or sometimes out in the open even in the city centre. In 1890 the first of the *Tubes* was opened with the line sunk much deeper. In due course as these lines were extended to the suburbs they came to the surface away from central London. The first of these lines was the City & South London Railway, now a part of the Northern Line and ran from Stockwell to King William Street. In 1907 this line was extended to Euston (King William Street station was abandoned for technical reasons) which was really the end of its independent existence.

Another part of today's Northern Line was authorised in 1893 with the approval of the plans for the building of the Charing Cross, Euston and Hampstead Railway. In 1907 this line was completed with all the stations opened between Golders Green and Charing Cross.

Demands for improvements in transport for London and suburbs between the wars led to the setting up of the London Passenger Transport Board in 1933, their first tasks being to improve facilities and then attract new custom.

In 1923 a new stretch of line with two stations at Brent (now Brent Cross) and Hendon Central was opened, and in August 1924 the line reached its fullest northern extent with the opening of Edgware station. Colindale and Burnt Oak followed a few months later, Burnt Oak as a direct result of the Watling Estate which was being developed by the London County Council. This was the strongest competition yet for the old steam railway that ran through Mill Hill, Finchley and Highgate to Kings Cross and meant that Hendon and Edgware were now firmly established as commuter suburbs of London.

At the same time as the line was being extended northwards a similar expansion was taking place south of the Thames, although with the exception of Morden, the terminus, all the stations are below ground. When Morden was opened in 1926 the line was renamed the Morden-Edgware Line.

The new station built for the *Underground* at Edgware was to a design quite unlike anything else on the network. It has only one storey and with its columns has a distinctly Italian look about it. This was to be a combined facility for the *Underground* with proper space for a bus terminus. Later on there were plans to build a link with the LNER Edgware station.

By the mid 1930s the newly formed London Passenger Transport Board was beginning to have firm plans about the integration of the various lines serving the Northern Heights. The Midland line was not involved in these changes but all the other services were. There were to be six main developments:

* To extend the *Underground* line which terminated at Highgate (later named Archway) underground to surface south of East Finchley station, side by side with the LNER line from Kings Cross and build a new Highgate station below the Highgate surface station.

* To lay double track from Finchley Church End to Edgware.

* To construct a connection between the LNER station at Edgware and the Edgware *Underground* station.

* To extend the line from Edgware to Bushey Heath.

* To convert all the lines where steam powered to electric traction, including the new line to Bushey Heath.

* To extend the Northern City line from Drayton Park to run into a new platform to be built on the eastern side of Finsbury Park LNER station.

Construction began on all this work in November 1936 but the outbreak of hostilities in September 1939 brought all these projects to a halt.

The intention behind all these developments was to introduce three new services of *Underground* train operation: between Moorgate and Alexandra Palace or East Finchley, between Bushey Heath and Kennington via Finchley and Charing Cross, between High Barnet and Morden via East Finchley and Camden Town.

At long last the line from Mill Hill East to Edgware was to be converted to double track and Finchley Church End, which would be a major junction, was to be demolished and completely redesigned and rebuilt.

To permit the laying of the extra track from Mill Hill East to Edgware the trains between Finchley and Edgware were replaced by a single deck bus on some Sundays from autumn 1938 and totally from September 11 1939. Thanks to the *'Phoney War'*, the slow start to actual hostilities, works proceeded on a modest basis and electrification to High Barnet was completed enabling the *Underground* to commence on April 14 1940. *Underground* trains had already reached as far as East Finchley on July 3 1939.

With the arrival of the *Underground,* Finchley Church End was changed to Finchley Central and the Mordern Edgware line was now renamed the Northern Line. At this time steam trains were still running to

Alexandra Palace, but from March 2 1941 steam trains no longer ran into the newly rebuilt East Finchley station, at least not on a scheduled basis. For some time goods trains continued to run on the lines to both Edgware and High Barnet and there were even some special excursions, mainly to seaside resorts, and visits to railway 'shrines' for enthusiasts.

For mainly military reasons the Edgware branch line was opened to the *Underground* as far as Mill Hill East on May 18 1941. A second track with conductor rails had already been laid as far as Mill Hill for the Hale, but the service used only one set of rails (there was no points system for switching tracks at Mill Hill East). The second set was removed soon after the *Underground* was inaugurated.

The service was between Mill Hill East and Morden on weekdays until 7.00pm, at all other times it was a shuttle service with Finchley Central.

At this point the railway bus between Finchley Central and Edgware was withdrawn although the special tickets were retained for some time, it being permissible to use them on ordinary buses operating the route from Edgware to Mill Hill East. This created a very strange situation because these tickets could be purchased at Edgware *Underground* and Mill Hill LMS stations, so it was possible to purchase an LNER ticket at an LMS station for travel on a London red bus for use on an ordinary scheduled run.

A year or so later, presumably under pressure from the war office, the goods yard that was situated on the north side of Mill Hill East station was extended to accommodate the additional military traffic for Mill Hill Barracks.

THE END OF THE EDGWARE LINK

The line to Edgware was not quite dead yet and for a decade or so the occasional steam train found its way past Mill Hill East. But it presented a problem and something of an anomaly. The new signals installed for the *Underground* trains had to be placed to coincide with steam train performance and the steam trains were limited in length. And of course fitting steam freight trains into a busy *Underground* schedule always posed difficulties and risks. In addition the dangling link on the guards van was often dangerously close to the centre 'return' rail, and sometimes even touched it resulting in a shower of sparks.

All these steam trains were supposed to be fitted with automatic tripcocks so that they would be brought to a halt should they try to pass a signal at danger. This instruction was not always adhered to.

For the trains to travel past Mill Hill East a special procedure was necessary. First the driver or guard had to obtain the key to the Edgware ground frame from the Finchley Central signal box, the Mill Hill East platform signal was then passed at danger thus operating the tripcock which was reset. The train proceeded on its way westwards with the driver keeping a sharp lookout for children on the line. If anything went wrong the train crew had to leave the train and return to Finchley Central by bus for assistance.

In 1956 there were still nine freight trains daily each way to East Finchley of which seven travelled beyond. Four were coal trains for Mill Hill Gas Works. That year the gas works closed and domestic fuel supplies were transferred to a centralised depot at Enfield Chase. The last real use for the line to Edgware had gone and the end was in sight. Economics and the determination to maintain the Green Belt at all cost led to the cancellation of the proposed extension to Bushey Heath. This extra line would have needed a long viaduct and the piers for this were in fact partially constructed and some still remain visible to this day as a reminder to us of what might have been.

The station buildings at Edgware were demolished in 1961 to make room for an office block but the goods yards both here and at The Hale remained for the time being: until May 1961 for Edgware and February 1964 for The Hale. From the time that the line westwards of Mill Hill East closed for electrification in 1939 it never again opened for passenger transport. The line from Mill Hill East to Edgware was closed to passengers on September 11 1939 and to all traffic in June 1964. All the track past Mill Hill East was finally lifted in September of the same year.

Alas there is not much to see of this bit of railway history now. Looking westwards from the Mill Hill East platform is a sorry sight of twisted and rusted rails running a few metres past a fixed red light, and although the actual route of the line is still discernible, it can only be followed by the line of a hedge leading to the bridge in old Sanders Lane (this bit of the Lane now downgraded to a footpath). The bridge in the main part of Sanders Lane was in the days of the railway a narrow hump-backed structure but it was rebuilt not long before the line was ripped up.

From the first bridge in Sanders Lane to Page Street the track is now a bridle path except for about 400m which is a (private) London Borough of Barnet nature reserve. From Mill Hill East to Page Street the concrete supports for the track cables erected in 1940 can still be seen. The Page Street bridge has long since gone, replaced by a footpath in a tunnel under the road. On the other side of this road is one of the buildings belonging to the contractor John Laing, which ironically would have been abandoned by them if their planned relocation away from London had gone ahead.

All signs of the railway vanish at this point but there are still bits of the old LNER three open bar railway fence for the observant spotter to find. The railway arch of the bridge that takes the Watford Way over Bunns Lane became a spur for the M1 but this has since been abandoned in favour of new spurs at Fiveways Junction.

The track of the line from this point vanishes into the M1 but reappears as the bridge in Bunns Lane by Mill Hill Broadway station, thereafter it is visible only as a completely overgrown cutting to Deans Lane which is the boundary of Mill Hill.

All this history for 6.5km of railway, of which 5km never had a future right from the day it was laid down, in spite of various schemes and attempts to make it into a success.

There is no point now in taking a Luddite stance with regard to the closure of branch lines and the transfer of traffic from railways to the roads. Except for large industrial complexes railways cannot transport door-to-door any easier than the canals could. Off-loading and reloading takes time and costs money. Nevertheless it is a great pity that even some of the largest trading estates no longer have usable railway lines within their perimeters. In earlier times it would have been possible to construct a new line to make rail deliveries to the Bittacy Business Centre opposite Mill Hill East Station but this was developed after the line was closed to goods traffic. As for the Mill Hill Industrial Estate in Flower Lane this has only existed since the old Great Northern line to Edgware has been dismantled.

In the future it may well be necessary however to look very closely at the total transport package and calculate which method causes the least concern with regard to all ecological standpoints. We all enjoy the freedom to come and go as we please that road transport gives us but concern about possible climatic changes that could result from our ever increasing abuse of the atmosphere may in the years to come lead to us being compelled to do what is best for mankind at large: use our feet a bit more and certainly make better use of public transport.

A FUTURE HOPE

It is now nearly 30 years since the line onwards from Mill Hill East was dismantled and vanished for good, or so we thought. In July 1990 a new plan was announced by *London Underground* which detailed a proposed extension of the line to terminate at the Copthall Stadium, which they say would provide this sports venue with the opportunity of becoming the equivalent of Crystal Palace in North London. *London Underground* state that the Stadium is host to 800,000 visitors per year, and this number would increase if transport was improved, at the moment it is very poorly served. With the possible, redevelopment of the old Mill Hill Barracks an extra station and a better service would certainly make this part of the Northern Line much more important.

The track of the old railway where this would be built now mostly belongs to the London Borough of Barnet and they were not immediately in favour of the plan, probably because they were not advised of the proposals before they were officially drawn up. It is hard to see how Barnet Council can have a valid objection, and there is probably an element of pique. After all a double track from Finchley Central, with an extra platform at Mill Hill East would be a great improvement, and it could also lead to some building at Finchley Central, something planned and started over half a century ago. In fact *London Underground* do claim that at the same time they would improve the service to Barnet.

The total scheme would cost something over £1m and could be ready by 1997, however if Barnet Council object strongly then *London Underground* say they would abandon the project. Most people would agree that substantial improvements to much of the Northern Line are long overdue.

CHAPTER X

THE HISTORY OF PRIVATE PROPERTY

From the earliest times there were really only two kinds of basic land ownership; the King or Chieftain, together with his family and associates and appointed ruling class, and the Church. Much of the Country is still in the hands of these two classes even today. In the Middle Ages some new land owners made their appearance: the independent farmers and city merchants. The farmers' houses were utilitarian but those built by the merchants were often fine buildings that vied with the manor houses in size and magnificence.

With the end of villeinage it was inevitable that the Lords of the Manors would lose influence. Although serfdom did not end with the 14th Century the bonds that held the villeins were relaxing everywhere, whether the Lord liked it or not, and none did. Agricultural workers were demanding higher returns for their labours and when this was not forthcoming they left and offered their services on a free market. This situation was amplified by the Black Death which so reduced many communities that there was a serious shortage of labour, particularly at harvest time. By the middle of the 14th Century the Lords were no longer the only employers of labour, there were even instances of relatively prosperous peasants who in addition to working on the lands of the Manor also built up holdings of their own and employed labour to help run it. There were serfs who were freelance shepherds as well as workers for the Manor: they not only looked after their own sheep but also took in flocks from other owners.

THE ARRIVAL OF PRIVATE FARMS

Under the system that had prevailed since the Conquest each villein had a number of strips of land, but all in different fields, so that there was much trecking involved from one field to another. Many of the villeins had managed to gather their strips into one field by swapping with other villeins on the Manor. This was the beginning of the private farms, even though they were still within the confines of the Manor.

Probably the first man to lease Hendon Manorial land was John atte hegge. His lease was for meadows and pastures for £24pa. Throughout his 40 year career he negotiated leases for enterprising farmers who wanted release from the rule of labour and dues in kind. John and the new leaseholders were also free to sublet.

When John atte hegge died he was a rich man by the standards of the age. He was certainly something of an entrepreneur: from comparative youth he had not only leased land for himself but also managed all the other land in the Manor for the Abbey showing loyalty to both the Abbot as well as to his own people. In addition he also acted as something of a peacemaker during the troubled times that followed the Peasants' Revolt.

The changes that have been detailed were of course not peculiar to any particular area, they were happening everywhere. People were becoming more self assured and aware that they should have rights. The Peasants' Revolt was a brutal reminder, (even though in many ways it was a failure), to the people in power that changes were inevitable.

The Mortimers and Scropes mentioned earlier were large families at this time with property, many of them were knights. Some were faithful King's supporters (Henry III) and one was his most successful commander.

MANOR INTO MANORS

The Manor of Hendon of which Mill Hill was one of the hamlets went through a period involving many changes during the 16th and 17th Centuries. Some appear to have been as a result of incompetence and the rest were due to political chicanery of one kind or another. In addition private property was developing so that the all embracing control, and power of the Lord of the Manor, was beginning to crumble. The result was that other manors were being carved out of the whole, and the hamlet of Mill Hill developed into a village in its own right.

The first of the 'new' manors had in fact already been in existence since the 14th Century. Although not mentioned in the *Domesday Book*, Frith Manor is of considerable age, and was probably detached from the Manor of Hendon by Gervase de Blois. The owner in 1366 is on record as being Richard Rook, the Knight of the Shire. The Manor of Frith was a large area from the day that it was created.

In ancient documents the Manor of Frith is described as Hendon Frithe, or Fryth in Hendon. In the King's books it is valued at £13 6s 8d (£13.33) and the ownership given as the Monastery of St Peter at Westminster. The annual rent was £1 6s 8d (£1.33) and for additional land 10s (50p) value with rent of 9d (4p).

It is on record that Rook gave a messuage (house and adjoining land)) two copses, 646 acres (261ha) of arable land, 39 acres (16ha) of meadow, 100 acres (40.5ha) of woodland and rent amounting to £2 7s 6d (£2.38) to the Abbot of Westminster. There appears to be a deliberate falsehood in the description of the lands because the arable land is described as 'so dry and stony so as to be worth only one penny per acre, and it could not be cultivated without a great expenditure for manure'. Now anyone familiar with this part of Mill Hill will know that at almost any time of the year the land is damp and in the winter mainly very sticky clay. It is certainly not stony and the stony parts of Mill Hill are few and far between.

The Manor was known as Frith and Newhall and was established in the northwest of the Parish. The first mention by this name was in 1500 but almost certainly included lands in the Manor of Hendon granted to the Abbey c1244-46 by Walter le Frith and Ernald, son of Roger del Frith. Gilbert of Hendon had already made grants to the Abbey (c1226-28) of two crofts formerly held by Vial which stretched from the lands of Ernald del Frith to the River Brent.

At the beginning of the 18th Century, when accurate maps first began to appear Frith is just shown as a dot, but on John Rocque's map of 1754 Frith Green is a manor of some importance and takes up most of the land that is now the Finchley Golf Course.

In 1754 Frith Manor consisted of the farms of Dollis 69 acres (28ha), Frith 153 acres (62ha), and Partingdale 54 acres (22ha), plus an additional 100 acres (40.5ha). The Manor estate was split up after 1809 and the farms were owned in 1828 by Sir Charles Flower Bart of Belmont on The Ridgeway (Dollis Farm), Thomas Fentham (Frith Farm), and R Franks (Partingdale Farm). Sometime after this Partingdale became known as Partingdale Manor.

WESTMINSTER ABBEY IN CONTROL

The monastic institutions of the mid 16th Century lacked the zeal that obtained before 1400. In the last 150 years only eight new houses had been founded, many of the older ones were declining and no religious or historical chronicles were being written. Although printing had to a large degree reduced the need for hand written manuscripts nothing of note was being printed and no religious author of distinction existed. The Abbey of Westminster was a monastery before all else and these comments applied to this institution as much as any other.

In 1534, after a number of small religious houses had been dispersed and their assets seized by the crown the stage was set for the King (Henry VIII) to present a Bill to the Commons whereby all religious houses with an income of less than £200 per year were 'to be converted to better use'. This was done on March 11 1536. Presumably the sum of £200 had no real significance because it is impossible to accept that the smaller houses were necessarily the ones that did not carry out their religious duties with proper devotion, much the reverse. All lands and properties were transferred to the crown. Although the gain to the exchequer was considerable it still did not balance expenditure and there is no doubt that the larger institutions were already destined to follow the path of the smaller houses that had already gone. The days of Westminster Abbey as a monastery were numbered.

Towards the end of July 1536 Thomas Cromwell set up a committee to put in force the *Act for the Dissolution of the Monasteries* and a general order was issued that all images, relics and shrines were to be taken away, and figures over the altars were to be destroyed. Westminster held out longer than most but the golden shrine together with the plate and all the jewels that adorned these articles were taken. The black day was January 16 1540 when the 24 monks and abbots of Westminster signed the 'Voluntary Deed' (sic!) by which the Abbey and all its estates were surrendered to the King. This was the first really big change of ownership of the Manor of Hendon since *Domesday*.

Henry rewarded the obsequious monks well. Because the Abbey had immense revenues he could afford to. On December 17 1540, *Letters Patent* were issued to make Westminster Abbey into a cathedral church with a bishop and a see. Thomas Thirlby, Dean of the Chapel Royal was appointed Bishop of Westminster with nearly all of Middlesex, and it was also directed that a dean, 12 canons, and a number of lesser officers of the church were to be appointed. Most of these came from the monks. By 1542 the change-over was complete. The bishopric was endowed with a considerable annual revenue and the Bishop was given the Abbot's house as his palace.

Unlike the Manor of Hendon, after Dissolution the Manor of Frith did not form part of the endowment of the Bishopric of Westminster but rather it was granted to Bishop Thirlby and his heirs personally. Even after the reduction of the See, the Manor remained Thirlby's property. Eventually it passed out of this family to that of the Peacocks.

Ownership by the new Bishopric of Westminster was of short duration and the Manor passed into lay hands. In 1550 Edward VI granted ownership to Sir William Herbert who became the Earl of Pembroke. When his second son, Edward, was married in 1569 he gave the Manor of Hendon to him as a wedding present. Shortly after the marriage some of the tenants were ordered to draw up a survey that took nearly two years (1574-1576) to complete. The landlords of the 16th Century could not guess how land ownership would develop in the years to come. Even before the Survey was finished a lawsuit was drawn up whereby the

Manor was conveyanced as belonging to Sir Edward and his heirs for ever. In the introduction of the Survey are the names of the Customary Tenants who carried out the work. There are 24 of them, and of these six are of the Nicoll family and six are of the Marsh family.

The entry on the Marsh family details the holding:

"WILLIAM MARSH holdeth one tenement called Slattens and
renteth yearly to the Lord.........ii^s vi ^{d}
For service...............................ix^s viii ^{d}
and tenn bushells of otes"

The Marsh family was one of the largest in the Manor and from this we see the detail of just one of their holdings and the rent payable.

The Manor then passed via the family of the Earl of Pembroke to the Duke of Powis. In the time of Elizabeth I the Manor House was the property of Sir Edward Herbert and the residence of Sir John Fortescue. When Sir William died in 1595 his son succeeded to the title and to the Lordship of the Manor. He confirmed the tenancy of Hendon Place to Fortescue. Sir William, the new Lord of the Manor married Eleanor Percy, the daughter of the Earl of Northumberland, and in the same year, 1629, was created Baron Powis.

The son of Sir William, Percy, was knighted and made baronet in 1632. At this time his father handed over the Manor to him but not before yet another survey had been carried out. Once again the Nicolls and Marshes are prominent amongst the names of tenants making present-ments. The boundaries are unchanged from the previous survey and are set out again, and ancient customs of the Manor are detailed. There is a list of copyhold and freehold tenants together with holdings, rents, and dues.

In 1688, because of his adherence to the cause of James, the lands of the Duke of Powis were declared forfeit and it was not until 1722 that ownership was regained by his son.

For the greater part of the 17th Century the house was occupied by the Nicoll family. Towards the middle of the 18th Century the house was sold to Thomas Snow who demolished it and built a new house.

THE END OF COMMON LAND

In the 18th Century the Manorial waste or common lands were granted away without any apparent consideration of the effect in years to come. Today there is virtually no such thing as common land. Starting in 1758 with 'land six perches wide' being granted to Elizabeth, wife of Anthony Vere the sorry tale continues with waste and common land being handed over to almost anyone who applied for it, and in particular anyone who already had lands and money. The list for Mill Hill is considerable, here are a few examples:

> To John Franklin in 1754 'seven poles by 22 feet at Highwood Hill'
> To Samuel Rutter in 1786 'eight poles in front of his house in Mill Hill'
> To John Stillman in 1786 'some waste at Thrift Green near Mill Hill'

In 1816 two pieces of waste land in Lawrence Street were enclosed.

There is a rhyme in *A Social History of England* by Asa Briggs. It is not original and has appeared in numerous books with alterations on emphasis. Nevertheless it does describe the unfairness of this land grabbing rather well.

> They hang the man, and flog the woman
> That steals a goose from off the common.
> But leave the greater criminal loose,
> That steals the common from the goose.

Occasionally the applicants were disappointed and permission was refused and there is even one instance of a piece of land being returned to common use, but this is very exceptional. The steady march to ownership of all land was irreversible. One notable parcel of common land was a large green at Holcombe Hill that disappeared bit by bit between 1754 and 1828.

Entries in official records for this period give an indication of land values. In 1722 the Parish sold 36 acres of waste at Dollis for £9 16s or about 5s 5d per acre (in today's money 67p per ha). During the same year nine poles at Highwood were sold to a Mr Carter for 9s and 131 poles in three lots at The Hyde for £6 9s. This was arable land and was valued at £8 per acre.(£19.76 per ha).

THE NICOLL FAMILY

The family associated with the Hendon area more than any other, and for over 500 years is Nicoll, and an early mention is made of the lands belonging to a William Nicoll in the *Memorandum Roll* of 1448. Indeed we have evidence that he was residing in the area before the Wars of the Roses. An earlier historian (Norman G Brett-James) claimed to have a deed dated 1434 that recorded the transfer of Goldbeater's Farm from John and Eva Clark to their daughter and son-in-law. Among the witnesses were John Breynt and William Nicoll who was apparently already residing in the area where the family seat, Copt Hall, would eventually be built. Then again in 1574 Richard Nicoll of Mill Hill is mentioned in a survey of Hendon carried out for Sir William Herbert as being a responsible freeholder who provided information.

The Nicoll family over the centuries owned a great deal of property and were also responsible for the construction of at least five important buildings. Alleyne Nicoll, who was in all probability the grandson of William Nicoll mentioned above appears in local records of 1524 as residing at Ridgeway House.

Other Nicolls of property were John Nicoll of Heywood (Highwood), and William Nicoll of Hendon Place and The Ridgeway; he was a citizen and grocer of London. Many more members of this family are listed as having property and important civil positions in the 16th and 17th Centuries.

Apart from their various lands there were two houses of note belonging to the Nicolls, unhappily both are no more. The older of these was listed as Cookes in the *Court Rolls* and was prob-

Copt Hall a mansion built in 1637

ably situated between the *Adam & Eve* inn and the Priory and was reputed to have been built during the reign of King Edward IV (who reigned from 1461 to 1483) and demolished shortly after 1820. At around 350 years old it was the oldest house in the Village.

According to records of the time it was a fine old timber house with projecting lattice windows with a great deal of carving both internally and externally. The interior was decorated with religious paintings and frescoes on both walls and ceilings. For the last 20 years or so of its existence it was let out in apartments: a sad end for its magnificent rooms. The owner had the place demolished rather than pay for the cost of refurbishment and we do not know what happened to all the valuable interior decorative work, if indeed any of it was saved.

The other Nicoll edifice, Copt Hall, was a mansion and was rebuilt between 1624 and 1637 by Randall Nicoll. The house was constructed of red brick and had copings of carved stone. The flat front of the house was flanked by gabled wings and tall chimneys with decoration typical of the period. About the time that the house was built the area was referred to as Borgers Mead and this name still appeared in a deed dated 1717. It remained almost exactly as built, except for alterations to the gables and ornamentation in the 19th Century, until demolition in 1959.

For the last 27 years of its existence this house was also subdivided into apartments, and has now been replaced by a block of flats. Modern and for the residents no doubt a most desirable development but such a pity to destroy 300 years of history and about 600 years of heritage in one act of officially approved vandalism. The reason given at the time was that the structure was dangerous, but many buildings have been restored that were in far worse condition. The flats carry a Blue Plaque stating that it is the site of Copt Hall, home of the Nicoll family.

The house was in Page Street with the main entrance across a cobbled courtyard with stabling along one side. From the north side of the house a grass avenue led to Wise Lane. Copthall Park is now a municipal playing fields and stadium, mainly in Hendon. North of the track of the old GNR railway line is Mill Hill.

The name of Nicoll continues to appear at frequent intervals and this family seems to have appeared in every kind of document and been involved in just about everything of importance that happened in the Manor and surrounding district.

THE MANSIONS OF MILL HILL

Elsewhere mention has been made of the sale of the Manor to David Garrick in 1756. This marked the beginning of a new era in the history of Hendon and therefore Mill Hill. The slow change of the last 700 years was being overtaken by events. As communication with London improved the society based upon farming and the farmhouse began to decay in favour of the estate with its mansion or country villa with its garden. The progress of this change was continuous right into the 20th Century. Certainly some of the larger estates were worked as farms but the basic social structure of Mill Hill had changed forever. If a comparison is made between the 1754 map by Crowe and that of Cook in 1796 there is very little change but the difference between these and the first OS map of 1822 is considerable.

From the middle of the 18th Century we see a big and by comparison rapid increase in the number of private estates and large impressive houses. Many of these were built on The Ridgeway and in the Highwood Hill area which had reached its peak of importance as a desirable place for people of influence to live. Later this polarized the classes residing in Mill Hill. The gentry tended to build in the places detailed above whereas all the estates that were built in the early part of the 20th Century are around Mill Hill Broadway Station on the Midland

Railway and distinctly middle class. The development of private property in Mill Hill during the 18th and 19th Centuries was predominantly in large houses with extensive grounds.

It must be said however that The Ridgeway was not all big houses if for no other reason than the gentry needed suppliers and artisans. These were the real local people, less peripatetic than their rich neighbours who moved in and out of the district as fame and fortune arrived or deserted them. In the late 19th Century the range and scope of traders along The Ridgeway was quite comprehensive. Obviously there were inns and public houses and of course a blacksmith and farrier, but the existence of baker, confectioner and butcher, grocer and even a florist are a little more surprising. There was also a firm of builders. Some of the old weatherboarded houses predate the mansions and with the prices of houses, particularly old ones, being what they are today they are now worth a great deal more in real terms than when they were built.

Some...old weatherboard houses

The 20th Century is completely different, the days of the mansion are over. We have come to the age of the developer and the housing estate and no matter how hard the architects may try an estate is an estate and it is where most of us live. We buy a house in an estate, and spend the rest of our lives moving from one estate to another. Like most other suburbs Mill Hill away from the Village is a collection of developments, separated and surrounded by main roads.

MOAT MOUNT HOUSE

Rocque's map makes no reference to Moat Mount and by all accounts Moat Mount House had not been built at that time. The Estate was described at the end of the 18th Century as 'a piece of land, extent one acre, surrounded by a moat'. The presence of a moat no doubt means that there was a building on the land at some period, but there was no trace of any building at that time. With few exceptions moats were dug between

1150 and 1500 with the majority being completed in the middle of this period. Whatever the house that originally occupied this site it must have been of considerable size and importance. There is some evidence that a house existed some time in the 18th Century but there is no record of what it was like or the date that it was levelled.

The nearest moated castle was at South Mimms but its active life was short. It was rather a simple affair, a typical motte (high mound) and bailey (enclosure). Little more than a stockade with an encircling dry ditch. The castle was almost certainly constructed during the civil war between King Stephen and the Empress Matilda c1142.

Moat Mount house was erected by Abel Browne and was occupied by William Browne in 1828. The whole estate was 60ha. A guide in the 1920s described the house as an imposing mansion standing in spacious grounds. The house was at one time the residence of E W Cox. Cox was born in December 1800 and at one time intended to enter the Church but subsequently changed his mind and became a lawyer. Starting as a solicitor he was called to the bar in 1843 and joined the Western Circuit. Later he was made in succession recorder of Falmouth then Portsmouth, and in 1870 deputy assistant judge of Middlesex Sessions which brought him to Mill Hill.

Cox was also a journalist and his first venture was the *Somerset County Gazette* which he sold on being called to the bar. In 1843 he decided that there was a need for a weekly legal paper and therefore founded the *Law Times*. He also started *The Critic* and the *Clerical Journal*. In 1854 Cox purchased the copyright of *The Field,* at that time of little reckoning, and transformed it to a much respected magazine, later he took control of *The Queen* and gave it the same treatment by altering its management and tone.

Cox was awarded the title of Sergeant-at-Law and thereafter was known as Sergeant Cox. When the order of Sergeants was abolished he purchased the Society's hall, had it carefully dismantled and re-erected in his own grounds exactly as it had been before. He died quite suddenly in 1880.

CHAPTER XI

MIDDLE CLASS ESTATES

I n the period between the turn of the century and the mid 1920s the population of Hendon increased from 2,245 to nearly 110,000 and it doubled between 1921 and 1931. Mill Hill took its share of this increase and the centre of Mill Hill shifted from the Village on The Ridgeway to the area around Mill Hill Broadway. Three completely new housing estates came into being, the Birkbeck Estate which is known locally as Poets' Corner and lies northwest from Dawes Lane (all the roads are named after famous poets and dramatists: Byron, Milton, Shakespeare etc), Mill Hill Garden Village, and the Uphill Farm Estate. Later on there were further developments to either side of the A1 Barnet by-Pass north of Apex Corner.

There was no real resistance to the building of these three estates. New housing was the big thing, the majority wanted to be a home owner in their own modern home (although there was still a demand for rented property). The main concern was to maintain a reasonable quality with a low density. Later on when the Reddings Estate was proposed on the western side of Lawrence Street many people felt that Mill Hill had gone far enough in accommodating new urban developments. People had come to Mill Hill because it was rural and were anxious to keep it that way. The battle to prevent Reddings was lost, but people were alerted and further developments on this scale seem to have been prevented and appear to be unlikely. It would mean developing up to The Ridgeway, in the Totteridge Vale, or into Moat Mount. All

FROM UPHILL FARM ESTATE BROCHURE

very improbable and certainly undesirable.

The only likely developments are in the small areas between existing buildings and possibly the field to the north of the cemetery whose entrance is in Milespit Hill. Plans for building houses here have been rejected on a number of occasions already but if past experience is anything to go by the developers will win in the end even if the density that they originally requested is reduced.

The building of the A1 Barnet By-pass and A41 Watford Way created another attraction for the developers. The triangle formed where these two roads parted was dead land, being hemmed in by Mill Hill Golf Course and two main roads. A small estate was built here, the Golf Course Estate (1935/6) which quickly spread to fill all the available space. The developer and estate agent advertised this as Stoneyfields Estate.

During World War I there was a considerable amount of industrial and residential development along either side of the Edgware Road, Mill Hill escaped the worst of this type of building and agriculture remained the chief industry. By the time World War II arrived the industrialization of the Edgware Road had continued right into Edgware and beyond.

The great increase in house building after the cessation of hostilities in 1919 brought in its wake three things which the Hendon Urban District Council (which controlled Mill Hill) was anxious to avoid at all costs: jerry building (cheap building methods with poor materials), ribbon development, and excessive density. Mill Hill was to be reserved for residential purposes, mainly of private ownership. Discussions about a Green Belt to stretch from Ruislip in the west to the Lea Valley in the east were already under way and Mill Hill in the middle of this was reasonably safe. The developers of the three estates mentioned above were at pains to point out in their literature that jerry building was to be prevented. Some ribbon development did proceed along the Barnet by-Pass when this road was built but the houses in the main are large and impressive and have stood the test of time. In the Uphill Farm Estate at least the density was limited to 20 per ha (8 per acre).

The prices of the houses were roughly the same as were being quoted in other outer London boroughs. In 1930 houses in the Uphill Farm Estate (all freehold) were priced at £895, the cheapest, for a semi-detached house without garage to £1,000 for a detached house with garage. Monthly repayments were from £5 14s (£5.70) to £6 6s 8d (£6.32) and any house could be secured with a deposit of £10.

Having bought your home, or rather taken out a 25 year mortgage at these mammoth monthly repayments and interest of around 3% how did the man of the house earn the money? Almost certainly he commuted to London. He could have used either of the railways, Midland or Great Northern, and they both quoted exactly the same fares. Today these seem unbelievable: in 1925 a quarterly from Mill Hill Broadway to St Pancras cost £6 First Class, £4 8s 6d (£4.38) Second Class and £4 2s 2d (£4.11) Third Class. Today there are only two classes and the relevant price for a Travelcard, Zones 1 to 4 is £236.26.

Taking the prices of houses given above, a three bedroomed semi in either of the estates cost around £1,000 and today would fetch £150,000 to £200,000 which is an increase by 150/200 times. On this basis the increases in the price of rail travel are reasonable. However if we take a senior clerical officer of some authority in 1925 who would have been fortunate to earn around £300 pa and today is paid £15,000 to £20,000 then you are only looking at an increase of 60 times. Whatever may be said to the contrary the burden on the average house owner in mortgages and fares is much greater than it was 65 years ago.

MILL HILL GARDEN VILLAGE

In 1919 when Sir Ebenezer Howard planned Welwyn Garden City he was designing a self-contained residential and industrial complex with a proposed eventual maximum population of 50,000. It was a grand opportunity to start a town layout from scratch. There would be no excuse for narrow streets, houses with a back-yard instead of a garden, and a lack of facility for public amenities and entertainment. Truly a place fit for heroes to live in. In many ways it was and is a success: it has retained its identity, the design and layout has not become out of date, and industry is still there. True the population has been a bit slow in getting to the planned level (which in many ways is a blessing) and the town is not self-contained because a high proportion of the working population commute to London. Hampstead Garden Suburb, (which was designed by the same man to the vision and forward thinking of Dame Henrietta Barnett) in spite of being surrounded and hemmed in all sides by later developments has still managed to keep its name.

If a stranger arrived in Mill Hill today and asked to be directed to Mill Hill Garden Village could anyone help? Almost certainly no. And yet in 1910, ten years before Welwyn Garden City, this great development was being advertised with the all usual developers' and estate agents' hyperbole. The fat brochure (price 6d) went into great detail about Mill Hill, 'one of the prettiest and healthiest in Greater London', 'extraordinary natural beauty and diversity of scenery', 'magnificent panoramic views', and so on. All true no doubt in 1910, and to be fair still largely so for those who are fortunate enough to live in the Village, on Highwood Hill or The Ridgeway. But for most of Mill Hill they were using the wrong crystal ball.

Where today is, or rather would have been, Mill Hill Garden Village? On a map it would fit quite snugly in the triangle formed by the M1 Motorway, Mill Hill Broadway, and the A1/A41 Watford Way. Obviously this is not at all what the developer had in mind: the Barnet by-Pass was not even a dream, and as for the motorways the first one was nearly 50 years away.

Even within the 'Garden Village' little followed the plan shown in the actual brochure apart from the street layout and even here the road names were not all kept: Goodwyn Avenue was meant to be Mount View and Newcombe Park was first named Highwood Park. The old farm house and farm which were to be converted into a club house and recreation ground vanished under the Barnet by-Pass and all that remains is the small sculptured garden on the northern side of Mill Hill Circus. True this small recreational garden is usually well maintained and quite pretty but in the middle of so many busy roads it is hardly the place to leave the children whilst doing the shopping. The open space indicated half way down Mill Hill Broadway (still shown as Lawrence Street) and another open space in the middle of the development and a bowling green failed to materialize.

But more significant than any of these was the actual houses: the plan was as far as possible for plots to be sold and the buyers to have their own houses designed and built. The brochure promised that there would not be a host of onerous restrictions on the types of house. There are many desirable houses here, and a considerable variety of design, in fact as an estate its houses are some of the best and most varied anywhere. Today they are of course worth a great deal of money, but in the main they do not appear to be the individual architect designed homes that were intended.

Setting aside the usual copy writer's silly excesses (such as *Ye Olde Plough Inn* instead of the real no nonsense name *The Plough Inn*) what would the prospective buyer have been offered that certainly would not be found in this area today?

'There are no main roads through the district with the consequent motor dust and noise'.

The 'Village' is now surrounded by main roads.

'The whole of this area lies undisturbed and peaceful, yet within easy walking distance of the Edgware Road with its service of trams'.

Not a bit of it, and not many people would regard a walk to the Edgware Road to pick up a bus to town at all favourably.

'Travelling is quite clean and comfortable (by train) and totally devoid of overcrowding'.

A bit optimistic!

'The rates and taxes are lower than those charged in most suburban areas, whilst from a health point of view it has one of the lowest death rates on record'.

Come to Mill Hill and become immortal. Presumably they meant premature death, but even so there is a law about making such claims today. Strangely enough the developers actually quoted figures to prove that Mill Hill did indeed enjoy a very low death rate per 1000 residents.

'A considerable portion of the estate borders Lawrence Street (Mill Hill Broadway) with its natural wide grass margins and magnificent trees'.

You will search in vain for these.

No doubt the planners and developers meant to achieve all this (after allowing for their usual exaggerations) so what went wrong? Unfortunately people and money got in the way. The difference between a somewhat visionary planner with his advertising copy writer and reality is simple. No-one guessed how much the population would increase, how densely the suburbs would be built up, and most of all how many motor vehicles would be on the roads in a few decades. All these led to bigger, wider trunk roads and unfortunately Mill Hill is in the thick of them. Certainly the people moving into Mill Hill in 1910 and for the next 20 years or so were looking for peace and quiet, and there are parts of the area which have managed to keep it that way, at least by today's standards. A short ride, or even a walk, up to Wise Lane, The Ridgeway or Highwood Hill and you can still find a touch of rural Mill Hill and we hope will continue to do so into the 21st Century.

THE DEVELOPMENT OF MODERN MILL HILL

The new estates, the development of the arterial road network, and big increases in population meant the inevitable end of rural Hendon and to some degree of Mill Hill too. The farms which had formed such an important part of the social structure for hundreds of years were doomed with the arrival of the 20th Century. Age old lanes and footpaths were bisected by main roads and therefore often ceased to have any proper function. The list of new roads is impressive (if you like roads) and by 1927 all those that were to influence Mill Hill (except of course the M1) were opened. Hendon Way from Finchley Road and Barnet Way were begun in 1924, and in 1928 the Hendon section of the North Circular Road and the Great North Way were built. Bunns Bridge was built in 1927, and with Hendon Way completed to the North Circular Road this road was now operational to the northern boundary of Mill Hill.

In the *Ordnance Survey* map of 1863 the locations of 38 farms were shown in the area, many of them within the bounds of the Mill Hill of today. Before the outbreak of World War II most of these old farms had already disappeared, sometimes because they had been in the way of a new road but more often because some other development was planned. It is interesting to record when some of the Mill Hill farmhouses were demolished and the lands taken over, and where they were located.

GOLDBEATERS FARM *Demolished 1924*

Sited west of Bunns Lane. This farm was in the way of the route to be taken by the Great Northern Railway on its way from Finchley to Edgware so some of the lands were lost at the time that the line was laid down. The line was actually cut through the farmlands in 1868. The farm finally lost all its lands when the Goldbeater's Farm Estate (later named the Watling Estate) was built. At its prime Goldbeater's was one of the largest farms in the area at 154ha (380 acres).

DOLLIS FARM *Demolished 1930*

On Holders Hill Road west side near to the entrance of Hendon Park Cemetery.

UPHILL FARM *Demolished 1931*

This farm was in Lawrence Street on the edge of what became the Uphill Farm Estate. The farmhouse was supposed to have been converted into a community centre but was demolished in 1931. The farm had in fact been renamed Cherry Farm by the time that the estate was built. Uphill Farm was at one time a part of the greater estate of Moat Mount, purchased by Sergeant Cox in 1877.

DOLESTREET FARM *Demolished 1937*

The farmhouse was in Page Street near to the junction of Milespit Hill and Wise Lane. Unfortunately this farm was in an area under severe pressure and finally gave way to compulsory purchase when a Council housing estate was built in 1931. In any case part of the farm lands were lost to the Great Northern Railway in 1868. For a time this fine example of a typical Middlesex farmhouse survived as a private dwelling.

Of course this is merely part of a continuing process that had been

Dole Street Farm... typical Middlesex farmhouse

going on for generations, land ownership has never stood still and other farms such as Bittacy Farm and Hale Farm had vanished at an earlier date. The lands of Bittacy Farm were taken over by the War Office when Mill Hill Barracks was built in 1904, and the lands of Hale Farm are now all built up.

116

CHAPTER XII

THE NATIONAL INSTITUTE
FOR MEDICAL RESEARCH

T he Institute is of course much more than a building, but even if it were not its position and imposing size would necessitate an important place in a history book on Mill Hill. It stands on The Ridgeway, its green roof clearly visible like a beacon for miles in nearly every direction. The enterprises that are carried on within its walls serve all mankind, both the peoples and their animals.

BACKGROUND TO THE NIMR

During the 19th Century, this country was concerned primarily with world power, and the exploitation of the resources of the mineral and vegetable wealth that were to be found in the British colonies around the globe. To achieve these successes meant developments in manufacturing and other industrial processes. In spite of progress in these areas we lagged behind countries such as France and Germany when it came to scientific application applied to biochemistry and medicine. To ensure true progress in these fields it is necessary to proceed with research on a systematic basis using both government money and endowed private funds, which were not forthcoming at the time. Later on the Lister Institute was to become active in this role but government funding was urgently needed.

The spur to setting up a government backed research project was the *Insurance Act* of 1911 introduced by Lloyd George, which among its measures proposed that one penny from each individual contribution should be set aside for medical research purposes: scientific research for medicine was to have a properly regulated budget at last. The Medical Research Committee of 1913 came about as a direct result of this. This body resolved that to further their ambitions and to ensure that the money made available was correctly channelled where it would be most effective a central research institute should be established in London. Later in the same year appointments were offered to a number of eminent medical men of the time but no overall medical director was appointed until 1928 (the first nominee declined). The National Institute for Medical Research (NIMR) had arrived.

Little could be done with staff and money but no headquarters so a search was made for suitable premises. A number of buildings were considered and finally an offer was made for the Mount Vernon Hospital or North London Hospital for Consumptives in Hampstead. According to a guide book of the time the hospital which consisted of a main building and nurses' home plus just over one hectare (2.4 acres) of grounds was started by public subscription in 1880. The nurses' home was originally the manor house of the estate, and subsequently the official residence of successive directors of the NIMR. The purchase price was £35,000 and the date March 1914. Unfortunately the declaration of war prevented any conversion work being put in hand and the buildings reverted temporarily to their original use of hospital.

It was not until 1920 that the NIMR was eventually admitted into the completely refurbished building with its brand new laboratories. Before long it became obvious that Hampstead was far from ideal for animals, there was insufficient space and the location and building were unsuitable so additional accommodation was sought. In 1922 a farm in Mill Hill of 13.5ha was purchased for £6,000 and the present NIMR buildings and animal husbandry facility stand on this site.

It is worth noting that when the NIMR was first set up it absorbed 35% of the Medical Research Council budget, but by 1980 this had shrunk to 8.2%. True there are lots of other establishments (mainly universities and hospitals) that deserve extra fundings but nevertheless the NIMR does seem to be obtained on the cheap.

THE NIMR IN MILL HILL

By the middle of the 1930s it was already apparent that the building in Hampstead was quite inadequate and in many departments was bursting at the seams. The Mill Hill farm site was in many ways an ideal place for a completely new research institute: the land was already owned by the Medical Research Council, there was plenty of space for expansion, and the environment was very pleasant without being too remote, although it must be admitted that a past deputy director of the Institute wrote in 1983 that a site nearer to a major centre of learning such as Cambridge or Oxford would have been better. However today with computer links, fax machines and the like the inconveniences of distance have been minimised.

With amazing speed for such a huge project preliminary studies were completed and Maxwell Ayrton FRIBA was commissioned to work on the design which he commenced in 1937. The main structure was completed at the beginning of World War II: the second time that the NIMR was prevented from moving to new premises by the outbreak of hostilities. Occupation of the great new building had to be postponed. In

1942 the building was requisitioned by the Admiralty and from then until 1946 was used as a training depot for WRNS personnel.

If it was true in 1937 that NIMR Hampstead had reached bursting point then by the actual date of removal to Mill Hill in 1950 the position was much worse. Every available area was fully occupied, even the corridors, and this congestion was hampering efficient working. The new building must have been heaven to the hard pressed staff with its working space of well over 8,000m². Indeed the laboratories, other areas of work and the refectories were so good compared with most of those in hospitals and other research institutes that there were no problems with finding suitably qualified staff.

Ayrton's design consisted of a central block seven stories high with two oblique wings at each end, these to have three stories above ground

The Institute, much more than a building

and two below, but because of the slope of the land these basements at some aspects would enjoy natural light. Such a building today, as we approach the 21st Century, would cost many millions of £s whereas the actual estimated capital cost (excluding the scientific equipment) was a mere £820,000. Truly a far sighted investment without parallel.

The building is truly massive, almost awesome when viewed from close up, and yet with the supporting wings appears curiously stable and complete no matter from which direction it is seen. It has weathered well and still looks clean in spite of its 50 years. Obviously the design is functional, after all it is very much a 'working' building, but because it has a pitched roof it looks finished, unlike many of the buildings of the 1960s that could probably gain or lose a couple of floors without affecting the design (sic!).

Today the NIMR of Mill Hill consists of the main building, the Fletcher Memorial Hall (the General Stores is housed in the basement), various farm buildings, the nutritional block, the Collaborative Centre in Burtonhole Lane, and Fir Island, a rather splendid Victorian House in the triangle formed by The Ridgeway and Burtonhole Lane that is used to accommodate some staff and visitors. In addition the NIMR has excellent sports and recreational facilities, probably the best in Mill Hill.

THE WORK OF THE NIMR

In a nutshell the role of the NIMR is as far as possible to act as a central research institute on the National level and at the same time to co-operate closely with all other similar research bodies overseas. Because of the Institute's relations with other research bodies it helps to reduce over duplication of effort without in any way restricting competition. The main functions can be classified under a number of groupings.

The NIMR provides a basic nucleus of research workers covering a wide range of non-clinical activities which complement the work of the more specialised units. In addition to short term practical studies long term basic work is also carried out.

Central government (which provides the bulk of the funding through the Medical Research Council) requires of the Institute certain statutory obligations. These include monitoring and surveillance duties with regard to such diseases as influenza and leprosy. The World Influenza Centre is one of the responsibilities of The Division of Virus Research. The Centre identifies the strains and mutations of influenza viruses that are collected from outbreaks and epidemics around the World.

The facilities of the Institute are made available for meetings of scientific societies, and conferences and discussions are arranged on a regular basis. In addition educational and post-doctoral training is carried out together with formal PhD work.

Apart from the essential collaboration between departments there is also much external co-operation with universities, polytechnics, and hospitals at both theoretical and clinical levels. This co-operation facilitates multidisciplinary approaches to biochemical problems.

In the early days the NIMR actively liaised with the British drug industry, companies such as British Drug Houses and Burroughs Wellcome, particularly to help in the development of chemotherapy agents for the treatment of cancer and certain tropical diseases. This liaison with the drug industry is now of lesser importance.

THE NIMR's ACHIEVEMENTS

THE STANDARD DOSE

When the NIMR was set up there were no standards by which the activity of drugs could be measured. H H Dale, one of the founder members had worked on the standardization of the drugs used to treat syphilis, and was therefore already familiar with the necessity of properly measured dosages of known strength. When insulin was identified and separated by F G

Banting and C H Best in Toronto, Canada in 1921 Dale realised that it was absolutely essential to have an accurate standard if the correct dosage was to be arrived at and so reduce the suffering and premature death of diabetics. The concentration of blood sugar, (in normal people between 800 and 1000 milligrams per litre of blood) has to be controlled very precisely. Dale proposed that the unit of insulin should be defined by comparison with a standard stable preparation that would be held by a central agency similar to the way that standards of weights and measures are kept.

The suggestion was accepted and this led to the creation of the Department of Biological Standards which shared the responsibility with the Serum Institute of Copenhagen. The man responsible for the setting up of this department was P Hartley, and by the time that he retired in 1946 the Standards Division of the NIMR included antibiotics, antitoxins, blood group antigens, drugs (such as digitalis, ergometrine and tubocurarine) hormones and vitamins.

The work load of the Biological Standards Division continued to expand year by year. Indeed shortly after the NIMR moved to The Ridgeway the standards department moved back to the old laboratories in Hampstead and from 1972 until 1987 a quite new and separate National Institute of Biological Standards and Control had its offices and laboratories in the old NIMR building. In 1987 the NIBSC moved to new premises in South Mimms in Hertfordshire.

PREVENTION NOT CURE

By comparison with most viruses, bacteria are huge. There are in fact viruses that attack bacteria (bacteriophages). In 1914 when the NIMR was founded little was known about these agents that could pass straight through a filter which would retain bacteria and yet whose effects could be so devastating. The study of viruses was one of the first investigations of the new Institute and has continued to receive a high priority.

Those of us who are old enough will remember the sorry sight of our pet dog, dry-nosed, runny-eyed and listless, stricken with distemper. A highly infectious influenza like disease which was often fatal. Seventy years ago the disease was very common and feared by dog lovers everywhere. Today the disease in this country is virtually unknown. The search for a vaccination or cure was sponsored by the *Field* magazine.

Distemper was an early NIMR success; they discovered and isolated the virus that causes the disease and in 1927 a successful vaccine was prepared. Within a year it was in commercial production. Today the list of 'firsts' that can be attributed to NIMR research is probably unsurpassed by any medical research centre anywhere in the world, and the list grows year by year.

Bit by bit many other facts were discovered about viruses. Some are type specific and can only infect one animal or plant type, others are transferable, such as influenza which infects man and some rodents, rabies that has a natural vector in various canines and bats as well as man, psittacosis, the parrot disease which can be fatal to man, and tobacco mosaic disease (TMV) that can be a serious problem for tomato growers. In many cases an animal (and this includes man) that has recovered from the disease is then immune to further infection by the same virus. This is the basis of immunology and the success of vaccines. With the invention of the electron microscope, and particularly the scanning electron microscope, viruses can be 'seen' although it must be said that Barnard and Smiles working at the NIMR had developed a method of photographing viruses before this by using ultra-violet light which has a shorter wavelength and therefore greater resolution than visible light.

We now know what viruses look like, how they work, how antibodies function, and in many cases how to prevent infection. Much of this work has been done at the NIMR.

After the success with distemper some of the other most notable events in virus work were the isolation of influenza and common cold viruses, the development of a method for measuring virus size, and the discovery of interferon, a naturally occurring anti-viral agent.

With all the work that has been done with regard to viruses it does not mean that other infecting agents have been ignored, for instance much work was carried out on the Salmonella group and cholera between 1926 and 1949. Bacteria, fungi, protozoa, amoebae and many others still cause the sickness and death of millions of people per year and the diseases related to these are therefore just as important to the NIMR as those caused by viruses. In spite of all the efforts of the NIMR and elsewhere so far only one disease has been completely eradicated from this planet and that is smallpox.

OTHER SUCCESSES

The work of an establishment like the NIMR cannot stand still so that between the times of writing and publication this list will already be out of date.

Other firsts are new drugs for use in tropical medicine, obstetrics, surgery, and for the treatment of hypertension, the isolation of the first pure vitamin (Vitamin D2, Calciferol), and techniques to study the effects of drugs on the brain. Actual discoveries include the chemical structure of cholesterol and antibodies, the natural source of cortisone, and the active thyroid hormone which contains iodine.

Some discoveries do not appear to have a direct and immediate relationship with clinical medicine, the establishment of the chemical transmission of nerve impulses is one of these. However any developments in this area are of great importance in helping to understand the nature of degenerative disease and why nerves in the central nervous system fail to regenerate after injury.

A great deal of work has been done regarding the tendency of microbes to develop strains that are resistant to antibiotics. An effective treatment for amoebiasis has been developed and there is now a satisfactory vaccine for scrub typhus. Big strides have been made in cryobiology (freezing cells, tissues etc.), the nature and function of sex hormones and pheromones and organ transplant immunology, all thanks to the NIMR.

FUNDAMENTAL MOLECULES

An entire book could be devoted to the work and the discoveries of the NIMR relating to fundamental molecules. The effects of alkaloids and their comparison with similar molecules that occur naturally in animals, internal and external glandular secretions and their influence on bodily functions, identification, separation, and in some cases synthesis of hormones and vitamins are some of these. All these studies have lead to a greater understanding of what makes life tick and eventually stop ticking.

In some cases substances that occur naturally have had their molecular structure 'improved' so as to enhance their effectiveness or reduce unwanted side effects.

THE UNGLAMOROUS SIDE

Elsewhere in the NIMR are departments relating to applied physics such as optics and crystallography, the chemical laboratories where routine work is carried out, even an engineering shop, and of course the library. Devoted people who seldom make the headlines. It is from these departments that such developments as gas chromatography (an extremely accurate method of quantitative analysis that only requires a minute specimen) and the apnœa alarm mattress (which gives immediate warning if a child stops breathing) originated.

Add to all this the work on human physiology: high altitude

research, deep sea diving and sea sickness, the measurement of physical efficiency, biomechanics and so on and we have something in Mill Hill that is unique in Britain. The NIMR may not be the most exciting building in Mill Hill, but it would be hard to find any others that are more important. It is difficult to assess its true value, certainly it cannot be calculated in financial terms alone, nevertheless a few simple facts are interesting.

Tenured and short term doctoral posts number about 140 in an average year. There would normally be about 100 visiting and attached workers, 70 or so Medical Research Council and non-MRC postgraduate students plus a few MRC training fellowships. Research officers and technicians number about 230. Salaries amount to the biggest single cost at around £10m. To these must be added scientific equipment at around £2.5m, any necessary building works and recurrent costs at about £5m.

CHAPTER XIII

THE ENIGMA
THAT IS LITTLEBERRIES

In many ways Littleberries is one of the mysteries of Mill Hill, indeed for many years no-one was even certain who actually had the right to the *Title Deeds*. The house was built on the site of an earlier house. Today it is well concealed within the buildings of the Convent of St Vincent de Paul and behind a high wall, but close to the public road, The Ridgeway. Any visitor or rambler unfamiliar with the district would miss this piece of local history unless equipped with a guide book. Because the house was built on the side of a hill there are different levels to the garden. There was a pool on each level (although one was filled in a long time ago), but strangely neither of the fountains detailed in earlier descriptions is to be seen.

According to many writers Littleberries is supposed to have been built for King Charles II and to have been used as the residence of two of his favourite women, the Duchess of Portsmouth with her son, the Duke of Richmond and Lennox, and Eleanor (Nell) Gwynne and her little son, the Duke of St. Albans. Sadly there is no evidence of this. We know that Charles lived a profligate life style, what with racing at Newmarket, brothels in Covent Garden and many established mistresses (and the bastard children of whom at least 14 can be positively identified), but as to the residence of them at Littleberries this is wishful legend.

If the association of the house with James II is tenuous then it is interesting to relate a supposed connection with some notorious people of a different hue. In the early 18th Century two brothers both wine makers, Daniel and Robert Perreau are reported to have lived there with a friend Mrs Rudd and this trio were involved in the forgery of £70,000 worth of Bank of England warrants. The trial caused quite a sensation at the time, and the accused were found guilty and sentenced to death. This is another mystery because these people are not to be found in a list of the copyholders of the period.

Littleberries is an old red brick house within the compound and school of the Order of St Vincent. Today it is really a shell without any of the carvings and other works of art that adorned the building in earlier times. Writing in an earlier book (*The Story of Mill Hill Village*) Brett-James talks of a portrait of the Duke of Richmond (amongst others) which was in the house until 1885, this may appear to give a little credence to the story of the residence there of his mother, the Duchess of Portsmouth. Also prior to 1885 there were many rich carvings, ornate ceilings, and full size copies of famous paintings by Corregio, Rubens, and Van Dyck. As if this was not enough there were portraits of a later date: George II and his queen Caroline of Anspach, and of William III.

The last private owner was Lord Aberdeen and during his period of tenure Gladstone was an occasional guest. But let us return to the beginnings.

The site that is now occupied by St Vincent's on The Ridgeway has been important to Mill Hill for over three centuries. What we can now see is a complex of buildings representing the additions and alterations by a procession of owners over this long period, such that the original plan is now completely submerged under the bricks and mortar of following generations.

In a survey of the Manor carried out in 1574 this plot of land on The Ridgeway was described as containing a house and garden. In 1685 another survey was commissioned and in this it shows that Edward Coderin (like most names of the period this name has various spellings) surrendered his 'customery messuage (mansion house), together with yards, stables, outhouse, orchard gardens and carriageway' to George Littlebury and his wife. Littlebury was a bookseller of the City of London and was married to Mary Snow. The Snows were a well established important family residing at Hendon Place. This would seem to be the reason for the Littleburys taking a house on The Ridgeway. The surviving parts of the earliest house owe their existence to George Littlebury.

In 1711 the alterations to the house began when Littlebury mortgaged the property to Charles Kent for £250, the money raised being used for enlargements. A year later £18 15s (£18.75) was paid to Lord Powis for improvements to the residence and gardens. The improvements were to include the pavilion and the layout to the garden. The grounds from the house face due north over the vale of Totteridge, a superb view with the land dropping 30m to the Folly Brook, and then rising 45m to the ridge that carries Totteridge Lane. A truly excellent spot to design a garden. The somewhat strange aspect of the design is that although it was obviously the work of a competent gardener it is restrained, almost conservative, compared with the decorations in the house.

In 1721 George Littlebury died and as he had not redeemed the property it was surrendered by his wife to Thomas Snow, a citizen and goldsmith and probably Mary Snow's cousin. Thomas Snow died in 1746 and his son Robert was admitted to the title in 1747. Robert was now a powerful man in the district with title to all the Snow estates: Hendon

Place, numerous small houses in Hendon, extensive land, and now Littleburys. George Littlebury's additions were continued by the Snows, mainly by Thomas, and the wings joining the pavilion on the north elevation plus the entrance facade date from this period. Robert Snow died in the latter half of 1771 or early 1772 and his son George was admitted to the property, but his tenure was short lived and in 1777 he surrendered all the property to Samuel Bonham.

From this date until the time that St Vincent's took over, the property changed owner or tenancy many times, which is probably why the actual title holder was considered to be in doubt. Strangely the *Manorial Courts* still referred to 'formerly inhabited by George Littlebury' even though at this time he had been dead for 50 years and the Snows had lived there for much longer. Nevertheless it would seem obvious that the house took its name from Littlebury with the slight corruption of the name to Littleberries.

Samuel Bonham was the title holder until 1788 when he surrendered it to James Rankin who in turn passed it on to Thomas Kerr in 1800. The Kerr's ownership lasted for nearly 50 years although they did not occupy the house for all of this time. One of their tenants was a Mr Wilkes (from 1824-6), who some consider was responsible for the building of the Gothic lodges, but there is no documentary evidence of this. A Manorial survey of 1796 does not mention them but they are detailed in a survey of 1828, so construction was between

Littleberries - one of the mysteries of Mill Hill

these two dates. There is also confusion regarding Mr Wilkes and some have taken this to mean John Wilkes the radical politician (qv) but this is most unlikely because he died in 1797. The *Wishaw Survey* of 1828 lists Thomas Carr (should be Kerr) as the owner, and described the house as 'an old brick mansion with neat Gothic lodges'.

The Kerrs gave up the property in 1847 and the next owner was J F Pawson. The Pawsons were a family from Shawdon, a hamlet in Northumberland, (now a part of Cumbria) and their arms were added to the summerhouse. More alterations were carried out in the mid-19th Century, and since the Sisters of the Order of St Vincent moved in further buildings, including the Chapel have been added. The chapel served the Catholics of Mill Hill from 1887 until their own church was consecrated in 1924.

The oldest and most imposing part of the house is the garden front; with the pavilion raised above a semi-basement are three bays with a projecting pediment. Two windows flank the door which is reached by a double flight of stairs from the garden. The pavilion is built of red brick with headers of black, the windows have stone architraves and rusticated stone quoins. Because of the position of the pavilion it could never have been a symmetrical design. The main entrance is on the south side of the building but not in the same plane as the pavilion so it would seem that the pavilion was added to an existing building. The choice was not arbitrary because it is part of the symmetry of the garden rather than the house.

According to various surveys for the Manor of Hendon the property which belonged to this house was a rectangular plot with the long side facing on The Ridgeway and from this land a long tongue extended northwards. This land being meadow it in no way related directly to the house. When the garden was being designed it was obviously considered as giving great scope for landscaping, which of course it had. The pavilion was created to close the vista at its highest point and for the view to be down a long terraced tree lined avenue.

In 1855 the house was stripped of its pictures and some of the interior decorations which were sold in the gallery of Foster's in Pall Mall. They realized the trivial sum of £15 8s (£15.40). Even before the sale many of the carvings had all ready been covered up with white paint. When the Sisters moved in they decided that all the remaining finery was incompatible with their status and everything movable was sold. Clearly they should have sought guidance elsewhere. It would be hard to guess what the two lots would be worth today, and how much more could the Sisters have made over the years by charging visitors an admission fee to view the treasures.

E T Evans in his book quoted at length a description of the house taken from *Notes and Queries* (6th Sr 41) by George Scharfe, secretary of the National Portrait Gallery. Evans could not verify any of this because when he carried out the research for his book the decorations had already been disposed of. We obviously have to rely on the written word. However because the house interior was unique and so interesting we propose to quote the same passage.

'This residence stands close to the public road, but is sufficiently screened from observation by a line of thickly planted trees bordering the lawn. The northern side of the mansion, away from the road, abuts on the brow of a steep slope, which descends to a considerable distance, and is broken into green platforms with two distinct pieces of water on different levels, one round and the other square but adorned with fountains (the round pond was filled in sometime in the 1930s). The effect of this, as seen from the house, is very pretty, and the vista is terminated by a summer house in the form of a classic temple, with a pediment and four Ionic columns, having arched windows between them. The length of ground between this temple and the house itself is bordered on each side with thickly planted trees, giving the appearance of green walls or lofty hedges.

'The mansion viewed externally, is an ordinary square building of red brick with irregular corners, and has been much added to at various times. The rooms are irregular, enclosing a central apartment, which appears to have belonged to a former and much more important residence. The apartment contains an amount of rich wood carving and mural decoration rarely to be met with in buildings of such a size and so situated, and being profusely gilded, is known as the 'Gilt Room'. The tone of this elaborate ornamentation is in the taste of the first half of the 18th Century, that is from the period of Queen Anne to the reign of George II.

'The walls between the dado and the cornice are divided into large panels, containing showy painted copies, full size, of celebrated pictures by Reubens, Van Dyck, and other artists. The subject of the panel to the left of the door is the *'Union of Earth and Water'*, consisting of two figures of Neptune and a nude female. It is mentioned in The *English Connoisseur* 1766 p72 under the title of *The Marriage of Neptune and Cybele*. The companion panel to the right of the door, is also after Reubens, from a magnificent picture in the dining room at Blenheim Palace. It represents the Hesperides gathering fruit, assisted by Cupid perched on the branch of a tree. Another composition from Blenheim, *Time Clipping the Wings of Love,* painted by Van Dyck, may here be recognised in a tall panel to the right of the fireplace on the east wall. The corresponding tall panel, between the fireplace and the window, is occupied by a naked figure of Venus standing in a shell, with a Cupid crouching at her feet, gliding over the sea, drawn by two doves, which she guides by silken reins held aloft in her right hand. Two other Cupids follow her, hovering in the air with drawn bows and a dart directed forwards. The remaining picture is described, beneath a shield of arms encircled by the Garter in letters of no great antiquity, Charles Lennox, Duke of Richmond and Lennox, born 29 July 1672, dyed 27 May 1723.

This picture seems to have been inserted into the panel as a substitute for something else. Two smaller panels beside it, now filled with looking glass, under broken pediments, may have once contained pictures. This full length of the Knight of the Garter is the only painted portrait in the room.

'In the centre of each wall, is a large circular medallion containing a white plaster representation of a crowned sovereign the size of life, seen to the waist, and spiritedly executed in alto-relievo. These clearly form a part of the original decorations of the building. Above the fireplace, the medallion contains a portrait of Caroline of Anspach, Queen Consort of her husband George II. On the opposite wall is a portrait of her husband, George II. On the side facing the door, and over the windows, the medallion exhibits a portrait of George I. Over the door is a well-modelled relief of William III. Each medallion is supported by two white plaster figures of naked children, extremely well-modelled. The choice of portraits for these medallions would appear to be as a celebration for the accession of George I in 1714, with William III being odd man out. His inclusion would point to early 18th Century for the ceiling decorations. The subjects of the portrait indicate that work continued after 1712.

'The chimney piece, which occupies the entire length of the east wall, deserves particular attention. It is elaborately carved in wood, with two prominent figures, in full relief, of Justice and Peace embracing, surrounded by mouldings, complicated curves, and borderings in ultra-French taste of the Louis Quinze period. This heavy mass of carving appears to have been imported from elsewhere, and rests on a low square chimney piece of white marble, and more recent design.

'Throughout the whole building there is no indication, either by coronet, garter, or heraldic cognizance, that the place ever belonged to any person of rank or distinction. The only exception where heraldry appears is in the pediment of the summer-house at the end of the grounds. There the arms of the Pawsons, of Shawdon, in Northumberland, are carved on a plain shield, and may be referred to a period when the front of the building was altered, and the spaces between the columns filled in with windows of coloured glass. The interior of the summer-house, both on the walls and a shallow domed ceiling, is highly decorated with figures and ornaments in low relief, all in white plaster. They include portrait medallions of females, supported by sphinxes, mermaids, and tritons. These faces are all in profile, full of individuality, and probably represented members of the family who then occupied the house. On the east wall is a curious circular medallion, containing a view in white plaster alto-relievo of the mansion as it formerly appeared from this spot, showing the different levels of ground, and reproducing the building in its original state, including the Gilt Room and steps leading up to it. One piece of ornamental sculpture in white plaster remains to be noticed in the house itself. This adorns a niche at the foot of the stairs, and is hollowed in the thickness of the wall outside the Gilt Room, immediately beyond the picture of the Hesperides. It was probably connected with a fountain. On the upper part of the round-headed recess, and cleverly adapted to the concave surface, are two naked sea-nymphs, seated back to back on a rock, each resting her feet on a separate dolphin. One female supports her long tresses with her hand, and the other pours out water from a shell. The figures are pure in form, and extremely well modelled. The figures approach that type which distinguishes Leonardo da Vinci'.

It is a dreadful pity that it is not possible to see any of the treasures that made Littleberries such an amazing house with all its portraits and sculpture. Even in the 18th Century it must have cost a great deal of money to produce copies of so many celebrated paintings, and these plus the carvings and plaster work no doubt kept a team of artists busy for a very long time. Such extravagance would probably be considered to be vulgar today, and was excessive even 200 years ago. Perhaps George Littlebury and the Snows were trying to prove something, that they had 'arrived'.

Winston Churchill said in a radio broadcast in 1939 'I cannot forecast to you the action of Russia. It is a riddle wrapped in a mystery inside an enigma'. Littleberries is certainly not as perplexing as that but an enigma it most definitely is.

A new era began in the late 19th Century which has continued in a more sedate and orderly way to the present time: Littleberries was opened as St Vincent's Orphanage and there have been no further changes of ownership.

The British Province of St Vincent de Paul purchased Littleberries and its 40ha of grounds in 1885. A seminary block was begun in 1886 and in 1887 a large stone chapel in the Perpendicular style was opened. The architect was F W Tasker. In the early 1930s the chapel was gutted by fire, and was rebuilt and recommissioned in 1935.

In 1969 the convent was the administrative and training centre for 1,200 sisters of the British Province. There is also a school for deprived children, nursery for abandoned babies, and college for children's nurses on an adjacent site.

CHAPTER XIV

THE STORY OF
HIGHWOOD HOUSE

E lsewhere in this book will be found detailed accounts of the lives of the two most notable men who resided at Highwood House: Lord William Russell and Sir Stamford Raffles. Russell was a son of the Duke of Bedford and lived at Highwood towards the end of the 17th Century. Raffles; traveller, administrator, and botanist died in 1826 at the early age of 45 after a very short tenure at Highwood.

The first house to be built on the spot where the present building stands was probably owned by one of the early Nicolls. In those days it was certainly remote from other habitations with commanding views over the countryside. It stands some 135m above sea level with the land dropping away on all sides except the northern aspect, here it rises to the highest point in the district (in Mote End Farm :145m).

Part of the original Nicoll Highwood House is said to have been incorporated in the present building. This is interesting because there are no other Nicoll houses or parts of them still in existence. A family whose branches owned Copt Hall, Cookes, and Highwood House must have had considerable wealth and great influence. Whether the house as lived in by Lord William Russell and his wife was the Nicoll house without much alteration and rebuilding or whether it had already been almost entirely rebuilt we do not know. In the south-west corner of the present house are some walls that are nearly 2m thick, these are reputed to be a part of the original building.

The 2m thick walls from the Nicoll house form deep recesses where there are windows. In earlier times these would have formed ladies bowers or retiring rooms when enclosed by a tapestry. In this part of the house the ceilings are low and the rooms have small windows. They are connected by winding passages, and the upper rooms are reached by a tortuous staircase.

In 1681 Russell was almost certainly involved in a Whig plot to prevent the Duke of York, a staunch Catholic, from succeeding to the throne. This plot was mixed up with another and this lead to the arrest and conviction of Russell and some others. Russell was imprisoned in the Tower of London and sent for trial which was a complete mockery. His wife, Lady Rachell, acted as his secretary throughout this ordeal, and somehow they managed to keep up their resolution to the last.

Russell was found guilty of high treason and beheaded in Lincoln's Inn Fields on July 21 1683. His body was brought back to his home by faithful friends and buried as a temporary measure in a shrubbery in the garden. Lady Rachell had four yew trees planted in the form of a square and this area was thereafter referred to as the cemetery. At a later date the body was exhumed and reburied in the family vault in Chenies, Buckinghamshire.

Highwood House

As for the legend to the effect that Russell was sleeping in the house when he was arrested there is no hard evidence of this so it has been discounted. Certainly there are no writings by Lady Rachell to confirm this and this story does not surface until a much later date. It is an interesting tale none the less.

A magazine article in 1874 said that one of the rooms is by tradition 'haunted', we assume by Russell. But then what would an old house be without a haunting? Whether Russell was apprehended at Highwood House or not it was one of his residences and therefore he obviously had a bedroom there, but why would he haunt it, we usually associate hauntings with the place of death. His ghost may well walk in Lincoln's Inn.

To preserve the legend every writer has described the window, 'A small circular swing window of an adjoining closet', and a window of this description does exist in the south-west corner of the house. After escape Russell was supposed to have been pursued up an avenue of trees that extended to the north-west but was overtaken by the King's messengers and arrested.

Until the middle of the 19th Century the avenue of trees was still in the grounds of Highwood House. Part of this land was sold separately and by 1874 was included in the Moat Mount estate of Sergeant Cox.

After the execution of Russell the house was extended somewhat. The extent of this building work is not known because during further developments at a later date most of the house was rebuilt. Lady Rachell lived in the house for some years after the execution of her husband. We know that she devoted her time to the education of her daughters but there does not appear to be any firm record of the date that the house acquired its next owner.

By all accounts Lady Rachell was a very pious lady and well liked and respected by the local people. She is on record of being a close friend of Queen Anne. Presumably by then Lord Russell had been posthumously rehabilitated. Records mention a chalybeate spring in the garden that she endowed to the poor of the district, which was known locally as Lady Russell's well. It was supposed to have had healing powers and has been compared favourably with other more famous springs such as Cheltenham Spa, which probably means that it tasted just as foul. The spring is described as, 'A circular wall built pit about 10ft in diameter and seven feet deep. Access is obtained by an old moss covered flight of steps. The mineral spring flows unceasingly into an oval basin, dyed red with iron and all bordered with moss and lichen'. A plaque was placed on the wall above with the inscription in old Roman capitals.

MRS. RACHELL
RVSSELL'S GIFT
JVNE YE 10TH 1681

This was placed before Russell's execution, and in fact when his elder brother was still alive. He had not inherited the title so that the inscription refers to 'Mrs' rather than 'Lady'.

No doubt there are many owners between the Russells and the purchase by Sir Stamford Raffles in 1825. There were 142 years between the two. Almost certainly there were also a number of alterations to the property and the outbuildings would have changed.

In *Cooke's Survey* of 1796 the freeholder's name is given as William Brown Esq. The description of the property is very detailed and comprised 7acres 3roods 13perches (3.17ha) with mowing grass and tythe measure, extended to 13acres 2roods 32perches (5.54ha) with hedges and ditches:

'At Highwood Hill, a large house, with pleasure grounds, gardens, yards, coach-house, stables, out-offices etc. with the fields or pieces formerly called the Well Field; the cherry orchard, the apple orchard, the barn pightle, gravelly field, and the house pightle, now converted into pleasure grounds, etc. Likewise, a farmhouse, stable, and garden, included in the above measure; (a coach-house, on the waste, and part of a pond)'.

When Raffles took over the house the *Rising Sun* public house was part of the estate. In 1796 the man who became the owner of Highwood House, John William Anderson, owned a considerable amount of property in the area, viz:

'At Highwood Hill, the Sun Public House (Rising Sun), with garden, stable, large barn, and small piece of ground enclosed in front. Likewise, two cottages and gardens adjoining the above' and 'At Highwood Hill, two cottages, with cart-house, stables, garden, etc. and a large barn; all at the left hand corner of the road from Mill Hill.'

Presumably it was Anderson who created the estate by purchases between 1796 and 1825, at which time Raffles purchased it.

After Raffles died his widow lived in the house for another 32 years and died on December 12 1858 aged 72. She is buried in the churchyard of St Paul's Church on The Ridgeway. No doubt many will have wondered why husband and wife were not buried in adjacent graves or at least in the same graveyard (Raffles is buried in the churchyard of St Mary's Church Hendon).

The vicar of Hendon at the time was not enthusiastic about burying Raffles and refused to conduct the ceremony. Raffles was buried in an unmarked grave that was discovered during building and renovation work when part of the churchyard was taken into the church. His actual burial place is now denoted by a stone tablet let into the floor to the left of the altar at the end of the communion rail.

A bronze statue of Raffles is a landmark in Singapore. Some years ago the government of Singapore requested that Raffles' remains be sent to them for re-interment at the foot of the statue as a kind of homage. Hendon Borough Council refused. A copy of the statue in plaster was made for the Wembley Exhibition of 1924-25 and for many years this stood in the entrance of Hendon Town Hall in the Burroughs. It has since been moved.

Most of the house to be seen today dates back to the early part of the last century. Demolition of the older house and rebuilding work was carried out for William Anderson and was completed just prior to 1817. Perhaps the most notable part was added later, this was a rather beautiful conservatory that occupied the recess between two abutting parts of the north-west frontage. This addition by Lady Raffles was designed to communicate with three rooms. Raffles introduced mahogany into this country and many of the doors and part of the landings were changed into this wood.

Between 1858 and 1872 the estate had a number of owners: Mr Urquart, Mr MacEwan, Captain Dent, and Mr Grey, who then sold it again to a Mr Lockett.

In *Wishaw's Guide* of 1828 Lady Raffles was shown to be a considerable land-owner with Highwood House being the largest single unit. As will be seen the lands are not all together:

	A	R	P
At Highwood Hill a Farm House in two tenements, with Stabling, two Cottages, Yard, and Paddock.			
A Piece in front from Waste	3	3	32
Spratt's Close	3	2	05
Willingham's by Lilley Lane (now Uphill Road)	6	1	18
Sander's Mead	9	3	36
Gibb's Close	9	2	25
At Highwood Hill (Highwood House) A Handsome stuccoed House, the country residence of Lady Raffles, with Lawn, Shrubberies, Plantations, Park, Out-offices etc.	51	0	21
Tree Fields	8	1	24
Upper Hankins	6	0	37
Moat Field	7	0	23
Lower Hankins	6	0	01
Farther Hocomb Hill	3	2	32
Hocomb Hill	4	2	12

The total of all these is 120.66 acres, which is equal to 48.83ha.

At the beginning of World War II the house (and estate) was still privately owned but was vacant for a time at the early part of the War. It was requisitioned by the local authority and used to house families that had lost their homes in bombing raids. At one time seven families were living there. The house was handed back to the owner in 1948 when it was no longer required as a half-way house and the families were moved out.

Not long after the end of the War there was a plan to create a club as a memorial to those who had died in the Far East, particularly in the Malaya Campaign. This was to have had a reference library and other leisure activities. The Governor General and other Governors in Malaya did not agree and felt that any memorial to Raffles should be in Singapore so the scheme was abandoned. In retrospect there must have been justification for both schemes, in any case survivors of the War were hardly likely to journey to Singapore, and before long the Colony gained its independence.

In October 1951 the property was put up for auction and at that time described as a freehold property consisting of Highwood House, the Studio House, and others. According to the prospectus all the separate parts (it was now four individual residences) had been completely refurbished and modernised but retaining period features.

Only 2½ years later and the roof was completely gutted by fire during renovation work. (How many times has this happened to a building in course of restoration?). It may seem odd that extensive work of this nature was necessary after such a short time, but the main house was being converted into a home for the aged (hospital patients) to be run by the Red Cross. The restoration work was completed in December 1954 and the Home was officially opened by the Queen Mother.

There was a letter in *Country Life* in November 1945 signed by Harold Whitaker. He claimed 'When I lived in Highwood House the place was still remote and 'old world', Even in this century at Christmas-time the mummers used to come round to act their traditional play with the characters of St George, Pompey, the Apothecary, and others I cannot remember. Instead of sheepskins, the mummers wore bulky coats of shredded paper to produce the same effect. Otherwise the play appeared to be unchanged after centuries of repetition'. Unfortunately Mr Whitaker did not give any dates.

The house carries a Blue Plaque indicating that Sir Stamford Raffles lived there, but it will come as no surprise that there is no mention of Lord William Russell who lived there rather longer. The blue plaque, fresh white paint, and neat front garden give a good impression of orderliness. At present the grounds at the rear do not, and today they are certainly not something of which Lady Raffles would have been proud. The house and 'estate' is now only a shadow of its former self with the separate parts mentioned above quite divorced from the main.

CHAPTER XV

UNIVERSITY OF LONDON
OBSERVATORY

The heavens themselves, the planets, and this centre
Observe degree, priority, and place,
Insisture, course, proportion, season, form,
Office, and custom, in all line of order.

(*Troilus and Cressida*) Shakespeare

E very day thousands of vehicles of all types hurtle up and down the Watford Way. To most of the drivers it is just a route to somewhere, they see nothing except the road in front and many are travelling well above the speed limit. This is a pity because there is something different here in this otherwise boring road, nestling behind the now mature trees and neatly clipped hedges and lawn is the University of London Observatory.

The first building to be erected here is now over 60 years old but still looks bright, white and shiny. The characteristic shape of the main buildings set them apart from any others in the district and because of the very nature of their science there is an air of peace about the place. There is a feeling of permanence and belonging too. To those who may be interested the Observatory is open to the public (by appointment) twice per month.

THE EARLY YEARS

Dr W E Wilson was an astronomer and lived in the family seat in Daramona, Co. Westmeath, Ireland in the last century. He was elected FRS in 1896. When he died his son J G Wilson offered to the University of London the telescope that had been in his father's private observatory and the gift was accepted. The instrument had been constructed by Grubb of Dublin in 1881. It was transported to University College in 1928. The University now had a telescope but no suitable site to construct an observatory. Many places were considered, most were unsuitable because of location and lack of accessibility with the College. Eventually an arrangement was made with the Hendon Urban District Council to lease a site in Mill Hill at a nominal rent for 999 years. At that time the Watford

Way had not been built but Mill Hill Broadway Station on the Midland Line was close at hand.

The Observatory building was designed by L Rome Guthrie using the material favoured at the time, reinforced concrete, and constructed by Leslie & Co. The building work was commenced in July 1928 and finished in 1929. The Senate of the University made a grant of £5,000 towards the cost and additional fundings were provided by Bedford, East London (now Queen Mary and Westfield), King's and University Colleges and The London School of Economics. (To many people the gift by the LSE came as a bit of a surprise). The official opening was performed by the Astronomer Royal, Sir Frank Dyson FRS on October 8 1929.

nestling behind ... mature trees
University of London Observatory

The original building contained the dome for the Wilson telescope (a 24in reflector), a spectrographic laboratory with darkroom, a computing room and a workshop. Additional development before WWII was made possible by another gift. In January 1930 H R Fry of Barnet presented the University with an 8in refractor made by Cooke of York in 1862. A new building was erected in 1931 to house the Fry instrument and the University were fortunate in obtaining a second-hand dome from a house in West Wickham in Kent. Mr Fry met most of the cost of reconditioning the refractor and its subsequent re-erection.

In 1934 the Radcliffe Observatory, which was in Oxford, was being relocated near Pretoria in South Africa. The Radcliffe Trustees offered the University a twin 24in/18in astrographic refractor that they did not propose to take to their new location, this was accepted. This telescope had also been made by Grubb of Dublin (in 1901) and it was dismantled and brought to London in 1935 together with its dome and rising floor. Some further land adjoining the original site was leased from the Hendon UDC and a new building was constructed between 1937 and July 1938. This new building cost £2,300 plus an additional £1,000 for auxiliary equipment, furnishings, the re-erection of the telescope and dome, and the rising floor. The official opening was by the Astronomer Royal, Sir Harold Spencer Jones FRS on July 1 1938.

TROUBLED TIMES

At the outbreak of the War in 1939 the Observatory was officially closed, as were the smaller teaching observatories in University College at Gower Street W1 although some dedicated staff still carried on from Mill Hill. The lenses of the only recently installed Radcliffe telescope were removed and stored for the duration as a safety measure. University College suffered heavily during the War however and a 10in telescope was destroyed by enemy action.

The Observatory buildings at Mill Hill came through the War unscathed and the Wilson telescope was used during this period on a programme of spectrographic research. The blackout imposed during the War had its advantages and the observers benefited greatly from the absence of background light. The wartime research programme did have unscheduled interruptions and it was not always easy to carry on when the bombs were falling and the anti-aircraft guns going mad. On the night that the V1 came down at Mill Hill Circus the observers were the Director C C L Gregory and his assistant Miss E M Peachey, who later as Dr E M Burbridge became the Director of the Royal Greenwich Observatory. (See also *Mill Hill in the Wars*)

When the War ended in 1945 the Mill Hill Observatory was officially reopened. The telescopes at Gower Street that had survived the air raids were brought to Mill Hill in 1946.

DEVELOPMENTS SINCE WORLD WAR II

Up to this time the Observatory had been under the direct control, and an institution of the University. In 1951 the administration was transferred to University College and the Observatory was incorporated into a newly created Department of Astronomy. Back in 1943, during the War, the University had been left a bequest by F Perrin which was to be used for the development of optical astronomy, and this was used to create the Perrin Chair of Astronomy in 1951. The bequest has been used for the further development of the Observatory and a north wing extension was built between October 1952 and April 1953. This building was designed to provide office space, a library, and a lecture room. In 1960 a further development followed with the erection of a south wing. This was completed the following year and as far as the main buildings are concerned the Observatory site was by then much as it appears today. The south wing contains additional teaching and office accommodation and a spectrographic laboratory.

Although the Mill Hill Observatory was now much larger than

when first built the rapid expansion in astronomy brought about by the arrival of the Space Age meant that the Watford Way site was now overcrowded and could not be suitably extended further. An annexe was acquired in the mid 1960s by converting some premises in Daws Lane which runs nearby. Initially these premises were used to house an IBM 1130 computer and other research facilities.

The Daws Lane facility was extended in 1967 by the addition of a lunar laboratory. Lunar research was very much in the news at this time: President Kennedy had promised in 1961 that an American astronaut would land on the moon and return to Earth within a decade. This was achieved when Apollo 11 left Pad 39a at Cape Kennedy for the Sea of Tranquillity on July 16 1969 carrying three men, Armstrong, Aldrin, and Collins. Neil Armstrong stepped onto the lunar soil on the evening of July 20 and there made the profound statement, 'That's one small step for a man, one giant leap for mankind'. He was followed down by Aldrin whilst Collins remained in the command module. Specimens of the rock from the Moon were sent to 142 universities and laboratories around the world for analysis and study.

In 1972 the Department of Astronomy was merged with the Physics Department to become the Department of Physics and Astronomy. An obvious move in many ways; it would be difficult to understand and appreciate modern astronomy without a comprehensive knowledge of the laws of physics.

The telescope that formed the beginning of the Observatory, the Wilson 24in reflector was retired in 1974 and since that time has been on permanent loan with the Merseyside Museums. Its replacement was a new 24in reflector of modern design made by Ealing Beck of Watford which was named the Allen Telescope after Professor C W Allen, the Director of the Observatory and first Perren Professor (from 1951 to 1972). The new telescope was officially 'opened' by Professor D W N Stibbs, Napier Professor of Astronomy at the University of St Andrew's on May 22 1975.

THE OBSERVATORY TODAY

Even before World War II it had become increasingly difficult to carry out some types of research in a meaningful way, and since the War research from the Mill Hill site has deteriorated further. In an ideal world the whole facility would be transferred elsewhere, to a stable environment where there is little or no background light and no traffic vibration. There is always a glow over central London and Mill Hill is criss-crossed by well-lit major roads: good for safety but hopeless for astronomy. Modern research of faint astronomical objects is impossible and even study of the planet Mercury for instance that never rises far above the horizon. Additionally this country is not renowned for its cloudless night skies. The cost of negotiating a new site and building a new observatory would be prohibitive unless a very rich benefactor could be found.

Mill Hill still has an important role to play in providing the facilities for undergraduate teaching in practical astronomy and in supporting researches in interstellar physics, the theory of star and planet formation, geological surveying of planetary surfaces and cosmic abundance studies. The Observatory is conveniently located for access to and from University College and the very comprehensive range of equipment does provide the best teaching environment in Britain for practical work in astronomy. The observations of remote astronomical objects are now carried out by UK national research facilities and from remote controlled telescopes on board satellites in Earth orbit where there is no interference.

The Radcliffe refractor is at present undergoing extensive renovation and reconstruction including replacement of the dome and rising floor, the addition of a modern digital control system, and a new drive. A UBV (Ultraviolet, Blue, and Visual spectral regions) photometer, an infrared photometer, and a medium dispersion spectrograph have been built for use with the Allen telescope (the first two as projects by undergraduates). The Fry refractor was dismantled in 1981 and during its absence its place has been taken by a recently restored Joynson 6in Cooke equatorial refractor made in 1863. Next in line for refurbishment, as part of the continuing programme of restoration and updating, is a 7½in Coelostat solar telescope commissioned by the Observatory in 1929.

In the summer of 1990 the control system of the Allen telescope was replaced by a new computer controlled system made by DFM Engineering of Boulder, Colorado which is based on a Mackintosh computer. This telescope has also been equipped with a Wrights Instruments Peltier cooled system which has the advantage that it can be used as a direct camera, spectroscopic camera or photometer.

In 1985 when PCs became readily available a computer room was installed at the Observatory for the use of undergraduates. The original IBM 1130 which had provided access to the main College and University based facilities was replaced by a GEC 4000 system which was in turn replaced by a set of PCs. It is fair to say that the computers at Mill Hill are continually being improved and updated.

In 1990 a VAX 3100 station was installed for process work and to form the basis of a STARLINK node and at the same time another station was acquired for processing and analysis of of the data accruing from the Magellan Venus mapping mission.

Today we can only wonder how scientists (and others) managed without computers, calculators, fax machines and all the modern electronic equipment that we take so much for granted. We would certainly not like to go back to logarithm tables and slide rules, and many of the younger generation could not even use them. The beginning of the 1990 season saw the Observatory at the forefront of astronomical teaching in the UK. They employ the very latest detector system (which gives the students good observational experience in spite of the atmospheric problems) backed by a substantial distributed computer system with excellent communications with larger computing facilities.

The costs involved in setting up the Observatory and replacing the equipment is not really relevant because most of the instrumentation has been provided as a result of gifts and bequests. However it is interesting to note that the Allen telescope that was purchased for £44,000 would cost at least £½m if it had to be replaced today.

It would be nice to say that some great discovery has been made at Mill Hill but unfortunately this has not so far been the case. There is always an element of luck in these events. The Observatory has however always been heavily engaged in much systematic astronomical work. As early as the mid 1930s definitive studies were carried out on the spectrum of γCas by the assistant director E M Peachey and in the 1950s and 1960s the emphasis was on solar physics and studies of the solar corona.

A great deal of work has been carried out to determine the abundance of elements (in addition to hydrogen and helium) in the Sun. These studies have been extended to other stellar atmospheres, in particular with regard to a rather special kind of star called *Peculiar A stars. The presence of these elements gives us a guide as to the age of the star and how long it will last in its present form. This research is all a part of the overall studies in the determination of star formation and understanding of the interstellar medium. Nearer to home, with distances in millions of kilometres rather than light years, there have been many satellite surveys of the planets in our own system and the data that has

---

*The make-up of these stars is peculiar. They display strange anomalies in the composition of their constituent elements (for instance gallium, manganese, mercury, or yttrium) with over abundancies that are not possible with normal star development, and these have not been fully explained.

come back will take years to completely analyse and the Observatory is deeply involved in this.

It will be immediately obvious from the equipment in the Observatory that the research and instruction of undergraduate students concentrates on the visible wavelengths. With so many developments taking place all the time in other spheres it is hardly surprising that from time to time there is a tendency to wander into the infrared and ultra-violet parts of the spectrum.

CHAPTER XVI

SOME OTHER
IMPORTANT BUILDINGS

T he residents of some less well endowed London suburbs may well feel that Mill Hill has more than its share of old and interesting buildings, and we would have to agree. There are some magnificent mansions and there are also some smaller houses equally interesting, there are buildings that started life as houses and have become something else, and vice versa. There are the special buildings, such as the observatory on Watford Way and the National Institute for Medical Research on The Ridgeway, and many, many more. In a book of this kind it would be impossible to write even a paragraph about every structure that has a history or an interesting story to tell, so all that can be included is just a selection.

Some buildings have chapters of their own, their stories are too interesting to be confined to a couple of paragraphs. These you will have found elsewhere in the book. Unfortunately many fine old houses, particularly the farmhouses and inns that were so important to the Mill Hill of earlier centuries, have been demolished, in many cases in the last 60 years or so. If they are interesting in the development of the locality then they have been mentioned elsewhere in the book.

We will start by looking at some of the larger buildings that have been such an important part of the old Mill Hill, and to some extent remain so.

HIGHWOOD ASH

This fine house is opposite Highwood House. It was built on the site of an earlier house in which Celia Fiennes, the intrepid traveller and diarist of the late 17th Century lived when not on her travels around England. Highwood Ash today has a stuccoed finish and contains parts of an earlier timber framed building.

The first record of a house on this site is in the *Hendon Manorial Survey* of 1632:

'James Blott holdeth a house and an orchard with the appurtenances being a parcel of the tenement of Highwood Hill, now Peter Franklyn and rents to the Lord of 3½d'.

There is a strong possibility that a house existed in 1574 because in an earlier survey James Blott is described as of Highwood Hill but there is no mention of house or orchard in the list of freeholders. James Blott (or Blatt) of the later date may well be one and the same.

In the returns for the infamous Hearth Tax for 1664 Blott is assessed for one hearth. He was also liable for a Church Rate of 9/- (45p) in 1657 and 4/1 (20p) in 1663 (for church repairs). In 1669 the property was owned by John Blott who must have enlarged the house considerably because his Hearth Tax levy was based on five hearths and remained so for the Tax returns of 1672 and 1674. The 1685 Survey for the Manor of Hendon makes no change however to the entry of 1632. James Blott and John Blott also owned a croft known as Gussoms.

Highwood Ash

In October 1950 this lovely old residence and its lady were very fortunate to survive, on that day a Dakota of British European Airways crashed in the garden because of engine failure. One engine failed shortly after take-off from Northolt (Heathrow was not in operation then) and the pilot made a desperate attempt to make a landing at Hendon aerodrome but without success. The plane had been on route to Glasgow: 27 adults and one infant died either in the crash or the fire that followed.

HENDON HALL

Not far from Highwood House, and on the same side of the road once stood Hendon Hall, the mansion of the Wilberforce estate. All that remains today is the lodge, now converted into a modern residence. Some development has also taken place in the grounds. Nan Clark's Lane, which once divided the Raffles' and Wilberforce estates remains unspoilt and as leafy as ever. Our only reminder of *The Crown* public house, a part of the estate that once stood here are the modern houses of Crown Close. The inn was demolished in 1937.

In May 1834 the executors of William Wilberforce put the whole estate on the market to be auctioned in lots unless sold by prior private contract. The advertisements listed the property as 'his former residence and estate, known as Highwood Hill or Hendon Park'. The lands were described as being at a fine elevated healthy spot only 12 miles from town. The buildings were said to be a mansion together with suitable office buildings plus stabling, gardens (with hothouse), entrance lodge, beautiful timbered grounds and paddocks totalling 60 acres (28ha). There were also considered to be some beautiful sites for the erection of villas.

With the home estate went meadow and arable land, the small inn mentioned above with brewery, more farm buildings, bailiff's house, dairy, and sundry cottages. One of the comments made about St Paul's Church on The Ridgeway (built on the instructions of Wilberforce) was that inferior bricks were used made from clay dug on the estate. In the advertisements one of the fields was said to contain good brick earth so perhaps there was some truth in the claim that home produced bricks were used. The complete estate was given as 146 acres (61ha) and considered by the vendors to be an excellent speculative investment.

THE CLOCK HOUSE

This interesting house stood at the top of Milespit Hill but unfortunately there is no record of its design. It appeared on all maps and Parish records for up to 150 years. In the late 17th Century it was the residence of a branch of the Nicoll family, others were at Highwood, Cookes and Copt Hall. In 1828 the designer of the marine screw propeller, J P Smith lived here.

THE PRIORY

This is another building that has been constructed on the site of an earlier one. The previous building in this case was the Clock House which was built in the mid-18th Century. The Priory dates from 1875. Although built in the style of a great house The Priory is truly enormous. Even the description 'mansion' does not do it justice. The house stands well back from the road (The Ridgeway) on the corner of Milespit Hill and is well concealed in spite of its great size.

BITTACY HOUSE

In the 19th Century Bittacy House was of some importance locally. It was a long low stuccoed building quite unlike any others in the vicinity, and described at the time as 'A handsome modern house'. In 1937 the entire contents of the house were sold by auction.

It gave way in 1950 to Watchtower House which as a building does not deserve mention; it is certainly not historic, (it was built in 1950), it is not a worthy piece of architecture and would not earn an accolade from the Prince of Wales. This building is the United Kingdom headquarters of the Jehovah's Witnesses. All that can be said in its favour is that many fine trees have been preserved in the grounds, including an ancient cedar.

PARTINGDALE MANOR

By 1898 Partingdale House had been renamed 'Manor' although there was no historical justification for this. Part of the house is quite old, most being early 19th Century but there have been many additions over the years. The construction is of brick. The lands associated with the house were transferred to the farm from those of Frith Manor.

The house has now been divided into two independent residences, Partingdale Manor and Manor End. The gardens are exceptionally beautiful and slope gently down towards the Vale of Totteridge.

FRITH MANOR

Unlike Partingdale, Frith Manor is entitled to this name having been detached from the Manor of Hendon in the 14th Century, (see also *'The History of Private Property'*). The original manor house was sold by the descendants of the Peacock family, (Richard Peacock), in 1720 to John Lade and was demolished, who rebuilt it in 1790. The house was a stuccoed building with wings and according to some records contained a 16th Century stone fireplace and linenfold panelling taken from another (unknown) house.

It was inherited by his son Sir John Lade, a man of somewhat dubious morals. After Sir John's death Lady Mary Lade, his widow, held the Manor until 1810 when it was sold to T J Fentham. In 1898 the owner was Frank Heal who opened the furniture store by this name. The building was destroyed by fire in 1957.

In the 1920s the farm lands became the property of Express Dairy and were used as pasture. Milk deliveries were made from this depot. Later on it became a rest home for horses, still owned by Express. In those days, and indeed for a while after World War II milk deliveries (twice daily) were made from horse-drawn floats. Today an equestrian centre is located here.

NETHER COURT

This fine house built by Henry Stubbs JP was the largest Victorian house to be built in the Parish of Hendon. It was locally the final fling in this age of grandeur. As a house it was quite amazing even by the ostentatious standards of the age. The main building material is brick and there are stone dressings. The whole is surmounted by a steeply pitched gabled roof. There are tall brick chimneys and the north-east angle has a massive tower. In 1883, not many years after the house was completed a golf course was set out in the grounds. The house and grounds are now Finchley Golf Club and clubhouse.

At the eastern boundary of the grounds is the Dollis Brook which was landscaped with artificial islands, fine trees and bushes, and rustic bridges. On the opposite side of the brook another fine house called Rocklands was built (in Gordon Road, Finchley) and much of the grounds around the brook were absorbed into this garden when the golf course was laid out. Today it forms a part of the new footpath, an extension of Brookside Walk, that runs beside the Brook all the way from Woodside Park to the viaduct that carries the *Underground* from Finchley Central to Mill Hill East station. Rocklands was demolished some years ago and a block of flats with the same name now stands on the site.

RIDGEWAY HOUSE

Jeremiah Harman, a banker and a Quaker was the grandson of Colonel Harman, (an officer of Cromwell's Ironsides). He lived in the original Ridgeway House, which he later sold to Michael Russell, the father-in-law of Peter Collinson. Peter married Mary Russell in 1724. When Michael Russell died Mary inherited the property (as well as Dollis Farm) and the Collinsons lived there until Peter died in 1768.

Ridgeway House was the home of the first Dissenters' School which opened in 1807. It still retained much of the garden as laid out by Peter Collinson. Eventually the building was demolished to make way for Mill Hill School and the gardens were absorbed into the School grounds, but without disturbing any more of the valuable trees than absolutely necessary. Collinson's gateway to the garden can still be seen in the wall facing The Ridgeway (the actual gate is modern) and inside is a short stretch of path probably much as it was during Collinson's time.

BELMONT HOUSE

This fine mansion was built in the style of Robert Adam about the middle of the 18th Century. It was once the home of Sir Charles Flower Bart (who gave his name to Flower Lane) and of John Wilkes. Both of these men were Lords Mayor of London.

This house contains a curious spiral staircase surmounted by a glass lantern. The Oval Room, so called, has a fine plaster ceiling and deep low windows which look out on to beautiful lawns and apparently open countryside. A piece of pure 18th Century splendour in well wooded surroundings. In the garden of Belmont stands a strange building that is a cross between a chapel and a cottage. A rather well appointed hermitage that did not entail leaving home comforts for too long.

Because Belmont is now a school, the preparatory school of Mill Hill School, some alterations and additions have been made and some features have been lost. How-

... rather well appointed hermitage

ever this in no way detracts from the magnificent proportions.

HOLCOMBE HOUSE

This house is also pure 18th Century and was designed by John Johnson in 1775 for Sir William Anderson, then a City alderman. He later became Lord Mayor of London. One writer described the house as having;

'A hall of sheer delight in white, with blue mouldings picked out in gold, and a circular staircase smaller than that of Belmont but more delicate in style'.

How splendid it must have been to have been entertained here when this house was a private residence. The superb dining room has Grecian figures looking down from the walls, these are in raised stucco. The drawing room is more ornate still with catkins and acanthus leaves as the motifs of decoration plus dolphins and griffons. There are also two excellent ceiling paintings which are reputed to be the work of Angelica Kauffmann who is known to have been working in Mill Hill at this time. Indeed much of the decoration in the House has now been authenticated as being Kauffmann's work. Considering the fate that has befallen Littleberries it is comforting to learn that many genuine Georgian elements still survive in the house, for instance a superb portico with a most elegant fanlight, and of course the staircase already mentioned. At one time there was a domed Grecian style temple in the grounds but this was demolished after World War II.

Angelica Kauffmann was a Swiss Rococo decorative artist and portrait painter. She worked in England from 1766 to 1781, and was a friend of Joshua Reynolds and a founder member of the Royal Academy. Kauffmann worked on many interiors. In 1781 she married Antonio Zucchi, a Venetian decorative painter who probably assisted her with her work at Holcombe House. After their marriage they settled in Rome.

Cardinal Vaughan stayed in Holcombe House, and used it as a base whilst planning St Joseph's College, and during his many trips overseas drumming up support for his plans. In 1866 Holcombe House became St Joseph's Foreign Missionary College until it was relocated in the new college buildings in 1871.

In 1881 Holcombe House was acquired, on the instigation of Cardinal Vaughan, for the recently founded Congregation of Franciscan Nuns of the Regular Third Order. The house was then renamed St Mary's Abbey. A convent wing was added in 1883 and in 1889 the wooden chapel was replaced by a large brick cruciform building in plain early Gothic style with a central tower surmounted by a pyramid spire. From here nuns began missions in the 1880s and established several schools. In 1952 a separate missionary was established and by 1969 the Mill Hill sisters were engaged only in education. Holcombe House is now surrounded by the buildings of St Mary's Abbey of which it forms a part.

COVENTRY FARM HOUSE

The land and farm once formed the estate of the Earl of Coventry in the north of the Parish in a ward named Boysland. The farmhouse dates back to the middle of the 17th Century, with alterations and additions in the 18th Century. It has a Grade II listing as being of historical interest, and stands at the east of the Mill Hill Golf Club clubhouse on Barnet Way.

Coventry Farm was for dairy produce and the farm buildings were converted into the clubhouse. The actual dairy was made into the main building, the cow sheds were converted into the professional's shop, ladies locker room and trolley sheds. The barn which was used as mixing room and fodder loft is the Artisan's Club House. (See also *Millhillians in their Leisure Time*).

NICOLL ALMSHOUSES

In 1696 Stephen Nicoll, the Village miller, erected six almshouses which were endowed in perpetuity for poor persons. There is an inscription on the stone lintel 'For the use of ye Poore'. The almshouses are at the top of Milespit Hill. Even sufferers from vertigo would have no problems working on these houses. The cottages were built with the absolute minimum of appointments and total economy, with the roofs starting immediately above the little doors. No doubt just the same they have been very welcome to many people over the last three centuries. Considerable repairs and refurbishments were carried out in 1893 and again in 1923 so that the present occupants are at least living in the 20th Century.

OTHER WEATHER-BOARDED HOUSES

Many of the smaller houses in Mill Hill (and some of the not so small) are finished with weatherboarding and it is quite clear that this has been a

favourite style in the local- ity at least since the 17th Century. Elsewhere in the text there are many men- tions of houses of this type, not all are still in existence. Detailed here are some other interesting examples.

Rosebank Cottage is a long low weather- boarded cottage on The Ridgeway. It is one of the

Some...old weatherboard houses

small number in Mill Hill that is blessed with a Blue Plaque and is a Grade II listed building of 17th Century origins, and almost certainly dates from 1678, with alterations and extensions in 1693. It was constructed with a timber frame with brick and mortar infill and was built on a piece of land that was leased for £5 per annum. The building was used as a Quaker meeting house in the years between 1678 and 1719. In 1898 it became a refreshment parlour run by a local lady. Rosebank is now private houses and when the conversion was made an extra floor was added.

In recent years very extensive refurbishing work has been carried out and at one stage all that was left was the timber frame. In the latter half of 1989 the Hendon and District Archaeological Society received a letter from the Barnet Planning Office to say that a well had been found in the grounds during this refurbishing work. Because of the age of the house it was thought possible that the well has 17th Century origins too. At the time of writing, methodical excavation work had not commenced so the origins of the well had not been ascertained.

With the refurbishments now complete the house and barn (as described by the selling agent) does not really look 17th Century at all, or any particular date for that matter. Using old bricks and old timbers an exact replica could be built anywhere. So much for preservation orders.

Close by at the junction of Highwood Hill, Holcombe Hill and

Lawrence Street is the Old Forge. This picturesque collection of buildings, partly timber clad, was the home and workshop of the Village blacksmith, Barham, and later his successor in the trade, Mathews.

In more recent times the premises have fulfilled other roles, most notably as a tea-shop and meeting place for social groups: everything from the local allotment holders to the district literary society. It is now a private house.

The Old Forge... home and workshop of the village blacksmith

Near the top of Hammers Lane is the Mill Field, the traditional location of the mill. A few steps from here is the Post Office Cottage. This neat house is set off by a small cobbled yard and neat picket fence. This is another house that is Grade II listed. From this point, and round the corner into Hammers Lane is a row of weather-boarded cottages including the Village butcher's shop. This whole row was built in the 18th Century. Beyond these are a few more houses including Laurel Cottage.

A short walk down Wills Grove and we find another well preserved example of weather-boarded house nestling among the trees, again with a picket fence but in this case a little more decorative.

Next to the Nicoll Almshouses at the top of Milespit Hill are some modern houses that have been designed to blend with the older houses on either side. Just down the hill from here are three rather special houses: The Welches, Hillview and Hillside. These are all well preserved and constructed from part brick part weatherboard. All three are Grade II listed.

SOME MORE INTERESTING BUILDINGS

Modern Mill Hill, that is the estates around the Broadway and the houses along the Barnet by Pass is not of any particular interest architecturally. True there are some fine houses scattered among the ordinary but nothing worthy of a particular mention. Old Mill Hill is different, having developed over a long period there is a variety of styles, using every kind of material.

The estate of Hyver Hall is on the northern boundary of Mill Hill. The house was built and occupied by 1863. In 1754 this place was known as Hiver's Hill. This is a large house with extensive grounds, well protected with fencing and security devices.

Between Post Office Cottage and the Mill Field is something totally different, the Mill House. This is all in brick with a striking front at ground level, rather like a piece of Dickens' Curiosity Shop transported to the countryside and selling the same sort of merchandise.

A short distance down Hammers Lane stands the house where Sir James Murray lived with his wife and family before he moved to Oxford. This was his home during his years at Mill Hill School and while he was working on what became the *Oxford English Dictionary*. Later he moved to Oxford so that he could devote all his time to the project.

Murray's name for the house was Sunnyside and he lived there for 15 years. Much work has been done on the house in recent years and it has been renamed Murray House in his memory. With the elegant iron gates closed there is still a pretty

cottages of 18th Century origins

courtyard to be seen from the road. The rear of the house and garden has much of the country cottage look.

Where The Ridgeway divides and the western arm becomes the High Street is an interesting house called Blenheim Steps which takes its name from the battle (it was built that year). Although the house is Georgian in style the windows are not the originals having been added about 65 years ago. For many years this was the School tuck shop but has now reverted to its proper use. The facing cottages, all lovingly preserved, are 18th Century, they have no foundations, or as they would be described in some country areas 'built on the turf'.

Next to the Sheepwash Pond is a row of pretty cottages of 18th Century origins. Considered quite ordinary in their day they have recently been completely refurbished without apparently destroying any original features and are now very desirable properties. One has the distinction of having a path made from inkwells from Mill Hill School, although the casual visitor would probably not realise what they are. Behind these cottages is the house of the vicar of St Paul's Church.

Just south of the Sheepwash Pond on The Ridgeway are three

interesting houses. The most important of these is The Grove which is now the home of the headmaster of Mill Hill School and has been since 1945. It was purchased by the School in 1908. This house is much larger than first impressions would have you believe. It is sideways on to the road with a secluded garden that has many interesting shrubs and conifers. The house is reputed to be the oldest continuously inhabited house in (what was) Middlesex. The oldest existing parts date from 1590 and there are also some 17th Century features. The house was completely restored in 1912.

The house next door called Cleveland does not (unlike The Grove) have a DoE preservation order. It is a nice old square building with Georgian appearance to which has been added a modern low annex and is used by Mill Hill School as a masters' common room. The third house is a bit of an oddity, it is called The Bungalow but certainly is not. The middle is quite old but it has been added to over the years and is a bit like Topsy, it just grew. There is an upper window that appears to be tight against a chimney breast and the whole house looks rather like a weird ship trying desperately to sail across the road. Mill Hill School acquired The Bungalow in 1932.

THE LISTED BUILDINGS OF MILL HILL

These buildings are considered to be of historical or architectural interest and are registered as such by the Department of the Environment. Alterations to any of these is not permitted without Ministry permission.

Blenheim Steps	High Street
The Grove (Headmaster's House)	The Ridgeway
Littleberries (St Vincent's)	The Ridgeway
Ionic Building (St Vincent's grounds)	The Ridgeway
Mill Hill School	The Ridgeway
Post Office Cottage	The Ridgeway
Rosebank	The Ridgeway
Holcombe House (St Mary's Abbey)	The Ridgeway
St Paul's C of E School	The Ridgeway
Highwood Ash	Highwood Hill
Rising Sun Public House	Highwood Hill
Highwood House	Highwood Hill
Hillside and Hillview	Milespit Hill

Nicoll's Almshouses	Milespit Hill
The Welches	Milespit Hill
Coventry Farmhouse	Barnet Way

LONDON BOROUGH OF BARNET BLUE PLAQUES

In 1864 an anonymous correspondent wrote to the *Journal of the Society of Arts* suggesting that memorial tablets be displayed on certain buildings where notable people had resided. Six months later the suggestion was taken up by *The Builder* and shortly after that a committee was set up to deal with these 'memorial tablets'. Two years later the first list was agreed and the first plaque appeared. Between 1867 and 1900 36 plaques were put up by the Society.

In 1901 the responsibility for selection, production and fixture (in London) passed to the London County Council but their responsibility was limited to the Metropolitan area and therefore few of these plaques are to be found in the outer suburbs.

At a meeting of the General Purpose Committee of the Hendon Corporation in 1957 a report was received from the Mill Hill and Hendon Historical Society that recommended the placing of 17 plaques within the Borough of Hendon. The report was adopted and as a result two plaques were placed in the first financial year and four more in each subsequent year. The plaques to be found within the boundaries of Mill Hill are:

NAME	IN MEMORY OF:
Highwood House	Sir Stamford Raffles
Ridgeway House (site of)	Peter Collinson
Three Sunningdale Gardens	G L Jessop
Hendon Park (site of)	William Wilberforce
Copt Hall (site of)	The Nicoll family
Rosebank	Quaker meeting house
Murray House (formerly Sunnyside)	Sir James A H Murray

CHAPTER XVII

TWO GREAT REFORMERS

During one short month in the year 1826 two famous men were neighbours on Highwood Hill, William Wilberforce and Sir Stamford Raffles. Wilberforce MP and philanthropist is best known as the man responsible for the abolition of slavery, and Raffles, administrator and botanist who also the loathed the sickening slave trade.

Sir Stamford Raffles was a colonial governor and administrator. He took part in the capture of Java from the Dutch in 1817, and while he was governor of Sumatra (1818-1823) he was responsible for the acquisition of Singapore. Unfortunately he frequently fell foul of his superiors and associates because he could not accept their attitudes towards the natives; he gave them responsibilities and emancipated slaves.

WILLIAM WILBERFORCE

Wilberforce was a Yorkshireman, he was born in Kingston-upon-Hull on August 24 1759. As a child he was small and frail. He had a strong voice

William Wilberforce —
abolition of slavery

which he used to good effect in his campaigning speeches. He first expressed his loathing of the slave trade in a letter to the *Yorkshire Gazette* at the age of 14 and then spent the rest of his life on this great passion. Wilberforce entered Parliament for his home town at the age of 21, one year before William Pitt (The Younger), and they became great friends.

Many of the businesses of the day, and the rich and powerful people in the Country owed their fortunes to the slave trade so opposition to its abolition was very strong. Every year Wilberforce proposed motions or attempted to introduce anti-slave bills but he was always defeated until the year 1807. In that year the *Bill for the Abolition of the Slave Trade* was introduced into the Lords and was passed by a majority of 64. The Commons then approved by 283 to 216. Wilberforce, in tears, was given an ovation.

Pitt the Prime Minister of the day, was also against slavery but because of his inscrutable nature (he rarely confided in anyone) he managed to keep his ideas for reform under wraps until a suitable occasion was presented. Wilberforce meanwhile threw his whole political life and future behind abolition and in April 1792 moved resolutions to end this awful trade. Pitt had tried to talk Wilberforce out of precipitate action at this time, but nevertheless on the night made a superb anti-slavery speech himself:

'That noxious plant by which everything is withered and blasted, under whose shade nothing that is useful or profitable to Africa will ever flourish or take root'.

Other people too were beginning to see how wicked slavery was and incompatible with a Christian country and administration. In 1793 a group which became known as the 'Claphamites' had gathered round the church of the Rev. John Venn. They were intensely evangelical and amongst their members were Hannah More (one time actress and blue stocking who had turned to good works), Thornton of the Bank of England, Granville Sharp (another seasoned radical and campaigner) Lord Teignmouth, and of course Wilberforce. All rather sarcastically referred to as the 'Saints of Clapham'.

More than another decade was to pass before the dream of Wilberforce was to be fulfilled. He had commented that the Church of England clergy were at best indifferent to the sufferings of negroes and at worse openly obstructionist to his proposed reforms. His main support was amongst non-Conformists. In the end a new power was organized, public opinion, and this swept slavery into the history books in 1807 against all the fumings of powerful vested interests.

Unfortunately the landowners had possession of their slaves legally. They had purchased them in the open market in the same way as any other goods or commodities, and it would have been unfair to just release the slaves because their owners would have been ruined. The compensation needed to free every slave was the staggering sum of £20m, sufficient thought the opponents to kill the proposal. Not so, public opinion had changed so much and the populace was now so enlightened that the necessary money was voted by Parliament in 1833.

This was not the end, after his triumph at home the movement pushed even harder so that in the year that Wilberforce died slavery was officially eliminated throughout the British Empire. But to halt the transportation of slaves was one thing, to free existing slaves from their bondage was more difficult, particularly in the far flung parts of the Empire.

When Wilberforce retired from Parliament because of ill health he passed the banner to Foxwell Buxton. On his death bed (he died in a cousin's house in Cadogan Place in 1833) he heard that the measure that he so desperately sought for so long had been approved: every slave must be set free.

The (now almost forgotten) historian Reginald Coupland declared that midnight on July 31 1834 signalled one of the greatest events in the history of the World. At this time in the region of 800,000 slaves officially became free men. No one person had contributed more than Wilberforce. However he would be saddened today, 160 years on and slavery and enforced prostitution live on in many parts of the World.

When Wilberforce died a letter was sent to his son which had been signed by all the leading men of both houses of Parliament. Considering for how long they had prevented his every attempt at abolition its content was both surprising and delightful:

> 'We being anxious on public grounds to show our respect for the memory of
> the late William Wilberforce, and being also satisfied that public
> honours cannot be more fitly bestowed than upon such benefactors of
> mankind, earnestly request that he may be buried in Westminster Abbey,
> and that we, with others who agree with us in these sentiments, may have
> permission to attend the funeral'.

To the Abbey he was brought, all public business was suspended for the day, and people of every rank followed him to his grave.

Wilberforce was not only involved in efforts to reduce human suffering. He was also distressed by the appalling treatment of animals and he was partly responsible for the setting up of the first society to protect them, the SPCA. Only 170 years ago when bear and bull baiting and cock fighting were socially acceptable 'sports' Richard Martin MP supported the introduction of legislation (in 1822) to reduce the suffering meted out to animals. In 1824 Martin was joined by Wilberforce and a London vicar Arthur Broome and at a meeting held at the time the SPCA was set up. The Society was later awarded Royal Patronage by Queen Victoria and renamed the RSPCA.

In the 19th Century bear and bull baiting were quite legal, today they are banned, but the work of Wilberforce, Martin and Broome is not finished, animals are still neglected and maltreated, we still have hare coursing, fox hunting, and stag hunting (all legal) which are morally no better than dog fighting and badger baiting though these are carried out in secret.

Wilberforce purchased Hendon Park on Highwood Hill with its

58ha (140 acres) of land when he retired from Parliament in 1826 and lived there until 1831 at which time to his great regret he was compelled to leave. There was a large household, including two married sons and their families.

During the time that he was associated with Mill Hill he was in dispute with the despotic and rather intimidating vicar of Hendon, the Rev. Theodore Williams. Wilberforce had sought permission to erect a private chapel in his own grounds for the use of his family. When Williams discovered that the project had developed into a church for Mill Hill with its own incumbent which would deprive him of part of his congregation and the collections that he obtained from them plus considerable pew rents he was furious. First he tried to have the new church banned by the ecclesiastic authorities and when this failed he campaigned (successfully) for the church to be outside the Wilberforce estate on The Ridgeway. Most people today would regard pew rents as quite wrong.

To the growing population of Mill Hill their own church would be a considerable advantage. The road from Mill Hill to the Burroughs at Hendon is some distance and in winter this could be very unpleasant even if you had your own carriage. In spite of the strong protests by the vicar to the Bishop of London the church was built, in defiance of William's affidavits and all his posturing. The church which is known as St Paul's Mill Hill was consecrated in 1833, shortly after the death of its patron.

It has been said that one reason for Williams' objection to Wilberforce's church was because his family enjoyed considerable income from the slave trade which Wilberforce was determined to abolish. There appears to be no documentary evidence of this although it obviously remains a distinct and strong possibility.

SIR STAMFORD RAFFLES

Stamford Raffles (1781-1826) was the only surviving son of Benjamin Raffles and was born at sea on board the Ann off Port Morant, Jamaica. His father had for a long time been a captain in the English West India trade and the Ann was his ship. The main business of his father's ship was the 'triangular' transport: slaves from Africa to the West Indies, cotton, rum, and sugar on the return journey to Britain, and then back to Africa for more slaves. Possibly this gave Raffles the wanderlust that kept him on the move for most of his life and lead to his intense dislike of slavery.

Raffles was an intelligent child and attended school in Hammersmith for two years until family poverty forced him to leave. At the age of 14 he became a clerk in East India House in Leadenhall Street, the offices of the East India Company. His salary was £70pa, and this he used to support not only himself but also his widowed mother and sisters. During his leisure hours he studied and mastered French and studied natural history. Raffles' diligence at work attracted the attention of the secretary to the directors, and on his recommendation Raffles was appointed by Sir Hugh Inglis as assistant secretary to the establishment sent by the East India Company to Penang. By this time Raffles was married and he sailed with his wife Olivia and landed in Penang in September 1805.

Raffles natural affinity for languages enabled him to become fluent very quickly with the local Malay tongue, this and his tenacity convinced the governor and council to promote him to secretary in 1807 and registrar of the recorder's court. Unfortunately excessive hard work, hours spent at study, and the very unhealthy climate brought on an illness in 1808 which nearly proved fatal. On recovery he went to Malacca to study the resources and

Raffles hoisted the British Flag in Singapore

prevented its intended cession. He returned to Penang but his health broke down again in 1809 and he travelled to Calcutta to recuperate and because he wanted to obtain the governorship of the Moluccas. To his dismay this had already been promised to someone else.

From this point on Raffles became deeply involved in politics. His correspondence with Dr Leyden the oriental scholar, and the Asiatic Society in Calcutta on the languages and customs of the Malay peoples brought him to the notice of Lord Minto. When Holland had been annexed by the French Lord Minto undertook the subjection of Java taking advantage of the depth of Raffles' local knowledge. The situation was full of plots and intrigue and Raffles was sent as governor's agent to Malacca to collect information and to prepare supplies. Raffles recommended a route which would take the ships along the south-west coast of Borneo and Malacca to Java.

After some opposition Raffles' plan was adopted and the entire fleet was brought safely to Batavia: he did not take part in the military operation. For his efforts Raffles was made lieutenant-governor of Java. This was a very tough assignment for a man of already poor health; the island is large with a population that was around six million and the climate is trying. Unfortunately the position held by Raffles was subordinate to the governor-general in Bengal to whom he had to report for funds. His demands inevitably exhausted the patience of the senior administrators.

The Dutch had relied on a system of forced labour with feudal dues and payment in kind which Raffles abolished. He travelled the island widely and studied their history and languages. Raffles administration was on the basis of trust; he refused guards and escorts and made himself available at all times. The people were given lands on long leases, the policing was carried out by native institutions, and trial by jury was introduced.

Whilst his governorship was increasingly peaceful and prosperous and he was much respected by the people of Java his drastic change of land ownership embarrassed the government and from their point of view the results did not justify it.

Raffles was then in dispute with the commander of the resident forces about the number of troops required for effective control, Raffles wanted them reduced to save costs and because he saw no need for them, the general wanted the strength to be maintained. Lord Minto appeared to agree with Raffles and because there was some doubt whether control of Java would be retained by Britain (as part of the territories of the East India Company) when the war ended Raffles was transferred to Fort Marlborough at Bencoolen, Sumatra. The slighted general now presented a sweeping indictment of just about every facet of Raffles' administration to the governor-general and although he was exonerated on the charge of misconduct he had to endure anxious months of waiting and worrying.

Java was returned to the Dutch by treaty in 1816 and although it would have been to Raffles' benefit to take up the post on Bencoolen his deteriorating health forced a return to Europe. To add to his miseries at this time his wife, to whom he had been married for 11 years, died while he was in Java.

On the long journey home Raffles visited Napoloen, now held captive on St Helena. In spite of the poor treatment by his employers Raffles was given a warm welcome in London. As recognition for his services, and the book that he had just published on the history of Java, he was knighted by the Prince Regent.

Whilst in London Raffles married Sophia Hull, and true to tradition their first child, a daughter, was born at sea.

When Raffles health had improved the Court of Governors confirmed the governorship of Bencoolen and he took up the post in 1818. Once again he found a disorganised administration; the buildings had been wrecked by earthquakes and the pepper plantation, the only real reason for the outpost, was totally neglected. The main source of revenue was by the breeding of gamecocks and there was little respect for persons or property. All this had to change, once again Raffles emancipated slaves, reorganised the police and cultivated friendly relations with native rulers. Although others believed that the interior of the island was impenetrable he crossed from one coast to the other on foot often sleeping on the forest floor.

During the time spent in Bencoolen four more children were born. But tragedy so often a feature of Raffles life struck again and four of the five children died, leaving just one a daughter named Ella.

At this time Raffles was becoming increasing worried about the machinations of the Dutch because they appeared to be setting out to control the entire East Indian archipelago and he recommended to the Marquis of Hastings, (Governor-general of Bengal) that Britain should take control of Singapore to secure the passage of British ships. The almost uninhabited island was purchased from the Sultan of Johore and Raffles hoisted the British flag there in February 1819. This was probably Raffles' greatest success and of enormous service to British maritime supremacy.

Raffles directed the development with such zeal that in four years he had transformed an island that was largely a useless mangrove swamp into a thriving settlement with an annual trade exceeding £2.5m.

Raffles quitted Singapore in failing health in 1823 and returned to Bencoolen and planned his return to England. He departed on February 2 1824 but a few hours after sailing the ship caught fire due to the carelessness of the steward. Although no lives were lost the escape was made with minutes to spare before the ship's load of gunpowder exploded. The ship's boats were many hours in reaching the shore and the crew and passengers lost everything. Raffles was devastated: he lost all his notes, over 2,000 drawings, his notes for a history of Java and Sumatra and his huge collection of specimens. The disaster was absolutely irreparable, there was no insurance and even if there had been there was no way to recreate the lost material. In addition Raffles lost something over £20,000. He sailed again without money or belongings and arrived in Plymouth in August 1824.

His first task was to draw up from memory a report of his

administration. In the eyes of the Court of Directors it did not justify his actions, they censured his emancipation of the Company's slaves and whilst they approved in general of his motives they disliked his zeal: he did too much too soon. As far as the East India Company and the British Government were concerned Raffles was a fine colonial administrator but sometimes over enthusiastic and premature with his changes. Equally important but largely unrecognised was his contribution to his country, much misunderstood at the time. In the troubled Far East he ensured free passage for British ships in otherwise hostile waters.

He was just as important then and is certainly more significant now as a naturalist and botanist. Everywhere that he went he collected specimens and made notes and drawings and in 1820 he sent home a large collection of preserved animals. On his expedition into the interior of Sumatra when he crossed the island he and a Dr Arnold discovered what turned out to be the largest flower in the World, and subsequently named after them: *Rafflesia arnoldii*.

This plant is totally parasitic on the roots and stems of *Tetrastigma*, large tropical vines of the grape family. The flower is almost 1m across, reddish or purple-brown with five large lobes. It lasts five to seven days and all the time emits a foetid smell which attracts carrion feeding flies and these are believed to be the pollinating agents. The life cycle lasts two years and ends with the withering of the flower after less than a week.

The fruit is somewhat bigger than a large grapefruit and contains thousands of seeds. Squirrels and rodents feed on the seeds which stick to their paws and whiskers and they are then transferred to other parts of the vine.

Unhappily *Rafflesia* is another plant under threat from mankind, the logger and the bulldozer are destroying the forests and therefore the vines upon which it lives. And to make matters worse some native tribes consider that the seeds have aphrodisiac properties so they gather them in large quantities. There are 14 known species, one is believed to be already extinct and the rest are in danger. The life cycle is very delicate (male and female flowers have to bloom at exactly the same time and be adjacent for pollination to take place), and even without disturbance, precarious. They are only found in Malaysia and certain islands of south-east Asia. A life size model of the flower can be seen in the Museum of Natural History in London.

Sometime later another plant was named after Raffles, *Nepenthus rafflesiana*, this he discovered in Singapore.

Raffles said of Highwood House on arrival '*A happy retirement in a house small but compact with grounds well laid out and 112 acres*

(47ha) *in grass'*. No-one today would regard this house as small and certainly not the garden, but then times and priorities change.

Raffles was looking forward to his new neighbour when he wrote *'Wilberforce takes possession tomorrow so that we are to be next door neighbours and divide the hill* (Highwood Hill) *between us'*. Unfortunately their association was very short lived, Raffles wrote this on June 16 1826 but died less than a month later on the fifth of July. He had crammed more into 45 years than most people could hope to attain in twice that number.

Raffles' funeral was at St Mary's Hendon. The vicar was the Rev. Theodore Williams who had little time for Raffles or his neighbour Wilberforce and refused to conduct the service, indeed he would not even permit a memorial tablet. During reconstruction work in 1915 Raffles' remains were rediscovered, they were re-interred and an inscription was then added. The vicar's refusals add credence to the suggestion that his family's fortunes were made in the slave trade.

At home Raffles was recognised for the great man that he was, he was awarded LL.D and elected FRS and became a member of many other learned societies. Raffles was sincere and pious, a benevolent man whose hatred of slavery would make him a natural neighbour for Wilberforce. For a short while they lived as neighbours on Highwood Hill, side by side in the north aisle of Westminster Abbey are statues of these two great men.

Raffles knowledge of natural history earned him much respect among like minded people in England. He was involved with zoological societies and helped in the founding of the London Zoo, becoming the first President. Unfortunately his tenure did not last for very long, the fit of apoplexy that killed him came less than two years after arriving back in England.

With all the serious financial problems surrounding the London Zoo and its administration it seemed at one time to be very unlikely that the Zoo would survive into the 21st Century, at least not in its present form. However once the governors realised that Government funding was not forthcoming they tightened their belts, and now have plans for a leaner and fitter establishment. This will probably mean that our children and grandchildren will continue to enjoy that which people like Raffles started so long ago.

The remaining daughter died at the tender age of 19 and alone Lady Raffles, continued to live in the house for many years. She was known as a warm-hearted, generous lady and was visited on various occasions by Baron Bunsen the liberal Prussian diplomat, scholar and theologian who was Minister to England. (At that time the most important post in the Prussian Foreign Service). It was fitting that Bunsen who defended personal and religious freedoms at a time of rigidity and suspicion should visit Lady Raffles, the widow of a man whose life was largely devoted to freeing men from forced labour. Baroness Bunsen, the Baron's English wife wrote in her memoirs:

> *'A visit to Highwood gave an opportunity for commenting upon the dignity, the order, the quiet activity, the calm cheerfulness with which Lady Raffles rules the house, the day, the conversation'.*

A Wedgwood cameo bears a kneeling negro slave in chains. It carries the legend, 'Am I not a man and a brother?' No quotation is a more fitting epitaph to two great men, Wilberforce and Raffles. Erasmus Darwin (grand-father of the famous naturalist) reproduced the legend in his poem *'The Botanic Garden'*. Darwin lived from 1731-1802 and was therefore more or less a contemporary of the two reformers.

CHAPTER XVIII

WHERE BOTANY BEGAN

The discipline of biology really became a true science in the 18th Century. This was the time when a proper system was developed that classified living things into organised groups and sub-groups. Until this time they were known only by the so called 'common names'. This meant that the same plant (for instance) could be known by many names, each one peculiar to a particular area. In addition no-one had really set out to show that certain types were related.

There must be something about Mill Hill that has made it attractive to botanists. Peter Collinson lived on The Ridgeway for many years, and Carollus Linnaeus the man responsible for the international Latin system of biological nomenclature was certainly in touch with Collinson and almost certainly visited him in Mill Hill.

One other botanist, Sir Stamford Raffles, who studied and recorded everything that he saw, particularly in the Far East, lived briefly in Mill Hill. Because the most important part of his career was colonial administrator he is included elsewhere, nevertheless his contributions in botany would make him important even if he had achieved little else.

PETER COLLINSON

Peter Collinson (1694 to 1768) the botanist, deserves to be much better known than he is. He was without doubt one of the most dedicated botanists of his age, and indeed any age. His interest in plants was life long. He began a collection whilst living at Peckham with his grandmother which he developed after moving to Mill Hill. During his life he made great improvements to the existing English system of horticultural nomenclature and for his work he was elected a FRS on December 5 1728.

Collinson's father, also Peter, was a haberdasher and citizen of London. His mother Elizabeth Hall was the daughter of a Southwark mealman. He was only two when he was sent to live with his grandmother. Much of his extensive knowledge was self-taught, he was a keen observer and kept comprehensive notes of everything that he did. The formal education that he had, little that it was, was provided by a Quaker school.

In 1724 Collinson married the daughter of a prosperous weaver and landowner, Mary Russell. They had four children, two sons both named after their father died in infancy but a son and a daughter Michael and Mary survived them. Collinson and his brother James took charge of the family business about the time of his marriage (their father had died some years before) and ran the shop in Gracechurch Street until James died in 1762, then Peter continued it alone for another four years.

Although both brothers were Quakers they carried out various duties that were expected of citizens of London: churchwardens and vestrymen in the parish of St Benet, which they conveniently regarded as local government rather than religious. Peter also held the positions of constable, bensher, (senior member of an inn of court) and later in life as overseer of the poor in the Bridge Within Ward. Although Peter was not an active Quaker for much of his life he served as correspondent of the London Meeting of Sufferings which was primarily concerned with relations between Quakers and the State. His political contacts made him an effective lobbyist.

Peter Collinson the Botanist lived on The Ridgeway

From early childhood Collinson was interested in natural history and devoted himself to study of the metamorphoses of insects. Whilst still a young man he attracted the attention of other notables of the age, in particular Sir Hans Sloane, the Earl of Bute (who gave him much encouragement), and Sir Charles Wager who sought his assistance in his own studies. A large part of Collinson's collection was eventually deposited in Sir Hans Sloane's Museum. Collinson was also a lover of antiquities and was active in the formation of the Society of Antiquaries, of which he was a founder member and frequent contributor.

In the broadest sense Collinson was a capable gardener, and a very imaginative one at that, and he displayed great skill in introducing exotic foreign plants into this country and reproducing them. Eventually he developed a network of agents around the world, but his biggest business was with American merchants. Sometimes he found a more reliable source of new material such as Mark Catesby whom Collinson assisted with patrons whilst he was in America between 1722 and 1726. He further aided him at this time by lending him money without interest.

Because of his developing reputation as a collector of curiosities

168

and possibly assisted by Catesby, Collinson became a part of the group centred around Sir Hans Sloane who was the greatest collector of that time and president of both the College of Physicians and The Royal Society. It was because of Sir Hans' sponsorship that Collinson was elected as a fellow in 1728. Collinson was an active member of the Society and rarely missed meetings during the summer months. Unlike many of the members of that time he took part in the proceedings whenever he could and made comments and gave his own contributions. His most important contribution concerned the migration of swallows which most people at that time believed hibernated under water.

The Bishop of London, Henry Compton, had an easy way of obtaining specimens of new and unusual plants and trees; he told his missionary priests to be always on the lookout for them and then to send then back to him. Collinson developed a different kind of missionary. The first American botanist of any note was John Bartram, also a Quaker and the son of a settler who lived in Philadelphia and farmed on the banks of the River Schuylkill. By a happy chance he was told about Collinson and his interests and that he was looking for an American to collect plants and seeds for him. Collinson's business contacts put him in touch with Philadelphia's first scientific institution, the Library Company of Philadelphia, for whom he served as London agent from 1732. Through the good offices of the Company secretary Collinson was introduced to Bartram and from this developed the most fruitful botanical partnership of the 18th Century. Correspondence between the two botanists began in 1732 and continued until Collinson died over 30 years later.

Collinson obtained customers for the seeds that Bartram collected and these ended up in many of the great gardens of the time (such as Kew and Ken Wood) as well as the estates of the landed gentry, including the Dukes of Argyll, Bedford, Norfolk and Richmond. This was the time of Lancelot (Capability) Brown and the return to natural landscaping instead of the geometrical designs which under French influence had been in favour for so long. His use of trees in ones and twos gave excellent scope for the new imports from overseas. By the time that Brown died he was rich, honoured, and had seemingly returned to nature a greater area of land that any man before or since.

Bartram discovered over 200 hitherto unknown species which he found by wandering about on lands still occupied by American Indians, a rather hazardous enterprise. One genus was named *Collinsonia* in commemoration, it is of the order *Diandrous monogynia* (coarse herbs: horse balm, horse weed). The dispatch was not all one way, many European species were sent to America by Collinson, among these were the cedar of Lebanon and the horse-chestnut, and specimens of these were planted in the first botanic garden to be laid out in the New World. Following Collinson's advice the American settlers were encouraged to invest in industries that would thrive, and this lead to the cultivation of flax, hemp, sisal, and vines.

When Collinson moved to Mill Hill Village in 1749 he took with him a huge collection of species new to this Country, many of them exotic plants from the Americas. He is credited with the introduction into England of around 180 new plants, of which more than 50 were American. Among these 'new' types were the hydrangea and the yucca.

It was also through the Library Company that Collinson was introduced to Bejamin Franklyn and he visited Collinson a number of times whilst he was living on The Ridgeway. Although Collinson was not responsible for creating Franklyn's reputation in the same way that he did for Bartram he certainly played a very significant role in his life. It was Collinson who sent some simple equipment and relevant notes to the Library Company which started Franklyn on his studies of electricity.

After Franklyn, Collinson was never again so successful in promoting new experiments but nevertheless remained a sort of international scientific worrier, middleman, and sometime entrepreneur right up to the time that he died. Collinson remained an active member of the Society of Antiquaries, and his last action for them was a paper *Observations on the Round Towers of Ireland* which was printed posthumously.

Collinson's gate

Ridgeway House, the Collinson's house on The Ridgeway, became the site for Mill Hill School and it is believed that many of the trees in the grounds were planted by him. Ridgeway House and Dollis Farm were inherited by Collinson's wife from her father. Whilst living at Ridgeway House, Collinson was almost certainly visited by Carollus Linnaeus, the great Swedish botanist and explorer. Linnaeus once declared that John Bartram was the greatest botanist that the World had ever known, and he was also highly complimentary about the works and achievements of Collinson. Because Collinson was restricted in travel to his own country this limited his potential for discovery, however his agents achieved for him what he could not do himself. Another contemporary Dr John Fothergill, a biographer of the 18th Century also reckoned Collinson to be a leading authority on botany and natural history at that time.

Throughout most of his life Collinson enjoyed good health (apart from an occasional attack of gout), which is just as well considering the energy with which he pursued his many and varied interests. His death came rather suddenly as a result of a strangury (retention of urine) which he suffered while on a visit to Thorndon Hall, Lord Petre's seat near Brentwood in Essex. He returned home and died in Mill Hill and was buried in the Quaker burial ground in Long Lane, Bermondsey.

CAROLLUS LINNAEUS AND DANIEL C SOLANDER

Linnaeus was born on May 23 1707 and came from South Rashult in Sweden. He was a botanist and explorer and the first person to create a uniform system for naming genera and organisms. In 1732 Linnaeus explored the vegetation of Lapland, only two years after he took a lectureship in botany, He settled in Stockholm where he practiced medicine. His first system of biological nomenclature was published in 1738. Linnaeus' actual name was Carl von Linne, which he Latinised.

It is strange however that such a brilliant man could have held the unshakable belief that swallows spent the winter in a state of hibernation under water. Linnaeus did, and although Collinson knew from a sea-going friend, Admiral Sir Charles Wager, that they migrated (he had seen them over the Mediterranean) Linnaeus refused to be convinced. Collinson spent much effort in trying to prove the real facts to Linnaeus.

Not many people today are very concerned about the times that the blossoms of flowers open, although most people are aware that the evening primrose opens at sun-down and withers in the morning sunlight. Linnaeus must have been an early riser because he prepared a floral clock *(Horologium floræ)* from his observations and noted that the major convolvulus *(Ipomœa purpurea)* is the first to open at 2am followed by the bindweed *(Calystegia sepium)* between 3 and 4am, buttercups *(Ranunculus)* at 5am and so on right through to *Mesembryanthemum noctiflorum* and evening primrose *(Oenothera)* from 7 to 8pm.

Some biographers say that when Linnaeus visited Peter Collinson in Mill Hill two cedars were planted in memory of his visit. This is the reason for his inclusion here. Unfortunately some heavy storms in recent years have taken their toll and many large branches are now missing.

There is however no mention of Linnaeus' visit in Royal Society records although earlier writers claim that letters left by Collinson confirm that it took place. The evidence would certainly point to the fact that Linnaeus visited Collinson at his house on The Ridgeway. There was a long article on Linnaeus in *Encyclopaedia Brittanica* 9th Edition (published 1882). Later editions have rather less to say. This article confirms that Linnaeus visited London in 1736 and a colleague warmly recommended him to Sir Hans Sloane. He was however received coldly.

Linnaeus travelled to Oxford and was greeted in a more cordial fashion by Dr Shaw. The first professor of botany at Oxford, Johann Jakob Dillenius, although unpleasant at first eventually relaxed and Linnaeus stayed with him for a month, after which he visited other notable botanists. There are also reports of visits to a number of scientists of the time but they cannot be proved and we have no hard evidence of actual visits. As a result of the reception given to Linnaeus in England his pupil Daniel C Solander came to Mill Hill and Collinson was largely instrumental in getting him here. Linnaeus died in Uppsala on January 10 1778.

Linnaeus had two sons, one died in infancy and the other had difficulty in living up to his father's reputation and fame. He never married so the family name became extinct. His mother sold the collection and books to Dr J E Smith, the first president of the Linnaen Society in London. When Smith died a subscription was raised and the herbarium and library were purchased for the Society. Although Smith sold the collection of minerals in 1796 the remainder is much as it was when Linnaeus last used it.

CHAPTER XIX

SOME OTHER NOTABLE PEOPLE

I n earlier chapters much has been made of the isolation of Mill Hill. It was away from main roads, perched on a high ridge. These facts plus the dense forest that surrounded Mill Hill in historical times acted as a defence and a deterrent to possible intruders. The people of the hamlet probably kept very much to themselves, not wandering much farther afield than the limits of the Manor. There were visitors, and people of rank passed through but certainly few of influence or importance came to live there.

The 18th century saw the beginning of the expansion of London: its population, its commerce and its area. Many prominent people began to look at places like Mill Hill with a view to building country seats there, either moving out of the City completely or keeping a place in London and a more spacious residence in what are now the suburbs where land was cheaper and more plentiful and the air a bit cleaner.

Some of these were famous and important people. But they are not all remembered today. Some are now almost forgotten, so who is to be considered famous? Some are obvious, national figures of whom most people know something. Others were once on everyone's lips but like news and fashions no longer get the 'front page'. And for us here there is the remainder, those people important in a particular walk of life or of strictly local interest to Mill Hill but not well known to the Country at large. They are all worth a mention, particularly in a history of this kind, nevertheless some readers will feel that a notable person has been omitted whom they would certainly have included.

Some of Mill Hill's famous people are worthy of more than a potted biography. These were national figures and as such deserve something in greater detail to be written about their lives and exploits. They are in separate chapters. In addition many people connected with the arts have also resided in Mill Hill or nearby, and because there are so many they too have a chapter of their own.

GEORGE FOX

Fox, the son of a weaver, was born in Drayton, Leicestershire in 1624. He founded the Religious Society of Friends. As a child he was something of a prig and claimed that he was taught how to walk to keep pure. Before he was twenty years of age he went to a fair and witnessed how his

Puritan friends were (in his opinion) misbehaving. In disgust he gave up his job, left family, relations and friends and travelled the Country questioning and reasoning with anyone who professed religious wisdom at this time, the early days of the Commonwealth.

None of the advice that was offered appealed to him: to join the army, get married, to be bled, to take physic, to sing psalms, or to take tobacco. Later on he did marry, to an early convert named Margaret Fell. Despairing of human help Fox turned within himself, he said:

> '*I saw that there was an ocean of Darkness and Death, but an infinite Ocean of Light and Love, which flowed over the Ocean of Darkness, and in that also I saw the Infinite Love of God: and I had Great Openings'.*

When Fox proclaimed that 'The Lord God opened to me by his Invisible Power how that Every Man was enlightened by the Divine of Christ' he was accused of blasphemy. When he began to gather adherents to his beliefs he was persecuted. He organised Silent Meetings with no prearranged order of service, and without sacraments or ministers. Declaring that women had souls too he gave them equal status in his organisation.

Fox was sent to prison in Derby in 1650. In all he endured this punishment seven more times. When questioned by the Court he declared that he was without sin, but denied that he considered himself to be Christ. At one of these hearings he told Judge Bennett that they should tremble at the Name of the Lord, for this he was given the nickname of Quaker which stuck.

George Fox... stayed in Mill Hill 1677-1680

There was an active Quaker community in Mill Hill for many years which met in a building called Rosebank, now refurbished and divided into private homes. Fox visited this group many times (see also the chapters on Important Buildings and Religions). In his writings he said that in 1673 he went into the country with his wife and daughter to Hendon, and to William Penn in Rickmansworth. He also wrote that he stayed with a widow named Hagley in Mill Hill in 1677, 1678 and 1680.

By the time that Fox died in 1691 there were Quaker communities as far apart as Carolina and the Baltic States and he had managed to visit nearly every one of them.

LORD WILLIAM RUSSELL

Bearing false witness is as old as civilised mankind, hence the Ninth Commandment, Thou shalt not bear false witness against thy Neighbour. Throughout history people have suffered imprisonment, torture and death because someone else is prepared to lie, either to save his own skin, for revenge, spite, jealousy of another's success, or for personal gain. In modern parlance Lord William Russell was framed, and because he could not prove his innocence and said what he believed he was executed.

Was there ever a Popish Plot? Almost certainly not, and definitely not the plot that the liar Titus Oates and his associate Israel Tonge invented and laid before a Protestant magistrate in 1678. According to Oates the Pope had given orders for the Jesuits to overthrow the British government, kill King Charles II and place his brother James (who supported the Catholic cause) on the throne. All this to be followed by a general slaughter of Protestants. Fantasy? Yes, but coming so soon (in September 1678) after the Gunpowder Plot of 1605 and with the populace deeply suspicious of all Catholic behaviour a usually sane and sensible people had become gullible. Nevertheless it is still difficult to understand how anyone, let alone a magistrate, could be induced to believe Oates, look at his past: an indictment for perjury nearly ruined his career in 1675 but he escaped from imprisonment in Dover Castle, he had been expelled from school, from a naval chaplaincy and even a Jesuit college. He called himself 'DD' but had no right to any degree because his studies at Cambridge did not lead to a qualification of any kind.

Much has been written about this period of English history, perhaps because we like political intrigue. There is plenty of imagination and lots of exaggeration. What Oates and another 'informer' William Bedloe did achieve was to maintain an anti-Catholic hysteria which lasted on and off for some time. When the examining magistrate, Sir Edmund Berry Godfrey was found dead (probably murdered with his own sword but by whom we will never know) the suspicions of the people were heightened. There is certainly no evidence that Catholics were responsible. Unfortunately two of those implicated in the 'Plot' were Edward Coleman and his wife, and it transpired that Coleman had indeed been in touch for years with French agents and Jesuits. At the end of 1678 Coleman and three others were tried and executed for their alleged parts in the 'plot', and altogether some 35 people were put to death by one means or another.

The next four years were spent in further intrigue with accusations and counter accusations. The anti-Catholic fervour was maintained and by order of Parliament no Catholic could become King. Opponents of the King had their position rendered even more hopeless by the dismissal of any judge who resisted the King's will. Edward Fitzharris, an informer, was executed in 1681, the Earl of Shaftesbury was imprisoned in the Tower on a treason charge but escaped execution. Shaftesbury fled to Holland where he died two months later. The Government used its control over the judiciary to eliminate those Whig leaders who actively opposed them.

And so to the Rye House Plot. The three most important Whig leaders were Lord William Russell, Algernon Sydney, and the Earl of Essex. They were charged with implication in a plan to assassinate the King at Rye House near Hoddesdon in Hertfordshire on his way home from the races at Newmarket. Without doubt there was a scheme whereby pressure would be brought on the Government, using arms if necessary, and Russell certainly knew of this. Some other Whigs wanted to take the plan further and hatched a plot to kill the King and his brother. Unfortunately scheme and murderous plot were confused together, fake witnesses were procured who gave King's Evidence.

The 'evidence' was vague and circumstantial and certainly would not stand up to examination today. Nevertheless Russell and Sydney were executed and Essex committed suicide in the Tower before he could be brought to trial. Today we wonder whether there was ever a plot at all. There was of course something in the story on which Oates fabricated his version of the events. Hugh Trevor Roper (author, one time Regis Professor of Modern History at Oxford, and Master of Peterhouse Cambridge) compared him to a much later treachery:

> 'I was reminded of that other half-crazed witch-hunter in our history, Titus Oates, who could not also be wholly refuted, for the Popish Plot was not a complete myth: a small nucleus of truth lay buried under the unscrupulously manufactured hysteria'.

We do know that Russell, Sydney, and Essex and others belonging to the Green Ribbon Club had discussed ways and means of convincing the King to adopt a more liberal and fair-minded policy (towards Catholics in particular). Certainly Russell had been a prominent Whig but he had supported the *Exclusion Bill,* and in the beginning even believed much of the rantings of Titus Oates about the absurd Popish Plot. But all this was conveniently forgotten in the travesty of a trial.

According to popular legend the King's messengers were sent to

Highwood House to arrest Russell but he escaped out of a small window and made off down the green lane through which Wolsey had ridden a century and half earlier only to be chased and captured. Alas there is no hard evidence of this even though the story appears in a dozen publications (they have probably all copied the original writer). In all probability Russell was arrested in his London apartment.

Russell faced his trial with great fortitude and refused to deviate from his principles or change his story. He was beheaded in Lincoln's Inn Fields. Throughout the trial his wife gave counsel and made notes for his defence. He was buried as a temporary expedient in the grounds of his home at Highwood House where four yews were planted to mark the spot. His body was later exhumed and reburied in the family vault (of the Bedford family) at Chenies in Buckinghamshire. Highwood House later became the home of Sir Stamford Raffles

After the death of Russell his wife remained loyal to his memory and devoted her life to the education of their daughters. The days of their marriage, the trial and the execution were observed with great solemnity throughout the remainder of her life.

The emancipation of Roman Catholics did not come about during the reign of Charles II, or indeed for another 100 years. King George III was against such a move but in the final reckoning could be over-ruled. Country squires who had accepted the abolition of slavery as a piece of misguided legislation introduced by a handful of do-gooders regarded any proposals to relax the restrictions concerning the control of Catholics as treachery: putting power into the hands of ignorant Irish peasant voters. And this was at the end of the 18th Century! The Whig government fell, not the first time or the last that the 'Irish Problem' would see off an administration.

CELIA FIENNES

Ride a cock horse to Banbury Cross
To see a fine lady upon a white horse,
With rings on her fingers and bells on her toes,
She shall have music wherever she goes.

As children we all learnt this rhyme, did we know its significance? The 'fine lady' was in fact Celia Fiennes, 'fine', merely being the way that her name was pronounced. She was born in 1662 and best described as an English gentlewoman. At a time when travelling could be extremely hazardous (the late 17th Century) Celia travelled widely throughout

Britain on horse-back and made detailed notes about what she saw. Her writings became invaluable for architectural, economic, and social historians, not only because of their precise nature but also because her account was the first since Elizabethan times. Her spelling is somewhat wayward and she spells the same words in a variety of ways. Celia was a lady of some wealth and a Dissenter. She was the granddaughter of the First Viscount Saye and Sele. Banbury is not just one of the places that Celia visited, it refers in particular to her uncle's seat at Broughton Castle which is about 1.5km south-west of the town. It is worth noting that her journey of curiosity was undertaken 25 years before Daniel Defoe published his book, *Tour Through the Whole Island of Great Britain.*

Celia's travels are detailed in *The Journey of Celia Fiennes* by Christopher Morris (1947) and her diaries are a frank and altogether delightful description of life, often at the rough end of society. The travels took place during the reigns of William III and Anne. For much of this time England was at war with France and Celia recorded that the people in Penzance had to cook over a fire of furze because there was no wood (Cornwall's forests had been cut down long before this time) and French warships prevented deliveries of Welsh coal. There were no proper roads and obviously canals and railways did not yet exist.

Even in the Midlands dried cow dung was used as fuel because of the gap in time between the end of the forests (and a regular supply of wood) and the development of the Midlands coal industry. In another part of the diary Celia describes in great detail the arrival of coal barges 'from Bristol coming up by river through Bridgewater to a place within three miles of Taunton'. Evidently some places did enjoy regular supplies. Celia also had interesting things to say about some of the towns that she visited: she declared that Leeds was 'the wealthiest town of its bigness', Liverpool 'very handsome, a London in miniature', Norwich a 'rich thriveing industrious place', and Nottingham the 'neatest town that she saw'.

Celia Fiennes lived in a large house at the top of Highwood Hill, Mill Hill when not on her travels. The house Highwood Ash stands there today.

BENJAMIN FRANKLYN

Franklyn is said to have visited Mill Hill on a number of occasions from 1767 when he came to this country representing the people of Pennsylvania to the Court of St James.

Benjamin Franklyn, the American statesman, scientist and writer was born of poor parents in Boston Mass. As a young man he ran a printing press with such success that he was able to retire to scientific work in 1749 at the age of 43. He proved that lightning is a form of electricity, and he invented the lightning conductor. He also discovered that electricity has positive and negative poles: these three brought him instant fame and international acknowledgement.

Benjamin Franklin
American statesman,
scientist and writer

Franklyn was elected to the Pennsylvania Assembly and in 1754 put forward the first plan for a federation of the American colonies. As agent for Pennsylvania in England he was here between 1764 and 1765 and he used his influence to obtain the repeal of the *Stamp Act*. During this time he became a firm friend of Peter Collinson and visited Mill Hill many times. Collinson introduced him to the Royal Society. When Collinson died Franklyn wrote to his son:

'Dear Sir,

Understanding that an account of our dear departed friend Mr Peter Collinson is intended to be given to the Public, I cannot omit expressing my approbation of the design, as the characters of good men are exemplary and often stimulate the well-disposed to an imitation beneficial to mankind, and honourable to their successors. He encouraged the design of a subscription library in Philadelphia by making valuable presents to it and procuring others from his friends. And for 30 years he undertook the
choice, collecting and shipping of our books without ever charging for his trouble. . . . . . .'

Later in the same letter he explained how he came to investigate electricity, and it is obvious that it was Collinson who directed him down this path:

'*In 1745 he sent me an account of the new German experiments in electricity together with necessary instruments to repeat them . . . . This was the first notice I had of that curious subject which I often afterwards prosecuted with some diligence, being encouraged by the friendly reception he gave to my letters. Please do accept this small testimony of mine to his memory, for which I shall ever have the utmost regard'.*

When Franklyn returned to America he helped to draw up the *Declaration of Independence*, became ambassador to France 1776 to 1785, negotiated an alliance with France, and the peace settlement with Britain.

Franklyn was president of Pennsylvania from 1785 to 1788 and took part in the drafting of the *American Constitution*. He died in 1790.

PETER HAMMOND

Hammond was a man of some substance with considerable lands and property in Mill Hill in the 18th Century. Little is known about this family and there is nothing to indicate what happened to him and the lands after his death in 1794. His wife Anne died in 1769. Husband and wife are buried together in St Mary's Parish Church, Hendon.

JOHN WILKES

Wilkes was one time Lord Mayor of London who chose to retire in Mill Hill. In his time he was City Chamberlain, Sheriff, politician, editor (of the *North Briton,* which he used as a platform to attack the Court), and of course City alderman. He retired to Mill Hill in 1790 and to quote his own words 'As a fire burnt out'.

When Wilkes came to Mill Hill it seems that he did not wish his exploits to be remembered, and indeed he spent the last seven years of his life in almost total obscurity. Possibly by this time Wilkes was ashamed of some of his earlier life.

Patronage was a minor misdemeanour (members of his family controlled one government post for almost the entire 18th Century) compared with some of his other misdeeds. Up to 1757 when he separated from his wife, Wilkes showed all the signs of a man climbing the joint ladders to social and business success. He had been educated fashionably (at Leyden University), purchased a military commission (colonel in the Buckinghamshire Militia), and Parliamentary seat (member for Ayles-bury). From the end of his marriage he changed completely by mixing freely with most undesirable people, some were known criminals. He got into financial difficulties and lived on his wits.

Later Wilkes' attacks on Crown and Parliament led to trouble with the law and nearly ended with imprisonment in the Tower. Fortunately for him his offences were not considered to be a breach of the peace, a felony, or treason (which are all outside the privilege of Parliamentary Immunity) so he was released, but it was a near thing.

In his public role Wilkes stood for political and civil liberty against a King who wanted to revive the earlier powers of English monarchs. Wilkes disagreed violently with the policies of George III, and with the House of Commons which he considered too aristocratic and out of touch to represent the common people, a fair analysis. To some therefore he was the finest man in the land, but to others who only looked at his morals a figure to be despised.

Wilkes died at Christmas time in 1797 at the age of 70. A man who had fought many battles for the ordinary people yet strangely whose private life was in many ways reprehensible.

SIR JOHN ANDERSON BART

Sir John lived with his wife Dame Dorothy in Holcombe House at Highwood at the end of the 18th and beginning of the 19th Centuries. He was a glover and citizen of London. Sir John was the second son of William Anderson, a merchant, and Lucy (nee Sheldon). He was born in 1735.

Mill Hill seems to have been a popular place of residence for ex-Lord Mayors of London: Sir John was another one. Having been a City alderman for some years he was Lord Mayor in 1798 and made a baronet on May 14 of the same year. Sir John was also one time MP for Okehampton in Devon and later for the City of London. He married in 1762, his wife was the daughter and coheiress of Charles Simpkins of Devises in Wiltshire.

There was no issue to the union and the title therefore became extinct. Sir John died in 1813 and his wife in 1817. They are buried in the graveyard of St Mary's Parish Church, Hendon.

SIR CHARLES FLOWER BART

The magnificent house at the northern end of the Village called Belmont is now Mill Hill Junior School. It was built in the style of the Adelphi in London for Sir Charles Flower, then Lord Mayor of London. Flower Lane is named after him.

Sir Charles was a man on whom life endowed much. Apart from his house, mentioned above, he owned a considerable amount of property in Mill Hill and Totteridge. Belmont, then called Belmont House, was built on land expressly given to him for this purpose. Sir Charles was born on February 18 1763, the eldest son of Stephen Flower, a cheese monger with a business in The Minories in the City of London. The Flower fortune seems to have originated with sales of war materials, that is the sale of provisions, to the Government during the war with France.

In 1799 Sir Charles was Sheriff and was elected as alderman in 1801, to the Aldgate Ward according to one source but to another Cornhill. He was Lord Mayor in 1808 and created a baronet on December 1 1809, the year of King George III's jubilee.

Sir Charles was also connected with a number of important City business houses including the Pelican Life Assurance Office and Phoenix Fire Insurance. He also had a long standing interest in John Cass's School, of which he was treasurer for many years.

He was married to Anne, the eldest daughter of the Squire of Plymouth. Unfortunately she died young leaving a family of one son and six daughters. Sir Charles lived to the age of 72 and died at his town house in Russell Square in September 1835.

The only son succeeded to the baronetcy and estates and resided at Eccles Hall, Norfolk. He died without issue and the title became extinct. Under the terms of Sir Charles' will the property was then divided between his daughters.

SIR WILLIAM TITE

Sir William was an architect of considerable renown and is important to us as the designer of Mill Hill School. He lived from 1798 to 1873.

The selection of Sir William as architect is interesting because there appears to be a direct link with Samuel Favell one of the founders. Favell was Master of the City Company of Clothmakers. In the 17th Century when the Plantation of Ulster began lands were offered to the Clothmakers Company, they were horrified and complained that their members were far too poor to be involved. However due to pressure they acceded and were allocated an area of 5,445ha. By the early 19th Century the Clothmakers in Ireland were badly off financially. Later on, in 1836-8 Tite visited Ireland for the Irish Society and designed cottages for the 'Irish Peasantry', for the tomb of Colonel John Mitchelburn (governor and commander-in-chief during the siege of old Londonderry in 1689), some more splendid dwellings for erection between Londonderry and Moville and most important, 'Government House' the official residence of the Irish Society's agent.

Back in London in 1839 Tite was commissioned as adviser to the Royal Exchange for an architectural competition for their proposed new building (the original 16th Century building in which the Nicoll family had been involved had burnt down the previous year). Tite ignored all the other proposals and the new Exchange was built to his own design, this decision earned him much deserved criticism. Certainly his conduct in this affair was to say the least questionable and always likely to invite criticism.

As an architect Tite was almost spectacularly successful. He quite obviously had influence in the City as well as advising the Irish Society (which also had Plantation lands). In 1835 he was elected to the Royal Society, he was knighted in 1869 and made a Companion of the Bath in 1870.

At the time that Tite designed Mill Hill School his years of real fame were still to come. Did Favell make possible his involvement in the works in Ireland or is the connection with the Clothmakers Company a happy coincidence? We can only guess, certainly a few years later and Sir William Tite as he then was would have found it more difficult to have devoted the necessary time to the Mill Hill School project.

When Tite drew up the plans of the School it was a complete entity. Unfortunately because of the subsequent growth it has been necessary to add and alter so all that is visible today is not of one style or continuity of design. The most conspicuous addition is the classical gated memorial arch facing The Ridgeway.

WILLIAM EWART GLADSTONE

Gladstone...
often seen walking The Ridgeway

Gladstone's visit to Mill Hill School in 1879 was considered at the time to be more than just an acceptance of the the School but also of its principles. Even at this time it was still a courageous thing to do. No-one in his position would have dared to visit such an establishment even half a century earlier. By all accounts Gladstone spoke to an enthusiastic audience of pupils past and present, plus their parents and the masters for 50 minutes during which time it rained in torrents. This was not much fun as the address took place in a 19th Century marquee.

Gladstone was also a frequent visitor to Lord Aberdeen when he lived at Littleberries. By this time Gladstone was no longer premier. He was often seen walking The Ridgeway chatting to local people and generally busying himself in the affairs of the Village.

SIR JAMES A H MURRAY

James Augustas Henry Murray was born on February 7 1837 at Denholm Roxburghshire. He was the son of a clothier of Hawick and was educated at Cavers School near Denholm and at Minto School. He became a schoolmaster at Mill Hill School, officially being responsible for the instruction of English and Geography, although according to a pupil of the time 'In his classes you learnt about everything'. He was passionately interested in history, natural history and philology, he wrote a book on the

once the home of Dr. James Murray

Scots dialect and edited the poetry of David Lyndesay, a 15th century Scots herald. Murray was renowned during his own lifetime and still remembered, but chiefly as a lexicographer, a maker of dictionaries.

Murray was a schoolmaster from 1855 to 1885. During his time as a teacher he wrote an article on the English language for *Encyclopaedia Britannica* (1878) for which he became famous. Murray also served as president of the Philogical Society from 1878 to 1880 and from 1882 to 1884.

In 1879 Murray was appointed editor of the *New English Dictionary on Historical Principles* for which he laid down the basic approaches. The Dictionary was intended to be an inventory of words used since the mid-12th Century and in some cases earlier. The acceptance of any word was to be on strictly historical and descriptive principles, with each definition accompanied by an example with date and usage. The first section was published in 1884 (A to Ant). Printing was by the Clarendon Press at Oxford.

The Dictionary was later renamed the *Oxford English Dictionary*, the name by which it is still known today. Although Murray was overall editor the project was too big for one man, nevertheless he still compiled about half and was directly responsible for A to D, H to K, and the single sections O, P and T, and he worked on the main design and the scope of the whole project. It was estimated at the time that some three tons of paper slips arrived from all over the world over a period of six years from correspondents interested in the production and content. These were stored in a building known as the Scriptorium and then sorted. Initially Murray worked on the dictionary in his spare time (he had little of that), but this soon became an impossible burden and he left teaching and went to Oxford to work on the dictionary full time. Murray lived and worked in Oxford on the enormous undertaking until he died in 1915, a perpetual inspiration to all his successors. For his work on the Dictionary Murray was knighted and thereafter known as Sir James Murray.

Dr Murray put Mill Hill on the map wherever English is spoken. His treasured Scriptorium where the dictionary enterprise materialised was presented to the school as a reading room when he transferred his work base to Oxford. Unhappily this shrine was burnt down in 1902, subscriptions from the boys however enabled the governors to build a new Scriptorium in memory of the great man. In 1985 the Scriptorium was converted into the first of three new computing centres.

Dr Murray's home in Mill Hill was for 15 years 'Sunnyside' now renamed 'Murray House' to honour his name. It is opposite the *Three Hammers* public house.

REVEREND ROBERT HARLEY

It is very unlikely that Robert Harley ever considered himself to be a notable and he certainly never sought fame. By our standards he certainly was notable and for good reason: he was a Congregational minister and a mathematician such that it is impossible to decide which of these was most important to him. Today we would have to say that the mathematics was and is more important to posterity.

Harley's father was originally a merchant but then became a minister in the Wesleyan Methodist Association. This necessitated frequent travels on circuit, to the detriment of his son's education. Robert had a natural affinity for mathematics however which quickly developed and he was appointed to a mastership at Seacombe near Liverpool before his seventeenth birthday. This could not happen today. Later he served in a similar capacity in Blackburn.

In 1854 Harley entered the Congregational ministry and was stationed at Brighouse in Yorkshire for 14 years. During the latter part of this time he also occupied the chair of mathematics at Airedale College.

The next stop was Leicester where Harley was pastor of the oldest Congregational church from 1868 to 1872, then he moved to Mill Hill School to become vice-principal. He also officiated at chapel. In Mill Hill he erected a public lecture hall (where total abstinence was expected) for popular entertainments and instructional talks.

Three years in this post and he was off again, back to Yorkshire to be principal at Huddersfield College from 1882 to 1885, then south again having been appointed minister of the Congregational Church at Oxford. Whilst in Oxford he was made Hon MA.

For six years Harley was much farther afield, in Australia, then back again for another ministerial post in Halifax. In 1895 he decided that the time had come for him to retire from his religious duties and his wanderings. He concentrated the rest of his life on his great love outside religion; higher mathematics. He researched higher algebra, a branch called quintics, the general equation to the fifth degree for which he was elected to the Royal Society in 1863. Harley published a number of papers on mathematical subjects. He settled in Forest Hill in south-east London where he lived for 15 years until he died in 1910.

J P SMITH

You will need to search in very specialized reference books to find any mention of J P Smith. He is certainly more important, at least in terms of his invention, than many others of his times and yet almost unknown. As a one time resident of Mill Hill he certainly deserves a mention here. He was registered as a farmer but when he took out a patent in the spring of 1836 it had nothing to do with ploughshares or harrows, reapers or balers. Smith's invention was for the first practical marine screw propeller.

Some references credit the Scandinavian Ericcsson with the 'first'. He may well have been working along the same lines but Smith certainly did not know this and in any case Smith's was the first to be tested. Today apart from a few vessels operating in very shallow water such as rivers and lakes (which still use paddles) and hover-craft the marine screw still rules the waves.

At first the Royal Navy were not convinced, they could not see how the device could be effective. A test was conducted using two ships of the same weight and draught in stormy weather in the English Channel. The screw driven vessel won easily, which may not have been the case in calmer waters. The Government then commissioned a ship of 888 tons, and named it the Rattler, it had more powerful engines and a modified screw with blades less prone to fracture. Smith's invention revolutionized ship design and building as much as the change from sail to steam.

Like all good inventions the principle of the marine propeller is simple. Thrust is given to the ship by giving momentum to the water it displaces astern of the ship. In other words the propeller drives the water backwards which in turn develops a reaction force which thrusts the vessel forwards.

J P Smith lived at the Clock House, having moved there in 1823. This house was at the top of Milespit Hill.

GILBERT LAIRD JESSOP

By the time that Jessop came to live in Mill Hill (3 Sunnydale Gardens NW7) he was already spending more time writing about cricket matters than actually playing the game. But nothing could in any way diminish the exploits of this great all-rounder, to many the most complete cricketer of all time.

Jessop was a dy-namic and often violent batsman, who only knew one kind of cricket, to attack, and furthermore he was just as much feared as a fielder in the covers because of the power and accuracy of his returns to the wicket. Without all this his bowling alone would

three times Jessop scored 50 in 20 minutes

have earned him a place in any team. Jessop was nicknamed *The Croucher* because of the stance that he adopted when batting: it was not very elegant and for the purist lacked style, but for him singularly effective.

Jessop was educated at Cheltenham Grammar School and went up to Cambridge in 1896. He captained the University cricket team in 1899, his final year, and Gloucestershire from 1900 to 1913. He actually played for the county from 1894.

Although the travelling part of cricket was then much more arduous (nearly one hundred years ago) Jessop toured Australia twice and played in five Test series at home. His total tally of Test Matches was 18.

Jessop was a man for whom statistics do not do justice: his average for all first class matches was 32.63 runs and for test matches 21.88.

There are many batsmen with figures that are much more impressive. It was the manner of his scoring that puts *The Croucher* in the league of superlatives. On the attack from the first ball some of the game's analysts have said that he tried to score too fast, too soon, or lacked patience against the best bowlers of his day. But who can argue with the facts? These are some of his scores that found their way into the record books:

286 out of 355 in 175 minutes

233 out of 318 in 150 minutes

234 out of 346 in 155 minutes

101 out of 118 in 40 minutes

161 and 128 in one match, and the 161 was out of 199 in 95 minutes including 61 off four overs.

Three times Jessop scored 50 in 20 minutes. In 20 years (before his health failed during World War I) he scored 26,698 runs including 50 centuries. In 1900 he scored 2,000 runs and took 104 wickets. His centuries were made at an average of 82.70 runs per hour and his five double centuries at just under 100 per hour. Jessop died in 1955 at the age of 81. There have been other belligerent batsman and there will be more, nevertheless it is unlikely that we shall see many cricketers again with his combined abilities of fielder, bowler, and often violent batsman.

GRAHAM HILL

When a person has been engaged in a dangerous sport, becomes very successful in spite of accidents and lives to retire, only to be killed in a crash of another kind the death seems in a way to be more cruel. Graham Hill was killed in a plane crash in Hendon in bad weather in 1975.

Hill was the charismatic driver of the 1960s and became a well known face (and a well known voice) at a time when the sport was full of characters. His first Grand Prix win was in a BRM at Zandvoort in Holland in 1962 and he went on to win 11 more Grands Prix. Monaco, one of the most difficult circuits, almost became his own; he won here five times. Hill won the Indianapolis 500 in 1966, only the second non-American to do so, and also shared the driving in the winning car at the Le Mans 24 hour race in 1972. Graham Hill was never World Champion but he was winner of the Drivers' World Championship twice, in 1962 and 1968.

When Hill retired it was his intention to run his own racing team. Also in the plane when it crashed in November 1975 was his protégé

Tony Brise, designer Andy Smallman, and four of his team members. After the accident the whole project was cancelled.

Graham Hill was educated at one of the schools that went to make up Mill Hill County High School in 1984.

RICHARD DIMBLEBY

Richard Dimbleby attended Mill Hill School in the 1920s and left to become one of the best known figures in radio and television. He was born in 1913 and died in 1968.

His career started as a newspaper journalist and in this period he worked for many different newspapers. He joined the BBC in 1936 as news observer and in 1939 became their first war correspondent. Having covered the action in many of the worst places he was the first British radio announcer to broadcast from Berlin in 1945 and the first to talk from the infamous Belsen Concentration Camp.

In 1946 Dimbleby left the BBC to work freelance and covered every type of major event and became probably the best known face on television at the time, and certainly one of the most recognisable voices. He specialised in royal occasions from Ascot to the Coronation and weddings. He will be remembered particularly for his dramatic tones as a commentator at the funerals of Sir Winston Churchill and President J F Kennedy.

In 1951 Dimbleby was in the first Eurovision relay and the first broadcast from the USSR in 1961. For his services to television and broadcasting he was awarded the OBE and CBE.

NORMAN HARTNELL

Few people would recognise a photograph of Norman Hartnell, but most have heard of him. Hartnell was born in 1901 and was also a pupil of Mill Hill School and went from there to Magdalene College in Cambridge where he graduated. He set up his own business in 1923 at the age of 22 and became famous as a couturier and dress designer. In 1940 he was awarded the Royal Warrant and became the Court Dressmaker. From 1946 to 1956 he was the president of the Incorporated Society of London Fashion Designers.

Hartnell was responsible for the wedding dress for HM The Queen when Princess Elizabeth and for her coronation gown. Outside his royal duties Hartnell also designed costumes for many leading actresses, and at the other end of the scale was responsible for the design of wartime 'Utility' dresses and the uniform for the WRAC.

FRANCIS CRICK

Francis Harry Compton Crick was born on June 8 1916 in Northampton, he was educated at Mill Hill School. During World War II he interrupted his education to help the war effort and worked for the Admiralty as a physicist designing magnetic mines for naval warfare.

At the end of hostilities he turned his attention to biology, and the structure of large molecules, at the Strangeways Research Laboratory, Cambridge University (1947-1949). He became interested in the pioneering work then being worked on by a number of prominent scientists and transferred to the University's Cavendish Laboratories where the Medical Research Council had a team.

When the young American biologist James D Watson came to Cambridge in 1951 they formed a rather unlikely liaison, but what turned out to be a very special and successful one. Two years later they had worked out the structure of deoxyribonucleic acid (DNA) and were able to construct a model consistent with what they now knew about its physical and chemical properties.

DNA is the fundamental genetic material and it is the chemical substance that is responsible for hereditary control of life functions. The discovery of its structure, a double helix, and the way that it replicates is widely regarded as the most significant event in 20th Century biology. This biological discovery has probably inspired more researches, and been the key to more understanding than any other and has caused a veritable explosion in interest in the science of molecular biology.

For their work on DNA Crick and Watson and the New Zealander Maurice Wilkins were awarded the Nobel Prize for Physiology or Medicine in 1962.

The story of the events leading up to the discovery were related in a book by Watson *The Double Helix* published in 1968. It reads like a science thriller but unfortunately offended many other scientists, some of whom had been working on the same problem but were beaten to the post. The book was republished in a more critical edition in 1981 but a much more comprehensive account of the story is in *The Eighth Day of Creation* .

CHAPTER XX

SOME IMPORTANT FAMILIES

There are a number of families whose names have been associated with Mill Hill and the surrounding area for hundreds of years. They have occupied positions of power and authority, they owned large houses and estates, they were benefactors and businessmen. Strangely not one of these names is to be found here today. They managed to survive plagues and wars, famine years and good years, and yet when survival became easier they succumbed. Did they move away from the area, was there a predominance of female babies and an overwhelming mortality amongst male children or were all these families just unlucky? Whatever the reasons the names that can be found time and time again in every kind of official document appear no more. They are a part of the history of Mill Hill but not of the future.

THE NICOLL FAMILY

If there is one family who's name is inseparable from the Mill Hill district then it has to be Nicoll. The name Nicoll appears literally hundreds of times in Court Rolls, deeds, registers, and surveys. The various branches of this family were land-owners, and occupied positions of importance in Mill Hill and the surrounding area for 500 years. The name was first entered on official documents in the 14th Century and continued to be mentioned into the 20th Century. The *Black Survey* of 1321 lists Stephen Nicoll as a freeholder with messuage (a dwelling house with buildings and lands) of 15 acres and 12 acres.

Many of the lanes of Mill Hill are named after prominent people who lived in the locality (see also *Roads, Lanes, Paths and Tracks*) but there is no obvious connection between the Nicoll family and the name of any local thoroughfare. It is true however that Colin, Nicoll and Nicholl are contractions of Nicholas and therefore a rather tenuous association between Nicoll and Colin Deep Lane is possible. This is of course pure conjecture and the name Colin Deep may well have a much simpler and more direct meaning and origin. There was a John Collin living in the area in the early 18th Century (1710) and Collin's Deepe could just have been some low lying land owned by him.

In *Court Roll No 1* (1461 to 1474) the family (spelt Nycoll) takes up page after page with references, mostly concerning land transfers. The *Court Rolls* contained details of villein and tenant services and dues.

Similar entries appear in *Court Rolls* up to the 17th Century. In other chapters mention is made of the Nicoll's property on The Ridgeway, Highwood, Cowleaze Farm, and Hendon Place and of the two houses most associated with them, Cookes and Copt Hall. But this is not all, old Ridgeway House which was built around 1525 was the residence of a branch of the Nicolls for 150 years and eventually became the home of the original Dissenters' school (before Mill Hill School).

The last Nicoll to own Copt Hall, the family seat, was Mr Nicoll-Hodgson and the earliest Nicoll on record was living at this place before the Wars of the Roses. The family was probably well off by the time of the 16th Century: they are reputed to have made a considerable amount out of the building of the Royal Exchange. However the architect Sir Thomas Gresham, the man responsible for this project was much criticized at the time for engaging a Flemish architect, Henri de Pas, and foreign workmen, so the part played by the Nicolls is not immediately obvious. The building was burnt down in the Great Fire of 1666, rebuilt and burnt down again in 1838.

In the children's section of Finchley Public Library in Hendon Lane is a stained glass window containing three coats of arms. The inscription reads 'The families of Hastings, Frowicke and Nicholl' and these were all at one time connected with Grass or Groats Farm and the records of this land can be traced back to Henry III (1216-1272). The name Nicholl also appears on graves in the burial ground of Hendon Parish Church. Although there is no apparent connection between the two families of Nicoll and Nicholl they may well be one and same and have a common origin if you go back far enough. In any case it is likely that the two families intermarried from time to time.

In 1545 Christiana Nicoll died and her will described her as 'A widow of Hendon'. Her will was a long and detailed affair with many bequests, the first being 'Unto Randall Nicoll my great table in the hall, my great cauldron, my great brass pot, and a cow.' She also asked that her body be buried in the churchyard of Hendon. Of some importance to her successors was her bequest for the upkeep of the road which ran from her house to the church (Sanders Lane).

The Nicolls of Page Street first appeared on the scene at the end of the 16th Century. Randall Nicoll who died some time prior to 1622 was mentioned in a *Chancery Bill* of that year that was filed by his son, also named Randall. This son was the builder of Copt Hall (it was built in 1637) and became a very important man in many aspects of local life. He lived in Copt Hall throughout the turbulent years of the Civil War, Cromwell's Commonwealth, and into the Restoration. Randall Nicoll died in 1665, the year of the Great Plague, leaving his wife, three sons, and a daughter. His wife died the following year.

The daughter Susan, by all accounts married into another branch of the family that resided in Highwood Hill. The eldest son, another Randall had four children by his wife Eliza, a son and three daughters, once again the son being named Randall and he was churchwarden at the Parish Church for many years.

Other Nicolls of the 17th Century were Ralph, listed as 'Collector' (presumably of taxes) in 1644 and Richard who held the position of 'Headborough' in 1645. This position does not have an equivalent in modern English law, being the chief of a tithing or frankpledge: in old English law members of a tithing aged 12 years or more were responsible for the good conduct and any damage done by the tithing's other members.

There was another Nicoll family residing in The Hyde that acquired extra land in Hendon in the 18th Century. The *Court Rolls* in 1786 admitted John Nicoll on death of Michael Nicoll 'A messuage, houses and gardens, five poles, called Vicar-

DRAPER'S COMPANY COTTAGES

age, with waste adjoining the house abutting on a field called Shallock Field, eight acres'. The lands extended to Finchley Lane and eastward to the Tenterden Estate. A road led to the estate from Brent Street called Vicarage Want.

William Nicoll, grocer and citizen of the City of London has already been mentioned in the chapter on property. He was one of the 'Clerkes of the cheque to the Fourty Messengers in Ordinary of Charles I'. His son of the same name was a member of the Company of Drapers in London, during the times of the Plantation in Ulster. The first phase of the building by the Company of Drapers started in 1614. The grand-daughter of this William Nicoll married Sir Charles Hedges, Queen Anne's secretary from whom is descended the Duke of Marlborough.

It will come as no surprise to learn that the name of Nicoll features frequently in the registers for births, marriages, and deaths. During the Commonwealth, clergymen were not permitted to sign the register as witnesses, and this duty had to be performed by a Justice of the Peace. The name Paul Nicoll features in this respect and amongst the marriages are John Nicoll to Susan Nicoll on December 13 1671, Eliza Nicoll to Richard Page on January 4 1672, Mary Nicoll to Daniel Kemp on February 15 1683, and Thomas Nicoll to Sarah Marsh on December 31

1728. It should be noted that the same family names appear again and again.

The early register of burials contains even more Nicoll references and they seem to be of all ages. We find two daughters of Randall Nicoll of Page Street in December 1756, and 'A maiden of Mr John Nicoll buried March 14 1667'. Many do not even have their full names being described as 'mother of John Nicoll' or 'wife of Randall Nicoll'. Paul, the Justice of the Peace mentioned above was buried June 9 1682. In these entries various Nicoll residences are given including the house called 'Cookes'.

In 1696 Thomas Nicoll built and endowed six almshouses for the poor of the Parish next to the *Angel & Crown* public house. It also appears that Thomas Nicoll had some work done on the houses in 1751. This inn was demolished in 1965 but the almshouses which are in Milespit Hill are still standing.

The graveyard in Hendon Parish Church contains the remains of many Nicolls. E T Evans in his book quoted a number of these and at that time many of the names were readable. With the passage of time (another century has nearly passed) this is becoming more difficult. The first Nicoll to be buried in the family tomb was Randall Nicoll who died during the Commonwealth, followed by his son, also Randall. There is also Lieut Col Thomas Nicoll of the 70th Regiment of Foot and his wife: he died in 1824 and his wife in 1808. The last interment in this tomb was in 1882, a Mrs Emma Mary Nicoll. Elsewhere in the cemetery is the grave of another branch of the family, Nicolls of The Hyde with another string of names. Yet another grave contains the remains of the Nicolls of Highwood Hill.

Apart from the positions of authority the Nicolls were also active with various charitable works. The Hendon Churchwarden's accounts for 1676 list Randall Nicoll as a subscriber to a relief for the people of Northampton.

Mr Nicoll-Hodgson mentioned above was the last direct descendant to occupy Copt Hall although in effect the name Nicoll, at least of this branch of the family had already become extinct. Towards the end of the 19th Century the house passed to Mrs C R Hodgson, the only daughter of Thomas Nicoll. In 1959 the house was demolished and replaced by a block of flats, a very sad end to 600 years of irreplaceable heritage and an ancient family home. The administrators of the estate of Mr Nicoll-Hodgson disposed of the entire contents of the house and garden by auction on September 22/3 1920.

In many ways it is strange that a family name with as many

branches as the Nicolls which had survived for over 500 years, has died out. They were of great influence in the district for centuries in just about every walk of life, both in commerce and with the Church. They owned a great deal of property and were responsible for the building of at least five important houses. Two of these were always owned by members of the family; Copt Hall and Cookes. One property had passed in direct line through eight generations and six of these consecutively were named John. The last John had only one daughter as heir to whom he left £100,000.

THE BRENT FAMILY

The map maker Norden considered that the River Brent took its name from the family of that name but this is discounted as nonsense by the historian Fuller who considered it to be much more likely that the family took its name from the river (see *Roads, Lanes, Paths and Tracks*).

This family can however be traced without difficulty back to the 13th Century. Fulke de Braint, a courtier of King John and Henry III's most successful general, and his family, were considerable land owners at that time. One of his descendants, William le Braint acquired some of the Manorial land from Robert le Rous, the remainder was assigned to Robert de Hamstede and his wife Marsilla. In 1285 these lands were vested in William le Brent and a charter held by the British Museum confirms this. The translation reads, 'Let it be known to all that may see or hear the present letters that I, son of Robert de Hamstede, by the consent and will of Marsilla my wife have granted, remised and wholly quit claim for us and our heirs for ever to William le Brent and his heirs. . .' These lands were apparently in the area now known as The Hyde.

King John, in a bid to ensure Fulke's loyalty, gave him in marriage Margaret, the daughter of his chamberlain Walter Fitzgerald who was the widow of Baldwin de Rivers. This act was not approved of, least of all by the intended bride because she considered him to be beneath her station in life.

Unfortunately Fulke was too good as a general and literally did himself out of a job by bringing order wherever there was a problem or an uprising. The most important 'adventure' in which Fulke was involved was the battle of Lincoln in the first 'Barons' War' in May 1217. In this skirmish the future King Louis VIII of France with the barons besieged Lincoln Castle. The King's men, approaching from the north-west were shown a bricked-up door in the wall which was reopened. The besiegers were amassed in the open space between the castle and the cathedral.

They were attacked and broken and fled down the steep streets to the lower town. The counter attacks raised by the French and the barons were repelled and within a few hours half of the knights (about 300) of the rebel army had been captured, and the rest fled in all directions. This almost bloodless victory was achieved as if merely taking part in a tournament.

After Lincoln, Fulke tried to keep the pot boiling by stirring up further strife, but the people were tired of civil unrest and refused to become embroiled. For this and various other crimes, including acts of robbery, kidnap and murder (which would have earned a lesser man summary execution) he was banished for ever. He lived out his days in Italy in total obscurity and died in miserable circumstances a couple of years later.

In *Court Roll No 1* of Edward IV (1461-1483) there is an entry stating that John Breynte Senior obtained a demise of land from the Lord of the Manor for 60 years at an annual rent of £40. On his death a few years later another entry admits his son John as heir. During the reign of Henry VIII Richard Brentt obtained the copyhold of land surrendered by Richard Foster, and during the same reign William and Agnes Brent obtained further lands surrendered by Richard Foster.

The names Breynte, Breynt, Brentt, Braint, Breant, and Brent (they are one and the same family) continue to appear in the *Court Rolls* for centuries, for instance Aleyn Breant died in 1548 and we can tell from his will that he was a considerable landowner. The simplest and most straightforward spelling of the name, Brent, does not occur in records until 1669. Most of the entries are concerned with transfer of land copyhold.

There are also mentions of the Brent family in the *Session Rolls* (details of criminal offences), for instance:

14 January, 10 Elizabeth (January 14 1568)

True Bill that, at Hendon on the said day, Thomas Lane, late of London, yeoman, stole five sheep, worth twenty shillings of the goods and chattels of William Brent and another sheep worth five shillings of the goods and chattels of Joan Brent. Putting himself 'Guilty', Thomas Lane was sentenced to be hung; but at a subsequent gaol delivery he produced the Queen's Pardon of his felony, under the Great Seal dated at Gorhambury, 29 March, 10 Eliz.

In other places there are records of sheep stealing, having sub-tenants in excess of the licensed number and even for destroying boundary stones.

There do not appear to be any identifiable Brent descendants in existence today or if they are they are not resident in the district. The last actual name in full of which there is a record is Christopher Paris Brent who appeared in a *List of the Gentry of Middlesex* of 1664. He was probably the head of the local family. The last entries show property of about five acres (2ha) at Highwood in 1756 and some land at Holcombe Hill in 1792, which were owned by a man named Braint. Fuller in his book *Worthies of Middlesex* published in 1662 said that the importance of the family had (already) declined.

THE MARSH FAMILY

This is another family whose members could not decide the correct spelling of their name. The earliest reference is in the late 15th Century during the reign of Edward IV, when John Mersh acquired copyhold on a parcel of land at The Hale. In the next 200 years we have Mersche, Mershe, Marshe, Mersh and finally Marsh.

Another ancient reference to the Marsh family is in a survey of the Manor of Hendon carried our for Sir Edward Herbert in 1574. In it we read 'by presentations of the homage' on October 19 1574, and among the freeholders who gave information were Robert Marsh and Richard Nicoll, of Mill Hill who were both styled 'customery tenants of the Right Worshipful Sir Edward Herbert' In the same manuscript Richard Marsh is scheduled as 'holding a parcel of tenement called Grauntes, being a messuage, one garden and three crofts, by estimation 10 acres and renteth yearly to the lord 12s 7d and payeth for service 4d'. This Richard Marsh died in 1615. A wall brass in St Mary's Hendon records 'Here lyeth buried ye body of Richard Marsh, yeoman, late of this parish'.

In the will of another Marsh, John Marsh of Myles-pitt there was a reference to William Marsh of Mill Hill. The historian Denoon considered it likely that it was the widow of William Marsh, Agnes, who successfully charged a yeoman of London named Thomas Brewer with highway robbery (at Hampstead in 1618) of a mare valued £7 and 4 shillings in minted money. Brewer had been convicted before and was therefore condemned to death and hanged.

In May 1618 Thomas Baker of Hendon and Edward Marsh of Hampstead stood as sureties for Robert Marsh of Hendon to appear before the Middlesex Justices charged with 'Touchinge the unlawfull huntinge in his Majesties Park called Hide Parke'. Another Marsh, Thomas, was appointed Collector in 1647, so that by the 17th Century the family had settled with today's spelling of the name.

The *Parish Registers* have numerous entries of lands owned by the

Marsh family, for instance in the 17th Century alone we find The Hale 1653, Page Street 1655, Mill Hill 1658, Button Hole 1660, etc. Other Marsh's are recorded as far away as Edmonton and we can assume therefore that Marsh is a very old Middlesex name.

At the beginning of the 19th Century the Marsh's were still of some influence. *Cooke's Survey* gives details of a number of properties owned by John Marsh, one more or less in Marsh Lane at Leveretts Close by Hankin Lane. Thereafter the position changed. In 1825 William Marsh owned land at Highwood near to the *Rising Sun* public house, but later in the same year he was declared bankrupt and his property was vested in Cuthbert Marsh. Nine years later John and Thomas Marsh surrendered land at Upper Hale and elsewhere to the Rev. Thomas Saddler, and a further nine years saw the surrender of nearly all the land held in the Manor by Thomas, John, and Jane Marsh to cover a debt.

By this time the family was not a shadow of its former self in influence and prestige. There is some evidence of two brothers as being the last to hold any of the old lands: Joseph a wheelwright and his younger brother an apprentice saddler were joint owners of some land in Hendon. These were the last of the once extensive lands owned by the family.

THE FRANKLYN FAMILY

This family also appears to have become extinct. The last member seems to have died at the end of the 18th Century. This man was appointed to the ancient title of Reeve in May 1754. It would seem that the title in effect died with him because we can find no later reference to this office. The Reeve was the chief magistrate of the district; its steward or bailiff.

Earlier in the reign of Elizabeth, in the *Court Rolls* of 1564, William Franklyn was admitted tenant and heir of the lands of his cousin Goditha Franklyn. Later the same man was prosecuted for closing a right-of-way, and because he failed to appear in court he was fined 10 shillings for contempt. It seems that nothing has changed, we are still battling to keep the same footpaths open over 200 years later.

The family resided at Highwood Hill. Evidence of this comes from the burial notice of Peter Franklyn of Highwood on August 9 1655, and of a piece of land admitted to the family measuring seven poles by 22 feet at Highwood. A few years later in 1664 George Franklyn, presumably related, paid out with John Marsh the sum of £35 for repairs to the Parish Church at Hendon.

THE WISE FAMILY

This family is another of those perpetuated in the name of a local lane. They do not however seem to have been of particular influence or significance for as long as many other Mill Hill families.

The first record of the Wise family (but spelt Wyse) dates back to 1584. *Court Rolls* from 1633 give frequent references to its member's appointments to official positions, e.g.:

1642	G Wyse	Constable
1642	E Wyse	Headborough
1663	Ennis Wyse of Dole Street	Constable for the North
1679	Thomas Wyse	Constable
679	G Wyse	Collector

In 1859 a list of church fees for the parish church at Hendon was published giving all the charges at that time. These include marriages, baptisms, and deaths and costs relevant to them. The list was authorized by Theodore Williams, vicar, and Jonathan Sparks and John Wise, churchwardens. Assuming that John is of the same family they still occupied official positions as late as the middle of the 19th Century.

CHAPTER XXI

ARTS AND ARTISTS
IN MILL HILL

I f we confine ourselves strictly to the boundaries of Mill Hill and to a narrow view of the arts then the direct associations with Mill Hill are rather limited. It is reasonable to assume however that the important and notable people who lived or worked just outside Mill Hill crossed into Mill Hill, even if only occasionally, and in any case some could see Mill Hill because of its lofty perch. Amongst the famous people who lived or worked not far from Mill Hill are some that we cannot ignore, for instance David Garrick, Oliver Goldsmith, George Frederick Handel, and Will Hay.

In The Arts in Mill Hill we are therefore concerned with people who have over the centuries had connections with the Mill Hill area. There have been various societies in Mill Hill in the field of arts, and for that matter still are, and in the brochure advertising Mill Hill Village mention was made of 'other local societies, both dramatic and musical'. We do not know which societies they were referring to, but it is interesting that a location with a population as small as Mill Hill was able to boast a dramatic society as early as 1910.

The people who have been included do not follow any particular pattern. They are from various aspects of the arts and cover two centuries, and we would like to think that each one has in some way contributed towards the making of Mill Hill as it is today.

MRS MARY ANNE PORTER

It is not known with any degree of certainty when Mary Porter was born; she died in 1765. She was an actress of some standing and was renowned for a particular type of role and was one of many of the period. Mary had been on the stage since she was a child so had considerable experience when she was asked to understudy the celebrated actress Elizabeth Barry. Eventually Mary took over her tragic parts. Mary Porter was a pupil of the actor and dramatist Thomas Betterton.

As a mature actress Mary Porter was considered by many of her contemporaries to have the ideal voice and bearing for the major tragic roles of the day and was named The Queen of Tragedy. She was tall and had a deep resonant voice which made her quite unsuitable for any kind of comic part. One of the critics considered her performance of Belvidera in

Otway's *Venice Preserv'd* to be the best interpretation of the part and was by all accounts in raptures about it. When passion was called for Mrs Porter could stir the coldest audience, but was equally effective in putting across grief and tenderness. Her first appearance was in the *Lincoln's Inn Fields Theatre* in 1699 and her last at Covent Garden in 1742. Among her original parts were Hermione in the *Distressed Mother*, and Alicia in *Jane Shore*. She is also known for her portrayals of Jessica in *The Merchant of Venice*, Desdemona in *Othello*, Portia in *Julius Caesar* and the *Duchess of Malfi*, the key role in the 1623 tragedy by John Webster. Many of Mary's performances were at the Drury Lane and Haymarket Theatres.

In her private life Mrs Porter was a quiet, and very respectable lady. After her last performance, she enjoyed a long retirement in association with her many friends at her home at Moat Mount. Mary Porter could also be very generous and understanding and an anecdote is related about her which tells a great deal about her character. Because many past writers appear to think that this tale is just as important as her acting successes we will repeat it here.

Some time in 1731 after a performance at *The Playhouse* Mrs Porter was driving to her home. It was her custom to drive home every night. On the way she was stopped by a footpad who demanded money. Because she knew that her servant was riding a distance behind she drew a pistol and levelled it at the aspiring robber. He broke down, and assured her that he was not a bandit by choice but only because he needed money to feed his starving family. The man's tears and emotional behaviour assured Mrs Porter that she had nothing to fear and rather than hand him over to the authorities and certain death she gave him 10 guineas on the spot and also promised to help him still further if he would say where he lived. At this point her servant arrived on the scene and the man ran off down a pathway between the fields.

Mrs Porter gave the horse a smart flick with the whip which caused the animal to run off the track. The carriage overturned and Mary's thigh was fractured. She was carried to her home in great pain where she lay for a considerable time. Eventually the bone healed but without the advantages of modern surgery she had a pronounced limp for the rest of her life and from that time acting was very difficult. This did not prevent her from fulfilling her promise to the footpad. She set him on his feet by sending him over £60 that she had collected from her friends, a very considerable sum in those days.

GEORGE FREDERICK HANDEL

Handel is considered by many to be one of the greatest English composers, in spite of being born in Germany, and without doubt much of his music is played more frequently and is more popular here than anywhere else. Handel was born in Halle in 1685, (the same year as J S Bach) the son of a barber-surgeon who intended that he would become a lawyer. Handel's early clandestine studies did not last long and he became a pupil of the organist of Halle, Zacheus. At 17 he was appointed organist of the cathedral but after only one year he left for Hamburg. He then played violin and harpsichord in the local opera house, but in 1706 he was

at Canons Park

Handel wrote two dramatic works

invited to go to Italy, which he accepted, and then spent over three years there.

Handel left Italy in 1710 and returned to Germany, this time to Hanover where he was appointed Kapellmeister, but almost at once requested leave to attend an appointment in London where his opera *Rinaldo* was being produced (early 1711). He returned to Hanover but applied for leave again and returned to London in the Autumn of 1712. Queen Anne commissioned Handel to write a *Te Deum* for the peace of Utrecht in 1713 and bestowed a pension on him. This time Handel deserted his German masters and transferred his affections to London where he lived for the rest of his life.

Unfortunately Queen Anne died the following year, 1714, and with a touch of unexpected irony the new king, George I, was his old employer. Luckily he was forgiven and the royal patronage was reaffirmed.

In 1717 Handel entered the service of the Earl of Carnarvon (he became the Duke of Buckingham and Chandos) who was at that time building his great mansion at Canons Park near Edgware. At Canons Park Handel wrote two dramatic works as well as 11 anthems for the modest orchestra and choir that was always retained there. Handel played on the organ in the church of St Lawrence Whitchurch (which had been rebuilt by the Duke). At that time he was Master of Music to the Duke.

Handel was a great extrovert, he enjoyed company and the society of the period which included such famous people as Congreve, Pope, Prior and Swift, but musical genius in England was a bit thin.

Today few people with any claim to culture could say that they are totally ignorant of Handel's greatest work, the *Messiah*. The man and this particular piece of music will live for ever. At the first performance in London (the premier was in Dublin) which was performed at the *Covent Garden Theatre*, Handel said of the *Hallelujah Chorus*, 'I think I did see all heaven before me, and the great God Himself'. The chorus had such a dramatic effect upon the audience that to a man they stood, with the King setting the example. A precedent maintained to this day.

The text for the *Messiah* was given to Handel by Jennens and the whole composition was completed in 23 days during August and September 1741. It was an amazing achievement even though the Messiah contains some re-worked passages composed earlier. Jennens said at the time that he was disgusted with the way that it had been hurried and would never trust Handel with another sacred work. Little did he know about the future that it held.

After *Messiah* other oratorios followed; *Samson, Judas Maccabaeus,* and *Jephtha* but none of these has ever enjoyed the same fame or popularity. Handel had given his inspired best and by now was a very weary man. At this time a tragedy struck him, he started to go blind, and eventually he lost his sight completely.

In spite of his terrible affliction, which was to him as bad as Beethoven's deafness half a century later, Handel still played the organ and conducted his own works. At one performance many of the audience were reduced to tears at the sight of the blind musician at the organ whilst the *Samson* aria was sung:

> *Total eclipse - no sun, no moon:*
> *All dark amid the blaze of noon.*

On April 6 1759 the *Messiah* was performed at Covent Garden to end the season. Handel conducted his great work but was carried from the hall in a faint. In less than a week he was dead.

Handel was a great traveller and philanthropist. In 1726 he became a naturalised Englishman. When Handel died he was buried in Westminster Abbey; the man and his music had become thoroughly English.

OLIVER GOLDSMITH

Oliver Goldsmith lived in what would now be part of Edgware, to be precise in a house at Canon's Park just off the Edgware Road. He took up residence there in 1768, in as much as he lived anywhere as a permanence. He was born on November 10 1728 in Co. Longford Ireland, the son of a clergyman. His early education was at various schools and at one of these he was infected with smallpox which disfigured him for life.

In 1744 he was accepted as a sizar (student paying reduced fees) by Trinity College Dublin, but unfortunately he came into conflict with a tutor and left in 1746. A friend induced him to return and he graduated BA in 1749.

Against his wishes the Church was chosen for him as a profession but when he presented himself to the Bishop of Elphin (in totally unsuitable clothes) he was rejected. He next became a tutor but when he had saved £30 he gave this up and spent his little savings. A long suffering uncle paid for him to go to London to study law but he only got as far as Dublin where he was fleeced once again. He then returned home to his mother's house, she was now a widow with a large family.

A period of idleness was followed by studying medicine at Edinburgh University until 1754 when he left there too, and went to Leyden in the Netherlands. After a year he left here too and started on a walking tour which took him to France, Germany, Switzerland and Italy. Apart from busking (he was quite an accomplished flautist) it is hard to see how he made a living or even paid his way because he departed from Leyden penniless. On his travels he is believed to have obtained a degree in medicine, probably in Italy, he also of course accumulated a vast store of experience and knowledge which proved to be invaluable for his literary endeavours which came later.

In 1756 Goldsmith reached London, once again without any money. Here he took on various jobs including paupers' doctor, apothecary's journeyman, and school usher.

The year 1757 saw the start of his literary career when he obtained a regular commission with the *Monthly Review*. In 1759 came his first important literary venture, *An Enquiry into the State of Polite Learning in Europe* which although published anonymously attracted some attention. This brought him other work and he obtained commissions from various periodicals. In 1761 Goldsmith met and became a friend of Johnson which led to introductions to others of his circle and membership of the *Literary Club*. A number of works followed, not very well known today but in 1766 his novel *The Vicar of Wakefield* was a success and has remained so.

In 1768 Goldsmith went into a temporary retreat in a cottage described as 'eight miles up the Edgware Road at the back of Canon's'. A Goldsmith biographer described it as 'very small with absurd decorations', but we don't know how small was small. He named it his 'Shoemaker's

Paradise' which was an association with something in his past, a 'Shoemaker's Holiday' or country jaunt to which he had been particularly partial. It is also believed that the house had been built by a follower of St Crispin, the patron saint of shoe-makers, which strengthened the nickname. The builder had apparently decorated the garden most inappropriately with flying Mercuries, fountains and other unsuitable ornaments. The whole place was something under 0.25ha. Goldsmith and his friend Bott would drive madly down to the retreat at Canon's often late at night. When the gig overturned, which it did only too frequently, Bott would lecture Goldsmith on cause and effect.

In 1771 Goldsmith withdrew to an even more remote retreat and lodged at Hyde House Farm on the borders of Hendon and Kingsbury. He took a single room meaning to be undisturbed to write a comedy. Always his behaviour was eccentric, although he boarded with the family he usually took his meals in his own room. At other times he would stand in the kitchen with his back to the fire, apparently miles away in thought, then suddenly dash off, presumably to commit some idea to paper.

When the mood took him Goldsmith would disappear to the fields, either to wander about endlessly or just sit under a hedge thinking. Sometimes he would vanish for days or even weeks at a time either to London or farther afield to visit friends. Evidently the family were very fond of him and although they considered him to be odd they referred to him as 'The Gentleman'. Goldsmith was apparently so happy

Oliver Goldsmith usually wore his collar open

here that he gave up a summer visit to Lincolnshire that had been proposed by Joshua Reynolds.

When indoors Goldsmith usually wore his collar open, nothing unusual about this now but in the 18th Century it just was not done. There is a portrait of him by Sir Joshua Reynolds in this casual mode. At night he read a lot, often into the small hours, at other times when he could not sleep he would lie in bed with the candle burning, which if not within reach would be extinguished by hurling his slipper at it: it is a wonder that he wasn't burnt to death along with anyone who happened to be in the house at the time.

When Goldsmith had visitors the parlour was given over to them. These included such celebrities as Dr Johnson, David Garrick, Sir Joshua

Reynolds, and Sir William Chambers. In 1771 Boswell paid a visit with a friend but unfortunately Goldsmith was not at home and in fact about that time he gave up the Hyde House lodging. It had been the creative home of the comic masterpiece *She Stoops to Conquer*, which was apparently inspired by an event in Goldsmith's youth.

That Garrick and Goldsmith became great friends is well known. An anecdote about the two has been related in various biographies which was originally taken from *Memoirs of Haydon* in which Sir Joshua's younger niece said;

'The most delightful man was Goldsmith. I saw him and Garrick keep an immense party laughing till they shrieked. Garrick sat on Goldsmith's knee; a table cloth was pinned under Garrick's chin, and brought behind Goldsmith, hiding both their figures. Garrick then spoke, in his finest style, Hamlet's speech to his father's ghost; Goldsmith put out his hands on each side of the cloth, and made burlesque action, tapping his heart and putting his hand to Garrick's head and nose, all at the wrong time'.

When *She Stoops to Conquer* was produced Goldsmith was 45, after which he published three more works, all in 1774. These were all totally different: *The Retaliation, The History of Greece*, and *Animated Nature*. In the same year he caught a fever and worn out with anxiety and chronic over-work he died.

Goldsmith's friends included some of the greatest and best of the land at that time. No doubt he was often the butt of their jokes but they obviously loved him. When they heard of his death Burke burst into tears, Reynolds painted no more that day and Johnson wrote the famous epitaph, *'Nullum tetigit quod non ornavit'* (He touched nothing he did not adorn). The stair to his lodging was crowded with the old, the poor, and the outcasts as well as the rich and famous. The poor wept for the benefactor who never refused to share what ever he had, often little enough, with anyone who asked. The rich and famous cried for the special friend that they had lost. Analysed today much of what he wrote is of little merit, except that it has a certain charm of style that is the essential Goldsmith. He wrote at high pressure, often literally to keep the wolf from the door: to buy his daily bread and to keep away the debt collectors.

DAVID GARRICK

Garrick's connection with Mill Hill began in 1756 when he purchased The Manor and Benefice of Hendon for £13,381 (see also the *History of Private Property)*. The Manor House now Hendon Hall, which has been an hotel for many years, has in its times seen many changes. As Lord of the Manor of Hendon, Garrick is reputed to have lived there in great style until 1778.

David Garrick, surely one of England's greatest actors was born in the *Angel Inn* in Hereford on February 20 1716 and was the son of Capt. Peter Garrick of the Buffs (3rd Foot). According to Burke he 'raised the character of his profession to the rank of a liberal art'. Garrick who was of Huguenot descent showed an aptitude for the stage very early in life having his first part in a schoolboy production when he was at Lichfield Grammar School. He studied under Dr Johnson at Lichfield and travelled with him to London and took part in amateur theatricals at the expense of a business career in the wine trade, which was soon abandoned.

Garrick was responsible for many theatrical reforms that are still with us, the most important being stage lighting which was concealed from the audience, and banning the audience from the stage, which was long overdue.

In the 17th Century many of Shakespeare's texts were altered and rewritten, often changing the story line completely. Garrick is credited with having restored the plays to the original but this should be treated with reserve because he was also guilty of some shameful 'corrected' versions of his own. For instance his *Hamlet* had no grave-diggers, his *King Lear* had no fool, and in his *Romeo and Juliet* the lovers were permitted a tender scene in the tomb before dying. Before being unduly critical of these

Garrick's connection with Mill Hill

so called improvements however it should be remembered that in those times a play had to be produced in a manner that would be acceptable to the audience if it was to be successful. In the 18th Century much of the genius of Shakespeare was not appreciated by theatre audiences.

When Garrick died he was buried in Westminster Abbey, and it is said that the carriages carrying the mourners reached from the Abbey to the Strand. Many of his friends felt that it was a personal loss, and Dr Johnson wrote the profound epitaph 'I am disappointed by that stroke of death which has eclipsed the gaiety of nations and impoverished the public stock of harmless pleasure'.

Unfortunately Garrick had many enemies, not all his own fault, even though it is acknowledged that he was vain, a frightful snob, and possessed a violent temper. He had a reputation for meanness, but this was encouraged by Samuel Foote one of his bitterest critics, so can be taken with a pinch of salt. His quarrels were legendary but were often caused by the petulance of unknown actors for whom he had found no part and authors whose works he considered unworthy of production.

From 1763 to 1765 Garrick travelled widely on the continent with his wife Eva Marie Violetti, a dancer of the *Haymarket* whom he had married in 1749. He was received in style everywhere that he went, particularly in France.

Both the *Garrick Club* and the *Garrick Theatre* in London were named after him. Joshua Reynolds painted Garrick many times but the portrait that Mrs Garrick considered to be the best was by Gainsborough (painted in 1766) but unfortunately this was destroyed in 1946 by the fire which gutted the Town Hall of Stratford-upon-Avon.

NATHANIEL HONE

Hone came originally from Dublin but settled in England and painted portraits. Much of his work was miniatures and on enamel. He had the good fortune to marry a lady of some wealth and this enabled him to spend two years in Italy. After this he settled in London and became a frequent visitor to Mill Hill. He became a founder member of the Royal Academy and was a regular exhibitor until his death in 1784. Hone was also an Associate of the Florentine Academy of Arts.

In 1775 Hone submitted a painting called *The Conjuror* which depicted a conjuror who looked remarkably like Sir Joshua Reynolds and is pointing with a wand to prints by Michelangelo, Maratta, Pietro da Cortona and various others, which quite clearly hinted at plagiarism. There was also a young woman, and Angelica Kauffmann considered herself to have been impugned and misrepresented and therefore maligned. At the time the actual relationship between Angelica and Hone was a matter for speculative debate.

Angelica petitioned the Council (she was in fact a founder member of the RA) and the painting was rejected, although it was subsequently exhibited elsewhere. The picture, which is now in Dublin, was rediscovered in 1944, and it is quite clear that the imputations have to be accepted.

In another painting a part was considered to be a profane illusion so was also rejected by the committee. Hone painted this out, but with an easily soluble material, and in 1775 the work was re-exhibited in its original form in a private exhibition.

There are other paintings by Hone in London, notably in the *National Portrait Gallery*, and the *Victoria and Albert*, and also in Birmingham, Cardiff, Leeds, Manchester and Oxford. Hone died aged 66 and was buried in Hendon on August 20 1784. His five children are buried with him.

ABRAHAM RAIMBACH

Another Mill Hill artist, although of a different discipline was Abraham Raimbach the engraver. He was associated with the Mill Hill district at the beginning of the 19th Century. He was born in 1776 and although he lived much of his life in a house in Fitzroy Square (where all his greatest works were executed) he is buried in the churchyard of St Mary's Hendon.

Raimbach's father Peter came to England from Switzerland as a boy of 12 and never left the Country. He married the daughter of a Warwickshire farmer. As a young infant Abraham fell from the arms of a nurse and out of a second floor window. It is said that he escaped serious injury, partly because his voluminous clothes inflated and also because he fell on some lights which broke his fall.

At 13 years old his father apprenticed him to J Hall the engraver having decided that he already showed signs of artistic ability. Two others had however refused to take him. When his apprenticeship was completed Raimbach entered as a student in the Royal Academy, and simultaneously began to take on freelance work for book publishers. At this time there were no cameras therefore all the illustrations in books had to be line engravings, and in any case the technology for reproducing half-tone pictures had not been invented.

It had now become difficult for Raimbach to decide how his art should develop: he was equally good as an engraver or painter of miniatures. He decided on the former. In 1802 he took advantage of the temporary peace with France and visited the Louvre. In 1802 he married and moved to the house in Fitzroy Square mentioned above.

In the same year Raimbach met the painter Sir David Wilkie and they became great friends. In 1812 he became Wilkie's engraver and produced many fine works after Wilkie paintings. Among these are *Village Politicians, Rent Day (*published in 1816), *The Cut Finger, The Errand Boy*, and *Spanish Mother and Child*. His works are exhibited in Edinburgh, London (*The Tate Gallery, The Wallace Collection, Well-*

ington Museum), Munich, New York and elsewhere.

Raimbach never employed an assistant and always completed the entire plate himself, *Rent Day* took him 2½ years during which he did no other work. He died on January 17 1843 and unlike many artists of the time he was by then well off. His autobiography was published posthumously the same year by his son.

HOLBROOK JACKSON

Hammers Lane was the home for some years of this man of such varied learning. Holbrook Jackson was born in Liverpool on the last day of 1874. He is now nearly forgotten by almost every shade of historian. He died in June 1948.

Jackson was almost entirely self taught, which in no way inhibited his output. He began to earn his living at the age of 15 and had his first articles published one year later. He wrote a number of critical studies, the first on Edward Fitzgerald (in 1899), then on George Bernard Shaw and William Morris. His titles include *Great English Novelists, The Eighteen Nineties, Occasions, End Papers, The Anatomy of Bibliomania* (probably his best known work), *The Printing of Books, Bookman's Holiday,* and *The Reading of Books.* His last title was *Dreamers of Dreams* in 1948. Jackson had a great sense of fun and edited and wrote the forward to the Faber edition of *The Complete Nonsense of Edward Lear.*

In addition to his books Jackson also worked as a freelance writer and in 1907 became joint editor of *New Age,* he also edited *TP's Magazine* and *TP's Weekly* (TP = T P O'Connor) and his own literary journal, *Today.* There is no hard evidence as to whether O'Connor (The Rt Hon Thomas Power O'Connor MP 1848-1929) actually came to Mill Hill or not, however as a friend and associate of Jackson this is more than likely. O'Connor was the founder and first editor of *The Star, The Sun,* etc and also wrote a number of books including *A Life of Beaconsfield* and *Life of Parnell.*

It is a trifle ironic that Gladstone and O'Connor both have connections with Mill Hill. O'Connor was an MP when Gladstone was PM but they had little else in common. O'Connor was a member of the (Irish) National League, a society pledged to fight for Home Rule, which was opposed by a majority of the British people (particularly the Protestants of Ulster) and bitterly so by Queen Victoria, she regarded such discussions as treason. At this time Parnell (who was not a Catholic) was considered to be the uncrowned king of Ireland but his adultery with the wife of another MP, Capt O'Shea, and the subsequent messy divorce case set some of the Irish people, and particularly the Catholic clergy against him. By this time Gladstone was in favour of Home Rule but the disgrace of Parnell and his fall from power set Irish aspirations back another 30 years.

Jackson was a great walker of the Mill Hill district and was often to be found in the *Three Hammers* public house talking with great enthusiasm to anyone who cared to listen.

DANIEL GEORGE

George was another literary man, but in a rather local sense and he is also almost forgotten. The main interest to us is that he wrote of a country walk through Arkley and Mill Hill. The writing was called *Tomorrow Will be Different* and is a dry and humorous account in free verse with much literary allusion.

Other works consisted mainly of literary criticism and anthologies. George lived in Laurel Cottage in Hammers Lane.

NORMAN G BRETT-JAMES

Brett-James was a local schoolmaster and historian and a familiar figure in Mill Hill in the 1930s. His books are on Mill Hill, Mill Hill School and Peter Collinson. Unfortunately he seems to have repeated errors contained in earlier writings by other authors and in some cases taken legend as fact. His book on Collinson particularly should be read with caution: the official biography in the Royal Society says 'Brett-James biography is marred with inaccuracy and should be supplemented'. It almost seems at times that Brett-James wrote down events as he would have liked them to have happened rather than what actually occurred, or at least repeated the errors of earlier historians without attempting to verify them.

In spite of these doubts regarding fact, Brett-James books are still worth reading, but unfortunately copies are very difficult to obtain. Little has been written over the years specifically about Mill Hill and his interest and enthusiasm for the district comes over in his writings.

MARK LEMON

Lemon was born in London in 1809 and became well known in Mill Hill and the vicinity. He was for a time the manager of a brewery before taking up a literary career. He wrote over 60 plays (including farces and melodramas) as well as some novels and many songs. He even wrote operas. Lemon contributed to *Household Words* and various other periodicals and was editor of the *Family Herald* and *Once a Week*.

Today Lemon is best remembered as one of the founders of *Punch* when it first appeared in 1841. He was joint editor in the early days and sole editor from 1843 until he died in 1870. Lemon's best known novel is *Falkner Lyle* which he wrote in 1866, others are *Leyton Hall* and *Loved at Last*. He also lectured and gave public readings and wrote children's stories, his *Jest Book* was published in 1864. Alas, after just over 150 years Punch is no more. Have we lost our sense of humour and satire or is today's appeal for something cruder and more simplistic? It is unfair to generalise, but we do know that no buyer could be found for the ailing magazine because no-one thought that it had a future any longer.

WILL HAY

The comedian and actor Will Hay was born in Scotland in 1888, he made his mark on the stage and transferred his character of the incompetent

Will Hay...lived in the White House

schoolmaster successfully to films. In is true but hard to believe that anyone born after 1930 cannot really remember World War II in any detail, it is a subject for the history books. Will Hay and many entertainers of his time had to do their bit during the war years to keep up moral by poking fun not only at the establishment but also at the enemy. They were always coming to grips with secret agents and spies, quislings and fifth columnists, and these people were always portrayed as not very bright. It was a light-hearted look at the seriousness of war.

Will Hay appeared in many films (often with the same actors) and these have now become classics in their own right. These films are still funny today without necessarily appreciating that there was a double meaning to the script. The Will Hay character was usually the same, an uninformed, bumbling and slightly seedy schoolmaster who went from one chaotic scene to another, and was then rescued by the boys. In *The Ghost of St Michael's,* a typical Will Hay film, he presides over his school which has been evacuated to the Isle of Skye. Ably assisted by his partner of many films the chinless, loopy Claude Hulbert they stumble from one calamity to another. But of course they come out on top in the end.

Will Hay was also a knowledgeable and enthusiastic amateur astronomer and built an observatory in his back garden. For many years he lived in the White House, a rather elegant house on the Great North Way on the brow of the hill just up from Fiveways Junction. He was a great entertainer and often had lively dinner parties. The house is on the southern border of what was Copt Hall Park, the home of the Nicoll family and certainly visible from Mill Hill.

Will Hay died in 1949, still a relatively young man, but he had moved from the White House before that time.

JEAN SIMMONS

In 1956 the number one box office film was Goldwyn's *Guys and Dolls* which starred Brando, Sinatra, and Jean Simmons, but it failed to win an award. Jean Simmons had to wait until 1983 to win an Emmy for her part in *The Thorn Birds*.

Jean Simmons was born in London on January 31 1929, she was educated at Orange Hill School (later to be amalgamated with Moat Mount School to form Mill Hill County High School) and then at the Ada Foster School of Dancing. She was exceptionally pretty as a child and young woman and could always be relied upon to give a good performance but never became a symbol like many actresses of her time. Jean Simmons has been married twice, to Stewart Granger in 1950 and Richard Brooks in 1960.

At 13 came the first film appearance in *Give us the Moon* and minor parts in *Caesar and Cleopatra, The Way to the Stars* and others (1942- 1944). Jean Simmons has appeared in numerous British films including *Great Expectations, Black Narcissus, Hungry Hill, Hamlet, The Blue Lagoon, Life at the Top, Trio, Clouded Yellow,* and *The Grass is Greener.*

In 1950 Jean Simmons moved to America and the films of her American career include *Androcles and the Lion, Young Bess, Footsteps in the Fog, This Could be the Night, Divorce American Style, Spartacus, The Happy Ending,* and the two films mentioned above *Guys and Dolls,* and *The Thorn Birds.* She has also had some success with theatre and stage work.

CHAPTER XXII

HOUSES OF RELIGION

T here is certainly every opportunity for the people of Mill Hill to follow their religious pursuits, whatever they may be. Just about every aspect of Christian belief is catered for, (there are four Anglican churches, a church for Roman Catholics and a United Reformed church), there is a synagogue for the substantial Jewish community, Watchtower House on Bittacy Hill is the UK headquarters of the Jehovah's Witness movement and many other smaller sects have meeting places in Mill Hill too. In addition to all these there are also convent orders, St Joseph's Missionary College and Mill Hill School, each with its own chapel. The Christian churches of Mill Hill are without doubt a very ecumenical group, not only do they have all sorts of combined meetings, religious and otherwise, but they also issue a combined churches newsletter.

Whether we attend a place of worship regularly, seldom, or even at all today is a matter for own leanings and conscience. This has not always been the case and in the 16th Century there were many cases of people being prosecuted for 'not going to any usual place of Common Prayer'. There are a few recorded instances of people from Hendon being charged but none of these can be positively identified with Mill Hill. Perhaps they were excused, at least in winter time, because of the arduous nature of the walk. The usual punishment for repeated refusals appears to have been a fine and imprisonment. The punishment for attending the 'wrong' service could be much more severe.

The first church to be built in the Village was in fact designed as a community hall doubling as a non-Conformist church on Sundays. Richard Swift, one of the founder members of the first school for Dissenters held services there from 1662 to 1701. The building was absorbed into Mill Hill School on its foundation in 1807. The first two chapels built as part of the School catered for the public's needs as well but this facility had to be withdrawn when the number of pupils increased. At this time the Union Church was built.

ST JOSEPH'S COLLEGE

Probably the most important religious community in Mill Hill is St Joseph's College of the Sacred Heart with its entrance in Lawrence Street. The College was founded by Cardinal Vaughan in 1866 after touring extensively in America and elsewhere on a fund raising tour. He died in the College, and the building was erected to his memory. As befits such a memorial it can be seen for miles.

Between the apse and the cloister is a square campanile 30m high which is capped by a magnificent gilded bronze statue of St Joseph holding the infant Jesus. The foundation stone was laid by Cardinal Manning in June 1869, the first part of the College was opened in 1871, and the buildings were all complete by 1873. The architects were G Goldie and Child. The total area of the grounds is about 16ha.

St Joseph's College

Some people have considered the buildings to be rather dismal and with some justification. However it must be remembered that it is a monastic institution, and its purpose is to train priests for the foreign missions, a serious vocation.

The building material is mainly stock brick with some bands and ornamentation of contrasting black and red. The design has been called Venetian Gothic by some and Lombardo-Venetian by others. As is to be expected the most notable part of the whole College is the chapel which most would agree is exceptionally beautiful. This occupies one complete side of the court. The chapel has a main nave and aisles with side chapels and sanctuary. There is a quadrangle or cloister court surrounded by cloisters and a semi-circular apse with processional ambulatory.

When built the College was intended to house 60 students plus their tutors. On completion of their instructions the students are sent to any country that is considered to be missionary territory.

ST PAUL'S CHURCH

The Anglican church of St Paul on The Ridgeway is a rather indefinite style and has been described as Late English or Early Gothic. It does not have a lot to recommend it as far as the exterior architecture is concerned, however inside it is neat, roomy, generally unfussy and well cared for. The structure is of brick, later stuccoed and painted. There are small spires ornamenting the angles. The south doorways and the windows are lancet shaped, the style associated with Gothic. The appearance would have been improved by the addition of a spire or tower but no doubt finance was an important consideration. When built, St Paul's consisted of nave and chancel with a west gallery supported on slender cast iron columns.

The only item in the structure really worth a mention is a panel of painted glass that is in the centre of the east window. This is reputed to be a copy of a painting by Annibale Carracci (1560-1609), an artist who lived and worked in Bologna with a brother and cousin. The painting on glass in St Paul's was the work of Charles Muss and an associate. Fortunately for us it is signed, the only known piece of his work that is. Muss had various commissions from George IV.

An increase in the population of Mill Hill had led to requests for a Mill Hill church since the early 19th Century but there had been no firm developments. It would fill a much needed requirement in the Village but was the subject of a dispute between the parish priest of St Mary's Hendon the Rev. Theodore Williams, (an irritable and rather forceful domineering man who considered it to be unnecessary) and William Wilberforce. Obviously it would affect Williams' church collections, and in addition he stood to lose part of his income from pew rents. When Wilberforce first proposed the chapel it was to be built on his own estate, but Williams first tried to prevent it being built and when he failed in this, insisted it be moved further south to The Ridgeway and for him to be in control.

Unfortunately need was not the only issue. William Wilberforce, was the man largely responsible for the abolition of slavery and as stated elsewhere the vicar of Hendon was reputed to have had, via his family, a considerable income from the slave trade. Williams' main grouse was concerned with the financing of the building work. Wilberforce was supposed to have financed the project himself, but it is fairly certain that others assisted with the obviously considerable cost. As it was originally intended to be a family chapel private funding would seem possible, but would-be parishioners contributed because they wanted a church in the Village. Once built St Paul's became a Chapel of Ease for the Parish Church at the Burroughs.

The church was built in 1830 on land given by Sir Charles Flower Bart, which according to some sources was the site of an old gravel pit, and consecrated in June 1836, a few days after the death of the founder. The first incumbent was Joseph Brown MA.

Near to the west door, but tucked round the corner out of sight is a rather well executed oil painting of the Virgin and Child. It appears to be unsigned but the signature may well be obscured behind the frame. The rather handsome (and singularly appropriate) blue carpet that adorns the floor from the chancel step to the alter is a part of that used in Westminster for the Coronation of HM Queen Elizabeth II.

The second wife of Sir Stamford Raffles, Sophia, is buried in the churchyard. Raffles was interred in the churchyard of St Mary's Hendon.

A number of people have written about the church in rather disparaging ways. They have referred to inferior bricks made from clay from the Wilberforce estate, a poor structure, cheap, a typical church of its time, etc. There is of course some truth in these claims (there usually is) but considering that unlimited finance was not available and the intransigence of the local vicar the best was produced in the circumstances. And in any event the church has withstood the elements for 150 years in a most exposed spot remarkably well. It has to be admitted however that some of the protruding parts have crumbled and urgent repairs appear to be necessary. Presumably in the future the cost of repairs will escalate, cement rendering on brick is not the most durable of building materials and once moisture seeps into cracks the bricks are quickly affected.

The church house stands behind the row of cottages that are to the north of the Sheepwash Pond. It was intended that the church would be the centre of the Village, and by having the Parish Hall to the north and the school (St Paul's Church of England School) to the south it has achieved this.

UNION CHURCH (UNITED REFORMED)

This is situated right on Mill Hill Circus and is constructed entirely of red brick. The design is massive in style with a tower that somehow gives the impression that it started out to be a spire and then the architect changed his mind.

The most notable feature of the interior is the unusual decor. It has been described as friendly although this is not really strong enough, perhaps homely and inviting is better.

ST MICHAEL AND ALL ANGELS

This is now the Parish Church of Mill Hill although originally intended to be a Chapel of Ease for St Paul's on The Ridgeway. The first brick church was dedicated in 1909, this became the church hall when the chancel and first two bays of the permanent church were consecrated on the adjacent site. The church became the centre of a new parish, separate from St Paul's Mill Hill in 1926.

The interior is rich in detail. The church was designed by Herbert Passmore and the east window is by A E Buss. Building commenced in 1921, the sanctuary was consecrated in 1932 but the church was not completed until 1957 when end bays of the aisled nave and a chapel were added together with a baptistery, vestries and porches. The style is late 15th Century Perpendicular and in uncoursed ashlar. The chancel has a barrel roof.

THE CHURCH OF THE SACRED HEART AND IMMACULATE CONCEPTION

Anyone arriving in the 'new' Mill Hill, that is the area around Mill Hill Broadway cannot fail to notice this church. It stands at the junction of Flower Lane and The Broadway with the elevated front facing almost due north. It is built in the Byzantine style with stone pillars on brick. There is

a decorative wheel window on the front which is much admired. The church was dedicated by Cardinal Bourne in 1924.

Although the windows are high and not particularly large the inside is bright and light. Square, fluted, unfussy, columns with no apparent taper give a feeling of height, and the

... built in the Byzantine style

lattice design ceiling in red and white with small gold crosses is decoration enough for this style of building. The pews are good, solid, and comfortable and the risen Christ looks benevolently down upon the devout.

This church has a particular meaning to the author because it was in this church that he was received into the Catholic Faith in 1956.

JOHN KEBLE CHURCH

This striking church is on the very borders of Mill Hill and stands in Deans Lane. With the main door facing due west we have in this church a return to the strict east-west layout followed by all of all the early churches and cathedrals.

The style of the exterior is modern without giving the impression that it will 'date', in fact after more than 50 years it still looks new and fresh. The design was by D F Martin-Smith and the church which was completed in 1936 is of yellow brick on a reinforced concrete frame with a tower crowned with a gilded cross. There are little thoughtful embellishments such as the crosses that surmount the gate posts.

Inside it is rather splendid and certainly unusual. The architect was ahead of his time because his layout with the congregation surrounding the choir and priest became common many years later. The interior of white stone is bright yet peaceful. In many ways John Keble Church is one of the more

striking church on the very borders

notable in the district. The square plan and flat coffered ceiling creates an exceptionally spacious interior unencumbered with columns. The altar is set in a recess in the east wall and there is a western gallery. The only link with the past is the old corn mortar which serves as a font.

The new parish was formed out of St Michael's and all Angels and St Alphage Burnt Oak in 1932 and was intended to serve the area around The Hale. For the first six months worship was in a hut in Deans Lane and then in a dual purpose hall and church. This became the Parish hall when the permanent church was built.

THE QUAKERS OR SOCIETY OF FRIENDS

There is no Quaker meeting house in Mill Hill now, but their presence in Mill Hill in the past is of some importance.

George Fox, the founder of the Society of Friends as they are correctly called came to Mill Hill many times, certainly in 1677 and 1678 and the Society had been associated with Mill Hill from its very beginnings. It is difficult to put a precise date on the founding of the Society in Mill Hill but it is fairly certain that a meeting house had been established at Rosebank in the Village by 1650 or thereabouts.

Because of their interpretation of the Gospels and their devotion the Quakers were subjected to fierce opposition and persecution. The name 'Quaker' was originally intended to be derogatory and was given to Fox and his friends because he told Justice Bennett in Derby that they should tremble at the name of the Lord. Quaker soon passed into common usage and is to be found in the records of the House of Commons as early as 1654.

The accessibility of Mill Hill to London, in spite of its relative remoteness made it an ideal spot for a religious order that had to operate in a clandestine manner. The Quaker house Rosebank (see also *Important Buildings)* was erected on a site for which an annual rent of £5 was payable.

By the early 1680s there were regular meetings in Mill Hill but attendance declined towards the end of the decade, recovered again and in 1693 the house was extended, presumably because of the increase in membership. In 1709 it was proposed that in future two meetings per month should be held instead of one. However this state of affairs did not last and before long local support began to decline once again, indeed by the year 1740 only the burial ground was left in Quaker hands. In the 1730s Rosebank was sold.

Presbyterianism and other new non-Conformist religions probably contributed towards the decline of the Mill Hill Quaker movement. In 1730 Mary Nicoll's house on Highwood Hill was registered by seven Presbyterians led by Celia Fiennes. Later on in the 18th Century John Wesley started the Methodist religion.

Apparently no minutes of the meetings were kept, but accounts of the time maintained by the *Meeting Houses of London,* record that the collections (yes, they had offertories in the 17th Century) on Sundays was anything between 2s 6d (12½p) and 8s (40p).

It was the custom for each meeting house to be attached to another in the locality. Initially the proposal was for Mill Hill to join with Hammersmith but when local interest waned Hendon and Mill Hill were linked with the Peel House in Clerkenwell. In 1715 a benefactor to the cause, William Jordan, left £20 for the repair of Rosebank and another meeting house at Guttershedge, and for the entertainment of guests who attended the Mill Hill meeting house. This would not go very far today.

THE JEWISH COMMUNITY

There has been a sizable Jewish community in Hendon for many years. Jewish families first began to congregate in the district shortly after World War I, and as long ago as 1922 the first synagogue was consecrated in Dunstan Road Golders Green. The building was actually completed in 1927, and that same year the building of another synagogue was started in Brent Street, Hendon. This was later moved to a more imposing building in Raleigh Close NW4 (which was completed in 1935) and another synagogue was eventually built on the Brent Street site.

In 1933 the influx of Jewish refugees fleeing the persecutions of the Nazis in Germany started to arrive. This immigration continued until the beginning of World War II and many of these found their way to Hendon. By 1959 it was estimated that about a quarter of the population of Hendon was of the Jewish faith.

As is to be expected some of these people spread northwards into Mill Hill and Edgware and it therefore became necessary for Mill Hill to have its own place of worship. The Mill Hill and District Hebrew Congregation began meeting just off the Broadway in Sylvan Avenue in 1950. This became the Mill Hill District Synagogue in 1960. The foundation stone for a modern impressive building was laid by Benjamin Silverman on September 12 1971 and the synagogue was consecrated and opened for worship the following year.

Round the corner in Brockenhurst Gardens is the smart Annie and Samuel Levy Hall which plays such an important part in both the religious and secular lives of the Jewish people of Mill Hill. The original hall was opened in 1969.

JEHOVAH'S WITNESSES

Watchtower House on The Ridgeway was built in 1950 in the grounds of Bittacy House that had been purchased and demolished to make room for this religious sect. The building is the United Kingdom headquarters of the Witnesses (or Seventh Day Adventists) and it is from here that their countrywide programmes to obtain converts are co-ordinated. *The Watchtower* magazine is printed here.

OTHER RELIGIOUS HOUSES

One rather unexpected addition to the religious communities of Mill Hill is to be found in the Village. The Wesleyan Methodist Chapel that was built towards the end of the 19th Century on the island at the top of Milespit Hill formed by The Ridgeway and the High Street is now the

Bethel of the Nigerian Brethren of the Star and Cross. At one time there was a Methodist chapel behind Mill Hill Broadway in Goodwyn Avenue but this was destroyed by fire in 1982.

Mill Hill East is a long way from the parts of Mill Hill around The Ridgeway and the Broadway and the other churches. There is a church to serve this part situated at the junction of Salcombe Gardens and Sanders Lane. It is modern with clean lines but does not have any particular merit architecturally. It was nevertheless a very important development in this area.

With the steady increase in the numbers of various ethnic minorities in the district, many of whom are Muslims, we must expect further changes to the emphasis of religious faiths in Mill Hill.

CHAPTER XXIII

EDUCATION FOR ALL

A history of the schools in a district give a good indication of the development of the area as a whole. They are proposed, designed, and built to satisfy an anticipated need, they develop and ultimately they may be demolished, redeployed or transferred elsewhere. It all depends upon that most unpredictable of statistics, the birthrate, and to a lesser extent the popularity of the place as somewhere to live and bring up a family.

Some good examples of popularity are the London Boroughs that were on the outskirts 100 years ago. Fine houses were built in places like Islington, and Poplar which over the years were neglected as the suburbs were built farther out. In some cases the roads deteriorated into near slums. Now they are popular again and houses that escaped the bulldozer and developer are being refurbished, frequently divided into flats, and are once again desirable environments. Unfortunately the families that were living in these areas when they were in a run-down state now say that they can no longer afford to live there.

In some respects Mill Hill is no different from any other semi-rural suburb. The range of schools at primary level is adequate and evenly distributed and because Mill Hill is a part of the very large London Borough of Barnet there is plenty of scope within the Borough for education at the higher levels. Mill Hill is a popular area and there do not appear to be any wild swings in the birthrate. In addition there are colleges in the surrounding areas that are more suitable for specialist disciplines, in particular Middlesex University (previously Middlesex Polytechnic) with its main building in The Burroughs in Hendon. In its first years this College was known as Hendon Polytechnic and then Hendon Technical College (its title when the author attended one of the first courses of engineering). In those days these Colleges were an end in themselves and it was nearly impossible to read for a degree having attended one of them, now fortunately this is all changed.

This is a far cry from the schools in the Mill Hill district before World War I when an assistant schoolmaster would have been paid a wage between £110 and £275 per annum and his female counterpart £98 to £180. In 1918 when the scales in Hendon had risen to £120 to £325 for men and £110 to £250 for women Hendon Educational Committee proudly announced that their scales were the best in the land. Maybe, but at this time there were certainly no signs of sexual equality.

The history of education and how it affected Mill Hill is a lot older than this and we must go back to much earlier times.

THE BEGINNINGS

After the collapse of the Roman Empire the standard of literacy declined. For centuries almost the only people with any education were those in religious orders: priests, monks, etc. Most writings were of a religious nature as will be seen from the ancient documents that are in museums, and books were few in number and precious. Little changed until the Norman invasion when another language, Norman French arrived, to supplement the official Latin. This would not have had much relevance to the people of Mill Hill, there were no religious orders in the vicinity and in any case education would not have been considered desirable or necessary for a population consisting of little more than peasants.

A study of the annals of senior officers of Church and State (they were frequently one and the same) in these times gives an indication of the amount of travelling to distant places that these people undertook. Certainly they were the educated few, but not in Dutch, German, Spanish, etc. The key was Latin, it was considered to be the most important subject taught in the early schools, and anyone of learning could read, speak, and write the language. It was international, perhaps we should have retained it as such rather than trying to introduce the entirely artificial language Esperanto, which is most unlikely to be successful.

The first big change came in the Middle Ages with the arrival of the guild merchants. Not only did they control merchandise by laying down rules for business and conduct and for maintaining quality but in many cases they also set up their own schools. Many of these later developed into the grammar schools. The guilds also introduced another kind of education, or rather properly defined training, the apprenticeship system. This would have been the first education to be of any benefit and have any relevance to the ordinary people of Mill Hill. As an acceptance of the standards of literacy amongst common people the oaths for these indentures could be in either English or Norman French.

Towards the end of the 14th Century William of Wykeham founded a grammar school at Winchester to improve the education of secular clergy. The scale was magnificent and far superior to anything that had come before. This became the model for other schools such as Eton and laid the foundation for the public schools as we know them today. The two ancient great universities, Oxford and Cambridge, already existed but they had not as yet become rivals because Cambridge did not achieve national importance until the 15th Century.

By the end of the 14th Century there were probably as many as 400 grammar schools in the Country as a whole, most of them very small. They were primarily concerned with the teaching of reading, writing and Latin with some mathematics and were under the control of monasteries or cathedrals, guilds and even hospitals. Clever boys (but not girls) from humble backgrounds could progress to clerks and the priesthood via these schools. There was no attempt to teach even basic learning to the great mass of the population until the charity schools made their appearance in the 18th Century.

At the time of the Reformation, education, like clothing, diet and accommodation, was strictly stratified both socially and culturally. Even though the number and types of places of education had increased dramatically, the inequalities in terms of availability for the poorer classes were exaggerated rather than improved. True there were small private establishments, often run by just one master and there were the by now well endowed grammar schools after the pattern of Winchester.

Before the present century there was almost no professional work available for women, and teaching was one of the only options open to them. Unfortunately in the 19th Century this did not guarantee that they were well educated or even competent to teach. In the mid-19th Century there were two private day schools in Mill Hill both run by women and there were no rules governing the curricula or indeed the discipline. Also in the Parish at this time there were three boarding schools each with a roll of less than 20, and one of these was also in Mill Hill. And this is a long time before there were any housing estates, just scattered farms and a few big houses so the children must have come from elsewhere.

The *Education Act* became law in August 1870. It had its limitations but nevertheless it was a start in education for all, no longer would a child be excluded because the parents could not afford to pay. True, compulsory education was limited to children under 13 and there were problems with accommodating religious differences but for the first time local expenditure on education was secured. Locally elected school boards had power to levy an education rate, build schools and recruit teachers, and they could compel the attendance of children if they were not already receiving suitable education. The biggest problem was to overcome the lack of parental interest and to convince them that education was more important than working, in the fields at harvest time for instance.

Strangely these small private schools remained a feature of

education in England almost right up to the present time. Most have now gone but at the beginning of World War II every locality had many of them, usually called preparatory schools and by now nearly always staffed entirely by women. It need hardly be said that the standards to which they taught varied considerably and many of the pupils experienced problems when they had to transfer to a different type of establishment at junior school level.

Mill Hill does however still have at least two independent schools. There is a sizable establishment in a fine old house on Milespit Hill, The Mount Independent School for Girls, and in Hammers Lane is Goodwyn School, a preparatory school for infants. (See end of chapter).

The Mount was established in Hampstead in 1925 and moved to Mill Hill in 1932. The School started with just six pupils and in the early years took boys and girls, but infants only. Today the School is strictly girls only and normally there are 450 pupils aged from seven to 18 years. There is a deliberate international policy and many Japanese girls attend, usually the daughters of diplomats and businessmen. They return home after three to five years, and frequently go straight to Japanese universities.

During the War years the School was evacuated to rural Amberley and the School buildings were taken over by the MoD as a nursing home for shell-shocked soldiers. In the 68 years of the School there have only been three headmistresses so continuity is obviously important.

RELIGIOUS INTOLERANCE

Throughout the history of Christianity followers have been prepared to suffer and even die to protect their religious beliefs. The residents of Hendon were involved in the changes that the Reformation brought in its wake. There were not any local martyrs but there was certainly persecution as Christian inflicted suffering upon Christian.

At the time of the Commonwealth, Hendon and Edgware both had Anglican parsons and they were dismissed, and two sympathisers named Francis Wareham and Richard Swift were appointed in there stead. Swift's appointment was to Edgware in 1656 by Parliamentary Commission. Prior to this, in 1650 he had been vicar of Offley in Herts and chaplain to Sir Brockett Spencer. Swift was born in Norwich in 1616 and was the son of a lawyer, he died in 1701 in Hendon. His father died when he was young so his education was restricted. Although he entered the Christian ministry there is no evidence that he was actually ordained. In spite of the manner of their appointments Wareham and Swift were popular with the local people. After Wareham was ejected in 1662 he was licensed as a Congregationalist and went to live in Upper Hale.

The rector deposed by Swift was John Whiston MA and at the Restoration he complained and they were summoned before the Middlesex Justices. Whiston's benefice was restored, you may conclude quite rightly. Swift was ejected and retired to Mill Hill. He moved into the house on The Ridgeway called Jeanettes and was imprisoned on a number of occasions for holding conventicles (forbidden religious meetings) in his house.

Swift was in fact just one of 450 so ejected between May 1660 and August 25 1662 (Bartholomew's Day). The *Third Act of Uniformity* of 1662 was designed to ensure that positions in churches, schools and universities were awarded only to Anglicans. The original date was Michaelmas (September 29) but was brought forward to prevent the deposed clergy from drawing their Michaelmas tythes before ejection.

Swift was by nature a philanthropist and in every way a very generous and pious man. The poor of the Parish remembered him particularly with great affection and he placed many of their children into trades. He studied the Scriptures daily but was greatly influenced by the Fifth Monarchists' strange interpretations of the *Book of Daniel* and the *Revelation*. There were many weird sects at this time: Levellers, Grindletonians, Muggletonians, Ranters, Particular Baptists and so on, each seeking its own path to salvation and convinced that the rest of the world was wrong.

Swift opened a school in Mill Hill, in all probability the first non-conformist school in the country. Mill Hill was outside any restrictions imposed by the *Five Mile Act*. This did not mean that he was now left alone to teach and practice his religion, and on more than one occasion he was incarcerated in Newgate Prison. The school created by Swift was the original Mill Hill School for the sons of Protestant Dissenters but there is however no actual link between this school and the Mill Hill School of today and indeed over a century separates the two.

The final number of English clergy forced to leave their livings as a result of the *Third Act of Uniformity* was probably over 1,900. Further restrictions on non-Conformists were the *Conventicle Act* of 1664 which banned any assembly of more than five adults unless held in accordance with the *Book of Common Prayer,* and the *Five Mile Act* (1665) which forbade preachers and teachers who had not taken the necessary oaths from going within five miles of any town or city, or travelling within five miles of the parish from which they had been ejected.

The *Act of Settlement* of 1701 vested the Crown in the Protestant

House of Hanover. Whilst this piece of legislation was aimed primarily at Roman Catholics it also severely restricted all types of Dissenters as well. Any person who would not take Holy Communion according to the rites of the Church of England was barred from holding any office under the Crown or even in the municipalities. The Houses of Parliament were closed to Roman Catholics and the universities to Dissenters of every kind. This may seem inconsistent because the *Toleration Act* of 1689 appeared to give a measure of religious freedom. Although non-Conformists (except Unitarians) were free to worship as they wished they were still barred from public life.

The treatment of Dissenters was very harsh, however it lacked the cruelty meted out in the years when Luther's writings first appeared. Then they were considered to be heretics and were tried before special commissioners. If found guilty they were usually excommunicated and delivered to the civil power for punishment. Three acts laid down the punishment for heretics of which the most important (and the most infamous) was the *Act for the Burning of Heretics* of 1401. By this act any person, man or woman, so condemned was to be burned alive in some public place in the district. If the heretic recanted the miscreant had to 'carry his faggot', a public ceremony at which he would appear, barefooted and in penitential garb carrying a faggot of wood on his back as a reminder of the burning that he deserved. No recantation was accepted for a second offence.

SCHOOLS FOR MILL HILL'S CHILDREN

Apart from the small private schools and boarding schools St Paul's Church of England School on The Ridgeway was the first school for the children of the Village and was opened in 1834. This was one year after St Paul's Church was consecrated and it was always intended that there would be close links between the two. The School's Trust Deed is quite clear about this and states that 'The School is founded so that the Christian Faith can be taught to the children of the District of Mill Hill'.

In the early days it was a charity school and at that time there was a similarly run school at The Burroughs in Hendon. The School has also been referred to as The National School but the proper name has always been St Paul's Church of England School. The School was opened 36 years before education became compulsory and it was not easy to convince parents that education was necessary or even desirable. The situation did not improve much when the *Education Bill* was passed in 1870, there was still the hay harvest to be gathered in July and probably acorns for pig food in October, not to mention other excuses such as expected epidemics (and the risk of infection) and bad weather. And in any case parents did not like paying the 3d (1½p) per week in fees.

The first schools inspector was appointed in 1878 and attendance improved dramatically. For much of the time in these early years the School struggled with one teacher and even the pay was not always regular. In 1885 a new headmaster was appointed who was really enthusiastic, he improved the whole position of the School and stayed for 36 years, and during this time he maintained good attendances.

... church of St. Paul on the Ridgeway

The building erected in 1834 still stands and is Grade II listed, as being of architectural interest. It is certainly most attractive and in the middle of the Village conservation area.

The School celebrated its 150th Anniversary in 1984 and to commemorate the events of the times that the School had been through the children performed a pageant illustrating Victorian times and through two World Wars to today. A service of thanksgiving was held which was attended by the Bishop of Edmonton. When the School first opened there would have been 50 children at most, 100 years ago there were 70 and today there are just over 200. They are aged from four to 11 years.

The next school to come to The Ridgeway was St Vincent's Roman Catholic Infant School. When first opened this was the Convent of the Daughters of Charity of St Vincent de Paul. The Convent is unique in the Village and occupies a rather special place in education in Mill Hill. It is difficult to decide whether to include this establishment under Education or Houses of Religion: it is something of both.

Until the 17th Century the religious communities for women were subject to rigid cloistering and were for contemplatives. The modern, more open communities all have their origins in a different type of establishment set up in Paris in 1633 by Vincent de Paul and Louise de Marillac (both subsequently canonised by the Roman Catholic Church).

The congregation set up by Vincent was the first non-cloistered order for females and it was devoted to the service of the poor and destitute, and other active charitable works.

At first the members nursed the poor in their homes but this developed quickly into the running of hospitals and teaching the children of the poor the rudiments of their religion. From this they went on to be involved in every kind of charitable work. During a number of wars the sisters worked at the front and for this work became known as 'Angels of the Battlefield'.

Littleberries and part of the grounds was purchased in 1885 and re-arranged into an orphanage for children from the London Poor Law Unions and home for abandoned babies. From a historical point of view one building here, Littleberries, is more important than the rest, and this is described in a separate chapter.

Older residents of Mill Hill Village will remember the previous dress of the order: stiff white linen winged cap (or corvette), and long slate-blue full dress which had been modelled on that worn by 17th Century French peasant women. In September 1964 a simpler habit was adopted consisting of a shoulder length white-lined slate-blue kerchief, and the dress was shortened and made less full.

In the 1970s the total membership of the order worldwide was in the region of 45,000, all subject to the Motherhouse in Paris.

A church in the Perpendicular style was added to the St Vincent's site in 1887 and when the elementary school was added in 1896 the necessary extra buildings almost surrounded and obscured the original building (Littleberries). The house next door was Jeanettes, previously mentioned in connection with Richard Swift, and was also at one time the home of a noted philanthropist Lady Anne Erskine. This house was absorbed into St Vincent's in the 1920s but was demolished in the 1930s to make way for an extension to the convent vegetable garden.

The cost of constructing the School was financed by voluntary gifts. Within a year the School was recognised by the Department of Education. From modest beginnings the School has developed to become an important part of the Catholic education of Mill Hill, and today there are 312 pupils at primary school level.

The two schools of St Paul's and St Vincent's were the only state run or assisted schools in Mill Hill up to World War I and no further developments took place until the 1930s. In 1931 two more were built, a combined infant and junior school and a high school, Deansbrook School and Moat Mount School. Deansbrook has always had the same name but Moat Mount amalgamated with the Orange Hill Schools in 1984 to become Mill Hill County High School.

The Hendon School Management sub-Committee met on November 26 1929 and reference was made to an earlier meeting when the provision of a school for children who lived to the west of the Midland Railway was discussed. The decision was deferred once again. Someone once cynically remarked that when more than two people are gathered together no decisions are made. Committees are the worst offenders but something had to be done. Much building work had been completed in the area including what had been designated as the Mill Hill Garden Village, plus all the new housing at The Hale and of course the Watling Estate was not very far away. Two further meetings later and a report was discussed regarding the purchase of suitable land at Deans Lane Mill Hill.

The surveyor was recommended to proceed with the purchase of the site and to take the necessary steps to erect a temporary school there. The land totalling just under 2ha cost £4,000 including legal fees.

On October 28 1930 the Education Committee agreed that the School should be named Deansbrook Elementary School and that it should accommodate not more than 400 pupils, infants and juniors combined. The School opened in August 1931. The existence of the new school was soon justified; after two years there were 451 children and this necessitated having two extra classes in the School hall.

The population in the district was still increasing, families tended to be larger than they are today and provision was made for the use of the John Keble Hall (for 100 children). This hall was used in this way for two years. In January 1933 approval was sought to divide the School into an infants department for five to eight year olds and a junior school. This to cater for 400 children to 11 years old and to be carried out as quickly as possible. On this occasion agreement was reached rather quicker and building work started almost at once.

After the summer holidays in 1934 the new infants school stayed in the original school building and the juniors moved into a new building near to the present school. Today the Infant School has 240 pupils aged four to seven years. The Golden Jubilee was celebrated in 1981, and 1991 was the year for the Diamond Jubilee.

At the peak the number of children in the junior school was 355 (1957). After this the catchment area was controlled and then the number of children levelled off and started to drop. Today there are 250 junior children.

Most schools can relate at least one event of importance in its history. Something they want to remember. Deansbrook has one that they would probably rather forget: the Junior School was very severely damaged by fire in November 1970 when three classrooms were gutted by fire along with the administration block. Sad times, but at least something was proved, the team spirit of the School meant that it reopened after only two days and even the examinations were held on time.

Deansbrook School is in the most densely populated part of Mill Hill, Mill Hill County High School is right on the northern edge and backs on to open country. Moat Mount was the name for over 50 years, until the great period of reorganisation began and schools were merged to make larger units. Many people are still wondering whether this led to higher standards. As far as Moat Mount was concerned there do not seem to have been too many problems, the various Orange Hill Schools: Secondary boys and girls, Grammar boys and girls, and High School junior and senior all amalgamated with Moat Mount to form Mill Hill County High School. This is one of the two largest schools in terms of pupils in Mill Hill with a current roll of 1,100 aged 11 to 18.

Copthall Girls School is the other large school in the district and also came about as the result of a merger. Copthall Grammar School was founded in 1937 and as the name implies has always been a Mill Hill school. Woodcroft Secondary Modern School was somewhat later on the scene and was not established until 1963. The two schools were amalgamated in 1973 to form the present school. With 1,150 pupils aged 11 to 18 Copthall is just the largest school in Mill Hill.

The two schools of Mill Hill County High and Copthall emphasize the flexibility of schools in the district with regard to their catchment areas. Clearly if there are 1,150 girls at Copthall and 550 or so at Mill Hill County High they outnumber boys 3 to 1 so either many boys aged 11 to 18 go to schools outside Mill Hill or a high percentage of Copthall girls come from the surrounding districts, particularly other parts of the Borough of Barnet. It is probably a combination of both factors. The location of Mill Hill County High is somewhat inaccessible to much of Mill Hill.

Since World War II three extra schools have opened that take both infant and junior pupils, that is from around 4 years to 11 plus and all are roughly the same size; 200 to 230 pupils.

The Fairway JMI School was opened in 1952 to accommodate children from the Stoneyfields Estate area. They marked their Silver Jubilee in 1977 with a celebration. Courtland JMI School joined the Mill Hill education system in 1954. They chose 30 years for their celebration and J Gorst MP came to help with the thanksgiving. The School lies to the east of the A1 Barnet by-Pass and caters for those children that live in the area north of Marsh Lane. This leaves one other primary school,

Dollis (Infants and Junior) School in Pursley Road.

In 1944 the Hasmonean Girls High School was established in Parson Street Hendon for girls of the Jewish faith aged 11 to 18. In 1975 the School was transferred to a new site in Page Street. The official opening was performed by Rabbi Dr Soloman Schonfeld. The normal attendance roll is 380.

The most recent (and maybe the last) new school to open in Mill Hill was originally called Northway Special School but was changed to Northway School one year after opening by request of the pupils. Pupils were admitted from September 7 1967 but the actual official opening was delayed for one year and was carried out by Cr V Usher the Mayor.

Northway School is designed and staffed for children with individual needs. There are usually about 90 at the School which caters for both sexes aged from five to 16 plus.

This school is in the last area of the Mill Hill district to be developed and like the whole of the area was once farmland. Just north of here was a large dairy farm and the site of Northway was once a pig farm.

In 1986 the School's own swimming pool was built and in 1988 the Princess of Wales visited the School through the Special Olympics.

Most school buildings erected since 1950 are square structures with flat roofs. In the last few years we have had a number of very violent storms and this type of building has suffered badly, in many cases the roof has been lifted off completely. Local authorities in the south east have learnt this to their cost and the London Borough of Barnet is one of them. Unfortunately this is unlikely to lead to a return to school buildings with pitched roofs (they look better anyway). We will have to wait for them to need replacement and hope that by that time the fashion has changed.

Mention was made earlier of Goodwyn School, a private infant school in Hammers Lane. This school is larger than many of the pre World War II preparatory schools or kindergartens, and now has 200 children attending aged from three to seven years.

This school was founded around 1925 as Langley Park and was then changed to Mill Hill High School for boys and girls in 1938. At that time the School was in Goodwyn Avenue (hence the name) and moved into the premises of Erlsmere School in Hammers Lane in 1946. The two schools were amalgamated. Erlsmere was founded in 1910 and had already merged with St Gabriel's of the Good Shepherd during the War when the MoD took over their premises in Flower Lane.

Geoffrey Chaucer started the composition of the Canterbury Tales in 1386 and in the (unfinished) Squire's Tale we find the passage;

Now may each cobbler send his son to school,
And every beggar's brat learn from his book,
Turn to a writer and get into a lord's house.

Nearly 500 years were to pass before education for the masses was established as a right. Perhaps before the beginning of the 21st Century agreement will have been reached by the experts as to what our children and grandchildren need to be taught and how it should be done. There have been so many changes in the last few decades that everyone must be confused, most of all the teachers and the parents particularly as the number of children leaving school at 16 barely literate or numerate continues to rise.

The author first attended school in the Summer Term of 1934 at St Mary's Finchley, which until recently was at the top of Hendon Lane, just outside Mill Hill. In those days the School was lit with gas lamps, and each class had an anthracite stove for heating. The School has now transferred to a new building elsewhere in the Borough.

In 1991 ex-pupils were invited (by means of an advertisement in the local press) to visit the School on its last day. The author attended with a sister. Pupils and teachers had many questions for the visitors, particularly regarding the facilities in earlier times and schooling during the years of World War II. They found it hard to believe that there was no dining room before the War because there was no need. In those days with few exceptions married women stayed at home, divorce was uncommon and the single-parent family was not even mentioned. This meant that children had to go home to lunch, so that from five-years-old onwards many children had to walk four miles or more every day. They certainly did not travel to and from school by car.

Many of these old schools, built in stone like St Mary's, have been converted into desirable homes. The majority were constructed about the middle of the 19th Century, or a little later. St Mary's had been much altered and spoilt long before it closed (by removal of the Gothic windows for instance) so that it was not suitable for conversion. In any case it was not in the right location.

CHAPTER XXIV

THE STORY OF
MILL HILL SCHOOL

Whenever there is a public school in a town or a locality it is frequently the most important single institution and the one by which the place is known to outsiders. Eton, Harrow, Marlborough and Roedean are good examples and so of course is Mill Hill. Apart from the position of Mill Hill School as the most important centre of learning in Mill Hill, it has also one of the most notable buildings in the Village, in an extremely prominent position. The School is also a very important land and property owner.

WHY PUBLIC SCHOOL?

Public Schools do not set out to be important for the sake of it, it is just that they have occupied a position of influence in educational thought for so long that they are a part of the history of the Country. They embody traditional values and standards in a fast changing world. That is not to say that they never change, of course they do, but their changes are more subtle than those of most state schools because they are not affected by the changing whims of local and regional educational authorities, anxious to show that they are 'doing something' by introducing modern trendy subjects and teaching methods. New subjects are added to the curriculum only when they are relevant to the future careers of the pupils, not as a cosmetic exercise. And because they are supported by fees they are able to maintain a high ratio of teachers to pupils.

Whether by coincidence or not these schools have another advantage, they are all in magnificent surroundings: Lancing high on the hillside, Harrow perched on its hill, Winchester tucked under the Cathedral walls, Roedean on the cliff facing out towards the Channel, Mill Hill on a high ridge with superb views all round and so on. It is easy to understand how and why the founding fathers when they first came upon this spot, decided that this was where their school in Mill Hill must be.

Many of the young men and women who attend our public schools today are from overseas. Indeed without their patronage some of these schools would find it hard to balance their budgets. They must be puzzled by the name 'Public School'. There is nothing public about them, the total number of students is strictly limited, and they are not free to all comers. The cost of everything from teachers' salaries to building maintenance has to be met from the fees paid by the parents of the students. And these schools by their charter are not run for a profit, they are in fact registered as charities. This is probably the only way in which these schools could be considered to be public.

The basis of most public schools is that the majority of their students are boarders (although from the earliest times there have always been some day students in the boys' schools). Therefore they are not really a part of the educational structure of the district in any narrow sense because they attract pupils from a wide area. Of equal importance with the schools' formal education, particularly in days gone by, is attending the services in the school chapel (which is usually a magnificent building). A fine example of a public school chapel is Lancing College in Sussex. Cathedral like in dimensions and style it stands on the hillside and is visible from the eastern and northern approaches from a very great distance. Religious education occupied a very important position in school life in all these schools and Mill Hill with its background of religious non-Conformism was certainly no exception.

THE ORIGINS OF MILL HILL SCHOOL

It is not possible here to give a full account of the history of Mill Hill School. To do it justice this would command a book on its own, and in fact at least two books on the School have already been published, albeit not in recent times. The origins of the School and the reasons for its foundation are well known and much has been written on this before in all sorts of books and publications. Nevertheless an outline of the beginnings has a place here.

Jeremiah Harman was the grandson of one of Cromwell's Ironsides and a Quaker, who came to live in (the old) Ridgeway House towards the end of the 17th Century. Together with some others of the same persuasion they built Rosebank (see also the chapters on Important Buildings and Religions) for their meetings, as well as a place of residence. When Harman eventually left Mill Hill in 1729 the house was passed to another Quaker, Michael Russell; his daughter married Peter Collinson (qv), a botanist of considerable renown. Collinson's garden is now a part of the Mill Hill School grounds. The present School is built near the site of Collinson's house, Ridgeway House.

When Collinson died in 1767 his botanical work was carried on by his son Michael, with help from another dedicated botanist Richard Salisbury. At about this same time another magnificent house was erected for the Lord Mayor of London at the other end of the Village. This is called Belmont and for many years now this has been the home of Mill Hill Junior School.

There were no further developments until the beginning of the 19th Century, to be precise in 1807, when a small band of non-Conformist clerics and merchants travelled to Mill Hill (it was still a very rural place then) to see whether the building called Ridgeway House would be suitable for a rather special school that they intended to found. At that time the universities were still closed to Dissenters and the older public schools were unwilling to admit them because of the possibility of sanctions which would affect their other pupils.

Much religious zeal and a great deal of courage was required because the house was in a bad state and in need of a considerable amount of repair work. Furthermore they were not rich. The siting however was superb which probably helped to convince them and they returned to their colleagues in London determined that Mill Hill and Ridgeway House in particular was to be the place.

The School was officially founded in 1807 but really came into existence in 1808. On January 14 a sermon was preached on behalf of the School and the first pupils (20 and all day pupils) were admitted on January 25. By 1810 the number had risen to 77.

From the beginning it was intended that the standard of education would be comparable with the best universities in the land, from both cultural and academic standpoints.

It is not really possible to name any one man as School founder. When the School first opened three men were responsible for the initial success, Rev. John Atkinson and Rev. Maurice Phillips together with Thomas Priestley (a grand nephew of Joseph Priestley the chemist and non-Conformist devine), who became headmaster. Of the handful of devoted men who risked all to this precarious venture in such a troubled period of our history two names stand out; Samuel Favell, Master of the Clothmakers Company, and Rev. John Pye-Smith LLD, DD, FRS.

The Pye-Smith family remained faithful to Mill Hill School and Philip Henry Pye-Smith, grandson of John was a pupil. He became senior censor of the Royal College of Physicians and consulting physician to Guy's Hospital as well as accepting many other important posts. He was also elected to the Royal Society and published many works on medical subjects.

It soon became obvious that Ridgeway House was quite inadequate in both size and appointments. In 1824 six architects were approached with a view to designing a completely new school, each was promised £20, with £100 to be given to the one who produced the winning design.

The schoolhouse was to accommodate 120 boys, five masters, a housekeeper and four servants, and the cost was not to exceed £315,000.

The design prepared by William Tite was accepted and the main body of the school was built in 1825. Building work commenced on June 16 and the official opening was in July 1826. The architect preferred the view to the south so that the School has its back facing The Ridgeway and looks over the valley to the home of its nearest public school neighbour, Harrow. The design consisted of a main centre block with a portico of six unfluted Ionic columns in Bath stone. Behind the portico is the dining hall which is 11m high. Two plain wings of nine bays flanked the centre, the appearance to be symmetrical. Today some consider the columns to be over heavy and the junction of bays and portico to be lacking finesse, the appearance is however impressive when viewed from the public footpath.

In the original drawing it was intended that there would be a pavilion linked by colonnades at each end of the building. Only the one at the western end was built to take the chapel.

The School was not always a success and after a change of headmaster there was a decline in the mid 19th Century which led to actual closure for some months in 1868. A loyal group of men, the most influential of whom was Thomas Scrutton, set out to put the School back on a proper footing and the School reopened in 1869 and earned a level of success that has been maintained with only one further hiccup. By this time religious intolerance was much reduced and the School was able to admit boys on a much broader basis.

In the early days before temporary closure the School was known as The Protestant Dissenters' Grammar School Mill Hill, but this was changed to the present title, Mill Hill School, when it was reopened. At the turn of the Century many of the older residents of the Village still referred to 'The Grammar School'.

Two of Scrutton's most able supporters in the revived School were Dr Murray who stayed as master for 15 years and was later to become Sir James Murray, and Rev. Robert Harley (see also Famous People for biographies of these two). Dr Murray left the School to work full time on the now world famous *Oxford English Dictionary*.

The School continued to progress for another decade or so and during this time Mr Gladstone gave a major boost to the School's prestige in 1879 when he agreed to present the end of year prizes. In 1882 further problems beset the development of the School, between this time and the turn of the century there were three headmasters and the School roll dropped to 50 or so. Now another man took over, Dr McClure, later to become Sir John, who immediately set about improving the situation.

The number of pupils began to increase again and in broad terms the School has never looked back. Sir John became the School's most famous headmaster, and was responsible for much expansion around 1900 both to the buildings and in acquiring extra land.

In the years before World War II there was already a wide range of religions represented amongst the School's pupils. An earlier writer said that there were Anglicans and non-Conformists, Roman Catholics and Jews, even Muslims and Buddhists, and this was 50 years ago! Today this sort of mix would probably apply to most of our public schools, particularly those that attract a high overseas intake. Because Mill Hill School was founded during a period of strictly imposed religious intolerance the School has always been determined to accommodate all shades of belief. The teaching of religion is open minded and the pupils are taught to appreciate all creeds, nevertheless all members are expected to attend chapel services.

In the past, great preachers have taken their place in the pulpit of Mill Hill School chapel: bishops, chaplains of famous colleges, a former president of the Methodist Church and so on. The rector of St Mary at Finchley, Prebendary Bernays, preached here before World War II. This in some way emphasises the ecumenical nature of the present school because Bernays was of Jewish origins. He was also chaplain to the Royal National Orthopaedic Hospital on Brockley Hill Stanmore. and the Rector of St Mary's when the church was struck by a bomb during World War II.

Apart from its renown as a seat of learning Mill Hill School has had other beneficial influences upon the neighbourhood and has done much to preserve the rural and gentrified air of the Village. The School and the 49ha (121 acres) or so of parkland that it owns; those to the south of Wills Grove, further land to the north of The Ridgeway, and the grounds of Belmont (the junior school) ensure that building and development in the area is strictly controlled. In fact the School governors probably exert as much influence in this respect as the local council.

THE SCHOOL IN THE 20TH CENTURY

In 1898 a new chapel was added to the west of the School complex, built to the design of Basil Champneys. The original chapel was then converted into an assembly hall and is known as 'The Large'. At this time a gallery was added. A sanatorium had already been built in 1877, designed by T Roger Smith.

Quite separate from the main buildings is a neat composition comprising the Murray Scriptorium (now a computer centre), the Winterstoke Library and the School Tuck Shop. This was added in 1907 and the architects were T E Collcutt and Stanley Hamp.

Collcutt was also responsible for two rather different School houses, Collinson House and Ridgeway House. Collinson House was built in 1902 and by comparison with some of Collcutt's other work is rather plain. It is in red brick with some stone dressings and part rendered. Collcutt's name is inscribed on the foundation stone. Ridgeway House built in 1911 is a complete foil for the earlier building. It is a large fine building with many unexpected details particularly in the composition of the windows. The arched porch of voussoirs (wedged stones) and other refinements are inventive without becoming extravagant.

Martin Shaw-Briggs, an ex Mill Hill pupil, is probably better known today for his books on architecture rather than for his actual buildings. He was at one time fully employed as a Government Inspector of Schools. Many of his designs are in and around the School. He was responsible for the McClure Music School (formerly the art school) which was built in 1912. The concert hall has a barrel vaulted roof and high north facing dormer windows to give excellent light without direct glare. Practice rooms and offices are contained in flanking wings.

The original Scriptorium (see above) was destroyed by fire and Shaw-Briggs designed the replacement building. He was also the architect of the rather elegant row of houses behind Hammers Lane and Wise Lane at the foot of Wills Grove known as Winterstoke Gardens. These semi-detached pebble dashed houses were built in 1912. Some years later (1924) Shaw-Briggs designed Winterstoke House, the large red brick neo-Georgian house in Wills Grove which is a complete contrast to his earlier large works.

In 1924 a science block was added. Another building attributed to Stanley Hamp but probably designed by Dixon. There is no decoration to this building, which was officially opened by the Prince of Wales, later to become (briefly) Edward VIII. The following year three extra bays were built to the south of the main building which rather spoilt the original symmetry.

Prior to World War II the headmaster lived in the house known as St Bees which is within the School complex, and was built for this purpose. When war broke out the School was evacuated to St Bees, near Whitehaven in Cumberland (now part of Cumbria) and the School was taken over by the MoD for use as a convalescent depot. When the School returned to Mill Hill at the cessation of hostilities the headmaster of the time preferred to live outside the School in the old house The Grove which is on the other side of The Ridgeway. This has been the headmaster's house since that time.

In 1959 a new Art and Design Block was opened. Art subjects play an important part in the School curriculum and are focal points for leisure activities. More recently there have been many other developments of considerable importance to the School starting with a new Sixth Form Centre completed in 1972. This incorporates five classrooms as well as two social lecture areas and two day-pupil houses.

In the mid-seventies came the most dramatic change since the School's establishment with the admission of girl pupils into the sixth form. Many of the other public schools now have girl pupils, some as young as 14 year olds, so in this Mill Hill is in line with current thinking. In the first years of admission there were only 20 girls, this doubled by 1980 and has now increased to over 60.

The Victorian indoor swimming pool was completely modernised along with all the ancillary equipment in 1981 and in 1983 the new sports hall was completed and opened. Mill Hill was in fact the first school to have an indoor pool as well as gymnasium and squash courts. A great number of sports are actively encouraged, the level of coaching available is exceptional and success in competition is encouraged. The establishment of Mill Hill School Enterprises, which enables the non-School community to make use of the School's facili-

magnificent house ... Belmont

ties out of hours, is an enormous benefit to residents in the west of the Borough of Barnet.

Mention was made earlier that new subjects are only added to the curriculum when they are relevant to the careers of the pupils. To this end business studies, information technology, and design technology, were added during the 1980s together with all the necessary plant and equipment which was a very substantial investment. These have been well supported. In the same period the number of senior pupils has risen by about 15% and now stands at around 570.

The junior school Belmont has not been left behind in all these changes. In 1988 boarding was phased out here and this permitted a very large re-allocation of the space available. The interior has been considerably upgraded and the number of pupils has been increased and is now 280. Prior to this reorganization Belmont built its own independent sports centre.

The Belmont bachelor quarters have been converted into an administration unit and renamed Walker House. Four staff cottages have been built in the stylish Millers Close adjacent to the Belmont grounds.

With a school like Mill Hill it is almost inevitable that many pupils will have gone on to become highly successful, even famous in their chosen careers. Many have become architects and those that have returned to design School buildings have been mentioned here. Amongst the others are Sir Francis Crick who won a Nobel Prize for his work on the DNA molecule, Richard Dimbleby the journalist and broadcaster and the Queen's couturier, Norman Hartnell.

SOME INTERESTING SCHOOL BUILDINGS

The School Chapel

Tite's chapel completed in 1832 was rather stark. The chapel built to the design of Basil Champneys is a complete departure from the somewhat austere designs of much of the original School building. It is constructed in narrow red bricks and Ham Hill stone. Much of the stone on the facings fronting the road is already showing signs of deterioration however and will need remedial work in the near future.

The Champneys chapel is a basilica in form with an apse at the west end and a wing on either side to accommodate organ and vestry. A bell tower rises above the junction of vestry and nave. The nave is supported by brick buttresses surmounted by small Ionic columns and these continue around the apse supporting a stone cornice. Fronting the road at the east end is the vestibule which is between two small towers. The stone architrave also rests on Ionic columns.

The interior has teak panelling and this wood is used for all of the woodwork. The aisle is paved in grey and white marble. A waggon roof is divided into five panels.

The Gate of Honour

Many of the School's Old Boys died in the two World Wars and other lesser conflicts. The Gate of Honour which the School and Old Boys erected on The Ridgeway is in Portland stone. It is attributed to Stanley Hamp FRIBA, but was probably designed by Dixon who was working in

Hamp's studio at this time. The carvings are by P G Bentham. The names of the fallen are on panels to be found within the gate. The grill of bronze is opened once per year. The gate is considered to be a good example of Beaux-Arts inspired classic design associ-

The Gate of Honour .... in Portland stone

ated with the Liverpool School of Architecture where Dixon had studied.

Cricket Pavilion

The cricket pavilion is not the biggest belonging to a public school, the one at Shrewsbury School is certainly larger and there are probably others. Size is not necessarily a virtue. The Mill Hill School pavilion is a fine building built in the traditional timber framed construction and clad in grooved weatherboarding, painted white. The balcony is supported on slender concrete columns. In the original design the scoreboard was in the centre of the balcony but presumably was often obscured by spectators and has been moved to the right facing. A Stuart Gray, an ex Mill Hill boy was the architect.

The front patio area with terracing and two flights of steps to the actual ground is something of which many a county ground would be proud.

Housing

A considerable incentive to would-be public school teachers is that these schools are usually able to offer housing in the locality. Not every teacher could afford to purchase a house at Windsor, Harrow or for that matter Mill Hill. These are all expensive areas. Starting in 1908 with the purchase of The Grove (the headmaster's house since 1945), Mill Hill School has added to this quite steadily over the years so that the School is a very considerable land owner in addition to the buildings actually concerned with education and sports. This also means that these properties are well maintained. Today the list of houses and the dates that they were acquired outside the School complex consists of the following:

Park Lodge	1926
Crown Cottage	1928
Church Cottages	1929
The Bungalow	1932
Park Cottages	1934
Garth, Wills Grove	1935
Ridgeway Cottage	1948
Shenley Cottage	1951
St Augustine's Cottage	1961
9 Winterstoke Gardens	1962
17 to 22 High Street	1963
1 to 4 Orchard Terrace	1972
5 Winterstoke Gardens	1974
Millers Close	1989

Other teachers are housed in more communal types of accommodation, for instance boarding House Tutors. There are four houses in Millers Close (and these are used for non-teaching staff) .

CHAPTER XXV

INNS AND HOSTELRIES

T he Village of Mill Hill is not on a main road and for centuries was preserved in a kind of limbo. The primary route to the north, the Roman Watling Street, passed to the west, but Mill Hill on its ridge was pleasantly isolated, just one of the hamlets that went to make up the Manor of Hendon. The size and style of public house is determined by the type of custom that can be attracted. Mill Hill inns have relied mainly on local trade, with some visitors, mainly casual labour at harvest time, but not on through traffic.

We do not find the typical coachmen's pull-ups that are so common in towns that sit astride the main arterial routes such as St Albans, Hitchin or Stamford. Many of these old inns are now converted into rather splendid houses but their original purpose is still obvious: the large double doors opening on to the thoroughfare through which the coach and horses could pass to the stables at the rear. Fishpool Street in St Albans and High Street Hitchin have a number of these. Because the inns of Mill Hill had to cater for a different kind of visitor, the immigrant worker from other parts of Britain, (particularly Bedfordshire), and Ireland it was almost a case of quantity rather than quality. These workers had no proper abodes whilst they were in Mill Hill so inevitably they would spend their spare time in bars.

The workers came in large numbers to help with the hay harvest and then returned home to work on their own corn crop. The inns were no doubt quite busy for a few weeks in the summer and then it was back to local trade.

The 18th Century saw the beginnings of Mill Hill's development as a desirable place in which to own property, but these people were rich and had no need for public houses. Another change was taking place too, ordinary people were beginning to travel and suddenly maps and guide books became a necessity, and the fact that the earliest guide books gave mention of Mill Hill it was bound to attract some visitors. And of course the building of the railways in the latter half of the 19th Century followed by the advent of private motoring after World War I ended the isolation for ever. The locality suddenly became accessible and very much a part of outer London. Young people particularly were prepared to drive some distance to a pleasant 'pub' that served good beer.

These changes were too late to have much effect upon public

houses already in existence although some have been enlarged in a manner not always in keeping with the style that one might have liked. In recent years new public houses have been built which look just like any modern licensed premises anywhere but fortunately Mill Hill has almost avoided these. The most attractive are without doubt the ancient inns that have managed to retain their character in spite of 20th century updating.

The part of the Northern Line tube which runs to Mill Hill East was once part of a line that ran on to Mill Hill the Hale and Edgware. At the end of this line was built the *Railway Hotel* (there must be hundreds of these around the country) and is a typical example of an architectural style that has been called somewhat contemptuously Brewers' Tudor. In fact although this type of building with precise timber work and accurate angles offends the purists most have weathered rather well and are regarded with much affection. Because they are a definite style of building and peculiar to a particular era perhaps one (at least) will be served with a Preservation Order.

In 1890 there were about 30 public houses in the whole Parish of Hendon and of these 10 were in Mill Hill. At the time this worked out at one to every 450 inhabitants for the Parish as a whole which is very modest by the standards of the time. With 10 inns in Mill Hill the number of inhabitants per inn was rather less. As mentioned earlier Mill Hill inns did not have to cater for a great deal of through traffic and there was no market day bringing a huge influx of thirsty visitors on a regular weekly basis, so the small number of people who lived in and around The Ridgeway and Highwood Hill were well served with seven public houses.

Let us approach Mill Hill from Hendon along the route that is almost as old as the Manor, via Holders Hill. At the junction of Holders Hill Road and Dollis Road is the roundabout known locally as Kelly's Corner which has on its western side a large public house called *The Mill*. This we will ignore because it is strictly modern. The only puzzle is why no public house appears to have been built on this site in earlier times so that horsemen and other travellers could take refreshments before tackling Bittacy Hill (or Drivers' Hill as it was then known). In fact there was an inn at the foot of Drivers' Hill in the middle of the 18th Century called *The Harrow* but it had already been converted into a private house before 1796.

A little farther up the road and tucked round the back of Mill Hill East Station in Sanders Lane is *The Railway Engineer*. An obvious bit of history here, the gas works was built in 1862 and the Great Northern Line to Edgware in 1867. The name therefore seems appropriate and would appear to date back to the time when the railway that ran through Mill

Hill was being constructed. The building is of this period but the original name was *The Railway Hotel*, which was only changed in recent years. Before the coming of the railway and the Gas Works there were few houses in the area, just the odd farmhouse. Houses developed around the gas works, the workers had to live somewhere, and railway construction workers were thirsty people. The building is typical of many built about this period and should last for ever.

Before the advent of motor vehicles the 800m climb up Bittacy Hill was heavy going, in fact it is only in recent years that double-decker buses have been able to tackle this. At the top as the road levels out is the most desirably sited *Adam & Eve* inn at the start of The Ridgeway. The original building was a weatherboard construction.

There has been an inn on this site since 1717 and the original was called simply *The Eve*. The name was changed in 1828. The weatherboard building was almost certainly built in 1751 and remained until the early part of the present century. The present building was erected in 1915. *The Adam and Eve* and the *Three Hammers* are the only public houses left on The Ridgeway. At the turn of the century there were four, or five if you include *The Plough* that stood at the top of Holcombe Hill.

—— *The Three Hammers... as it was in 1900*

Proceeding westwards along The Ridgeway we come to the Angel Pond and the junction with Milespit Hill. In earlier times another public house stood here called the *Angel & Crown* which dated from the early or mid 18th Century. This was a small weather-boarded building. The licence was not renewed after 1908 and the building was converted into a dwelling house. In 1965 it was demolished and the Angel Cottages, a Seifert designed terrace was erected on the site.

In James Thorne's book published in 1876, *Handbook to the Environs of London* the inn in Mill Hill is given as the *King's Head*. No other inn is mentioned in the section so presumably Thorne considered it to be important and note-worthy and the only inn worth visiting in the village. Obviously the owners didn't agree; it was demolished some years ago and the land recovered became a part of Belmont School playing fields.

The building dated from the middle of the 18th Century, with parts of the structure being considerably older. It was situated on The Ridgeway opposite the top of Wills Grove.

The next licensed house is on the corner of Hammers Lane and is a modern public house without any particularly distinguishing features. The building is in Brewers' Tudor. The original inn on this site was another of weather-board construction which according to Holbrook Jackson was once known as *Bunn's Bushes*. In its day the old building was the meeting place of many famous people, including Jackson who was a literary historian, a man almost totally ignored just 40 years after his death.

The original premises were built in 1754 and the present name is supposed to have been derived from the location; apparently it was possible to hear the hammers of the local forge, presumably the one at the foot of Holcombe Hill, the Village joiner and the stonemason. Joiners do not usually do much hammering (although carpenters may well do so) so he must have been very close by.

The next inn on our route would have been *The Plough* at the top of Holcombe Hill. Sadly this hostelry has gone the same way as the *Angel & Crown* and the *King's Head* and was demolished in 1931. Today we would do our best to preserve buildings such as these old inns, 60 years ago they were not considered worth saving even as private houses. This is a pity because they were a part of the continuing development of Mill Hill, its social history and its architecture.

Now another climb, this time up Highwood Hill to the *Rising Sun*. The original was

The Rising Sun

once owned by Sir Stamford Raffles

built in the 17th Century and unlike most others in the district which were weather-boarded is of brick. The style is typical of many inns built across the Country in the 17th and 18th Centuries as roads were improved and coach routes were introduced into rural areas. They were popular then and are just as popular today with both locals and visitors.

Many like the *Rising Sun* were built on hill tops to refresh the weary traveller after the long haul. But what about their horses, did all these inns have horse troughs? In the days before the motor vehicle when cattle were not transported as they are today the *Rising Sun* was a popular, and very necessary inn for the drovers.

In *Cooke's Survey* of 1796 the name is given as the *Sun Public House*. It is impossible to be certain whether this is merely an error in the publication or the common name at the time.

The *Rising Sun* was once owned by Sir Stamford Raffles. Much rebuilding and improvement work has been carried out since that time but the building has not lost its character There is now a DoE Preservation Order on the building. On the green, across the road from the Rising Sun is a Mill Hill Village sign, one of two made to a design by Martin Shaw-Briggs. He was a conservationist before it became fashionable, and an architect, an architectural writer, lecturer and traveller. The signs show a windmill of the type that we all recognise although as we now know the mill of Mill Hill was much more primitive.

In the year of the Great Plague 1665 a petition was got up by the local people who objected to the behaviour of the licensee. Unfortunately there does not seem to be any record of the heinous crime that he was supposed to have been committing.

Around the corner a little way towards Totteridge is Nan Clark's Lane. The tale of Nan Clark is detailed in the chapter on roads. By all accounts she was either the publican or the barmaid of the *Three Crowns* inn which stood at the corner of the lane which now bears her name. This inn was demolished in 1937 but had been unoccupied for many years before this time, and was once a part of the estate of William Wilberforce.

The old public house on the corner of Barnet Road and Barnet Gate Lane is called *The Gate*. It stands on the boundary of Mill Hill and it is doubtful whether it is in Mill Hill or not. High up outside is a white gate fixed to the wall inviting (with a simple rhyme) all to enter:

> *This gate hangs high, and hinders none,*
> *Refresh and pay, and travel on.*

This inn has been in existence since at least the middle of the 18th Century.

We now retrace our steps a little and head down Marsh Lane to Northway Circus, then down Selvage Lane to The Hale. At the beginning of the 18th Century there was little more here than Hale Farm and the *Green Man Inn*.

The Hale was a separate hamlet and Upper Hale was at the junction of Deans' Lane, Hale Lane, and Selvage Lane. The first mention of a public house on this site was in 1751 and the *Green Man* was there until quite recently. Alas, although this area is still referred to locally as Green Man Corner the pub is no more having been replaced by an American style eating house and renamed the *Everglades Exchange*.

In the 18th and 19th Centuries the *Green Man* was a favourite meeting place for sportsmen, particularly boxers, when the bouts were outdoors and fought with bare-fists to a finish. As many of these were not strictly legal, a secluded situation off the beaten track was essential to avoid the unwelcome attentions of the law.

At the start of this chapter mention was made of the *Railway Hotel* at Edgware and also of the *Railway Engineer* at Mill Hill East. It will be no surprise therefore to learn that there is also a public house near to where the other station on the section of the line from Finchley to Edgware once ran. This is the *Railway Tavern* in Hale Lane.

Before the coming of the railway the Tavern was a local farmhouse with the usual outbuildings catering for the needs of local passers-by. The construction of the line to Edgware was started in 1864 and the enterprising owner, a man named Crook decided immediately that there was money to be made out of selling cider to the railway workers. He renamed his premises the *Railway Tavern* and his turnover increased dramatically. The present building was erected in 1867, the year that the railway line was opened and is a solid square structure typical of many of the period.

The building of the motorways necessitated a completely new style of eating place. An inn implies a leisurely halt in congenial surroundings, a transport cafe good sound food with basic ambiance, and a restaurant good food and comfort. Motorway service areas have to cater for all types and ages quickly and efficiently, and we have one of these on the M1 in Mill Hill, *Scratch Wood Services.*

In the early days they failed to provide decent fare and they were uniformly ghastly. The food was not very enterprising, plastic plates and paper plates were frequently the norm and complaints in the media were commonplace. Fortunately *Scratch Wood Services* was not the first on the scene so that by the time they arrived on the M1 they knew what had to be improved. In addition to adequate varieties of food in the restaurant areas these services have to have shops for food, confectionery, reading material etc., adequate toilet facilities, plenty of telephones, and of course a fully equipped garage facility.

Even though *Scratch Wood Services* has had time to get the mixture right there is still a kind of love hate relationship with the public with all of these Motorway Services even though some are noticeably better than others. We know that they have to be there. Perhaps when we have time it is still preferable to leave the motorway and find somewhere more homely but no-one does, we never have the time.

CHAPTER XXVI

LOCAL INDUSTRY

Mill Hill is primarily a dormitory area and therefore there are few large employers. Nevertheless even with the restrictions that have always been put in the way of any large industrial development there is the odd pocket of light industry scattered around the district.

When the North Middlesex Gas Company (now within the North Thames Gas Board) opened the works at the foot of Bittacy Hill they became the largest single employer in the district. It was in its day quite a self sufficient plant. Towards the end it was however inefficient and wasteful with old horizontal retorts that leaked carbon monoxide rather badly. This could be seen burning with its typical eerie blue flames all round the retorts. There was also a water gas plant, the first one had used coke (which is a by-product of coal gas manufacture) but the last used coal so eliminated one stage of the production. But most of the equipment was well past its economical life, and even if North Sea Gas had not been discovered the Mill Hill plant would have had to be rebuilt or more likely drawn its gas from elsewhere. In any case with no convenient railway to bring in coal supplies transport was always going to be costly.

There have been industrial developments along the Edgware Road for many years, this really started during World War I. In 1911 Claude Grahame-White attempted to float a company with public money but unfortunately the proposals did not appeal to investors and the receipts were only a third of what had been hoped. The money was returned. Grahame-White then went ahead alone and launched Grahame-White Aviation Ltd. This was a success in the first year. Grahame-White was a great believer in air power and worked ceaselessly trying to interest politicians. Hendon Aerodrome with its annual air show and regular races became a social event to vie with Ascot and Henley, but the government of the day was unimpressed.

While all this was going on Grahame-White was engaged in building aircraft in a modest way using his own funds. When war broke out in 1914 his factory went into full production and he was permitted to leave the Royal Navy (he held a commission in the service) to concentrate on building planes and training the pilots. At the beginning of the War the factory employed just 20 men, in 1918 the number had risen to 3,000. The new aircraft industry at Hendon Aerodrome required all sorts of accessories and this encouraged the building of other factories west of

Edgware and later on further afield in Stanmore.

With the abandonment of Mill Hill Barracks by the military in the not too distant future it is quite likely that there will be some industrial development there. It is a pity that the area encompassed by Frith Lane, Partingdale Lane and Bittacy Hill cannot be transformed into a large public amenity, however in the light of current land values and shortages in the district this is probably naive. In any case the land occupied by the Barracks is already largely covered by buildings, many of which could be converted into factories for light industry without much change to exterior appearances or dramatic increases in heavy road traffic. The married families quarters is another matter and these houses would almost certainly end up partly in the private sector and the rest as council housing. The only change necessary would be modernisation.

In recent years a little light industry has come to the area. There is already a small industrial complex opposite Mill Hill East station known as Bittacy Business Centre and an extension of this into what is currently MoD land would make some sense.

Elsewhere in Mill Hill there is some industry around Mill Hill Broadway, and at the end of Flower Lane. The Flower Lane development is known as the Mill Hill Industrial Estate. From the road it lacks the obtrusiveness and ugliness of many of these estates and is quite well hidden. Industry, which after all is essential if an area is to be kept alive is much more acceptable if treated imaginatively. One of the biggest problems with trading estates is that because there are no residents little is done to make them attractive or if it is to keep them that way.

It would not be possible in a book of this kind to relate the story of every industry in Mill Hill, so three have been selected and their history is very different in every respect. Gas was and is a most important energy source, and before the discovery of North Sea gas was prominent in the development of Mill Hill. Electricity we certainly could not do without, but its arrival and early days in Hendon (and therefore Mill Hill) was from the start a complete bungle. The real success in Mill Hill is John Laing plc, the international building company that has had its headquarters in Mill Hill since 1926.

GAS: MILL HILL'S FIRST INDUSTRY

The first large scale developments in the destructive distillation of organic substances began in the 1790s when William Murdoch experimented with various materials including coal. In 1797 he used coal gas to light his premises at Old Cumnock in Ayrshire. The coal gas industry really began on a commercial basis in 1812. It was quickly realised that the gas was a complex mixture and the tarry residue even more so, but more of this later.

The first plant to be built in Mill Hill was in 1862 for the newly registered North Middlesex Gas Company. Coal deliveries must have been a problem because the Edgware, Highgate and London Railway (later to become the Great Northern Railway, and finally the LNER) was still three years away. The construction was by R Laidlaw of Edinburgh on a part cash, part share participation basis.

In the early days the carbonising plant was direct fired hand charged horizontal retorts and even with this basic equipment output in 1897 was 5,500m^3 per day. Records for the first few years are rather sparse but we know that the plant was run by William Porteous and his daughter, ably assisted by a handful of workers.

In 1898 a start was made in constructing a carburetted water gas plant (CWG), with two units giving a total of 56,000m^3 per day. In this process steam is passed over red hot coke giving the breakdown products of carbon monoxide and hydrogen. This was added to the coal gas to improve its calorific value.

In 1912 the original retort house was demolished and a new stage floored machine charged house was built with up-to-date coal and coke handling plant. The following year the CWG units were replaced with new ones giving 56,600m^3 per day.

World War I prevented any further expansion until 1920 when a third gas holder was added giving much needed extra storage. In the same year another CWG plant was built.

The Company's area of supply had increased to 4.25km^2 and 340km of mains had been laid. New housing estates had been built including the large Watling Estate and considerable private developments in Finchley, Golders Green, and Hendon so that the Company was having great difficulty in keeping pace with demand. In addition the market for coke had increased and something had to be done to release the coke that was being used in the CWG plant.

In 1926 and 1929 two new complete gasification plants were added which used coal instead of coke (making four in all) and this further increased capacity to 113,000m^3 per day. This additional plant employed a new technique. By 1933 the 1913 retort house had become inefficient to the point of becoming dangerous and plans were prepared for a new fully automatic horizontal retort house. This was built and went on stream in 1936.

The control of the Company was transferred to the South Eastern

Gas Corporation in 1937 which meant that extra funds were now available for necessary developments. At this time no-one dreamt of nationalisation, certainly not the discovery of gas under the North Sea which would eventually put an end to gas production at Mill Hill, and for that matter everywhere. The talk was still of increasing output, and as late as 1951 (two years after nationalisation and the creation of the North Thames Board) a new fully automatic CWG plant was erected on the site of the original retort house.

It is not really possible to talk of the romance of gas making, it was after all a smelly industry. But there was certainly romance in the people who worked the plant and developed it, and they were just as excited about new equipment and the latest technology as any other industry. Now all this has gone. Certainly the place looks the same from the outside, except that there are only two gas holders, but it is much quieter and no longer malodorous. It is now after all just a storage and distribution depot for a much cleaner gas. But what did coal gas consist of?

When coal is destructively distilled a mixture of gases is formed, various liquids, a tarry residue and finally coke. The inflammable gases are mainly hydrogen, carbon monoxide, methane, ethane, vapours of benzene and toluene and carbon disulphide and hydrogen sulphide. As far as possible it is necessary to remove the last two. In addition there are small quantities of nitrogen, ammonia, oxygen, and carbon dioxide. Once the gas had been through the scrubbing towers it was more or less odour free. This was obviously dangerous because it could not be easily detected and carbon monoxide is extremely poisonous. A small amount of a substance with a very unpleasant smell (called pyridine) was added for safety reasons which gave the gas its characteristic odour.

North Sea gas is almost pure methane and therefore odourless as well. As with coal gas a 'smell' is added so that it can be detected.

The old Mill Hill plant managers were very conscious of the value of the industry's by-products and went to much effort and expense to extract these and market them. Benzene was used in their own vehicles, they sold creosote and ammonia and of course coke. The tarry residue is known to contain upwards of 10,000 different substances many of which had value to the chemical industries as a raw material for drugs, plastics, explosives and so on, all the chemicals now made from petroleum. When everything useful had been extracted from the tar the bitumen that remained was used in waterproofing and for road finishing.

One of the chemicals that Mill Hill extracted was naphthalene. If a weed is just a wild flower growing in the wrong place then the weed of coal gas production was naphthalene. This white, crystalline, aromatic chemical is recognised by most people as moth balls, to chemists as a base material for dyes, drugs and much else and to the the gas companies as a source of extra revenue. Unfortunately if the naphthalene was not completely removed from the gas it tended to crystallize in the pipes causing serious blockages. The North Middlesex Gas Company was very good at removing this nuisance and selling it. They did not waste much.

ELECTRICITY: A LONG TIME COMING

The first place in Britain to be connected to a domestic supply of electricity was Godalming in Surrey, although part of the Thames Embankment had been lit before this, more or less as an experiment by the Metropolitan Board of Works. By the *Electric Lighting Act* of 1882 licences were issued to local authorities and suitable companies to establish electricity generating undertakings, with the option that the local authorities would purchase the companies at a later date.

By the turn of the Century, technical developments including the introduction of the electric motor (for both static and mobile power) had led to a big increase in the demand for electricity. The act of 1882 was proving to be an awful millstone to the infant industry, with a variety of small independent and grossly inefficient supply systems around the Country that strongly resisted mergers and rationalisation.

If it was technical constraints that delayed the widespread use of gas for lighting (there were no problems with gas for cooking where a luminous flame is undesirable) it was legislative stupidity that prevented the general use of electric power.

Swann began his experiments with an incandescent lamp in 1845, two years before Edison was born, but who is usually credited with the invention? In 1913, the year before World War I began the total output of the electrical industry in Britain was one third of that of Germany. But it was not only in generation that we lagged behind; when the London *Underground* was electrified in 1905 it was largely American enterprise in the shape of Westinghouse, and American finance that made this possible.

In Britain electricity generating grew at the slowest rate in the Western World. The price was also higher than anywhere else due to the disorderly assemblage of generating undertakings that Parliament had encouraged by the 1882 Act. Only one industrial region, Tyneside, had solved the problem to their benefit. A number of local engineering companies had got together to generate a common supply for their firms. This enabled them to sell themselves power at ½d per unit when it was as much as 6d or 8d elsewhere in Britain.

When the Tyneside syndicate tried to get an act through Parliament that would enable them to build two large power stations in London it was resisted fiercely by all the existing small companies, and by every local authority had that visions of going into the generating business. Under the 1882 act local authorities had to give approval before any company would be given approval. The Bill was rejected and London suffered the high prices for a further quarter of a century.

After the War the first steps were taken to organise the industry into a proper national structure so as to benefit from standardisation and concentration. In 1919 the Electricity Commissioners were set up as an advisory body to encourage reorganisation on a voluntary basis. This was followed in 1926 by the Central Electricity Generating Board whose job was co-ordinate the change to bulk generation by selecting the companies best suited to form the network. These companies were linked by the National Grid. By the time that the industry was taken into public ownership in 1948 only 143 selected stations were supplying 95% of all the electricity used.

HENDON HESITATES

It is hard to understand today the strength of the opposition to the supply of electricity for both private and business premises. At the time they were really only concerned with lighting, electric appliances did not really exist, but the electric motor was being developed quite quickly and had great potential for everything from refrigerators to electric traction. Electric motors could be used to drive pumps, which would be much more convenient and efficient than steam engines at sewage plants, and safer underground in mines.

But who were the objectors? Certainly not just the ignorant. Some were afraid and their fears were encouraged. The biggest deterrent was cost and the fact that the roads would have to be dug up to lay the mains not long after they had been dug up to lay gas mains. People were concerned that the roads (such as they were) would not be reinstated properly. Nothing has changed! But most important no-one could see into the future and appreciate just how important electricity would become in a decade or so. The people in Hendon were ill-informed and uninformed, and yet schemes to supply electricity were already well advanced in many other places.

Before any company could start installation work, or even consider generating, application for a Provisional Order had to be made to the Board of Trade. A number of companies applied for permission to work in Hendon, the first in 1888, then in 1891, followed by 1895, 1896/7 and 1898. The local Council had to approve any proposal and they objected to every one. It was their intention to make their own application when they were ready.

In July 1898 the Council passed a resolution that they should apply for a Provisional Order and a panel was set up to advise on the viability of various schemes. There was no obvious urgency on the part of the Council and one of the companies who's application had been rejected (Electrical and General Engineering Company) wrote to the Board of Trade detailing the Council's negative response to earlier requests and suggested that the Council's consent should be dispensed with. At a BoT enquiry the case for the Provisional Order was satisfactorily made out and to the surprise of the Council the Company offered to assign the Order to the Council on payment of their costs (£150).

The draft of the Provisional Order was received in May 1899 and the Council expected to be able to light Hendon with electricity before many months had passed.

THE PROVISIONAL ORDER

The Order required the Council to lay cables in certain roads within two years, and in some other roads within three years of May 17 1899. In addition mains had to be laid in any other road if six or more occupiers requested an installation.

The recommended system was three-wire DC 480/240v, feeders costing £4,545 with sub-stations at £3,000 each. This would require a generating plant of two boilers evaporating 2,300kg/hr coupled to two 100kw generators. The output would be equivalent to 6,000 lamps installed. The cost of this was estimated at £6,000.

At the consumers' premises meters would cost £5, fuse boxes £1, and the cost of wiring and connection £4. The total of this was estimated at £35,500. It was expected that 8,000 8cp lamps would be installed within three years each at 15kwh per annum. At 6d/kwh this would net £3,000 plus meter charges. Costs would be 56% of this leaving an operating profit of £1,650. With other charges there would be a net loss of £390 but as demand would grow this would be reversed. A further boiler and generator would cost £3,420 which would enable another 6,000 lamps to be added. The additional consumers may well be at Mill Hill necessitating a high-voltage feeder and sub/station. The extra installations would enable the Council to reduce the charge to 5½d/kwh. Compare this with Tyneside mentioned earlier.

The possibility of combining a refuse destructor with the generating plant was considered. It would consume the 8½ tons per day collected at that time, produce 109kwh, and reduce coal costs by £140/pa or reduce the charge by 1d/kwh. Finchley UDC built such a plant in Squires Lane Finchley which ran successfully for many years. Unless a special high-temperature incinerator was used today such a plant would be most undesirable: the high proportion of plastics and other synthetic materials in the waste would create cyanides, dioxins, and other toxic organo-chlorine compounds.

The man given the responsibility for making the proposals was Robert Hammond who was already known to the Council because of his involvement in a tramway project. One of his schemes was accepted with the provision that it had to include an extension to Mill Hill. Hammond was appointed consulting engineer and he was authorized to apply for a loan. When the scheme was presented to the full Council on October 9 1899 there was widespread opposition on the basis of cost. The Council was already committed to heavy investment in a new sewage system and the building of new Council Offices. One councillor objected because in one main road '1,000 yards of cable would supply six consumers at most'. The proposals were published in the press but there was insufficient response for agreement to be reached.

THE ARRIVAL OF NORTHMET

When the Council met on Jan 15 1900 they were told of the Bill then before Parliament about the proposals of the North Metropolitan Electric Power Supply Co. (Northmet) which was to deliver a bulk supply to much of north London, and Hendon was included in this plan. The prices quoted were 4d/kwh for the first 100kwh in any quarter then 2d/kwh. The Hendon Lighting Committee recommended opposition to the Northmet Bill. At a public meeting on April 4 1900 the motion to oppose the Bill was carried.

At this time the *Hendon & Finchley Times* had become enthusiastic about electric light in Hendon and spoke out against the delays and prevarication. In May 1900 Hammond discussed some amendments to his report and on June 18 the Lighting Committee met and accepted the revised proposals, and further recommended that the plans be prepared for the compulsory area with the extension to Mill Hill already requested. The Committee also rejected a proposal by Edmonton UDC that the councils of Middlesex should combine for generation and supply of bulk electricity.

In an editorial the *Hendon & Finchley Times* stated that they were convinced that the Northmet Bill would be passed and campaigned for

Hendon to cancel their schemes and hand over to private enterprise and thereby save the £17,810 of capital expenditure. The paper was unimpressed with the successes of Hammond, they were all in densely populated areas and Hendon was not.

The *Northmet Act* was passed in September 1900 and following a speech at the British Association (where it was stated that local authority boundaries were too small for electricity generation to be economical) the Council was urged to put their scheme in abeyance to avoid a waste of ratepayers money. Not to be deterred Hammond had lodged details of his scheme with the Board of Trade. If it was cancelled he stood to lose a substantial amount of money based upon the terms of his contract.

At a Council Meeting held on October 22 1900 the chairman of the Finance Committee, W S Booth, moved that the resolution authorising the Hendon scheme be revoked, but after a debate his motion was lost. Two weeks later the Lighting Committee debated the scheme as already agreed and decided to press ahead with plans for the compulsory area and to apply for the necessary loan. Hammond was to go ahead with the designs for the generating station. At this point Booth stated that the proposed site for the generating plant (Brent Cross) could not be used and moved that the plans based on Hammond's report should be referred back. The *Hendon & Finchley Times* still watching events closely agreed, and supported Booth and claimed that the Lighting Committee's scheme would cost a 3d rate. It was adopted nevertheless.

Advertisements inviting tenders appeared in November 1900 and by the closing date 82 had been received. The approval of the Board of Trade was already to hand. At this time both Booth and the local Ratepayers' Association strongly recommended that the Charing Cross, Euston, and Hampstead Railway (later to become part of the *Underground*) and Northmet be approached for quotations for bulk supply. This was turned down and the Lighting Committee proposal was adopted by the Council and they pushed ahead with confirmation of the Hammond agreement.

COSTS AND SCHEDULES

A public meeting was called because of the costs involved, which was poorly attended. The *Hendon & Finchley Times* described Hammond's proposals as fairy tales, but he won the day and convinced the Council that it was better for them to generate their own power rather than purchase in bulk. The North Middlesex Gas Co. tried to hang on to the business that they had already won and argued that with the new Welsbach incandescent burners (gas mantles) gas lighting would be far better and one seventh of the cost of electricity. They failed to convince.

So much time had been wasted that the Council could not keep to the time limits scheduled by the Provisional Order and asked the Board of Trade for an extension of three years. The BoT replied that they did not have this power but revoked the existing Order for one year which in effect gave an extension of one year.

By this time everyone had taken sides, and there were as many against electric lighting as there were for it. An anonymous correspondent to the press quoted 22 local authorities that were losing money on their ventures. The *Hendon & Finchley Times* was strongly against a local generating plant and recommended again that the cost of bulk purchase be looked into. They also stated that of the Provisional Orders already granted to local authorities at 215 no work had so far been started.

And so it went on with claim followed by counter-claim and Hendon being left farther and farther behind many other municipal undertakings.

On December 7 1901 a Local Government Board enquiry was held at the Council offices which attracted a large audience. There was much opposition to the Council's lighting plans but not all objected for the same reasons.

The Northmet Company and the North Middlesex Gas Company were alternative energy suppliers and were bound to object. Other objecting ratepayers represented were Mill Hill School, the Midland Railway, and the Catholic institutions of Mill Hill, to this was added a total of 624 ratepayers from both within and without the compulsory area, 63 tenants from an estate and 180 members from a working men's club. All this was backed up by a collection of petitions and signed cards.

Only two spoke in support, but their evidence was poorly presented, their reasoning was unconvincing and they were ambivalent. One large potential consumer was already producing its own supply and several houses on the outskirts of Hendon had arranged to purchase a supply from outside Hendon.

There were so many objectors that the enquiry was held over for five days, meanwhile the governors of Mill Hill School had withdrawn their objections since they had been assured that the School was to be included in the scheme, and therefore they would not be paying extra rates for a service that they could not enjoy.

The whole business of Hendon and its electricity supply had become a complete fiasco. There were those who objected to electricity on principle, (some without any experience said that they did not like electric light), plus others who objected to the Council's scheme (that is having their own generator). Some thought that Hendon was not yet ready for electricity, but did not say what they meant by this strange comment.

Worse still for the Council, electricity had now become not one of the election issues but the only issue in the coming election, with the distinct possibility that enough councillors could lose their seats over this one item to ensure that the Council's plans would have to be abandoned. This would lead to a waste of public money and further delays. In fairness to the Council they had not been able to present their case at the enquiry because only two of their speakers had been heard, whereas all of those that opposed had managed to have their say.

ELECTION AND AFTERMATH

It was now obvious that electric lighting could not be pushed out of the discussions, it was the only issue in the election campaign that was being aired. One third of the councillors had to stand for re-election.

At two ratepayers meetings there was a large vote against the Council's scheme but at another the audience came out in favour. Two councillors seeking re-election spoke out strongly in favour of the Council scheme, gave examples of where the use of electricity would lead to savings (at the sewage works for example) and also campaigned for the combined refuse destructor and generating plant. They were amongst those who lost their seats.

Council members could now see that opposition to their scheme was too vigorous to be ignored and further decisions were held over until after the election held on April 7. The result was that the supporters were defeated.

The newly elected Council was now in a mess. They had Parliamentary authority to proceed and had been granted a loan not as yet taken up. Neither approval nor loan now applied. They had also incurred considerable expenditure. The Local Government Board said that no action would be taken regarding the loan unless further applications were made. At a meeting of the Council it was decided to offer the Provisional Order for sale or lease, and also agreed that the BoT should be approached regarding an extension to the time limit for the Order.

Whilst the BoT did agree to a 'final' extension to the Order to December 31 1902 they could not permit the transfer of the Order to a company. The Council then had to apply for an Amendment Order: to provide an extension to the date by which work had to commence, to transfer the work to a company, and to give the Council the option of purchase, should they wish to, in due course.

The Amending Order as drafted named Crompton & Company as the company to which the Order was to be transferred. The *Hendon*

Electric Lighting Order 1899, Amendment Order 1903 made its way through Parliament and received the Royal Assent on June 30. A leader in the *Hendon & Finchley Times* greeted this with some enthusiasm and said that work would now commence because a private company would not dither like the Council had done. Not so, the only cables laid in Hendon that year were by Northmet for the Edgware Road tramway.

MORE DELAYS

If anything Cromptons turned out to be worse than the Council. In February 1904 they asked for a delay until January 1905 and only after being repeatedly prodded by both the Council and the BoT did they even sign the indentures (in June 1904).

On December 3 1904 the tramway between Cricklewood and Edgware was opened, but there was still no sign of any move towards providing Hendon with electric light. Throughout 1905 frequent enquiries were sent to Cromptons by the Council but all to no avail. Then in December of that year the Council was informed by Cromptons that they proposed to purchase electricity in bulk from Northmet which would save both time and cost. The *Hendon & Finchley Times* said that whilst this made some sense they had already delayed the installation work in Hendon beyond all reasonable limits and it was hard to believe that they had any real plans.

In April Crompton & Co. wrote to the Council announcing that they proposed to start cable laying the following month, needless to say this was greeted with some scepticism. The Council had completely lost faith in this Company and asked for a map showing the streets involved. Cromptons sent a map which showed that nearly every street was to have the cables. The Council certainly could not believe this and returned the plan on May 21, and asked for the plan to be amended to show the streets that would be disturbed in the initial schedule.

The answer was provided by Northmet. In July of the same year the peace of Hendon was disturbed by a large gang of men working seven days a week laying high voltage cables for Northmet. They were working inwards from Enfield and Edgware and meeting up at Brampton Grove, Hendon but not unfortunately for electric light. The primary purpose was to supply the north end of the tramway at Edgware. However Northmet was looking for business and had made provision for tappings of the cable at three points, one being at Brampton Grove to give Hendon a supply.

It was pretty obvious by now that Cromptons had never been up to the job and it came as no surprise when they announced their intention of handing over the work to the Electric Supply Corporation Ltd.

Relatively speaking the Corporation already had quite a history in the new industry. It was registered on July 8 1897 and had obtained orders in Scotland as well as Hitchin, Chelmsford, Stevenage, several parts of Devon, and now Hendon. More legislation was necessary to enable the transfer to take place, and at the same time another Bill was passed which made it possible for the powers of local authorities to be by-passed. There were also two Northmet Bills, one that enabled them to supply electricity to Hendon.

THE ARRIVAL OF HESCO

On June 27 1907 the Hendon Electric Supply Co. Ltd (HESCO) was registered and the Electric Supply Corporation took up 3,793 of the 10,000 £5 shares originally authorised for HESCO. The Corporation's bill passed through the final stages the same month and it was then necessary to obtain an order from the BoT to allow transfer of the Order to HESCO.

The *Underground* railway to Golders Green opened on June 22 1907 which further increased the demand that Hendon would have its electric lighting. HESCO acting as agents for Cromptons (the transfer bill had not yet been passed) sought to meet the demand and built a small temporary power station at North End, and supply commenced on January 10 1908 in the Golders Green area.

The Council had not been impressed by the small temporary supply that was planned and at a meeting on July 22 they gave notice that they would take legal proceedings if the provisions of the Orders were not complied with. A little of the heat was taken out of the situation in the autumn when a new resident engineer and manager was appointed to HESCO.

At last cable laying began and by early November 1907 they were in position along Golders Green Road to The Bell and in Finchley Road.

By 1911 HESCO had offices in The Promenade, Golders Green. In August 1912 they were able to invite tenders for the laying of suitable cables to bring electricity to the most important streets in Mill Hill.

By 1915 electricity meant much more than just lighting, and the HESCO manager organised some social evenings to illustrate the benefits of electric power. Residents were invited to receptions furnished with tables carrying electric kettles and toasters and invited to try out these implements while they were being shown the benefits of electric ironing, vacuum cleaning, and cooking.

The main offices of HESCO were in Brent Street, another was opened at Hendon Central when the *Underground* station was opened, a showroom was opened at Childs Hill and last of all the Mill Hill showroom was opened in 1932 at 19 The Broadway.

HESCO grew rapidly from 1912 and the financial results were most encouraging. This naturally affected the price that would have been necessary for the Council to take up their option to purchase the Company. They decided against this on each occasion. In 1912 the lamp equivalent installed was under 50,000 which had increased to almost 5m by 1938, and over the same period kW/h sold had risen from under 500,000 to 50m.

In 1938 Northmet made a bid for the Company and the Electric Supply Company which held 55,000 ordinary shares agreed to the offer. In any case Northmet had supplied power in bulk since 1908. By the date of the expiry of the offer over 90% of HESCO shareholders had agreed to the takeover. Under the Northmet Act of 1939 HESCO became a part of the Northmet Company from September 30 1939 so ending its 32 years as a separate company.

Ten years later the whole industry was taken into public ownership, a situation which lasted for over 40 years. Now of course, as a part of the policy of returning nationalised industries to the private sector the electric undertakings are back in private hands.

JOHN LAING plc

EARLY YEARS

In 1848 James Laing, a master mason, completed a modest contract in Sebergham in Cumberland (this has been a part of the county of Cumbria since 1965). This is hardly earth shattering history. Over a century later John Laing & Son Ltd completed a contract for the first stretch of the M1 Motorway on schedule, in spite of what appeared at times to be quite insurmountable odds. (The Company was renamed John Laing plc in 1978). It was the first major motorway in this country. Today we take motorways for granted, just complain every time that there is a hold-up for whatever reason.

On November 2 1959 the M1 Motorway, or rather its first section from near St Albans northwards for 90km was completed. It was a completely new experience for motor vehicles and their drivers. Many were unprepared, there were still waiting lists for new cars and although the majority of the cars and trucks on the roads had been built post-war never before had it been possible for them to be driven at full speed for so long. The number of failures and breakdowns was high, but this was not the fault of the road planners and builders.

When the first motorways were built there were no speed limits on these roads at all. The 70mph for cars and 60mph for heavy commercial vehicles followed later. It should be remembered that there was a 20mph limit on goods vehicles (trucks had a '20' plate on the rear) up to 1957 which was then raised to 30mph for solo goods vehicles, but heavy commercial vehicles with trailers were limited to 20mph right up to 1963. Because these vehicles had always been driven slowly many of the components (e.g. the cross-ply tyres with which the majority were fitted) just could not stand the strain of sustained high speeds. But what is the connection between Sebergham and the M1?

The family of Laing can easily be traced back to the beginning of the 18th Century. At that time they were stonemasons working around the hamlet of Harelawhill just over the Scottish border south of Langholm. David Laing subsequently moved to Sebergham, a village surrounded by steep hills, nearly 16km south-west of Carlisle. There at the beginning of the 19th Century he started a business of building repair and maintenance work.

David's son James (the third James Laing) married Ann Graham, a girl six years his senior. Ann was a strong, determined character and persuaded her husband to purchase a strip of land that fronted the roadway at Brow Top where he built three detached houses, one of these was for their own use. These still stand, although much altered, and one, Caldew House, has a stone tablet above the door on which is carved 'JAL 1848' (James and Ann Laing). This is where today's international business of John Laing plc really has its beginnings. In 1986 the house was fully restored and refurbished and handed over to the Salvation Army for use as a missionaries rest centre.

John Laing, the son of James, gave his name to the Company and established it in Carlisle in 1874 where his father later joined him. John William Laing (later to be appointed CBE), the son of John Laing Senior developed the Company into a national organization. In 1920 the Company became a limited company and in 1926 the headquarters was transferred from Carlisle to Mill Hill.

In 1926 Mill Hill was very rural and housing was limited and scattered. To ensure that the staff that came with the Company had somewhere to live houses were built close to the new offices for them to rent or buy. John Laing was cautious too: the first office building in Mill Hill was designed to look like a large house so that in the event of the London venture being a failure it could be sold without difficulty.

The next milestone was in 1952 when a public company was incorporated and the Company began to operate on an international scale. A complete reconstruction of the Business followed in 1978 when the parent company for all Laing activities became John Laing plc, with John Laing Construction as the principal subsidiary.

JOHN LAING AND THE M1

It is difficult to choose as an example one major construction from amongst the hundreds completed by Laings. The list is so diverse both in size and complexity, and locations. All of us are familiar with motorways, (the M1 runs through Mill Hill), and it is now difficult to imagine long journeys without them. Because Laings were involved right at the beginning with construction of the first part of the M1 and have also won a large number of subsequent motorway contracts their work on the M1 is taken as an illustration.

The first road built to motorway standards and regulations was the Preston by-Pass but this was such a short stretch it was almost an experiment. It eventually became a part of the M6.

The M1 was something different, 90km of problems with changes in the terrain, and flood risks in a score of places. Then add to this the weather, which in the first year was terrible, so that the road that started as a dream became a nightmare. But as is always said in show business 'It will all come right on the night', and so it did.

Discussions on a new road had really started before World War II with plans to build a by-pass for St Albans, to relieve one of the worst

bottlenecks on the old A5. The City's narrow streets and steep hills were the bane of all motor traffic. In 1951 the plans for the by-pass were incorporated into a much bigger scheme when the Ministry of Transport and Civil Aviation approached the consulting engineers, Sir Owen Williams and Partners to investigate a new kind of road that was required to run between the outer perimeter of London and south Yorkshire.

The M1 was something different

The work was exploratory and there was no guarantee that the scheme would ever get off the ground. In fact the idea of a road where only motorised traffic would be permitted was only made possible by the *Special Roads Act* of 1949. Many people were sceptical, not least the landowners over whose land the road would be built, and possibly the surveyors too.

But events were catching up with the planners even before the study was complete, the number of vehicles on the roads had doubled in the 10 years since the War ended. Nevertheless it was really a go-slow operation and any possibility of an actual programme of motorway building was way off in the future. There were objectors too who wanted to merely upgrade the A5.

There was now no holding back the motor car, every family wanted one and the waiting lists were getting shorter. It became obvious that no matter what was done to the existing roads they could never cope, and what is more the upgrading of the A5 would cost more than the completely new road. In February 1955 the Ministry announced the programme for the new road and the following July the momentous news was passed to Sir Owen Williams, who was asked the simple question 'How quickly can you get going'?

The next two years were for the work of the consulting engineers, surveyors and negotiators for the land purchases. The possible construction companies would have nothing to get their teeth into for a long time yet. The route had to be finalised, there were more than 130 bridges to be designed from foot bridges and cattle trails to viaducts, specifications to be worked out, curves and gradients to be calculated to make for the shortest haul distance for the spoil and so on.

In the beginning of 1957 odd bits of information began to appear in the construction press but there were still no hard facts to go on. In September the first announcement about the tendering dates appeared and a broad outline of the road. The Ministry and the consulting engineers had however kept interested companies informed so that they were able to carry out some preliminary work before the official documents were released. The contract had been divided into four sections and Laing had resolved that if they were given the chance they would tender for them all.

When the details for the tender finally arrived there were only nine weeks (with the Christmas holiday in the middle) for all the very complicated calculations. To make matters worse there were a number of possible alternatives to the specifications which meant much more work for the hard pressed estimators. To have made an error in the calculations could have been disastrous on a project worth £15m! Many things had to be answered: how many of their own staff would be required and where would extra labour be recruited, does each section require different machinery, were there adequate resources of sand and ballast along the route, how far would the hauls be from digging to dumping, where would the contractor set up base, and so on?

The quotations that had represented such a tough assignment for the estimators were finally delivered on Monday January 6 1958. Nine days later the Company directors were asked to attend a meeting with the consulting engineers and the Ministry, where to their surprise and delight they were asked whether they would be prepared to undertake the building of all four sections in the planned schedule of 19 months. Although Laings had been prepared for such an eventuality they were to say the least surprised, bearing in mind the stiff competition that they had been up against.

The story of the building is worthy of a book of its own, indeed a very interesting book was published by Laings when the contract was finished. (*The London-Birmingham Motorway* by L T C Rolt).

Every road builder from the times of the Romans had experienced problems with parts of the route as had the builders of canals and railways in the 18th and 19th Centuries. The Watford Gap with its waterlogged sands always caused difficulties.

To make matters almost impossible, 1958, the year of all the muck shifting was the wettest on record. Someone described the rain graph for June, July, and August as looking like the Himalayas. In one period 95mm of rain fell against an average of 21mm! Vehicles bogged down in the mud, and the chalk that is present for much of the route turned into a glutinous white paste. It was so bad that face shovels could not operate and in places they were swapped for draglines operating at normal ground level working their way backwards.

Prematurely that horrible year, the project was closed down for the winter. But not for long, 1959 was completely different with spring coming very early. Bad weather could have returned, or worse there could have been a cold spell. Nevertheless a calculated decision was made to restart in early March and most of the men who had been laid off only a few weeks before were re-engaged. It was now or never if the motorway was to be finished on time. The weather held and 1959 was a great year.

The fact that the motorway was opened to schedule is now history and few people if asked today would even know when the first 90km of the M1 were built. It is something that is there and we take it for granted. In some respects it is a pity that when the M1 was extended southwards through Mill Hill this contract did not go to Laings.

JOHN LAING IN THE 1990s

No doubt if Laings were asked to tender for 90km of motorway today, or 900km for that matter, they would just take it in their stride, such has been the development of the Company in the last 30 years. The size and diversity of the contracts completed and in hand must be the envy of most other contractors world-wide.

To name a few of the projects in Britain there are houses in Totton Hampshire, a newspaper plant in Manchester, hospitals in a dozen locations (and 250 contracts in 30 years), a theatre in Glasgow, a shopping precinct in Belfast, a leisure centre in Stourbridge, the National Museum of Wales, Sizewell 'B' Nuclear Power Station, sewage treatment works in Basildon and Tilbury, a 12 storey office building in Potters Bar, and the new terminal building at Stansted Airport. Overseas there are the Tekirova Holiday Village in Turkey, houses in California, the Marine Majlis in Dubai and the Santa Maria Golf Club in Marbella Spain. The list is endless.

As a Company, success must be measured in terms of turnover and profit. From 1985 to 1990 the turnover increased from £817m to nearly £1,530m and profits (before taxation) was still £20.1m in 1990 in spite of the recent difficulties in the construction industry. The John Laing organization is by all standards a highly successful international group employing some 12,000 people in the UK alone.

Without doubt it is one of the top companies in the field of construction, mechanical and civil engineering in the Country and probably in the World. The Company can offer a range of specialist or traditional skills for every kind of contract large or small. John Laing plc is not a factory, and does not manufacture in Mill Hill, what it does do however is to create work for a multitude of other manufacturers in this Country and elsewhere.

The chairman today is J M K (Martin) Laing, the eighth consecutive Laing to have had this responsibility. Sometime in the future we look forward to number nine.

CHAPTER XXVII

MILL HILL & THE MILITARY

No doubt people from the hamlets of Hendon served in the various wars that were fought between the Norman conquest and World War I but as war memorials are a feature of the 20th Century we have no ready record of deaths by enemy action or in civil strife. The men of Hendon must have taken sides in the Wars of the Roses (three battles, two at St Albans and one at Barnet were fought close by), and in King v Parliament in the Civil War, and it is quite likely that men volunteered for service in the war against Napoleon's France if only to escape from the drudgery of their daily lives.

Maybe they were neutral, the *Court Rolls* of 1597 would certainly suggest their lack of interest in military involvement. An Act of Parliament of 1521 was meant to encourage archery and to this end regular practice in the butts was compulsory throughout the land. In addition every male over 14 years of age was bound to be in possession of a bow and two shafts. There is record of at least one Hendon resident who was found guilty of failing to comply with this Act. The butts in Hendon did not materialize until 1597 anyway, and then only when the local constable had been reprimanded for failing to provide this facility.

In August 1988 an active service unit (so called) of the Provisional IRA planted an explosive device against an accommodation block of Mill Hill's Inglis Barracks. As a result of the explosion that followed the building was extensively damaged, one person was killed and nine others were injured. It is a pity that this will have been the first time that many people around the Country will ever have heard of Mill Hill. Fortunately there is much more to Mill Hill than terrorist activities and political extremism and rather sad that the media will have had to draw attention to Mill Hill for such a reason.

Mill Hill is a long way from the sea, it does not have any sizable streams and certainly does not boast a navigable river, and even the largest lake would not take anything bigger than a rowing boat. So we cannot expect Mill Hill to have any real association with the Royal Navy. There is not much left of Hendon Aerodrome apart from the museum and it was never in Mill Hill anyway, so apart from using the high spots of Mill Hill to watch the Hendon Air Pageant which was held annually between the two World Wars we cannot claim any direct association between Mill Hill and the RAF. However no harm is done with a brief mention. After all when Claude Graham-White opened the aerodrome in 1910 it was with Croydon one of the first purpose built aerodromes in the country (if not in the world). And now that airmail for overseas letters is the norm it is interesting to note that the first UK air post was from and to Hendon in 1911.

The British Army is something different because Mill Hill has had a long and direct association with the Army ever since Mill Hill Barracks was opened in April 1905 as the Regimental Training Depot for the Middlesex Regiment.

MILL HILL'S NAVY!

But let us return for just a few lines to matters concerning the Royal Navy. As anyone who knows Mill Hill will be aware the most prominent building in the area is on The Ridgeway, and it is clearly visible from all directions. This huge building, which belongs to the Medical Research Council, was completed just prior to World War II and promptly taken over by the Admiralty to become a training depot for the WRNS.

One must assume that German intelligence was reasonably efficient and that they quickly found out about this annexation, and it is therefore not surprising that attempts were made to bomb the building. They were, but fortunately unsuccessfully. The people who lived in the area at the time were certainly familiar with the assembled ranks of the WRNS recruits on parade in the streets around the building. In such a large building many hundreds must have passed through (and passed out) during five years of WRNS occupation.

MILL HILL - A GARRISON TOWN

The presence of the Army in Mill Hill goes back much farther, is much more obvious, and has been more enduring, although it is now coming to an end. Anyone who has in the past ever had any connection with the Middlesex Regiment will remember Inglis Barracks on Bittacy Hill. It was the home of the Middlesex Regiment Training Depot for over 50 years.

The people who live in garrison towns, and anyone who served in the armed forces a couple of decades or more ago will remember church parades, but not necessarily with any great affection. They meant a Saturday night devoted to cleaning and polishing when there were always more interesting things to do. To the local residents it was always a little exciting, particularly for children, to see the Sunday turnout with flags flying and band playing. The people of Mill Hill were certainly no strangers to martial sights and sounds for a great many years.

The Middlesex Regiment has its origins way back in the reign of George II when he decided that the fighting regiments should cease to be named after their colonels. Up to that time each unit carried the name and insignia of its colonel-in-chief who often behaved like a feudal lord. Under the new rule, regiments were given numbers, these ran from 52 to 61, and it was from the eventual amalgamation of the 57th and 77th Regiments of Foot that the Middlesex Regiment was created on July 1 1881.

In the years between this edict of George II and the creation of the Middlesex, the 57th and 77th saw service in all parts of the World and the list of these places reads like a gazetteer: Gibraltar, Minorca, North America (in both the war against the French and the American War of Independence), France, the West Indies, Bulgaria, the Crimea, India, Australia, Ceylon, Burma, and so on. It was during one of these overseas postings that the Regimental motto was born.

After a particularly gruelling time in the West Indies the 57th had returned to Britain for service in England, Jersey, Guernsey, and Gibraltar.

one of their finest leaders
... Major William Inglis

One of their finest leaders at the time was Major William Inglis. On July 15 1809 the comfortable home tour came to an abrupt end when the 57th was posted to the Iberian Peninsular and landed at Lisbon. Looking back at this bit of history today the ensuing battle seems to have been totally futile and an utter waste of young lives. This was to be a showdown between the forces of Napoleon and those of the Duke of Wellington. The 57th joined a brigade that contained the Worcesters and the Northamptons and these regiments had already distinguished themselves in the Peninsular Campaign and considered the 57th to be new boys to this kind of fighting. They were, but not for long.

The Battle of Albuera in the spring of 1811 was a confused slaughter with hundreds killed and wounded on both sides. One of the first to be killed was the commander of the 57th, Major General Hoghton, and this loss left Inglis in charge as the next senior. The enemy grapeshot was proving to be devastating and particularly effective. Inglis fell with his chest pierced with grapeshot but still had voice enough to call out to his men, 'Die hard 57th', which became the motto of the 57th and ultimately of the Middlesex Regiment.

According to regimental writers of the time Inglis saw out the battle lying in front of the Regimental Colours propped up on his elbows and even refused treatment until the fighting was over. When the slaughter was finished for the day Inglis was the only officer still alive above the rank of major and he was too badly injured to resume command. He was given an honour on the field of battle but more than that his command 'Die hard 57th' was adapted to the name by which the Middlesex Regiment would always be known, the 'Die-Hards; a unique compliment. Inglis saw much further service, became colonel of the Regiment, and died in November 1835. He was buried in Canterbury Cathedral.

On July 1 1881 the two regiments, 57th and 77th lost their identities when they were amalgamated to form the Middlesex Regiment. In April 1905 the Regimental Training Depot was transferred to Mill Hill into a brand new red brick barracks with such luxuries (for those days) as indoor wash rooms and a proper separate dining hall. The Barracks was affectionately known as 'The Garden' because of its location and the surrounding scenery. The big surprise is that 25 years were to pass before the Barracks was named Inglis Barracks.

Before World War II the Middlesex Regiment consisted of four regular battalions, three of these in days of Empire were normally abroad. In addition there were two special reserve battalions and four battalions of territorials.

After World War I there were 46 battalions of the Middlesex scattered around the World, almost everywhere that had seen fighting. These units were brought home one by one, then disbanded leaving only four. Two of these survived until 1927 when these were also broken up. The last to leave France was the 1st Battalion which came home in May 1919. An advance cadre under the command of Col L L Pargiter was sent to Mill Depot and a new 1st Battalion was built up. With the end of hostilities Mill Hill Depot was able to resume its proper function of peace time activity; the training of recruits and postings overseas to keep the battalions up to strength. These were busy years because at the same time as old units were being disbanded and men demobilised new recruits were being trained and units created. All this put a great strain on Depot personnel.

By 1922 the home base had been reduced to two battalions with one militia battalion. Depot operation continued on these lines until 1938 with overseas units looking to Mill Hill for physical and moral support during the long Regimental tours of duty abroad.

In 1938 the Middlesex Regiment was selected as the machine gun regiment which added to the work load of the Depot staff. This was merely a foretaste of things to come. In September 1939 war broke out again which meant a great expansion in machine gun training. Inglis Barracks became the Regimental Machine Gun Training Centre. The Regiment was much enlarged to two regular and six territorial battalions. Mill Hill continued in this role until September 1941 when dangers of heavy bombing led to the decision to move the Regiment to Chester. At this time the Middlesex consisted of 250 officers and 1,700 other ranks, a very big increase on peace time strength. A skeleton party was left at Mill Hill until the war was over.

Just prior to the outbreak of war in 1939 building work was commenced on a number of semi-underground reinforced concrete buildings within the perimeter of the Barracks. They were clearly visible from the road, and in fact as children we 'explored' the unfinished

"Die hard 57th"

... became the motto

structures during the weekends when there were no building workers about. Local people referred to these buildings as the 'munitions dumps', although that was probably not their main function.

World War II, like the World War that started 25 years earlier meant for the Middlesex service in every theatre of war. They experienced the humiliation of Dunkirk, they were used to try to stem the tide of the Japanese invasion of Hong Kong, (those who survived were transported to the Japanese mainland and were torpedoed on route by an American warship), they fought with the Desert Rats in North Africa, and from there they were involved in the Sicily landings and subsequent fighting on the Italian mainland. They were in fact involved in some of the toughest and bloodiest battles in Italy. And just to round off their achievements they were landed on the Normandy beach-head just 20 minutes after the initial landings.

The end of the War did not lead to the lasting peace for which everyone had hoped, certainly not in the Middle East. The Middlesex saw service in Palestine right up to the end of the British mandate in 1948. It was a miserable thankless task because it was impossible to separate friend from adversary. The hunt for the elusive EOKA leader in Cyprus, Gen Grivas, was just as bad and equally difficult. But both of these local essentially policing jobs were to prove to be mere exercises compared with what was to follow; the Korean War.

The years after World War II meant much change in the fortunes of the Middlesex as once again the British Army was reorganised from a fighting machine to (Korea apart) peace keeping and other public duties. Not that this meant less work for the depot at Mill Hill, but rather work of a very different kind.

AN ENTIRELY NEW ROLE

On January 31 1961 the Middlesex severed its connection with Mill Hill when the depot was closed. After 55 years Inglis Barracks was no longer considered to be the ideal situation for the training depot of the Regiment.

The Barrack's was now given an entirely new role. It became the Postal and Courier Depot RE. However lest anyone should consider this to be an unimportant role ask any soldier, particularly those serving overseas, whether regular mail is important and the chances are that he will say that it is of equal importance to food and good billets after equipment. As a matter of interest the Corps of Royal Engineers is the second senior corps in the British Army and has therefore been in existence longer than the Middlesex Regiment.

Mention has already been made of the bomb attack on Inglis Barracks in 1988. In the last few years the Provisional IRA and the other Republican terrorist offshoots have changed their tactics and now attack what they describe as soft military targets. Mill Hill would certainly fit into this category and has therefore attracted the attention of the terrorists. This has probably accelerated the decision to close down the whole of this establishment by the end of 1995. In any case if this decision had not been announced in May 1990 the reduction in the size of the armed forces in July 1990 would certainly have forced the same decision to be taken. An easing of the tension between the eastern and western alliances is bound to lead to a complete reappraisal of military needs. So after a little under 90 years of residence the army will finally depart from Mill Hill.

As to what will happen to the buildings and about 42ha of land, that remains to be seen. Some buildings, notably the Officers' Mess may be worthy of a Preservation Order and others could be converted into factory premises for light industry and even for housing. Whatever is done much care and thought is needed, particularly as regards the trees, there are many fine specimens as well as the wooded frontages to Bittacy Hill and Partingdale Lane and these should be preserved at all costs.

ARMY CADETS

Mill Hill does have one other association with the British Army, which may not appear to be nearly so important as the Middlesex Regiment. Public Schools are in addition to being seats of learning, quasi religious institutions. The chapel is an important part of the school function. Some public schools have naturally gravitated towards military matters, not so Mill Hill. It was after all founded by non-Conformist ministers and at that time there was also a strong Quaker influence in the Village.

It was inevitable nevertheless that some Mill Hill Old Boys would take up a career in the Army and as early as the 1840s there were officers in the Indian Army who had been educated at Mill Hill School. And again in the Boer War a handful of ex Mill Hill pupils served there too. As a direct result of this activity a rifle club was started at the School in 1910 and as this proved to be successful the War Office was approached with a view to starting a unit at the School of the Public School Cadet Corps and Camps. Three of the masters took commissions and by the time that permission had been granted the number of boys who wanted to join had risen to 120. At that time the School bursar was Lieut. Col Glunicke who had been Corps Commander at Bedford for many years.

Needless to say the masters had no more idea of soldiering than the boys and some sergeant instructors were 'borrowed' from the Middlesex Regiment. The Colonel-in-Chief of the Regiment gave permission for the Cadet Corps to wear Regimental buttons and badges which was considered to be a great honour. It was always an advantage for the Cadet Corps to be in close proximity to a famous regiment, particularly in its early years.

CHAPTER XXVIII

GOVERNMENT & THE LAND

Sometime in our lives most of us will live in a house that we have purchased. Once the land belonged to no-one, now everywhere has an owner, how did this situation develop? Whatever the reason it is something that cannot be undone. It is probably a part of human nature to possess. The fact that we can all in theory be property owners is at least fairer than the division of land even a few hundred years ago when a handful of big landowners could control almost an entire shire, and had land in more than one county.

Much of the land in Mill Hill is still owned by a few institutions, and the local authority, which is probably to our benefit, there is also a considerable area of farm land and ownership of farms is as old as Mill Hill itself. There is no common pattern in the development of land control and government at a local level. Hendon (and therefore Mill Hill) is not unique, but because for many years it was 'owned' by the Abbey of Westminster it is special in some ways.

FARMING THE LAND

Throughout the times leading up to the Dissolution of the Monasteries the Abbey of Westminster relied upon its Manors for most of the food that they consumed. Attached to the Abbey there would have been a mill, probably horse or ox driven, a bakehouse, and a brewery. Bread would normally be baked twice per week and beer brewed under the supervision of one of the canons, and was probably the safest drink. Wheat and malt would have been provided by the Manors and the secular and religious staff (abbots, canons, and priests) of the Abbey would each have been entitled to a share.

The monks and their successors at Westminster Abbey maintained very accurate records of the farm accounts for the manors under their jurisdiction. The first date with respect to Hendon is 1316, this was when the Abbot of Westminster took possession following the gift in 1295 by *Royal Charter* of Edward I. At this time, the 14th Century, farm accounts were usually kept by tally and because few farmers could read or write nothing was entered on paper so little has come forward to today.

In 1376 John atte hegge took over the responsibility of keeping the farming records of the Manor. He farmed his own land, collected the rents, and kept the accounts for 40 years. When he died in 1416 the standard of the records declined, probably because there was no-one else of his ability.

When Westminster Abbey became owners of the Manor they spent some time on a complete reorganisation. The incomes were largely used for restocking and for repairs to walls and barns, and most important to us, the mill was built about this time.

Many historians, particularly those writing mainly for children, like to create the impression that all was well during the reign of Elizabeth I, Good Queen Bess and all that. There was however much unrest in the countryside, largely brought about by the Enclosure of Land Acts on an increasing scale for pasture. Complaints about this activity reached the government from many quarters: Bedfordshire, Derbyshire, Hertfordshire, Gloucestershire, Kent, Monmouthshire, Norfolk and Worcestershire.

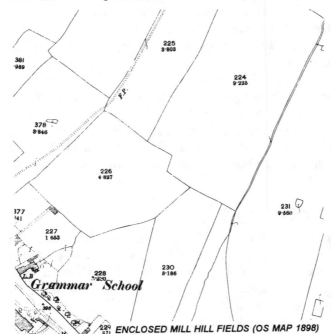

ENCLOSED MILL HILL FIELDS (OS MAP 1898)

There was no complaint from Middlesex which was significant: the County was almost entirely devoted to pasture and the hay crop already.

The main produce of the fields of Mill Hill for centuries had been hay, and up to the 1860s the whole of Hendon was considered to be a major hay producing district. Labourers from other areas, particularly around Bedford and from Ireland used to come every year bringing their own scythes to cut the crop. They brought next to no luggage, it was usually limited to what could be wrapped in a large kerchief, this was fine providing the weather was set fair, but the men and their families must have suffered miseries if the summers were wet and cold. No work meant no pay, and not even a change of clothes.

The next time that 'imported' labour was used was during World War II when trusted German and Italian prisoners of war were employed.

At the end of hostilities a number of these were not inclined to return home, knowing that their homes and families had vanished in the destruction of the cities during the bombing, or during the land warfare that followed. Worse still if their home town was now in the Soviet sphere of influence.

The fields of Mill Hill are still predominantly sown to grass and landowners have largely resisted the tendency over the centuries to change to corn production, or in more recent times to oilseed rape. Pictures of sowers in ancient times always show the sower with a basket scattering the seed by hand in simple broadcast fashion. A most haphazard and unreliable method. By the middle of the 18th Century Jethro Tull was beginning to convince farmers that it was far more accurate, less wasteful, and more productive to drill and sow in rows. The antiquated broadcast method of sowing grain was on its way out in most areas, albeit rather slowly. In Middlesex this was not so and the lead given by the farmers of Essex, Hertfordshire, Leicestershire, and East Anglia was not followed.

Other changes were taking place too. People were beginning to realise the benefits of added fertilizers and proper drainage. Chalk was used in the acid soils of Essex and hollow drains were being employed. Organic refuse from London such as horn shavings and chopped up rags as well as soot and ashes were being purchased as manure. But Middlesex in spite of being more conveniently placed than these other counties to introduce modern methods, and improve farming generally had not progressed at all. One tenth of the County was still common land, the roads were bad, and the farmers and landowners were uninterested and unenterprising.

At this point let us take a look at the land within the Manor of Hendon and compare it with the entry in *Domesday Book*. When the Normans came to England the greater part of the Manor was still forest and this must have been substantial because it was able to support over 1,000 swine. A survey carried out towards the end of the 18th Century revealed that of Hendon's 8,204 acres (3,418 ha) 7,700 acres (3,208 ha) were meadow, 300 acres (125 ha) were arable and only 120 acres (50 ha) were woodland. In other words in the 700 years since the Normans arrived nearly all the woodland had been cleared but little else had changed: most of the people were still engaged in agricultural pursuits and the crop was still primarily hay. Hendon was still largely isolated, most of the families had lived there for centuries and the tracks and paths were as ancient as the families.

It is interesting to note that throughout the Country as a whole 93% of the land under the plough in 1914 was already worked at the time of the *Domesday Book* in 1086. Probably the only county that had managed to show a big increase in arable land was Lincolnshire. By the beginning of this century the fens and marshes had finally been properly drained.

GOVERNMENT: NATIONAL AND LOCAL

At the time of the Norman conquest land administration was quite unlike anything today. There was no national government and for that matter nothing on a local level. In earlier chapters much has been said about the Manor of Hendon and the ten hamlets that were parts of it, and that it was under the control of the Abbey of Westminster up to the Reformation. This is not typical for the Country as a whole.

One out of 25 people lived in the 'large' towns, that is those with a population exceeding 2,000. The rural countryside was divided two ways, into manors and villages, and they did not necessarily share the same boundaries. A village may well have been divided between more than one manor and a lord frequently held more than one manor. The manor was an economic unit and run as such, the village was a community of people and not all had a resident lord. Just as not all villages were the same in size and wealth this also applied to the manors. There was not even a common structure, and two adjacent manors could be quite different in their customs and organisation.

The usual impression given is that below the lord all were peasants with no land and few rights. Apart from the fact that the term peasant was not used there were four different levels of society:

Villani (Villeins) 41% of the people with 45% of the land

Bordarii (Cottagers/smallholders) 32% of the people with 5% of the land

Liberi homines (Free men) 14% of the people with 20% of the land

Servi (Serfs) 10% of the people with no land.

From these figures it will be seen that the lord cultivated only part of the land, usually between 30% and 40%. It is not hard to understand how the private farms mentioned in an earlier chapter came about.

All this is a long way from any proper administration and divisions of responsibility. No-one was elected into a position of authority at a local level, the parish council was the only real administrative body.

Population was increasing steadily and by the early 19th Century it was clear that local government needed reforming. The JPs were the authority in the counties and the parishes were responsible to the justices. After 1815 much of the justices' work was taken over by central government, the biggest item being the administration of the *Poor Law*. In

1835 they lost their highway duties. In 1863 Hendon was under the jurisdiction of the new Edgware Highway Board and was entitled to elect two way wardens. From 1835 the justices' control of licensing and the police also weakened.

The parish councils were now trying to carry out duties for which they were ill equipped and the strain was beginning to show. Parish government had no common pattern, there was no uniformity regarding meetings. In most places a handful of important ratepayers met once per year, about Easter time, they discussed business and allotted responsibilities for the year. Corruption was frequently rife and one dominant man such as the Rev. Theodore Williams of Hendon could 'manage' the council for years in his own interests by intimidation.

An act of 1831 introduced elected assemblies with all ratepayers, men and women, being entitled to vote by ballot. All that was left for the parish councils was the levy and collection of church rates and when this was abolished in 1868 the parish as a unit of local government was no more.

In 1879 the Hendon Local board was formed with 12 members and was divided into three wards: Hendon, Childs Hill and Mill Hill with half of the members representing Hendon. The number was increased to 15 in 1895 when Hendon was upgraded to Urban District Council. Increases in population led to further additions and in 1915 the number of wards was increased to six and then to nine in 1931. By this time the councillors had risen to 33.

The Hendon UDC was enlarged by the absorption of Edgware in 1931 and the last development as a separate administration was promotion to borough status in 1932.

For the purpose of Parliamentary seats Hendon is divided into north and south, Mill Hill is in Hendon North. Both seats are traditionally held by Conservative members. In the Hendon UDC, Borough of Hendon and now the London Borough of Barnet there has always been a Conservative majority in the local council.

HOUSING

After the stagnation in building for the four years of World War I there was a shortage of 600,000 houses nationwide, in fact this is probably the first time that the phrase 'housing shortage' had been used. By 1923 the figure had risen to 830,000. At the end of the War a reconstruction programme was set up and Christopher Addison, a minister of Lloyd George's government introduced the far reaching *Housing Act* of 1919. In many ways this changed the whole basis of family life and in many places the appearance of the environment.

The Act gave to local authorities a duty; to survey the housing needs of the area under their control and to submit plans to central government for house building subsidised by State funds. It was this legislation that set in motion the principle of local authorities providing council houses, often on completely new estates. The Goldbeater's Estate later to become the Watling Estate was of course one of these.

Unfortunately this policy of housing at any price proved to be a financial disaster and houses built at the beginning of 1921 for £910 could be built less than two years later for £385. This caused an outrage. In July 1921 the grants for new houses were reduced and in 1922 stopped altogether so that all the houses in the programme were completed by 1923, nevertheless much had been achieved and Addison's plan had produced 213,000 new houses.

Not all the houses were in large estates. Some individual houses built in Mill Hill were tiny, and because they were built singly they were even more expensive. For £1,100 each and with virtually no garden you had two bedrooms, one reception room, and a tiny kitchen cum scullery about 2.5m x 2m which contained bath, copper, cooker, sink, and draining board. These barrack-like cottages were rented for 11/6 or 14/- (57½p or 70p) per week.

The private sector was not overlooked in the 1919 house building drive. A separate act, the *Housing (Additional Powers) Act* granted lump sum subsidies irrespective of whether they were for sale or rent. Builders did not expect the boom to last and were reluctant to take the risk of building without firm orders. When work did start bankruptcy often followed with a number of builders being involved before a street was finished.

In Mill Hill a £1,000 leasehold typical three-bedroom semi required a deposit of £300 and mortgage repayments of £69 6s (£69.30) for 16 years but £150 of the deposit could be borrowed as a second mortgage at 5% repayable over five years.

Three large estates of council housing have had an influence on Mill Hill, although only one of these is a actually within Mill Hill's borders. These are: the Watling Estate, built by the London County Council in the early 1920s, and one of the first developments of this type and to this scale anywhere in England, the Grahame Park Estate that was built after World War II on land from Hendon Aerodrome, and the estate to the east of Mill Hill north of Pursley Road which is in Mill Hill. There are also some smaller developments for instance around the Bittacy Hill area. Needless to say not everyone was delighted with the sudden influx of a large number of working class families into what had been a middle class area. They complained that the 4,000 families destined for the houses in the Watling Estate would equate to an additional population of some 20,000 and this would change the whole character and social structure of the district, which of course it did.

The Watling Estate has retained its identity but with the extension of private ownership in this type of development, and a less rigid meaning to the phrases middle class and working class, (and the almost relegation to history of the names white collar worker and blue collar worker) the existence of council estates so called is of much less consequence than it was. And in any case because many of these houses are now privately owned they are just as well appointed as their 'private' counterparts.

With the latest proposals regarding Mill Hill Barracks it is possible that a mixture of both types of ownership could exist there side-by-side and absorb the married families accommodation that already exists.

CHAPTER XXIX

MILLHILLIANS IN THEIR LEISURE TIME

In all probability the first team sports on any organised basis came to Mill Hill via Mill Hill School. Nevertheless many years passed before any regular teams were established and the 19th Century was in its last quarter before any visiting sides would have felt that it was worthwhile paying a visit here.

In the chapter on property we looked at four important 20th Century private housing developments; the so called Poet's Corner, the Uphill Farm Estate, the Mill Hill Garden Village and the Stoneyfields Estate. When these were built Mill Hill was still very rural, scantily populated, and not very well known except by the local people and those who lived in the fine houses of The Ridgeway and Highwood Hill areas. It was therefore necessary for the developers of these new estates to distribute rather elaborate brochures extolling the virtues of the district and the benefits to be obtained from residing there. Eighty years ago we were still very much wrapped up and restricted by the Victorian Prot-

> ### Recreations
> **Sports and Outdoor Games. There are ample facilities at Mill Hill for indulgence in all the favourite outdoor games- lawn-tennis, cricket, football, hockey, bowls, etc., in Mill Hill Park and elsewhere.** In respect of recreation, Mill Hill profits greatly by its proximity to the London Aerodrome, Hendon, the Country Club (at Colindale), and the extensive waters of the Brent Reservoir (generally known as the "Welsh Harp", from an old inn near it). On the Welsh Harp boating and angling may be enjoyed, and, when conditions permit, skating. At The Hyde, near the Aerodrome, are fine public swimming-baths, where on certain days mixed bathing is allowed.
>
> Certain packs of hounds occasionally meet within reach of Mill Hill - the Old Berkeley Foxhounds, Mr. Smith-Bosanquet's Foxhounds, and the Aldenham Harriers.
>
> **Golf.** Within a radius of six miles from Mill Hill there are some twenty excellent golf courses, of which we have not space to mention more than a few of the nearest. Clubs and positions of courses are as follows: Hendon G.C., Holders Hill; London Country Club, Colindale; Edgware G.C., Canons Park; Arkley G.C., near High Barnet; South Herts G.C., near Totteridge; and North Middlesex G.C., near Whetstone. All these except the Arkley Club's are 18-hole courses.

estant work ethic. Most people in authority frowned on leisure (the Devil finds work for idle hands etc.), the working day and week were still very long, and holidays were very short, if they existed at all for ordinary people. It is a little surprising therefore that any publicity was given to leisure activities available to future Mill Hill residents.

Needless to say some of the planned facilities failed to materialize, the land that they would occupy quickly became too precious. The Uphill Estate brochure mentioned 'six excellent golf courses within easy reach'. This is still true, there are three within the area now called Mill Hill and others are only a few minutes drive away. The brochure also mentioned private clubs for tennis, croquet, cricket and bowls, today we would add football and rugby. In addition to all these there were to be public tennis courts. If angling was to be the escape then there was the Welsh Harp and for the really daring with some spare cash there was a flying club at Hendon Aerodrome. The brochure for Mill Hill Garden Village made similar claims and even mentioned some more golf courses.

Today most types of sport are readily available within a reasonable distance. However not everyone enjoys vigorous exercise, and some would rather spend their spare time on an archaeological 'dig', in a local drama group, bobbing around in an aerobics class, getting involved in philately or dodging the washing-up by growing a private glut in the allotment garden. Mill Hill can cater for all these activities.

We are now coming to the end of the 20th Century. With the much shorter working week, longer and more frequent holidays and earlier retirement, Millhillians need all the facilities that are on offer.

One of the healthiest of exercises, and indeed essential for people with some disabilities, is swimming. Unfortunately Mill Hill does not have a public swimming pool within its borders. Until recently there was a pool in Daws Lane but in spite of much protesting by the local people this was demolished and has been replaced by a garden centre. If nothing else the pool's replacement encourages another leisure activity. At the time of the dispute there was a mysterious fire, no-one has suggested that this was started deliberately but even so it was certainly convenient for the developer. Today the nearest pool is at Copthall Stadium, just outside the Mill Hill boundary in NW4, this was constructed to the shorter length of 25m. Copthall has hosted the World Cup once, and the ASA on three occasions. Copthall is also the nearest athletics track.

Two of the largest institutions in Mill Hill (both on The Ridgeway) have very considerable sports facilities. The NIMR has a large sports field, three hard tennis courts, a squash court and facilities for badminton. The NIMR staff association organizes sporting competitions with those of other institutions. In addition there are separate clubs for chess, cinema, photography and other activities.

Recently Mill Hill School established Mill Hill School Enterprises which enables non-School Mill Hill residents to make use of the School's facilities out of hours. This has proved to be of enormous benefit to the the west of the Borough of Barnet. Mill Hill School was the first school to build its own indoor swimming pool, gymnasium, and squash courts, and rugby and cricket are very actively encouraged. In all the School has facilities for 25 major sports.

BEYOND THE BOUNDARY

'Now in Maytime to the wicket,
Out I march with bat and pad;
See the son of grief at cricket,
Trying to be glad'.

A E Housman

A walk through the Mill Hill School playing fields in early spring is a reassuring sight. The boys are actually coached in the cricket nets and many are obviously trying very hard, and with a lot of encouragement. Unfortunately this is becoming unusual for many schools. Even the old universities, so long a source of cricket talent, are not producing the goods to the same extent that they used to.

Is it just imagination or does the football season encroach on the shorter cricket season a little more every year? There is certainly a bigger overlap. Fortunately club cricket carries on regardless. It is not too demanding in terms of cost and commitment and no-one has ever dared to declare that it is a win at all costs exercise. The age of some of the players would confirm this. The secret is to try very hard indeed, but to give the impression that it is meant to be fun, and that only the game matters.

One of the first recognised clubs to be started up in Mill Hill was the cricket club that was established in 1868. There is nothing particularly unusual about this, a look in the directory of the Cricket Club Conference will show hundreds of clubs that came into existence about this time and many of them representing similar size villages to Mill Hill. At the turn of the Century in Middlesex alone there were 63 registered clubs.

Today Mill Hill has at least three clubs. There is the one mentioned above now known as the Mill Hill Cricket, Hockey and Squash Club, the Mill Hill Village Cricket Club, and the John Keble Cricket Club. The Village Club was founded in 1881, and John Keble in 1955. An apocryphal tale is told of a man who tried to join the Village team but was dismissed rather summarily and then joined the other team named Mill Hill. Of course the man is then supposed to have done rather well against the team that rejected him.

THE NOBLE GAME OF GOLF

'Ye see, professor, as long as ye are learning thae lads at the College
Latin and Greek it is easy work, but when ye come to play golf ye maun
hae a heid!'

Wise words from Lang Willie, a caddy at St Andrew's to a university professor who was proving to be rather unsuccessful at the noble game. With three courses having Mill Hill addresses and at least four more within 20 minutes drive there is every opportunity for Millhillians to prove that they 'hae a heid'.

The Finchley Golf Club is the oldest by 20 years of the three within the boundaries of Mill Hill. When Henry Stubbs JP built the mansion Nether Court just off Frith Lane it was intended to be a rather splendid home. It quickly became obvious that the gardens (which had once been a part of the farmlands of Frith Manor) would make an exciting and rather picturesque golf course.

The course was laid out in 1883 and the boundaries have remained much the same to the present day. A wide tree-lined public footpath (Lovers' Walk) divides the course in two. Stubb's mansion became a rather splendid clubhouse. In 1934 the land from the Dollis Brook to Frith Lane was transferred to the Finchley Urban District but in the reorganisation of 1965 reverted to Mill Hill.

In Sanders Lane is the clubhouse of the second of Mill Hill's golf clubs, the Hendon Golf Club. It has the distinction of having a Mill Hill address for the clubhouse but the entire playing area is in NW4. Ashley Lane, one of the oldest lanes in the district crosses the course and for about 0.5km this lane forms the boundary with the Hendon Park Cemetery.

The course was designed by H S Colt and opened at the turn of the Century. Colt is probably better known as the designer of the Eden Course at St Andrew's and the courses of Sunningdale and Wentworth. Today the membership of the Hendon Golf Club at all levels is around 550.

The Mill Hill Golf Club is the new boy of the three but nevertheless is still over 60 years old having been first opened in 1927. There are many interesting and unusual things about this club, the most obvious being that a dual-carriageway major road, the A1, separates the clubhouse from the entire playing area (except the putting green). Fortunately there is an underpass for pedestrians, the traffic on this road is rather unforgiving. There was a break in the central reserve of the road but only maintenance vehicles for the golf course were permitted to cross here, and in recent road works even this was closed.

The land between Mill Hill and Elstree was an ideal place to construct a golf course and when John Lewis Griffiths purchased 60ha of the Moat Mount Estate in 1923 he set out to make a dream into fact. The club was originally called Mote Mount Golf Club but this was changed to Mill Hill at a later date. There was no A1 Barnet by-Pass then, just open green fields and much of it taken up by a dairy farm. The farm buildings were converted and became the clubhouse with access via Hankins Lane.

Looking at the clubhouse today it is hard to imagine that it was ever anything else, the building seems so appropriate. The architect responsible for the transformation was Miss Anne J Cooke. Work on the course began in 1924 under the watchful eye of J F Abercrombie, a well known golf course designer of the time. Within the area was a lake of nearly 1.5ha which greatly added to the natural beauty. Water is pumped from this lake to all the greens. There was no particular hurry to finish the course and great care was taken to ensure that everything was as near perfect as possible before play would be permitted. The course finally opened in 1927.

In 1931 the layout was redesigned, the architect for this work being H S Colt, who has already been mentioned in connection with Hendon Golf Club. Provision was made at that time for an alternative starting point at the 10th Tee to relieve congestion, and five new greens were added.

By the end of 1937 an additional nine-hole course had been constructed, but this was turned over to agriculture during the War and never reinstated as a playing area. A reduced course of 15 holes was played for the duration of the War years and the War Office considered that the club house would be better employed as a casualty reception station. It was converted for this use and during this period the members had to make do with the barn.

In 1957 the route was decided for the M1 Motorway from St Albans north-wards. A few years later it was considered essential to extend the M1 southwards, first to the Bunns Bridge and then all the way to Staples Corner. This necessitated further changes to the layout and S Cotton was commissioned to carry out the design. His plans were not totally accepted and the Club professional, Alex Daniel, suggested further alterations which were agreed. The new course was finally ready in September 1965 and is nearly 67ha in extent. The current membership (all categories) is on average 550.

The (apparently pointless) roadway that runs across the course, crossing the first, tenth and third fairways is of historical interest. It was laid to give access to the sheephouse that stood at the back of the course near to the railway. It was a building of 17th Century origins but was demolished when the motorway was built.

In 1930 the course and clubhouse were sold to the Hendon Council for £41,000 and then leased back to the proprietor for £2,200 per annum. Some bad feeling was generated and a charge of broken faith was made by the committee. Eight years later there were further problems relating to the position of women in the Club and because of the adverse publicity the name was changed from Mote Mount Golf Club to Mill Hill Golf Club in 1939. In September 1944 the Club was made into a limited company.

In the early days of the Club it was quite common to meet a flock of sheep on the fairways. Presumably they were classed as natural hazards. A far worse natural hazard was the dreadful winter of 1962/3 when the course was forcibly closed for three whole months due to snow cover which greatly upset Club finances.

ANYONE FOR TENNIS?

'Pam, I adore you, Pam, you great big mountainous sports girl,
Whizzing them over the net, full of the strength of five.'
(*Pot Pourri from a Surrey Garden*) John Betjeman

It is always possible to play tennis on a municipal court and probably most aspiring Beckers and Sabatinis do just that. The great enthusiasm that builds up around the start of Wimbledon and then dies down only a few weeks after the new champions have gone into the record book. Club tennis is different. The image of cucumber sandwiches, long skirts and slacks and unsullied whiteness died with World War II but at least the bonhomie remains, fortunately we can still decide who we want in our private clubs.

Unless you already knew it was there it is hardly likely that anyone would come upon the Mill Hill Lawn Tennis Club by accident. The address is Sylvan Avenue but all that can be seen is an alleyway. The grounds fit rather neatly in land surrounded by Sylvan Avenue, Flower Lane and Woodland Way and you cannot join the 'Pams' at play unless you are a member.

The Club was definitely in existence by 1907 and it is possible that a club existed before then; it is now the only private tennis club in Mill Hill. Prior to World War II the Mill Hill Golf Club on Barnet Way had a tennis section, but unhappily where the courts used to be is now a car park. There was also a flourishing tennis club at The Hale which closed in the late 1960s, and on the 25in OS map of 1935 a tennis court is shown between the ends of the gardens of Woodland Way and the Midland Railway line (now taken up by the M1 Motorway). In the early days the courts were grass and in the 1950s the decision was made to change over completely to all-weather surfaces. The existing three grass and one red shale courts were changed to three all-weather and these have of course been resurfaced and relaid many times since then.

Today two of the courts are flood-lit which proved quite a battle; it took the Barnet Council six years to agree to this. The great 'switch-on day' was March 23 1991.

The Club can take up to 60 full members plus special categories (mid-week and six-day members) and there is also a flourishing junior section for up to 80 children aged nine to 16. Coaching is included as a part of their membership.

The present pavilion dates from 1968. The previous building had been in use since the beginnings of the Club. Some members remember the old building very well, particularly the men, they had to empty the Elsan toilets! In those days cooking and lighting were by Tilley lamps and Primus stoves and only updated to Calor gas in the latter years. The 'new' pavilion is something different being much better appointed and with all modern conveniences, it has also been added to over the years and further extensions are planned.

One man particularly was responsible for rescuing the Club from the doldrums into which it had sunk in the early 1950s. He was Jim Gladwin, chairman for 25 years and then president, until his death in 1989. He saw the Club through all the big changes and put the finances on a sound footing. Nevertheless fund raising activities form a major part of the members' commitments to their Club.

All the improvements have been carried out with loans from the Lawn Tennis Association and loans and grants from the National Playing Fields Association (now the Sports Council). Clearly it is to clubs like Mill Hill that in the long term we have to look for future international tennis successes.

LET'S PLAY RUGBY

Half Time Chat is a Carrollesque poem that appeared in the Mill Hill RFC *Golden Anniversary Celebration Book* and no apology is made for reproducing part of it here. Somehow it epitomises the spirit of amateur rugby, the kind of people who play it and for how long they contrive to do so.

> *The time has come, the captain said*
> *To talk of many things,*
> *Of scoring tries and kicking goals*
> *And passing to the wings,*
> *And why we're losing 30-nil*
> *And a host of other things.*

> *But wait a bit, the forwards cried,*
> *Before we have our chat,*
> *For all of us are out of breath*
> *And some of us are fat.*
> *No hurry, said the Captain*
> *And they thanked him much for that.*

With the amount of green space and open country in and around Mill Hill there would be something seriously wrong if there was no local rugby football team. It was nevertheless quite a long time coming into being and having been established it was some years before the players and committee managed to secure a permanent home.

It all began in April 1937 in the well known Mill Hill inn the *Adam & Eve* (it had to be a public house) on The Ridgeway when 13 men between the pints decided that Mill Hill needed a rugby football club and that they were going to create it. For the first 10 years the president was Norman G Brett-James, local historian and a master of Mill Hill School.

Setting up a club is one thing, but what about a ground, a pavilion or at least changing rooms, recognisable clothing and so on. And there have to be rules:

> *That the Club be restricted to 20 players with a waiting list of desirable*
> *players. The subscription be one guinea (£1.05) per season.*

These were two of the original rules, 'desirable' was not defined so we do not know what was intended. Later the rules were much extended (as is the way with these things) and one member remarked that as they were printed in the same space a magnifying glass was now necessary to read them.

A pitch was eventually found at The Radnor Hall Country Club and the facilities on offer included a changing room, a large bath, use of the Club's bar and snooker room. All this for £20 per annum with teas extra at 9d (4p). The first season was a great success with 16 wins out of 28 games played.

Unfortunately this high came to a rapid and unfortunately lengthy interruption when war was declared and sport had to take a back seat. Sadly in the course of the war three club members were killed, one in each of the services. In late 1946 the Club was reformed but unfortunately the pitch had been ploughed up in the 'Dig for Victory' campaign. At this time De Havilland RFC had moved to Borehamwood and Mill Hill RFC took over the clubhouse along with two pitches at Spur Road Edgware. Harrow RFC had also lost their ground and the two teams agreed to share.

It was an inauspicious re-start, the first autumn was the wettest autumn on record and this was followed by unrelenting cold. It froze on January 25 and stayed frozen until March 22 and there was no play at all in this period. In the summer of 1947 the Mill Hill RFC secured a lease on the sports ground of Mill House Preparatory School at Elstree and renamed the ground Chapel Field. Part of the deal was the right to sublet the ground in the summer months to Newlands Cricket Club for £100 per annum (for five years). Pity the poor cricketers!

After six years of war it was a mammoth task to refurbish the derelict pavilion and to convert it into an acceptable clubhouse for a rugby club. After much hard work the clubhouse was officially opened by the Mayor of Hendon in September 1947, and this remained the home of the Club until the lease expired. They moved out in 1956, and the land was then sold and redeveloped as a housing estate.

At this time the war-time wheat fields of the old Copt Hall estate were being developed as a sports complex and the Club successfully negotiated for a part of the playing fields. A site was agreed at a rent of £10 per annum, rising to £15 after four years, but there was to be a wait of two years before the pitches and clubhouse would be ready. The interim meant another move and two years at the William Ellis School with the *Railway Hotel* Edgware serving as the clubhouse. With a couple of qualified members in the team the cost of the clubhouse was kept down and in due course once again the Mayor of Hendon did the honours and officially opened the new Page Street headquarters. In 1963 the number of changing rooms was doubled and a shower area was added.

The winter of 1963 broke the record of 1947, this time there was no play for 10 weeks.

It is rather difficult to separate rugby football from clubhouses (which means the bar) and various public houses. The record of many matches, and particularly every tour, records this side of the sport as fully as what happened on the field of play. This led to two strange additions to the minutes of two Annual General Meetings:

'In the light of recent events, the sale of Merrydown cider would be banned from the clubhouse', 'The Road Traffic Act 1967 was having an adverse effect on bar profits, but it was hoped that this aspect would pick up when people got used to the breathalyser'.

There were no suggestions as to how the latter could be achieved.

Take any club, any sport, professional or amateur and there will be highs and lows, and in many ways Mill Hill RFC is typical. There would be no point here in giving a string of results, good and bad for the Club over the years of its existence. Sufficient to say that they have had some quite amazingly successful years when they have swept everyone before them and others when they have been really struggling. One in particular (1974/5) when the First XV did not record their first win until February 1. At that time the only team in England without a win.

Good seasons and bad, one thing is certain, Mill Hill RFC will be around for a long time yet, the completion of their second half-century already looks to be a certainty.

THE PAST, THE PRESENT, AND THE FUTURE

'The history of England is emphatically the history of progress'.

Macaulay

Whilst it is certainly true that people in general are more concerned with conservation and local issues than a few decades ago it is unfortunately equally obvious that there are still many vandals (although they would not like to be referred to as such) who are only interested in destroying or fouling the environment. Only too frequently we notice that a house has been sold and the new owner immediately removes all the trees in the garden. If they do not like trees it would be better for the the rest of us if they went to live on a prairie. Worse still is the developers' trick; buy a row of houses, demolish them, and then apply to build a block of unsightly flats. Whole streets are being ruined and Holders Hill Road is an obvious example.

Fortunately in Mill Hill we have three societies dedicated to the preservation of our environment and at the same time to learn as much as possible about the history of Mill Hill, which is for the benefit of all those who live there.

The first of these by many years is the Mill Hill & Hendon Historical Society (formerly the Mill Hill HS) which was founded in 1928. In this book some of the writings of past members have been used as reference. Over the years the Society has been responsible more than any other for drawing the attention of the local people to their past by books and other writings. From time to time Society members have submitted articles to the local press on specific subjects which for some reason or another are topical at the time. This is a useful way of putting over the issues, particularly for those who are unlikely in the first instance to purchase an expensive book.

Probably the most significant event for the Society was the discovery in 1931 of the original manuscript of the *Black Survey* of 1321. This document established that Mill Hill really is a village where a mill once stood and that all the years of speculation on the subject were well founded.

Second on the scene, and concerned mainly with conservation, was the Mill Hill Preservation Society founded in 1949. This was in the almost immediate post-war era when rebuilding and redevelopment were at their height. Whereas most other European countries that had been extensively damaged during the war restored where possible so that today it is often difficult to tell old from new the remains of our old buildings were usually destroyed. Now the post-war buildings are in many cases already considered unsuitable for refurbishment and are being demolished.

There are a number of buildings in Mill Hill that are guarded by Preservation Orders, but this does not only mean that they cannot be altered or destroyed, they have to be kept in good repair. In a recent case (not in Mill Hill of course) the owner of a large Victorian building has been charged £115,000 to cover the cost of preservation work carried out by English Heritage.

The Preservation Society are watchdogs for the total environment, not just the 16 or so buildings that have a Grade II listing. Anywhere that has a history or that is worth preserving, be it a view, a lane, a footpath, or a building is guarded tenaciously by the Mill Hill PS.

Fields and undeveloped land are important too, and the Mill Hill PS is very concerned (for instance) about the number of requests submitted to the planning authority to construct golf courses in the Vale of Totteridge. This could well spoil the untouched appearance of the whole area, and if footpaths were not actually removed or re-routed they could certainly become dangerous for walkers. These new facilities frequently have other sports incorporated in the clubhouse area such as squash and badminton and the necessary buildings for these are square and ugly and would certainly be obtrusive.

Last but certainly not least is the Hendon & District Archaeological Society (HADAS) which had its origins in April 1961 and was the brain child of Themistocles Constantinides. The original aim of HADAS was quite simple: to establish by discovery on the ground whether the origins of Hendon are Saxon. Today needless to say the brief is very much broader and covers every period from the Paleolithic to the present century, from flint axes to aircraft hangers. It is sometimes difficult to define what should be investigated, presumably that which interests the members, and therefore some of the HADAS newsletters cover items that would seem to be be more at home in the writings of the Historical Society, however better to be investigated by two societies than none.

Having started in a modest way HADAS has expanded both in

scope and in area of operation. The creation of the London Borough of Barnet gave the excuse (if one were needed) to increase the range for professional digs to cover the whole of the Borough. The Borough authority does in fact involve HADAS when it considers that something should be investigated (for instance the old well in the garden of Rosebank). With a limited number of field workers available the ability of HADAS to respond quickly is often rather stretched.

HADAS came into existence just about the time that metal detectors became readily available. A great boon and assistance to research in the right hands but can be a menace when possessed by fortune hunters. HADAS is only too aware of the harm that detector owners can cause and has taken great care to guide local enthusiasm through professional channels.

CHAPTER XXX

CIVIC SERVICES AND AMENITIES

I f Mill Hill is to retain its essentially urban character into the 21st Century then it is up to all of us to voice our objections when plans are drawn up that will alter the environment. Just after the turn of the Century there was much development for housing in the area but after a time the local people decided that enough was enough and resisted any further estates. It is unlikely that any proposals on the scale of the years from 1900 to 1935 would be tolerated again, but complacency would be foolish.

There are three organizations to thank for the amount of green space that we are still able to enjoy in Mill Hill, in addition to the Acts of Parliament that established the Green Belt. Sadly hardly a month passes without another assault upon our countryside which has to be fought off by the planning department of the local council. Fortunately Mill Hill School and the Catholic Church own large areas of land which they are very unlikely to even think of selling for development.

In addition to this safeguard the old Hendon Corporation purchased many large areas of land when they came on the market and these are likely to remain a part of the community lands in perpetua. Copthall Playing Fields, Mill Hill Park and Moat Mount are examples of these and Totteridge Valley seems to be safe too, except that this area is in demand for new golf courses.

If the diesel railcar with the facility for paying the conductor on the train had been designed and built a few years earlier there is a chance that many of our old branch lines would have been preserved. It came too late and when the lines were closed the tracks were ripped up so that there was no hope that they could ever be resurrected.

The same fate befell many of our cinemas, once every town and certainly borough had one, and this includes Mill Hill. The Capitol Cinema in Mill Hill Broadway was built in 1932 and demolished after World War II. Some were turned into warehouses, bowling alleys or bingo halls but the majority, like Mill Hill were just demolished and the sites redeveloped. Cinema they said was killed off by television, partly true but the death was largely self-inflicted by producing bad films. Now the interest in cinema has been rekindled and queues are even to be seen outside cinemas once again. The films have improved but for many places it is too late because like the railway lines the local cinema has gone. The baby has been thrown out with the bath water. As with hundreds of other places the people of Mill Hill have to go elsewhere.

Shopping is hardly a sport, even if there is sometimes a fight at sale time, and for every person who likes it there must be dozens that don't. Most families today rely upon the supermarket. They spend huge sums on convenience foods that only one generation ago would have been prepared in the home. Except for a few specialist shops few would go to Mill Hill for their main weekly or monthly shopping. The shops, which are concentrated in Mill Hill Broadway are really for the locals and for day-to-day purchases.

The large number of restaurants here and an apparent excess of 'fast-food' take-aways seems to confirm that the local residents like to eat out or at least consume food that they have not prepared themselves. Add to this the banks, estate agents and non-shop traders and there is a shortage of victuallers, although it must be said that many other high road shopping areas have fared far worse in this respect. There are a few shops also at the junction of Milespit Hill and Pursley Road and on The Ridgeway and these are certainly there to cater for strictly local demand.

THE LIBRARY SERVICE

Although there has been an increase in new book titles and purchases during the current recession, library borrowings continue to decline. The Government has talked of the privatisation of this service but it is hard to see how this could be a profitable investment for a potential buyer. Years ago shops like Boots and Harrods did have lending libraries where a lending fee was charged but the return was not worth the space occupied. With or without privatisation there has been a call for a charge to be levied for each book borrowed, or used in the reference department and amounts up to 20p have been suggested. Certainly it would be fairer to pay the authors more than the pittance they are paid by libraries now but a charge may well mean that the number of books borrowed is reduced even further.

Other means of introducing a commercial element into libraries have also been discussed, such as having shops on the premises selling cards etc., rather like the shops now to be found in large post offices. This could be a limited success but the space would have to be found and the employment of extra staff justified. One thing is certain, however the service develops the old haven of silence where staff and visitors spoke in whispers has probably gone for ever and that is no bad thing.

The Provisions of the *Libraries Act* of 1919 were accepted by the

Hendon Urban District Council but another decade was to pass before work was begun on a central library. This was planned for The Burroughs and finally opened to the public in December 1929. It is an imposing building designed in a neo-Georgian style. School libraries, organized and supervised by the Council, had in fact been in existence since 1927.

Clearly it was not enough to have just one library in such a large district, certainly if reading and study was to be encouraged. A programme of branch libraries was therefore called for, and up to the beginning of hostilities in 1939 two had already been built, Golders Green opened in 1935 and Mill Hill in 1937.

After World War II the Hendon Borough Council shook the dust off the plans drawn up in the 1930s to proceed with a comprehensive library building programme. Unfortunately, for some time building was restricted whilst more important work was attended to. To tide over this period a travelling library service was inaugurated in 1947 that is still very much a part of the library service today (but more of this later).

The building programme was restarted in 1950 and since then a number of new premises have been opened, notably at Burnt Oak, Childs Hill, and Edgware in the first phase and later on in Finchley. The Finchley library was housed many years ago in Avenue House (sadly almost totally destroyed by fire a few years ago but now completely restored), then for many years in rather inadequate premises near the junction of Hendon Lane and Regents Park Road and now in more salubrious quarters near to the church of St Mary's at Finchley. In the last few months a brand new library has been opened in Chipping Barnet behind the Spires Centre. No doubt in every way an improvement on the old and historic building near the church but rather impersonal and some people will probably prefer the inadequacies of the previous premises.

The Mill Hill library is a part of the London Borough of Barnet library service and fully computerized, a facility of which earlier librarians would be envious. Mill Hill has always been a part of something bigger and attached to the main library at Hendon, this is now the headquarters of the Borough library organisation. It is now possible to locate and reserve a book that is held anywhere in the Borough (or the south east of England). The other libraries of the Borough probably have the most to gain because the library in The Burroughs has always had the most comprehensive collection in the district. The Hendon library is just one of a whole group of buildings on The Burroughs, all impressive, which includes the fire station (also neo-Georgian), the town hall and a part of Middlesex University (formerly Hendon Technical College).

The library of Mill Hill is situated in Hartley Avenue, just off Mill

Hill Broadway and was officially opened on September 24 1937 by the Mayor of Hendon. Hartley Avenue was named after a vicar of St Michael & all Angels who was an incumbent during the 1930s. Exteriorly it is a little unexciting, but clean lines, symmetry of design and a rather over massive entrance porch give an air of importance. In its favour the brickwork has worn well and the structure looks much cleaner than would be expected for a building of this age. On September 25 1987 the Library celebrated 50 years of service to Mill Hill with a fête that was well supported by the local people.

On the inside much is as it was when built in 1937 and the temptation to replace furnishings and fittings with those of more modern times (which may quickly date) has so far been avoided.

A little bit of attention such as lowering the hedge and keeping it trimmed and ensuring that the area is free from litter would help to make the place attractive but little can be done about the location. Hartley Avenue is now a cul-de-sac, a very unprepossessing road full of boring buildings with dreary frontages, and the whole place seems to need a good clean. The road has all the disadvantages of a trading estate in miniature; a place where no-one lives and the people who go there never stay long enough to care, and where an overall plan never had a chance.

To add to the charm the public toilet adjacent to the pedestrian underpass of the A1/A41 seems to attract some of the most explicit graffiti in the Borough, and between cleanings is certainly a worthwhile place of study for any aspiring anthropologist or psychologist.

Mention has already been made of the mobile library. Because most of the population of Mill Hill is concentrated within 1.5km of the library in Hartley Avenue and this distance would probably apply to other branch libraries in the Borough and their relevant populations a mobile unit today would seem to be an extravagance. Up to now it has never been considered so. There are Mill Hill 'outposts' such as the area around the bottom of Bittacy Hill and Mill Hill East Station and also the estates north of Pursley Road for whom the library is in completely the wrong place. And this is just in Mill Hill, elsewhere in the Borough there are areas, that are a long way from any branch and for whom the mobile library is the only library. Add to this the aged and infirm, for them a library that comes almost to the front door is a necessity.

Even as this was being written the Council announced plans for a complete overhaul of the whole library structure which in some ways appears to be a reversal of their own earlier policies. On the positive side they plan better and more comprehensive storage of the historical records and documents section, (which at present is rather inadequately housed in the upper storey of a church social hall) and a more modern computer system. The computer will cost a considerable sum, but as the existing system is not that old one must wonder whether there was bad advice when the previous equipment was purchased.

Because of protests the plans that involved the scrapping of the mobile library service have been withdrawn. However a lot of money has to be saved somewhere to pay for these vehicles and the computer, to keep within overall library budgets. This means extensive cuts elsewhere.

The revised plans for the Borough amount to reduced hours for some branches (and this includes Mill Hill), the complete closure of some others, all the staff had to re-apply for their jobs, and some branches will not have a resident qualified librarian. Apparently many people were interviewed before all these decisions were made and a consultative document was prepared. Let us hope that before the dust settles the Council can arrive at the right answer and not jeopardise the future of the learning and reference of one of London's largest boroughs.

Somewhere in the decisions about new hours of opening there must be a provision for newspapers and magazines. After all they are important to many people as a part of the reference library service. But if libraries are to be closed for complete days this facility becomes much reduced in value, after all who wants a paper days old when seeking a new job?

In recent years we have witnessed one of the greatest revolutions in the history of newspapers: the circulation of local free-sheets, paid for by their advertising content. Perhaps the library management feels that there is no need to carry these because every household has them. When these first appeared their journalistic content was almost non-existent, with an absolute minimum of editorial. Not so today. Because they are paid for by what amounts to a kind of sponsorship they have to produce a balanced layout and copy that is acceptable to both advertiser and potential reader. They are much improved compared with their rather crude beginnings and obviously present a considerable threat to the established weekly local newspapers. Householders in some areas receive three or more different titles.

Mill Hill has never had a newspaper of its very own, there is not a big enough population to justify this. The Hendon Times Newspaper Group (established in 1875) has always included Mill Hill in its coverage.

CEMETERIES

It is easy to understand the tendency of inner city boroughs to build homes for its elderly, and buy up land for cemeteries in the suburbs and beyond. Land is cheaper, little demolition is necessary, and when buying the land it is often necessary to negotiate with only one land owner. Imagine the cost and problems involved in procuring the land for these amenities in central London. So we have for instance large homes for old people in Potters Bar belonging to the Borough of Haringey and a cemetery with its entrance on Milespit Hill in Mill Hill which belonged to Westminster City Council. It was opened in 1936 by Paddington Borough Council. The reasoning is fine, the problem is that those few miles make all the difference to visitors: the old are seldom visited in the old people's homes by their relatives, and the graveyards are unkempt and overgrown unless they are kept tidy by the appropriate authority because after a while few people visit the graves.

In Ireland they have a 'Cemetery Sunday' once a year. On this day fit and able relatives of the deceased are expected to turn up en masse and cut grass etc, and generally tidy up the graveyard. At least they accept it as their responsibility.

The 'local' cemetery for Mill Hill is Hendon Park Cemetery and Crematorium in Holders Hill Road which is just outside the boundary of Mill Hill. It was first opened in 1899 and because the total area available cannot be extended some of the early common graves have already been levelled and the ground will be reused. The author is quite familiar with this place, the funerals of two brothers have taken place there.

Three years ago the Westminster City Council caused a furore when they sold the cemeteries for which they were responsible for the trifling sum of 15p to a Swiss based development company, Wisland Investment Group. Because they owned three cemeteries this put a value of 5p on the graveyard and unused land of the cemetery on Milespit Hill. The repercussions from this sale will be with Westminster for many years.

Because of the increase in the number of cremations there is a large parcel of land (5ha) attached to the cemetery in Mill Hill which is not required for burials, and Wisland intended to develop this for housing. As a reciprocal deal they would maintain the graveyards. Unfortunately (for them) planning permission was refused and after a public hearing this was upheld by an inspector of the Department of the Environment. Nothing is final in the world of planning however and at a further hearing it appears that approval may well be given for a reduced number of houses to be built on this site.

The local authority will continue to resist because there is no suitable access to the site. At present the entrance to this land is via the Cemetery gate and this would hardly be desirable for a housing estate. All the property owners surrounding the field have indicated that they would refuse to sell enough land to build a road, but everything has its price.

To complicate matters further the District Auditor has stated that the deal was probably illegal in the first place and Wisland then offered to sell the cemeteries back to Westminster for £5.5 million. Obviously the relatives of the deceased were unhappy from the start, and particularly when maintenance by Wisland was suspended. Even if it is now proved that Wisland acquired the cemeteries legally they will be practically worthless to them unless they can develop the site in some way. They will certainly be unwilling to pay for cemetery maintenance without something in return.

PUBLIC UTILITIES

WATER OUT AND WATER IN

When in 1879 Hendon was divided into three wards with 12 members, one of the major plans of the new council was to build and develop a sewage system and treatment works. The works was opened in 1887. At this time The Hyde and Mill Hill were still without main drainage and indeed it was almost the turn of the century before most of the houses in the district were connected to the network. The lowest point in Hendon is Brent Cross and the sewage treatment plant was built here. The Toys-R-Us super store stands on the site today.

Many of the sewers are at a very considerable depth because of the high ridges that cross the area. Obviously it is necessary to go through hills not over them. The sewage from the whole Borough of Barnet today is taken a considerable distance for treatment, all areas west of The Ridgeway are connected to a main sewer which leads to the West Middlesex Purification Works at Mogden Lane, Isleworth. Finchley, Barnet, and the eastern part of the Borough are dealt with by a plant at Walthamstow.

Even today there are some farms and large houses that still have to use cesspools or septic tanks, (not actually in Mill Hill) notably on Totteridge Common. This means that filtered but partially treated effluent ends up in the Dollis Brook or the Folly Brook which is immediately apparent in dry summers when there is insufficient natural flow to keep the stream flushed. Some of the establishments have been rather negligent on a number of occasions and Borough engineers have had to deal with some severe pollution when a health hazard was threatened.

There are some very old tunnels in Mill Hill which almost certainly predate those constructed after 1887. The origins and purpose of these is obscure. There is a very deep tunnel which runs across the Vale of

Totteridge from near St Andrew's Church in Totteridge Lane to St Vincent's Convent. There used to be vents to this at the bottom of Burtonhole Lane but these were lowered many years ago and the cricket field is over these today. The tunnel was considered to be a security risk during World War II. There is also the remains of a tunnel under The Ridgeway from Littleberries to The Priory and another was discovered when the foundations to the Medical Research Centre were being excavated. The ends of all these have been bricked up and the vents capped off. Needless to say the old legend of Nell Gwynne surfaces again and the tunnel under The Ridgeway is said to have been used by King Charles II to get to Nell Gwynne clandestinely.

Considering that he was quite open about his mistresses this would be most out of character and the myth of Nell has already been disposed of. Other old drains in the area have glazed inspection manholes, in general these were first used in the beginning of the 19th Century when brick built drains were first used .

There are still some remote parts of the Country where mains water is not laid on, and there are still people who resist its arrival. In general piped water of acceptable purity is something that we take for granted: not so 100 years ago when there was still a good trade for water sellers in Mill Hill at 1d or 2d per pail.

The West Middlesex Water-works Company included Hendon in its outer limits in 1866 but the Company did not develop very quickly so that some years later the majority of the people still obtained

TYPICAL VILLAGE WATER PUMP

their supplies from springs, pumps, wells or the water seller. This applied particularly to those people living in Mill Hill. Town pumps were in Brent Street Hendon and near the parish church in Edgware.

In 1873 another supplier, the Cólne Valley Water Company was granted the right by Parliament to include part of Hendon in its supply network. Mill Hill was included in this arrangement and piped main water was laid on progressively throughout Mill Hill from this date. All of the new estates, built near to the Broadway since 1920, would have had piped water as a matter of course as would the newer houses on The Ridgeway,

Highwood Hill, Wise Lane, Marsh Lane, etc.

The West Middlesex Waterworks Company ceased to exist in 1902 when the facilities and the authority that they had been granted were taken over by the Metropolitan Water Board.

THE COMING OF GAS AND ELECTRICITY

The first gas street lighting in London made its appearance in 1807 when part of Pall Mall was gaslit for exhibition purposes. In 1814 the oil lamps of the parish of St Margaret's Westminster were removed and replaced with gas lamps and shortly after this Westminster Bridge was also converted to gas lighting. The manufacture of gas started in Mill Hill in 1862 and 40 years later the streets were still lit with oil lamps.

There is however a simple reason for this apparent tardiness. The early gas light was just a flat flame, and little better than a candle as far as illumination was concerned. One resident with gas lighting described it as 'A dim religious light'. Auer von Welsbach invented the fluorescent gas mantle about 1890 but supplies of the necessary rare earth salts, Thorium Nitrate and Cerium Trinitrate were only available in very small amounts and certainly not in commercial quantities. It was some time before the rich source mineral Monazite was discovered and 13 years before large quantities were refined.

Although mantles began to appear before this the development of large scale gas street lighting required a regular and reliable supply, as did house lights if they were to be any better than candles or oil lamps. If Mill Hill was late in getting gas street lighting it was also a long time before the last gas standard was removed. For some years gas and electric lighting ran side by side. Electric lights on main thoroughfares were arc-lights which, were quite unsuitable for minor roads: a photograph of Golders Green Road taken during World War I shows quite clearly an electric arc-light in the centre of the road and gas standards on the pavement. The contract was for this road to be lit by 12 arc-lights.

As late as 1934 tall gas lights were still around Mill Hill Circus and they stayed for some time after this. Gas retained its popularity with the local authority even for the new arterial roads, and only in 1936 were streets lit by both systems so that comparisons could be made. From then on electricity slowly superseded gas on all public lighting. New roads and estates were connected to electric lighting as they were built, but on the older suburban roads gas lighting could still be seen up to the beginning of World War II although the lamp-lighters on their bicycles had long since gone.

Mill Hill was obviously ideally placed for the supply of gas. It had its own gas works and being a commercial company, expansion was as rapid as technical constraints permitted. The new estates of Mill Hill, Burnt Oak, Golders Green and Finchley were connected to the mains as built. Consumers were not however always satisfied, they regarded the price as being too high and before the introduction of gas mantles the light provided was rather poor.

The Hendon Local Board (which became the Hendon Urban District Council under the *Local Government Act* of 1894) was approached by various people promoting the advantages of electricity, particularly for lighting, but the local authority was understandably reluctant to permit another monopoly to become established. There were many attempts to introduce electricity in the district but in the early days all were rejected, primarily due to the cost, and frequently Mill Hill was quoted as being uneconomical because of the scattered population. The obvious solution was to buy electricity in bulk rather than to generate within Hendon but this was fiercely opposed. To have (or not to have) an electricity supply in Hendon was an election issue for years.

The Rev. Dean Carter represented the Catholic institutions of Mill Hill and rejected electricity out of hand, he claimed that the rector of St Joseph's College did not like electric light. The governors of Mill Hill School also voted against the scheme, but mainly because the School was not to be included in the distribution network. Once it was shown that The Ridgeway was part of the plan the School's objection was withdrawn.

Hendon did of course get its electricity, and so eventually did Mill Hill with The Ridgeway trailing a long way behind The Broadway. The first connection was 48 The Broadway on December 11 1913 and Mill Hill School chapel (the first on The Ridgeway) on September 15 1919.

TELEPHONES

There are no records available of the dates that the first telephones were installed in Mill Hill premises, business or residential, probably because there was no exchange in Mill Hill. The estate agent that handled the property in Mill Hill Garden Village (built in 1910) was certainly 'on the phone'. All his offices appear to have had Finchley numbers which was presumably the nearest exchange. The offices were in Finchley, Hendon, Temple Fortune and Mill Hill.

On March 24 1921 a site for an exchange was acquired at 83 The Broadway and excavation work started on April 2 1925. Another 12 years were to pass before the exchange equipment was installed (March 31

1937) and the new Mill Hill Exchange commenced service to the area on June 30 1940. It is hard to understand how this process took 19 years, perhaps the equipment was not available or other installations were considered to be more important or there were insufficient subscribers and the exchange was an investment for the future.

THE FIRE, AMBULANCE, AND POLICE SERVICES

Hendon has had a fire service of sorts since 1855, and records exist of the purchase by the brigade of a manual Merryweather appliance in 1857. A team of volunteer fire fighters was founded in 1866 and named the Hendon Volunteer Fire Brigade. The voluntary contributions paid for the equipment (manual engine, truck, and 200ft of hose, scaling ladders and tools) but not for the fire-fighters uniforms. They were expected to provide their own. When the Urban District Council took over the responsibility for fire fighting in 1899 Mill Hill already had its own sub-station.

The Mill Hill Fire and Ambulance Stations are side by side in Hartley Avenue. This obviously makes some sense because the two services are frequently called out to the same emergency and should arrive together. The first Mill Hill Fire Station was built in 1889 and the present building in Hartley Avenue was built in 1929. The Ambulance Station was transferred to the same road a few years ago and is on an adjacent site to one side of the building. Unfortunately no attempt was made to design a building in sympathy with the Fire Station and it is rather like a tiled bathroom inside out.

There was no properly organised police force prior to 1829. The taking of offenders was purely a local affair. The high constable of the county was nominally responsible, but local JPs appointed parish constables. Officially these were unpaid and any male citizen was liable to serve, but as most were unwilling the service was generally undertaken by substitutes who were paid to do so.

In country districts like Mill Hill the system usually worked, there was no rapid transport for escape and the local bad characters were easily identified. In any event public opinion was against the creation of a force that could be used to reduce personal liberty.

The behaviour of a mob at the funeral of Queen Caroline convinced the Government that a stronger hand was necessary and in 1829 Sir Robert Peel was responsible for the *Metropolitan Police Act*. Even he had some misgivings, he thought it likely that it would be yet another system to provide easy jobs for the upper classes. Nevertheless the Act set up a commissioner and assistant at Scotland Yard and the Metropolitan Police was established.

The policing of Hendon still remained a local responsibility up to 1840, in that year Hendon was added to the Metropolitan Police District.

CHAPTER XXXI

RECREATION GROUNDS
AND OPEN SPACES

Thistle and darnel and dock grew there,
And a bush, in the corner, of may.
(Nicholas Nye) Walter de la Mare

T he London Borough of Barnet, an outer London borough is largely within the Green Belt. It is therefore no surprise that the Borough contains a considerable area of open land. There are some important reserves of natural grassland, an interesting nature reserve, woodlands, and conventional parks. The total area of the Borough is 8,593ha and of this Mill Hill represents 1400ha. Within Mill Hill is something in the region of 250ha of open space to which the public has complete access, add to this the nature reserve with restricted access, and the grasslands, (some of which are owned by the Borough and leased out). All are crossed by public footpaths, as is the Vale of Totteridge. There are also numerous sports grounds, some owned by the Council, and others private such as those owned by the NIMR and Mill Hill School. Taken all together, Mill Hill (that is the NW7 district) has a much higher proportion of open space than it has of built-up areas, for which we should all be very thankful.

There are also many other grassy areas that are not suitable for detailing here, either because they are too small to be of any real consequence, because they are roadside verges or similar sites, or they are 'private' for residents only. The playing areas within the grounds of Council owned housing estates for instance (no ball games allowed!) and the similar lands in the Mill Hill Barracks compound are in this category.

Mill Hill contains some of the most important natural grasslands in the Greater London area, and is notable for the examples of (deliberately preserved) grasslands on London clay. These herb-rich lands were once a feature of most of the old county of Middlesex but the larger part has since been lost to development and 'improvement', either for building works, for intensive agriculture or for traditional parks.

There are some good streams and ponds in Mill Hill, and one of the locality's few bogs is just outside the northern boundary. Most of the northern and eastern boundaries of Mill Hill are made up by the Folly Brook and the Dollis Brook and the latter is one of the longest and best habitat corridors in north-west London.

It is a long time since Mill Hill had a population of pigs to keep the ground clear, and grazing animals are selective about what they eat. Any area of grassland that is not properly managed quickly becomes invaded by coarse and tall plants, and the worst scourge today, bracken. In time brambles and hawthorns take over and finally the whole area becomes wooded. It is essential that the Borough keeps a tight control on the type and character of our open land, something that the Parks dept has very much in mind.

There must be many, many people that travel daily up and down the main thorough-fares of Mill Hill (A1, A41, M1) and the A1000 through Finchley and Barnet who never realise just how rural much of Mill Hill really is. They probably see little and are largely uninterested. If they would only take the time to leave the main roads they would find how much there is that is worth a closer look.

A number of separate *Acts of Parliament* have been passed over the last 100 years that assist local authorities in the acquisition of land for conversion into formal parks, recreation grounds, open spaces, sports grounds, gardens, public walks etc. These Acts fall into many different categories: housing, public health, the Green Belt, Town & Country planning, highways and so on. In some cases a parcel of land lost to the public because of a road development or other essential works has to be replaced and a *Compulsory Purchase Order* will be made on some suitable land nearby. In other cases land has been purchased by public subscription, and lastly there are those philanthropists who leave land in their wills for dedication to the public use.

Because of the great variety of parks and sports grounds in Mill Hill many Acts have been involved in the acquisition of the land.

The open spaces of Mill Hill to which the public have access, complete or restricted, can be classified under five types: conventional parks, ornamental parks, open spaces, woodlands, and nature reserves.

CONVENTIONAL PARKS

MILL HILL PARK

Mill Hill Park is the largest and most important conventional park in Mill Hill. It was acquired by the Hendon Urban District Council in 1924 and opened to the public on July 24 of that year. The total area is 16ha.

The HUDC did a good job for posterity when they purchased the farm land that went to make Mill Hill Park and protected it from the developers. Quite rightly a considerable celebration was made of the official opening. It was the first designated park in Mill Hill and a sure sign that the local authority was determined to cater for the recreational needs of the (at that time) fast growing population.

Today many would consider the opening ceremony to be over jingoistic and almost embarrassing. Not so in 1924. On the day, members of the Council, the Ratepayers Association (this association more or less vanished when local elections became party political) and school children assembled in Sylvan Avenue to make up a procession that was to go to the Park entrance via Daws Lane and Wise Lane.

They arrived band playing and flags flying to be met by Col. the Rt. Hon. Josiah Wedgwood DSO MP Chancellor of the Duchy of Lancaster who performed the official opening. The children sang Land of Hope and Glory and the assembly broke up after all sang God Save the King. Today we would probably recruit the services of a falling pop star or retired boxer to do the honours and Pomp and Circumstance No1 is reserved for the Last Night of the Proms. There would certainly be no National Anthem.

Some old barns and outbuildings of the ancient Daws Farm were demolished to make way for the entrance. Many years later the Park was cut in two by the A1/A41 Barnet by-Pass and an underpass was built to link the two parts. Probably the first time that such a thing was done.

LYNDHURST PARK

Lyndhurst is completely surrounded by houses and is rather plain compared with other parks in the district. There is very little in the way of attractions for children, or adults either for that matter and it seems to be used mainly as a short cut. There are two avenues of mature trees, one at right angles to the other that were probably the boundaries to an estate sometime in the past. One avenue runs down the centre of the Park.

The whole of this park is in Edgware but the main entrance is in Lyndhurst Avenue which just comes into Mill Hill. There is another entrance in Bunns Lane down a flight of steps by the bridge. Oh dear, the Parks dept obviously has a continuous problem here, the whole area is littered with rubbish and some of it most unpleasant. Why do people do this when the Council will arrange collection, even of awkward rubbish?

On the northern perimeter runs the track of the old GN railway line where it ran from the bridge in Bunns Lane (just south of Mill Hill Broadway Station) on its way to Edgware. It is getting on for 30 years since the track was lifted and is it now hard to see that a railway ever ran here so totally is it overgrown. There are now some quite sizable bushes and trees and some interesting herbage including various vetches and clovers and a variety of daisies.

Work had commenced on extending the *Underground* along this track before the whole project was abandoned. Remains of the concrete supports for the cables, in some cases with the cast iron brackets in place, can still be found.

WOODCROFT PARK

Woodcroft is entirely in Mill Hill with entrances in Blundell Road (Edgware) and Bunns Lane, in fact the side facing Bunns Lane is completely open. Woodcroft is all that Lyndhurst is not, and they are only 0.5km apart. There is a children's playground that is well kept and rugby football goal posts were still in position well out of season. The park is unfortunately just a little too convenient for people to 'exercise' their dogs.

The mature hedges contain substantial bushes and well established trees and are down both sides of the Park. Next to the Park on the southern side is the ground of the 'other' Mill Hill cricket club.

STONEYFIELDS PARK

Stoneyfields Park is in the angle formed by the A41 and the M1. This is a formal park in a residential area, it is not actually in Mill Hill but has been included because the Deans Brook which runs through the Park starts and ends within NW7. The only noteworthy element is the lake which has some interesting plants in and around its edge. The park is not wooded but there are enough mature trees for the park to be of use to birds.

BITTACY HILL PARK

Bittacy Hill Park is a little conventional park, situated at the top of Bittacy Hill on the western side, but is in some ways half way to being an ornamental park. Probably for safety reasons there is no entrance from Bittacy Hill.

The Park contains quite a large rose garden, and down wind with all the flowers in bloom it is possible to smell the perfume for 50m or so. Another nice touch are the little patches of unmown grass, left so that the different species can be seen, and there are many of them. The children's play area is well kept, and evidently well used too, and for older visitors there are tennis courts.

ORNAMENTAL PARKS

SIMMON'S MEAD

Simmon's Mead is the only truly ornamental park of any size in Mill Hill, and was originally a part of the Uphill Farm. The Mead is at the junction of the A1 and Lawrence Street and therefore it is impossible to escape from the noise of the traffic. In spite of this it still contrives to be a surprisingly peaceful place on a warm summer afternoon. The advantage of being in such a conspicuous place is that it reduces the risk of vandalism, and there is much to destroy.

The stream that crosses the Mead is quite remarkably clean and made more interesting by the rustic bridges. There is also a very enterprising collection of trees and shrubs for such a small area: a very fine weeping willow, various maples, a locust tree (false acacia), cherry, oak, alders, copper beech, laburnum, and many others. There are some interesting conifers, including a conifer hedge. A pleasant touch are the saplings that carry dedications, one to a lady who died aged 102. In view of the variety of trees and other plants it would be a thoughtful addition if the most notable at least carried identification tags.

OPEN SPACES

THE MILL FIELD

This open space which is the traditional site of the old mill is 4ha in area and was purchased in 1970. Because of its important historical associations it is right and proper that it should be dedicated to the people of the Borough.

The views from here westward are superb and when there is no haze, either weather or traffic, Harrow and far beyond to Windsor can be seen with ease.

The part nearest to The Ridgeway is kept mown, the remainder is natural grassland and on quite a steep slope. There is a sufficient variety of grasses and flowers to be of interest to naturalists. In the north the grasses are on sand and loam Claygate beds and London clay in the south. The most obvious grass is Yorkshire fog but there are many other kinds and there are at least 20 different wild flowers. Dog roses and honeysuckle are plentiful in the hedge.

Because of the view from here it would be helpful and interesting to have a direction plate (similar to the one in the churchyard on Harrow

Hill). It is always useful to know what we are looking at.

ARRANDENE OPEN SPACE

Looking into Arrandene from outside the main gate gives a completely wrong impression. It seems to be just a conventional park, but is much more than that. This open space, which is 25ha in area, was purchased on June 12 1929 and has been largely left in its original unspoilt state.

The site contains natural grasslands, hedges and woodlands. There is a considerable quantity of oat grass, Yorkshire fog, and many others in a rich profusion. In the rougher areas there are brambles and rose-bay willow-herb (this plant has spread everywhere, particularly into our back gardens) and young trees. The wooded places are mainly oak, ash, silver birch and sycamore. The elm trees that are regenerating (after the Dutch Elm infestation) are beginning to provide quite an extensive scrub.

A great number of wild flowers can be found, some quite rare in the Greater London area. The different fields that make up Arrandene are separated by mature hedges and streams. Most of this open space lies upon London clay but there are two small caps of the sandy Claygate beds on Featherstone Hill to the west of the site. The whole area is

BIRCH

undulating with the highest points to the north near The Ridgeway and at Featherstone Hill. The western side of Featherstone Hill drains into the Silk Stream and the remainder of the site drains eventually into the Dollis Brook. A small pond is the home of smooth newts, and common frogs breed here.

Many of the banks and ditches appear to be of some antiquity. Before World War II most of the present site was the lands of Dolestreet Farm and Meadow Farm. Some of the individual fields have at different times been cultivated (for corn crops) and as allotment gardens during the War. Part is still mown once per year which helps to keep the site as it is, it would soon be completely invaded by scrub if left alone.

MOAT MOUNT OPEN SPACE

This was another far-sighted purchase by the old HUDC and was acquired in 1923. The area that is freely accessible to the public is around 27ha, in addition there is a large amount of meadow land that is crossed by public footpaths.

It is a pity that the traffic roar from the A1 is ever present from any point in Moat Mount, but this apart it is still a delightful place, just sufficiently organised and no more. The trees are varied and it is not difficult to spot 20 different types whilst sitting in one spot. Add to these the bushes: hawthorn, elder, holly, willow, rhododendron and many more and for the greenery alone a visit is worthwhile.

From here take a walk across the footpath to Barnet Gate and in the upper fields is the nearest you will get to an old fashioned meadow with many different species of wild flowers, far too many to list here. In the wetter fields there are many species of marsh plants and several varieties of rushes. Because of the extensive hedges and shrubberies and undisturbed grass there is plenty of nesting habitat which is reflected in the number of different types of birds that can be found.

Moat Mount has been developed as a mixed amenity site and contains a picnic area next to the A1, a managed woodland (Nut Wood) and shrubbery, areas of rough woodland and open fields. Within the managed wood is the Leg of Mutton Pond, where the Dean's Brook has its source, a bit murky, but peaceful with its coots and geese. Until the 18th Century much of Moat Mount was demesne land (owned by the Lord of the Manor) but from that time has been divided, with parts now being incorporated into private estates.

The surrounding land is mainly London clay and in winter can be rather wet. There is a stretch of the sands and loams of Claygate beds and in the north at Hyver Hill is a cap of pebble gravel which has been quarried. Some of the field boundaries date back to the beginning of the 18th Century, or even earlier.

HIGHWOOD HILL AND HOLCOMBE DALE

These fields are not a public place but as they are crossed by a number of public footpaths the casual walker does have limited access. The rights of the owner should be respected by visitors at all times.

This is the place where the Folly Brook has its source and the area is predominantly on London clay although there are sandy Claygate beds. The site is best described as typical English countryside of the kind favoured by many famous landscape artists. The site is most notable for the fine mixed grasses with many wild flowers, some of them uncommon.

The trees are in the main mature specimens and varied, and the whole area is an attraction for much wildlife, most immediately noticed in the summer months are the butterflies and other insects. Some birds, not often seen in Greater London as a whole are nevertheless frequently seen in this area.

WOODLANDS

SCRATCH WOOD

This area has been woodland for a very long time and part is almost certainly a remainder of the ancient woodland that once covered most of Middlesex. Over the years Scratch Wood has been much modified and the centre is probably the only part of the original still remaining. The original trees are oak and hornbeam and to these are now added ash, maples, sycamore, hazel and birches. There are also smaller bushes such as hawthorn, rhododendron and laurels. On the southern side, near to the Mill Hill Golf Course, are horse chestnuts and silver birches with gorse and brambles.

SYCAMORE

Most of the site is on London clay but there are sand and loamy beds around the entrance of the railway tunnel.

Outside the woody areas there is grass, scrub and plantation which determines the ground flora. Where the scrub is less dense there are many interesting wild flowers. The plantation area contains some species of artificially introduced trees.

Much of the area has unlimited public access but it does run into the Golf Course without barrier or fence, which is private.

BARNET GATE WOOD

This small and compact wood is on the very edge of Mill Hill and may also be a remainder of the overall woodland cover of the area. The approach is either from the north of Hendon Wood Lane via a footpath or across the Moat Mount Open Space from Nan Clark's Lane.

Part of the wood has been invaded by rhododendrons which appear to be spreading rapidly, which will do if not controlled, and the floor has much scrub and the remains of fallen trees. Following paths and tracks can therefore be difficult.

NATURE RESERVES

DARLAND'S LAKE NATURE RESERVE

Darland's is artificial insofar as it was created by damming the Folly Brook. However this was done early in the last century so there is nothing about the Lake and surrounding area (the dam apart) that looks at all false today. The Lake is at the point where the boundaries of Finchley, Totteridge, and Mill Hill meet and only a part of this 5.1ha Nature Reserve comes within Mill Hill, it is however too important to be omitted.

As mentioned earlier in this book the Lake is on the migratory routes of some birds, notably teal, and when created it was intended to be a duck decoy. There are usually wildfowl on the lake at any time of year and although it is shallow some wading birds also visit the Lake, notably heron. Kingfishers have also been recorded. The grass

usually wildfowl on the lake

snake, which is becoming increasingly rare, also lives here. When the author last visited Darland's there were a few ducks and a coot with its flotilla of chicks.

Although owned by the Borough it is leased to the Hertfordshire and Middlesex Trust for Nature Conservation, and the Nature Conservancy Council has designated the Reserve, 'A Site of Special Scientific Interest'. The entrance is via a wooded lane from Totteridge Lane near to the Orange Tree. Darland's Lake Nature Reserve is always open and there is a conducted open day once per year.

The site has 18 known species of mammals, mainly nocturnal, including voles and shrews, and it is ideal for amphibians. The largest and smallest British bats, noctule and pipistrelle, may also be seen around the Lake. There is a great variety of fungi, over 120 species have been recorded. The site is important for many types of land bird, both residents and visitors, and the species lists for butterflies and moths, and arachnida is quite amazing.

The Lake has marshy borders and surrounding ditches that are rich in semi-aquatic plants. There is a wooded area extending from the Lake, with ash, elm, horse chestnut (two types), poplar, rowan, silver birch, sycamore, and scots pine. In places blue-bells grow and the reserve is particularly noted for the large colony of the rare British plant, snake's head fritillary. Unfortunately there is also widespread bracken which will take over if not controlled. In the Lake at the opposite end to the dam is a large bed of rushes and rough plants such as giant hogweed seem to like the shelter, one specimen was at least 3m tall in the summer of 1991.

DOLLIS BROOK NORTH

The northern part of the Brookside Walk and surrounding recreation grounds from Woodside Park has been in existence for at least 50 years. The part that we are concerned with is much more recent as an official public place but has been used without authority as a place for play by children for a very long time. This area was the south-eastern perimeter of the Finchley Golf Course and the end of the garden of the old house Rocklands.

Today there is a footpath some 4km long with the banks and surrounding green corridor, which includes a large pond. Taken with the part of Lovers' Walk from Frith Lane to Dollis Brook (which is now much more overgrown than it used to be) this represents an unusual wildlife corridor for a place so near to London. Unfortunately in many parts, over use by the public is causing some damage and conservation treatment may well be necessary.

The Brook itself does not contain very diverse flora (it is probably too fast flowing) but the pond is much more interesting in this respect. From the bridge in Lovers' Walk southwards to the viaduct over Dollis Road the footpath has been deliberately created and this corridor is well wooded. In the other direction an 'official' footpath now exists where the earlier one was made by children playing. This part also has good tree cover.

COPTHALL RAILWAY WALK

The Railway Walk is the section of the dismantled railway westwards from Mill Hill East Station but particularly from Sanders Lane to Page Street, and includes a small remnant of common land. The total area is 13ha.

The local school (Dollis Primary) has adopted part of the railway cutting and fixed nesting boxes to some trees. It is certainly hard to see when looking from the inside that this was ever a railway, but there are tell tale signs if you know what to look for (see also Lyndhurst Park).

From the outside it is a little more obvious, and the track looks like many others up and down the Country by the way that it follows the contours of the land and divides fields.

It is surprising how many species of plants and trees have made their homes in these artificially produced corridors, particularly in view of the poor 'soil' where the tracks ran. Apart from the 'wild' flowers, others such as golden rod and michaelmas daisies can be found that are probably emigrants from private gardens. The list of tree and bush types is extensive with most common species represented, and to these we can now add the cultivated shrub buddleia which was only introduced from western China in 1864 and is already a native, and such an attraction for butterflies. These are mainly peacocks *Nymphalis io* when the blossoms first appear, changing to small tortoiseshells *Aglais urticae* in early September.

The piece of common land is at the north-east corner of Copthall playing fields and has many types of grass together with sallow and gorse.

CHAPTER XXXII

IN SICKNESS AND IN DEATH

From time to time anthropologists and historians set out to recreate a copy of a Stone Age settlement, a village of the Middle Ages, or some other prehistoric or ancient domestic unit and live there for a period to see how modern people could cope under such privations. Usually they manage fairly well, but it is never a fair comparison because firstly they have a far greater knowledge than the people who they are trying to emulate and secondly they know that if something goes terribly wrong or some member of the group falls dangerously sick they can immediately be back in the 20th Century and its civilisation for treatment.

LIFE IN EARLY TIMES

Had you lived in Mill Hill in the Middle Ages (or any other similar settlement for that matter) there was no escape to another age. You just had to put up with the horrific living conditions: poor food, non-existent sanitation, very hard working conditions, and extremely bad housing, if house is the correct word.

Many of the sicknesses which today are routine and regarded as not serious were killers in the Dark Ages, and indeed remained so right up to the 19th century. The simplest operation was accompanied by excruciating pain and frequently death from septicaemia; there were no anaesthetics (save being dead drunk) or antiseptics. Maternity was always a high risk and if the mother and baby survived the actual birth there was still only a slim chance that the child would get through the first year, let alone reach maturity.

In the Middle Ages, Mill Hill was just one tiny settlement (and hardly even a hamlet) of the nine that made up the Manor of Hendon. Apart from the comparative luxury of the Manor House we can assume that for all the other tenants which ever hamlet they lived in the conditions were the same, crude in the extreme.

In Mill Hill, most of the inhabitants, which would have been a maximum of 150, all lived around the main street. The houses, typical of the period, were poor in construction and content, and indescribably filthy. A few posts with wattle and the whole plastered over with mud or clay would have been the limit, and a roof of whatever was available with a hole left to let out the smoke. Sometimes there would have been an upper storey reached by a crude ladder and this would have been on the outside.

There were no windows or chimneys and the smoke from the constantly burning fire would have escaped as best it may. It is unlikely that we could live in such an atmosphere for more than a few minutes. Passive smoking had nothing on this. There were no washing or other toilet facilities whatsoever and the floor would have been just bare earth. The Greeks, Romans and other early civilisations lived in better conditions than this many, many centuries earlier.

Furniture in these dwellings would have been an absolute minimum and limited to what the occupants could make themselves, perhaps a crude table, somewhere to sleep (certainly not a bed), a few poles, and probably a bacon rack. Animals would wander in and out of the house.

In spite of the many disadvantages, as far as we know the people were reasonably happy, and once they had fulfilled their duties to the Lord of the Manor and the Church they had a certain measure of independence. In any case most of the time they would have been too tired to worry and they knew nothing better.

MUMMERS FROM A MS OF THE REIGN OF EDWARD III

Their local interest would have been limited to that which affected them: how much the Lord of the Manor expected from them in dues and labour and how much would be left over, and the local Court and its rulings. The church, which they would all be expected to attend, was in the centre of the Manor.

The cultivation system was based upon the rotation of crops with the three field system: first year wheat, second year beans, third year fallow. Each tenant would have had one or more strips in each field so that his total holding would have meant a great deal of trudging from one field to the next. There was also common pasture where all tenants could put out their goats to feed and there was pannage for pigs in the surrounding forest.

Root vegetables were unknown so it was impossible to keep animals alive through the winter, except those required for breeding. Pigs were slaughtered, salted or smoked, and cattle were slaughtered and salted. There was no fresh meat until late spring when the progeny of the few animals that had been kept had grown big enough to make slaughter economically worthwhile.

It is hard to imagine that there was much fun of any kind in their dreary lives. Much later on, in 1734, we know that there was a maypole at

Drivers' Hill, Mill Hill certainly had its mummers, and some kind of rural sports were held on The Ridgeway outside the King's Head inn as late as the 19th Century. It should be remembered also that many of these entertainments had serious origins and started out before Christianity as fertility rites or to ward off evil spirits or sickness.

SICKNESS AND DEATH

The absence of green vegetables affected the human population as well. Rickets was common amongst children and scurvy was always prevalent and was responsible for many deaths. Another disease that regularly killed large numbers was Sweating Sickness, but because this malady appears to have died out we do not know exactly what it was. There were six severe epidemics, each one having a high mortality rate with death occurring as quickly as three to 18 hours after the onset of symptoms. Some people regard the most likely source as dirt and filth (although dirt does not actually kill and the ruling classes seem to have been more prone to the disease) but the most likely source was an insect vector. The start of the disease resembled a severe attack of influenza or typhus.

Later on the Black Death and the Great Plague (which are other names for Bubonic Plague) greatly reduced the population yet again. Strangely, in spite of Hendon's close proximity to London it does not seem to have been as seriously afflicted during the Great Plague as many other places near to the Capital. The Black Death was brought to England early in 1348 by ship, and by the end of that summer it had spread over the whole Country. London escaped until the winter. If Hendon was relatively plague free the surrounding areas certainly were not. The Abbot of Westminster perished in the Rectory of Hampstead with 26 monks, and presumably many of the villagers died also. The Abbey of St Albans lost the Abbot and 46 monks, and the Manor of St Albans lost over 400 tenants and their families.

It is clear from records that Hendon was a place of refuge for people fleeing from the plague. With so many dead in the London area church promotions came quickly for those that were left. The Abbot was dead and the small band in The Rectory in Parson Street had the task of reorganizing the abbotless monastery.

Records show that during these times the number of deaths in Mill Hill did not increase. The people were isolated from the main areas of infection but those who lived in the places where the disease was rampant fled and took the disease with them. Perhaps the sanitation in Hendon was better than most for the times, the people were particularly vigilant, or just rather fortunate. The people died from many other diseases too, smallpox claimed 8% of every generation up to the 18th Century.

In these olden times little was known about the causes of disease and the ways that they are transmitted. With frightening frequency an outbreak became an epidemic leading to enormous loss of life. In due course it subsided only for the whole process to be repeated at a later date. Other serious afflictions such as tuberculosis (at that time called consumption) took its toll year after year.

In the 800 years prior to the Black Death there were epidemics of leprosy, smallpox, diphtheria, measles, influenza, as well as bubonic plague and sweating sickness, plus of course many lesser complaints.

Because the origins of disease were a mystery they were invented; something rose out of marshy places, it was the miasma, the evil eye, punishment for past wickedness, and so on. The fact that infection was by a living agent and the non-existent hygiene helped the spread was never thought of. Ironically Robert Hooke first described cells and their structure the year of the Great Plague, 1665, but did not realise that other types of cell transmitted many diseases. We had to wait for the later part of the 19th Century for Joseph Lister to found antiseptic surgery.

Many of the diseases that were prevalent in this country in the Middle Ages and beyond are now rarities here and when isolated cases are reported it is usually because someone back from a visit overseas has come home with the infection. We are normally only reminded of these diseases when we are given a list of necessary vaccinations before we visit some exotic place on holiday.

Whether or not there is any foundation in the tales of Robin Hood we will probably never be sure, he is the sort of popular legend in whom we like to believe, but if he did exist it is unlikely that he was a benefactor of anyone but himself. In the last tale he is supposed to have died because he was bled, a common 'cure' until relatively recently. For the rich and famous particularly, this was a 'cure all ills' treatment. Catherine the Great, Empress of Russia, was bled so many times it is a wonder that she did not die from anaemia. Today for some of the same problems we would probably give a blood transfusion!

This age of superstition in medicine changed little until the 18th Century. Then at last the cases of premature death began to decline, in particular infant mortality. A serious hiccup occurred at this time, the cheap gin era. It lasted for little more than 30 years but in that period starting about 1720 it reduced the population of the capital severely with burials in the London region being twice that of the Baptisms. An *Act* of 1751 dramatically reduced the amount of spirits drinking and the death rate fell from one in 20 in 1750 to one in 40 in 1821. At a time when the population had doubled, deaths had remained constant, and apart from alcoholism the death rate fell steadily from 1730 onwards.

Medicine was at last becoming more scientific and for most people the conditions of life were improving. The great advances in food production meant that most had a better diet and changes in method led to higher wages so that the goods available were more likely to be within the reach of the ordinary people. The barber-surgeon was replaced by a specialist and the practice of midwifery was taken away from the well meaning local lady: proper training replaced the amateur.

In 25 years of the 18th Century most of London's major hospitals were built; Guys, London, Middlesex, St George's and Westminster. During the reign of Queen Anne the medieval hospital of St Thomas's had been rebuilt and St Bartholomews had become a major teaching establishment. And none of these were municipal undertakings, but came about by the initiative of individual people, their dedication and subscriptions.

It was still a long time before local authorities took a real interest in the health of the ordinary people. The people were certainly not immune to many of the complaints that cause distress today, and there were no regulations concerning who could serve food and how. The people of Hendon had to wait until 1881 for their first Medical Officer of Health and it was still only a part-time post.

Mill Hill has never had a hospital of its own, and had to wait until the 19th Century for hospitals in the vicinity. Today it is surrounded by a number of well established hospitals, many within the London Borough of Barnet. Amongst these are Barnet General (previously known as Wellhouse Hospital, and which is now due for redevelopment), Colindale Hospital (once the Central London Sick Asylum), the specialist hospital Royal National Orthopaedic Hospital on Brockley Hill Stanmore, and Edgware General Hospital. Some facilities have closed in recent years, or have been transferred elsewhere, and considerable complaint followed the decision to close the maternity section of Barnet General (Victoria Maternity) and merge this with the maternity section at Edgware General. The closure was unavoidable because the recruitment of sufficient qualified staff became impossible.

HEALTH TRENDS TODAY

The study of health and sickness today is more a case of the cause and its possible effects than ever before. We know which habits and substances are high risk and the types of work places that can lead to fatal disease, and therefore how to avoid them. Scientists have discovered that many of the so called hereditary diseases are caused by a tiny fault in a gene, and this is the first step in developing the cure. There will be proper treatment for the 'untreatable' and much misery, distress and suffering will be alleviated at last. Instead of tackling the symptoms we shall be treating the deficiency.

A rather sick young lady was recently found to be suffering from scurvy, a disease usually associated with ancient mariners and certainly not something we would expect to find in this Country today. It is caused by a diet deficient in Vitamin C. She never ate breakfast, usually bought a bag of crisps on the way to school and seldom ate fresh fruit and green vegetables never. Her diet seemed to consist of junk food and fizzy drinks. There must be many others who live perilously near to the same problem, something which can easily be totally avoided.

Perhaps the most significant development in the last three decades has been the scale of the involvement by the medical profession in both time and money with 'problems' that are not sickness, and in fact involve healthy men and women. We refer of course to contraception and abortion. Not everyone agrees with this trend, and it must be said that considering how many methods of contraception are available, abortion other than for pathological reasons (or when the pregnancy is a result of rape) should not be necessary. On the positive side an equal effort is being made with treatment for various reasons causing infertility.

We are now led to believe that in the near future there will be a contraceptive pill for men equal in performance to those currently used by women. One small problem remains; will women believe the men who say that they are 'on the pill'? The illogical fact is that many people have far greater scruples about genetic engineering (which is meant to ultimately relieve suffering) than they have about destroying a perfectly healthy foetus.

Then there is AIDS. The greatest scourge of the latter part of the 20th Century. Not long ago we thought that all the sexually transmitted diseases were now curable, no longer to be feared. Now we know different. The number of people found to be HIV Positive has been rising year by year and shows no real sign of levelling off. So far there is little hope for these unfortunate people.

MILL HILL: A HEALTHY PLACE?

In the chapter on estates mention was made of the advertising for the Mill

Hill Garden Village. This claimed that Mill Hill enjoyed a low death rate. Is Mill Hill still a healthy place? Figures published recently by the Director of Public Health for the Barnet Health Authority would appear to show that the residents of Mill Hill are less at risk from certain fatal diseases than many other parts of the Borough. The most notable diseases are ischaemic heart disease and cancer of the trachea, bronchus, and lungs, and this led to a newspaper headline 'The Rich are Better off'. The Standard Mortality Rate (a national average with the norm of 100) highlights the apparent risk areas: to be over 100 is bad.

It would be easy to misinterpret the figures and come to the conclusion that some areas in the Borough are inherently less healthy places to live than others. There are however adjacent areas with much lower mortality rates, so other causes must be responsible.

For the Borough as a whole the SMR is 93, comfortably inside the national figure. However the variation across the Borough from Brunswick Park in the east (the lowest) at 56.7 to Burnt Oak in the west (the highest) at 125.7 is very significant. Mill Hill, situated more or less in the middle was a very reasonable 77.6, and Hale between Burnt Oak and Mill Hill was 84.7. These figures are all for 1988. Other areas with figures over 100 were Woodhouse (102.8), West Hendon (104.6), and Colindale (110.8).

There does not appear to be any simple explanation for these wide variations without looking further. Normally we would associate an elevated SMR with poverty and deprivation, and in some parts of the UK those areas with large populations of ethnic minorities (recent arrivals living in crowded accommodation). It is not reasonable to accept that living in one ward of the Borough is much less healthy than the one next door. There has to be other contributing factors that cannot be directly influenced by the health services: housing, type of employment, income (and how it is spent), and most of all personal behaviour. Nevertheless the medical services do have a big part to play in education. The risks associated with smoking, alcohol abuse, drug and solvent abuse, casual sexual relationships, and inadequate diet with excessive fats and sugar are well known. They can all have an influence on life expectancy.

An important pattern emerges if we take the two diseases mentioned above and compare with the overall figures. The SMR (for people under 74) has been calculated to cover the three years 1986/8 for ischaemic heart disease and lung cancer. Burnt Oak is still at the top but Brunswick Park does not now feature quite so favourably.

The table is interesting. From the figures it becomes obvious that the most important factor is smoking and therefore much of the premature death can be avoided. The young particularly have to be convinced that they are at risk by even starting 'the habit' and that death from the diseases associated with smoking does not only happen to other people.

In the latest figures (by the Office of Population Censuses and Surveys) the number of smokers aged between 11 and 15 is given as 10% of the total in this group, and 25% of 15 year olds. The average consumption is 53 per week. In England and Scotland there is no difference between the sexes, but in Wales girls are more likely to be regular smokers than boys. It should come as no surprise to learn that the early smokers are also most unlikely to have ever been refused by a shopkeeper when they tried to make a purchase.

As a chemical compound nicotine does not have a particularly complex molecule but like many of the vegetable alkaloids it is exceedingly poisonous. In fact two or three drops taken orally can cause death in a few minutes. As a drug it is of course extremely addictive, probably more so than any other drug 'used' by mankind. Unfortunately because many people do not regard nicotine consumption in the same light as that of cocaine or heroin they do not accept tobacco usage as an addiction or regard smokers as drug addicts.

Tobacco was introduced into England by Hawkins in 1565 and quickly became popular. It was not long before some people realised that smoking leads to chest complaints, and even stunted growth was attributed to it. Certainly Charles Lamb (1775-1834) knew of its addictive powers when he wrote *Farewell to Tobacco* and the words;

> *For thy sake, tobacco, I*
> *Would do anything but die.*

AREAS	SMR	SMR/IHD	SMR/LC
Arkley	83.4	76.3	67.8
BrunswickPark	56.7	66.3	82.7
Burnt Oak	125.7	124.9	117.3
Childs Hill	79.7	57.3	91.0
Colindale	110.8	84.7	96.2
East Barnet	62.9	79.3	80.9
East Finchley	91.4	90.8	92.3
Edgware	97.5	83.1	89.4
Finchley	79.9	75.4	48.0
Friern Barnet	86.8	73.1	83.6
Garden Suburb	62.3	42.4	77.4
Golders Green	78.0	75.4	50.4
Hadley	62.8	57.9	62.4

Hale	84.7	62.3	81.1
Hendon	65.4	64.3	55.9
MILL HILL	77.6	46.5	73.9
St Paul's	79.0	87.3	41.6
Totteridge	64.2	63.5	94.5
West Hendon	104.6	86.2	117.6
Woodhouse	102.8	93.5	71.4

The North West Thames Regional Health Authority has been conducting a survey of the 3.5m residents in the area. The sample was 10,000 adults and some residents of Barnet were included in this. Preliminary analysis of the study reveal some interesting facts about ill-health, and health services, as well as what steps people take to improve their well being (or otherwise). Most residents in the area have access to good quality health services (and we would certainly include Mill Hill in this), although many only actually use these facilities when they require treatment.

Some of the findings are disturbing, but not surprising. A large proportion of all adults interviewed drink and smoke too much, and take far too little exercise. The life style of the unemployed and disabled is depressing, they tend to consume more alcohol and tobacco than the rest of the population, which probably contributes towards the fact that they suffer from more chronic illness.

Most of the people that drink felt that their consumption was reasonable, whereas the NWTRHA would regard many of these as heavy drinkers. No-one actually admitted to being a heavy drinker. Although 86% believed that smoking can damage people's health and 69% of smokers would like to give it up this does not apply to drinkers. Although 60% of drinkers agreed that alcohol can damage people's health very few would like to give it up completely.

The attitudes towards exercise are not surprising. Most people (58%) considered the amount of exercise that they took to be adequate to remain healthy, but 24% were not sure. Only 47% had taken any exercise during the last fortnight. The reasons for their apparent lack of energy were varied: a lack of facilities at work, no time, no money, no suitable transport, no-one to exercise with, and 2% do not intend to exercise at all.

In preventive medicine no surprises either. Over half (55%) were an acceptable weight, 28% were overweight, and 4% were obese. Quite a high percentage (8%) were underweight.

In the last year 57% of adults had been given a blood pressure check, and 63% of women had been for a smear test in the last five years. Most of the women who had not been tested declined to give a reason, but

2% said they had no time, and 5% gave their age as the reason. Of all those interviewed 7% had no natural teeth at all, 61% had visited a dentist in the last year, and 6% only do so when they have a problem.

One of the more disturbing statistics regarding the Borough's health is the number of incidents of poisoning by contaminated food, and the most common infection is by the organism *Salmonella*. It is hard to believe that there is anything new in this and it may well be that the population in earlier times developed a degree of immunity. Nevertheless most outbreaks are due to carelessness and could be avoided. Our ancestors certainly had other abdominal diseases to contend with, the most important being cholera, fortunately extremely rare in this country (visitors apart). Over the years 1988/90 the reported cases of intestinal diseases in Barnet numbered dysentery 75, hepatitis 66, typhoid and paratyphoid 18 and the inevitable 'food poisoning' 900.

Venereal disease has never held any respect for persons or positions. There are ample records of persons of influence that died from syphilis. When this disease became widespread in the early part of the 16th Century, control measures against prostitutes were introduced. Ibsen's play *Ghosts*, described by the playwright as 'extreme', was given a hostile reception in Scandinavia and violent reviews by London's critics. The subject of the play is the problems of inherited venereal disease, and considered by many to be unsuitable material for a play.

Fortunately after a cautious start AIDS is not having the same problem, and is getting considerable publicity which we hope will eventually lead to its defeat. However some of the unfortunate famous people that have died from the disease have caused raised eyebrows. Up to the end of March 1990 the cumulative total of people known to have AIDS in Barnet was 26, and of these 15 have died. The number of people in Barnet currently HIV positive is estimated at 200.

TOWARDS THE FUTURE

In the beginning of this book mention was made of changes in our atmosphere that will eventually affect everyone on this planet. The reduction in the ozone layer is a fact, and the so called 'greenhouse effect' may well be irreversible already. These may well introduce problems and diseases in their wake. Two important developments will be an increase in levels of ultra-violet radiation, and the elevation of the overall global temperature by up to 5%C in the next century.

An increase in the UVL levels could lead to increases in skin cancers and cataracts (not the geographical type), crop damage, and a cumulative destructive effect on the oceans' eco-systems. The main risk to us (in Northern Europe) by global warming would be widespread flooding and the introduction of diseases normally associated with the tropics or sub-tropics, such as malaria, denge fever, and spotted fever.

The Borough administration is taking an active stance with regard to 'Green' issues. Fuel conservation, destruction of waste with minimal pollution and proper use of the heat generated are all high on the agenda. The supplies department has to buy recycled goods, and purchase cardboard in preference to plastics wherever possible.

Is Mill Hill a healthy place? We think so, and we would like to keep it that way, but we are not an island and everything depends upon how the rest of the Country, the continent and indeed the World behaves.

POPULATION

In the times of *Domesday* the Manor of Hendon was nine hamlets of which Mill Hill was one. If we accept that the population of Mill Hill, was no more than 150, then the population of the Manor as a whole was probably about 1,500. When the London Borough of Barnet was set up the population was 316,000. In 1989 this had dropped slightly to 310,400.

We are often being reminded that we are becoming an ageing population. Certainly the life expectancy has improved century by century, although this cannot go on for ever. At the last count the Barnet residents aged 75 or more totalled 22,217 or 7.12%. The children under working age plus those at college or university made up 27%. If we assume that up to 50% of women do some kind of paid work (they probably do most of the house work too) then the working population is around 44%.

Of the population of 310,400 in 1989 48% were male and 52% were female. The breakdown by age was:

AGE GROUP	MALE	FEMALE
00-04	3.39%	3.24%
05-14	6.26%	5.92%
15-24	7.91%	7.19%
25-44	14.15%	15.48%
45-64	10.20%	10.51%
65-74	3.68%	4.69%
75-84	2.12%	3.66%

These figures are possibly much more even across the sexes than they would have been 100 years ago, or after a major war.

One last statistic (having said at the beginning of this book that they would be avoided), our mothers seem to be a fairly healthy lot if the weight of their babies at birth is anything to go by. The accepted desirable weight is 2.5kg (5½lb) and only 6.7% were under this weight at birth, against the National average of 6.8%.

THE FUNERAL

Today the main consideration for funerals is whether the deceased is to be buried or cremated, and various factors influence this decision. In country and rural areas people still prefer to bury their loved ones, but in the larger towns and cities the majority now opt for cremation. In earlier times people were more concerned with the 'quality' of the funeral and the fabric of the coffin linings and shroud.

There is nothing new about the 'protection' of a country's industry, and the imposition of legislation and controls to restrict imports is probably as old as trade itself. But the restriction is always one-way, to promote your own exports whilst preventing 'unnecessary' imports. Concern for the English wool trade had been expressed since the 14th Century and this came to a head in the period immediately after the Restoration. By this time there were already laws in existence that prohibited the import of cattle from Ireland (and administratively Ireland was supposed to have been a part of Britain) and corn from abroad. Although these measures did not take full effect until the early Hanoverian times it will not come as any surprise to learn that Parliament took steps to protect cloth manufacture as vigorously as corn growing.

Ironically the very laws that were being passed by the entirely male Houses of Parliament were being broken by their ladies. And because the clothes for men were to say the least, foppish, they also bent the laws.

In 1738 a law was passed which prohibited the use of silk for buttonholes: English serge had to be used. And people who wore French cambric or lawn in 1745 were fined. The East India Company was also strongly criticised because of the goods that it imported, particularly Indian muslins and silks. But these were in exchange for exported English manufactured goods. To be fashionable was a crime! The East India Company's imports had to be re-exported and not offered for sale in this Country. There was the usual claim frequently repeated over the centuries, cheap foreign labour would lead to unemployment at home, in reality it was the landlords who would suffer because without competition they were able to charge what they liked.

Today we can buy some very fine woollen fabrics, 250 years ago it was a different story and to dress everyone in wool only would have been as inspiring as the uniform of the Chinese under Chairman Mao. Even when it came to coffins the law still applied, only English wool cloth could be used for coffin linings and shrouds. But many people objected strongly enough to ignore the rule, they preferred to pay the resulting fine like a kind of tax and then to bury their relations in what they considered to be a worthy manner. The actual wording of the prohibition is very precise and could leave little doubt as to its intent:

'No person whatsoever should be buried in any shirt, shift or sheet made of or mingled with flax, hemp, silk, hair, gold or silver, or other than should be made of wool only; or be put into a coffin lined or faced of anything made of or mingled with, flax, hemp, silk or hair upon pain of the forfeiture of the sum of five pounds'.

An account in the reign of George III stated that up to that time people had been uniformly buried in wool. There is ample evidence to prove that many people were not buried in anything of the sort. In the Hendon churchwarden's account for 1693 there is an entry of £2 10s distributed to the poor of the Parish for the burial of Mrs Eliza Nicoll in linen, the other £ 2 10s going to the informer. Obviously the Nicoll family did not like to bury their members in the coarse flannel of the day. Is it surprising that with such stupid restrictions the smugglers and the highwaymen became heroes and almost legitimate traders, at least in the sympathies of the people?

CHAPTER XXXIII

SOME MORE SOCIAL HISTORY

This final chapter is about people and trends. The births, marriages and the population, work and workless, and the records that we keep. History yes, but the future too, a continuing process. They are all unpredictable facts and this is why they are so interesting for all of us, the ordinary people as well as sociologists, planners, and historians. Although Mill Hill will probably not change much in outward appearance its content will always be in a constant state of flux. The size and type of family unit, educational needs, public transport, and how we look after our retired folk (just to mention a few) will all develop or decline according to the needs and aspirations of the people.

POPULATION

Changes in population give the best guide to the development (or decline) of a living unit, be it a town or a village, or in this case a manor. The population at Hendon had slowly increased from the time of the Norman invasion and in 1700 stood at 1,900. In the next 100 years it rose to 1,955, an increase of less than 3%. But times were changing and ten years later the population had risen to 2,589, which represents an increase of over 30%, and although the Industrial Revolution was concentrating the population in towns this could not have affected Hendon, which was in many respects backward and never experienced any real changes until the arrival of the railways in the 19th Century.

By this time some speculative building works had led to further increases in population and by 1851 the numbers had increased to 3,333 which had more than doubled to 6,792 only 20 years later. The increases in Hendon continued throughout the 19th Century with any available land being taken up for housing. In 1801 there were 358 inhabited houses occupied by a total of 1,955 persons, the figures for 1887 were 2,296 and 13,295 respectively. Most of this new housing was on the southern part of the Manor in the Cricklewood area, and Mill Hill was hardly affected at all. This was to happen later, after 1900, when four new housing estates were built within 2km of Mill Hill Broadway Station.

By the time that the London Borough of Barnet was created in 1965 the likelihood of any further large scale housing developments was almost nil. Most land had been taken up where permission would be granted. Even with the large built up areas near to Mill Hill Broadway,

Mill Hill was still the least densely populated of the Borough. Compare Mill Hill at 22 per ha with Childs Hill at 64 and Burnt Oak at 84.

We are frequently told today that the number of couples that marry is declining, and at the present rate there will be almost no marriages at all before long. This is almost certainly nonsense because you cannot draw a simple straight line graph for such predictions. There will always be peaks and troughs just as there are with births. It is true however that with the number of children born out of wedlock exceeding one third in some areas this figure could eventually exceed those born to married couples.

A small number of marriages in any one year is nothing new. In the Hendon district for the early 18th Century the number of marriages must have been at an all time low. The records for the years 1728 to 1744 show that the average was only 10 per year and in 1736 there were only six. The first conclusion is that the vicar just did not get round to entering the rest, but this cannot be so because in the blank months it says quite clearly 'none married' and this is signed by the vicar. There is no obvious reason for this local reluctance to walk up the aisle except perhaps some underlying stress of the times which is certainly not apparent from the history books.

TIME FOR TIME

The innocent and the beautiful
Have no enemy but time

W B Yeats

It is difficult to appreciate today (when everything that we do is dominated by time) how remote other towns were from the Capital, and even more from each other, only 150 years ago. The journey by coach was long and transport by canal even longer. Time was by days and hours, minutes hardly mattered at all for most people for much of the time (the clock of St Margaret's Westminster has never had a minute hand). The coming of the railways was to change all this: it was not possible to run a railway without an accurate time-table. Major towns had their own time, there was no standard British time, so that Manchester time for instance was nine minutes behind London time. The correct calculation is four minutes for every degree of longitude.

A standard time had become essential and when Greenwich Mean Time was introduced all other places agreed to adjust their clocks accordingly, not all without protest. Obviously the introduction of a national time would have come about in due course anyway but the advent of the railways certainly advanced the date.

WOMEN'S WORK

When Cardinal Wolsey travelled through Mill Hill on his way to the Diocese of York he went with an escort of 600 gentlemen and servants (of course the servants were not all female), and it took 12 carts to carry the baggage. Prior to this journey Wolsey had been very concerned because the number of his servants had been reduced by the King as a way of informing others of influence that Wolsey's status and prestige were in question. The number of servants that people were permitted to have at these exulted ranks was limited by the sovereign.

The people of Mill Hill were only controlled by what they could afford, but no doubt personal aggrandisement was an influence too. An analysis of servants in Mill Hill towards the end of the 19th Century is interesting. We know about their ages and what they did, but unfortunately we do not know what they were paid in wages.

SERVANTS PER HOUSEHOLD

SERVANTS	1	2	3	4	5	6	7	8	13*
HOMES	25	8	6	5	0	3	2	1	2

*INSTITUTIONS

SERVANTS BY AGE

SERVANTS	4	51	58	28	11	11	1
AGES	<15	15-20	21-31	31-40	41-50	51-60	>60

SERVANTS BY OCCUPATION

General Domestic	House-maid	Cook	Nurse & Nursemaid	Coachman & Groom	Matron H'se-k'per
60	29	22	16	9	7

Boy	Governess	Indoor Manservant	Kitchen-maid	Parlourmaid
5	4	3	3	2

Lady's maid	Laundrymaid
2	2

The demands of the never ending battles of World War I changed forever the position of women in society. For the first time their skills in manufacture (of war materials) and the inevitable financial independence that resulted lifted them away from being mere servants. Whereas prior to 1914 it was considered a good opportunity for a young girl in the country districts to get a job in the 'Big House' or as a domestic in town, four years later servants and maids had become as precious as gold dust. In fact it had come to be considered almost degrading to do such work.

This freedom coincided with the invention and development of the typewriter (as first applied this name referred to the operator not the machine) and from now on there would be an increasing number of female staff working in offices. We are now nearly at the end of the 20th Century, not the beginning, and in many work areas we are still a long way from equality of opportunity for the sexes.

When the author's mother came to London in 1914 to go into service in Dulwich she was 18. This was quite old by the standards of the time. Not so a young girl named Miriam Carter, she came to Mill Hill to work at Hendon Park (the mansion that was once owned by William Wilberforce, now demolished) also in 1914 but at the tender age of 14. Apparently as well as her other more onerous duties this youngster had to carry the household washing to a convent in Lawrence Street every week and carry it back freshly laundered. On Sundays all the servants had to walk together to St Paul's Church on The Ridgeway for morning service.

There is no record of the starting wage, but after promotion to parlour maid Miriam's pay was increased to £10pa all found, which was still unattractive. Later she obtained employment at Highwood House because her sister worked there and the conditions were better.

To have run a house without servants would have been unthinkable. It is hard to see however how some of the households managed to support all these extra people on the modest incomes that they received, even accepting that the servant's pay was anything but generous. Lady Raffles for instance employed a staff of eight plus coachmen, which is as many as the household. In Highwood Ash opposite, the owner (the incumbent of St Paul's Church) had a staff of six, but then he did have 10 young children.

It is easy to be critical now, but in many ways and with some employers they were comparatively well off. What little they earned was their own, and they never had to worry about what and where they would eat or where they would sleep. Their accommodation and food was frequently better than the homes that they had left, but they would have needed to be, servants worked very hard and for exceedingly long hours. Edward VII once complained that without the alcoholic beverages and the sport staying in country houses would be unbearable, the houses were never warm and by the time that the food was served it was always stone cold. At least the servants got hot food, they ate in the kitchen.

There was a loose promotion structure so that kitchen maids and under nurses would have been 13-14, then housemaids a little older, say 15-16, cooks older still, and so on. And the most benevolent mistresses would even keep on their staff after retirement as an act of charity.

It is only in the last decade or so that 'housewife' has ceased to be a valid description of a woman's work. It has taken nearly 200 years of Income Tax for women to be accepted as responsible citizens and to be permitted to keep the details of their income to themselves.

Looking back 150 years, and certainly up to World War I, it is difficult to find any records of women in regular employment (from census returns). We know that the wives of the lower paid workers (general labourers, farm workers, etc.) took on extra work as a necessity, but this would have been limited to laundry work, charring, and similar menial tasks. The exceptions would usually have been widows or spinsters and some of these were actually recorded as having a trade. There were instances of baker, shop-keeper, licensee (possibly Nan Clark), but in the main the work was that which was traditionally done by women: making lace, hats and bonnets, corsets and stays, and dresses.

LOCAL RECORDS

The landed and historic families of Britain can usually trace their ancestry back through many centuries without recourse to parish registers or other official documentation. For other people it is a long and time consuming process, particularly for those with common names. In 1653, during the Commonwealth period an Act of Parliament was passed which decreed that every parish should keep a register of births, marriages and deaths. The only registers to remain the concern of the churches were those for baptisms and confirmations.

The available registers for Hendon commence at this time. The burial records 1653-1812 however are numbered III, IV, V so we must assume that there were records before the act was passed.

The vicar at the time of the execution of Charles I was Thomas Peake but he was deposed and Francis Wareham was appointed by Parliament. At the Restoration, in common with many priests installed during the Commonwealth he was forced to leave. The missing registers may well have been taken by Peake or hidden by him, in any case they have never been found. Peake did not regain his incumbency when

Wareham left and he was offered the position of rector of Much Hadham.

The historian E T Evans considered that this could be a clue as to the whereabouts of the missing records and arranged for a search to be carried out by the rector of the time (c1890). This was unsuccessful and we must assume that the missing records were just lost, destroyed by the Parliamentarians or even by Peake himself when he knew that he was not going back to Mill Hill.

Unfortunately during periods of national instability such as the Dissolution, the Reformation, and the Commonwealth, many records were deliberately 'lost' or destroyed. The resultant gaps in the records are very unfortunate because there is no way to replace the missing information.

The *Act* of 1653 was inadequate insofar as it detailed the information that had to be recorded but did not lay down precisely how and where the documents had to be stored. A further act was passed in 1813 which strengthened the regulations concerning the collection and the custody of parish records. Since the middle of the 19th Century the Public Record Office (formerly Somerset House) has kept a full and permanent record of all births, marriages and deaths from information supplied to them by district registrars.

The marriage registers for Hendon are also incomplete and although these commence in 1654 the first one contains information for the previous year, and as the first two volumes are numbered VI and VII five volumes have disappeared. No doubt at the same time and in the same way as those for burials. It is hard to imagine what possible use the registers would be to anyone outside Hendon, or for that matter why anyone would want to destroy them.

With the local registrar now responsible for the registration of births, marriages and deaths the local authority maintains statistics of a different kind. The official archives and various other departments store the information necessary to enable predictions to be made about future needs for nursery places and schools, libraries and sports facilities, sewage and drainage, and all the infrastructure of a modern society.

When immigrant families arrive at our shores from some overseas countries they cause confusion for the various authorities with their names: they do not have first names and surnames like we do. There is no family name as such. We are so accustomed to this method of identity that we tend to assume that it has always been so. It is in fact comparatively recent. Watt Tyler was of course Watt the Tyler and the Mill Hill entrepreneur John at Hegge merely tells us where he lived. Only in the towns did the family names develop early on. Today we have lots of names to remind us of the occupations of our forebears: Brewer,

Cooper, Fletcher, Smith, Tyler, Fuller and many more, Others give the locations where they lived: Beech, Hedges, Marsh, Oak (the author's name), Woods, etc.

In that strange (and unnecessary) framework called *Master Humphrey's Clock* used by Charles Dickens to set his novels *The Old Curiosity Shop* and *Barnaby Rudge* we find 'Jack Redburn - he was Jack Redburn at the first little school he went to where every other child was mastered and surnamed'. This was written in 1840/41. Clearly at that time the adoption of surnames was not complete.

An analysis of the birth announcements in daily newspapers shows that in spite of the use today of many new names the old faithfuls still take pride of place at the top: John, Peter, Michael, David, Paul etc. for the boys and Jane, Sarah, Mary, Anne for the girls. How many parents even realise that all the names have meanings (sometimes inappropriate ones) and that the new popular names are often just corruptions of much older ones, for instance Tracey = Theresa, Garry = Gareth, Mandy = Amanda, Rex = Eric and so on. Although the 19th Century is notable for the introduction of flower names (Hazel, Rosemary, Heather etc.) and words implying abstract virtues (Patience and Prudence) the records for Mill Hill show that at the end of the 19th Century they were not really common at all. The girls names registered in 1881 for instance were:

Elizabeth 38	Mary 38	Sarah 19
Jane 19	Emily 19	Mary Ann 15
Martha 10	Margaret 2	

POOR RELIEF

Although many people will doubtless say otherwise, there is today really no need to starve. There are organisations both government and on a local level that should give aid to the needy. Of course all this will never eradicate poverty and some folk will be thrifty and others will always live from crisis to crisis. Worse still are those who will not claim out of false pride, or claim and keep the allowances and live in squalor and even die from malnutrition. The idea of poor relief being a central government responsibility is a fairly recent development and in times gone by it was always a parish duty. Certainly there was help from one parish to another and in some cases these were quite a way apart, even in different towns.

According to the record books the number of people receiving alms (if only occasionally) at the end of the 17th Century was over 1 million, or nearly 20% of the population. This was mostly paid by the parishes.

The *Poor Rate* cost the Country £800,000 per year and rose to £1m during the reign of Queen Anne. There is no evidence that the recipients felt any shame in seeking help, and indeed why should they. Nevertheless there were complaints that the allowances were often so high that once people had accepted alms they never worked again, a complaint still heard about unemployment pay with supplementary benefits today.

The *Act of Settlement* was passed in 1662, partly because of the level of alms payments and also to restrain possible revolutionaries. By this Act any parish in which a person tried to settle could send them back to their native parish in case some time in the future they might become a burden on the local rates. This meant that 90% of the population (all except the large landowners) were at risk of being expelled from any parish except their own no matter how good their character, or how long and how reliably they had worked. For no crime save that of residence they were liable to summary arrest. It was as big an outrage as the notorious press gang.

To give an appearance of fair play no persons could be sent away until they had been 'examined' by two magistrates who would then issue the order. Needless to say there many of these evictions from Hendon. The whole procedure was frequently a farce because the parishes to which the poor unfortunates were sent often refused to accept them, so they became homeless. And local authorities spent great sums of money in serving the orders, finding out the origins of the people, and transporting them. Isaac Messeder, mentioned in the chapter on maps was examined in 1767.

Setting aside the wickedness of the Act much good was done by local alms, and a look through the records of Hendon is typical of any parish in any manor. There is a succession of entries which to us seem trivial but which were no doubt in some cases a matter of life and death to those involved. There are entries for coffins (at six shillings each) supplied to some desperate widows, burials (at eight shillings each), shoe repairs, placing children, usually orphans, into apprenticeships, financial help to nursing mothers, payment for rent arrears and so on.

Perhaps in a way this was a better system than that of today, after all the Manor was a unit where everyone was known and so were the claimants' problems. Today we have a faceless administrator sitting at a desk behind a security grill who is totally unfamiliar with the people who need assistance and who may not be very interested in their problems. Indeed it is quite likely that he or she knows little or nothing about the local community or the kind of people who live there.

For those who required residential care (orphans, the aged, and the infirm) there was the workhouse, one was near Ridgeway House and is mentioned in documents dated 1712. Unfortunately in many cases the inmates were treated more like criminals. It was probably closed when larger premises were opened at The Burroughs in 1735, in gardens adjoining six cottages already in use. These survived until 1934. The Parish also owned a house at Highwood Hill and another at The Hale which they eventually sold in 1837.

At the end of the 18th Century more concerted efforts were made with outdoor relief and in 1800 bread was distributed in Hendon according to the size of the family. In the short time that he lived in Highwood House Raffles commented that the local poor were not properly checked by any competent authority and were generally in a degraded state.

The people of Hendon are on record as being generous when it came to helping the poor. For instance official records give the amounts collected in the years 1813, 1814 and 1815 as £1,753, £1,760, and £1803. Modest by the standards of today, but this was 175 years ago. In 1887 this had risen to £3,771 but the population had risen sevenfold! It would seem that the new residents were less willing to part with their money. To return to the three years mentioned above we find that the average number of persons who received *Poor Relief* was 60. In addition there were 23 in the workhouse and 33 on average receiving occasional relief.

EPILOGUE

Three years and much reading, walking, and hard work have gone into the writing of this history. Whether it is too detailed (or not detailed enough), or whether it digresses too much will have to be decided by the reader. Certainly from the author's point of view it has been a source of fascination and very much worthwhile. If the whole exercise has become a bore for the family and close friends of the author at least they have been too polite to say so.

Perhaps with luck the book will inspire a few of the 'locals', and even some of those from outside the immediate vicinity, to discover what was there all along, if so then it has been a success. In this only time will tell. And for the children of Mill Hill and the seemingly endless school 'projects' maybe this book will sometimes help them too.

Unfortunately not everyone is interested in local history. In the course of researching for this book dozens of letters have been written to individuals, commercial undertakings, and official bodies. Of these about a quarter never bothered to reply, which of course added to the problems of gathering and checking information.

Nevertheless there is more interest in local history and the environment than ever before and perhaps this will lead to a greater awareness of our own little bit of the Country and what it means to the whole. Mill Hill is in many parts still largely unspoilt, and has much open space which should be the envy of the more built-up boroughs. Let us keep it that way. Perhaps it is best summed up by Byron, writing on another hill (and not very far away).

Lines Written Beneath an Elm in the Churchyard of Harrow

> *Spot of my youth! whose hoary branches sigh,*
> *Swept by the breeze that fans thy cloudless sky;*
> *Where now alone I muse, who oft have trod,*
> *With those I loved, thy soft and verdant sod;*
> *With those who, scatter'd far, perchance deplore,*
> *Like me, the happy scenes they knew before;*
> *Oh! as I trace again thy winding hill,*
> *Mine eyes admire, my heart adores thee still,*
> *Thou drooping elm! beneath whose boughs I lay,*
> *And frequent mused the twilight hours away;*
> *Where, as they once were wont, my limbs recline,*

But ah! without the thoughts which then were mine:
How do thy branches, moaning to the blast,
Invite the bosom to recall the past,
And seem to whisper, as they gently swell,
'Take, while thou canst, a lingering, last farewell!'
When fate shall chill, at length, this fever'd breast,
And calms its cares and and passions into rest,
Oft have I thought, 'twould soothe my dying hour,-
If aught may soothe when life resigns her power,-
To know some humble grave, some narrow cell,
Would hide my bosom where it loved to dwell.
With this fond dream, methinks, 'twere sweet to die-
And here it linger'd, here my heart might lie;
Here might I sleep where all my hopes arose;
Scene of my youth, and couch of my repose;
For ever stretch'd beneath this mantling shade,
Press'd by the turf where once my childhood play'd;
Wrapt by the soil that veils the spot I loved,
Mix'd with the earth o'er which my footsteps moved;
Blest by the tongues that charmed my youthful ear,
Mourn'd by the few my soul acknowledged here,
Deplored by those in early days allied,
And unremember'd by the world beside.

In past years many writers have contributed to our knowledge of the locality that we call Mill Hill with books, pamphlets, and newspaper articles. Unfortunately there is no comprehensive list of these so in writing this book something quite important may well have been missed. Unfortunately too, these writings frequently contradict each other so arriving at the 'truth' is sometimes impossible with any degree of certainty.

No doubt there are knowledgeable people in Mill Hill or who have lived there in the past who will be able to tell the author where he went wrong and all those important events and places that have been omitted. Unfortunately a book of this kind is only a record of what one person has found or observed, or as said in the *Introduction* an anthology of that which appealed to the author. And that is why it is titled 'A History' not 'The History'.

MAPS

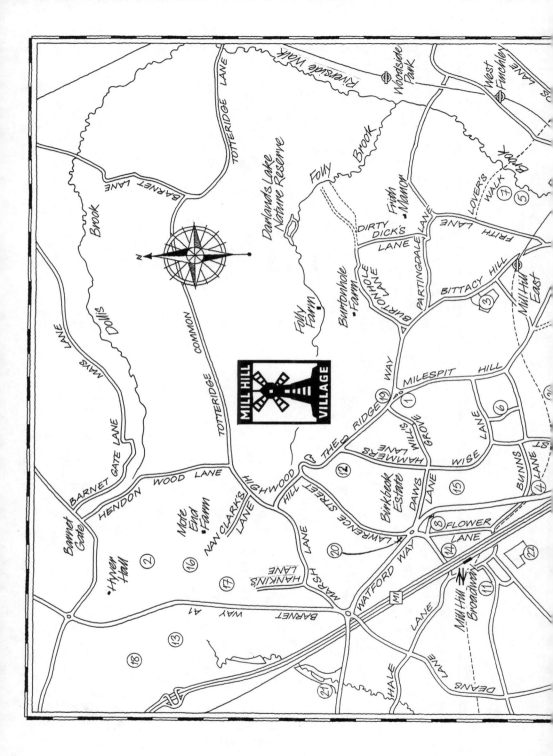

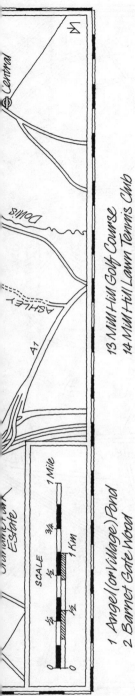

1 Angel (or Village) Pond
2 Barnet Gate Wood
3 Bittacy Hill Park
4 Burns Bridge
5 Brookside Walk
6 Featherstone Hill
7 Finchley Golf Club
8 Hartley Avenue
9 Hendon Golf Course
10 Hendon Park Cemetery & Crematorium
11 Lynchurst Park
12 Mill Field
13 Mill Hill Golf Course
14 Mill Hill Lawn Tennis Club
15 Mill Hill Park
16 Moat Mount Open Space
17 Nut Wood
18 Scratchwood
19 Sheepwash Pond
20 Simmons Mead
21 Stoneyfields Park
22 Woodcroft Park
23 Viaduct
24 Track of dismantled Railway

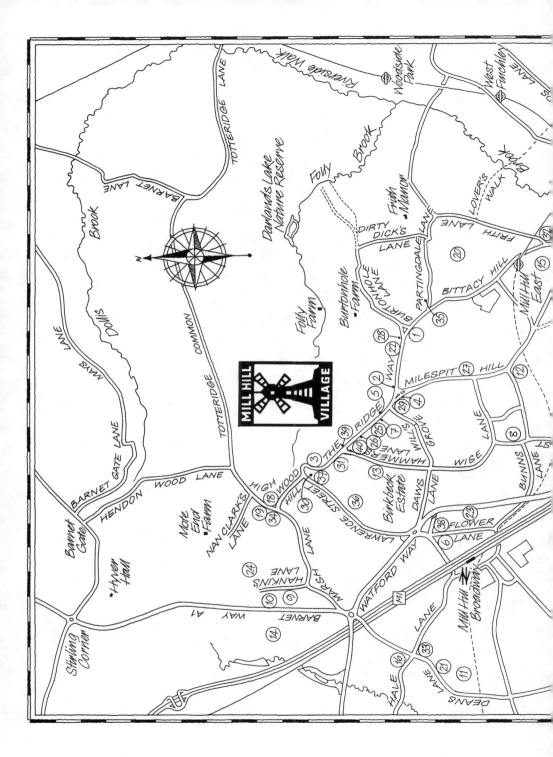

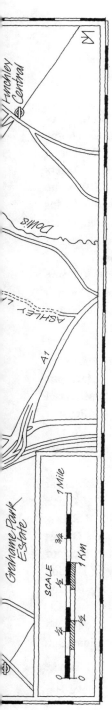

1 Adam and Eve Inn
2 Angel and Crown Inn (site of)
3 Belmont House
4 Blenheim Steps
5 The Bungalow
6 Church of the Sacred Heart
7 Collinson's Gate
8 Copthall Girls School
9 Courtland JMI School
10 Coventry Farm House
11 Deansbrook Elementary School
12 Dollis Infant & Junior School
13 Drapers Cottage Homes
14 Fairway JMI School
15 Gas Works
16 The Green Man
17 Hasmonean Girls High School
18 Highwood Ash
19 Highwood House
20 Inglis Barracks

21 John Keeble Church
22 Littleberries
23 London University Observatory
24 Mill Hill County High School
25 Mill Hill School
26 War Memorial
27 The Mount Independent Girls School
28 National Institute for Medical Research
29 Nicoll Almshouses
30 The Old Forge
31 Post Office Cottage
32 The Railway Engineer
33 The Railway Tavern
34 The Rising Sun Inn
35 Rosebank Cottage
36 St Joseph's Missionary College
37 St Mary's Abbey
38 St Michael & all Angels Church
39 St Paul's Church and School
40 Three Hammers Public House

BIBLIOGRAPHY

The Story of Mill Hill Village	Norman G Brett James
Handbook for the Environments of London	James Thorne
Paper 'How Mill Hill got its Name'	D G Denoon
The Blue Plaque Guide to London	Caroline Dakers
Regional History of the Railways of Great Britain	H P White
The History & Topography of the Parish of Hendon	Edward T Evans
Mill Hill (The story of Mill Hill School)	Norman G Brett James
Middlesex	Bruce Stevenson
The Middlesex Regiment	Gregory Bloxland
The Middlesex Regiment	Lt Cmdr P K Kemp
A History of Hendon	John Hopkins
The Oxford History of England	Various
Cooke's Survey of 1796	
Wishaw's Survey 1828	
Semi-detached London	Alan A Jackson
Who was Who	Harriman
Middlesex	A R H Moncrief
The Buildings of England	Nikolaus Peusner
National Institute for Medical Research	Various
Hendon & District Archeaological Society	Various Newsletters
Encyclopaedia Brittanica 9th & 15th Editions	
London's Underground Stations	Laurence Menear
The London Motor Bus	J G Bruce, C H Curtis
The Story of the London Bus	J R Day
A Social History of England	Asa Briggs
British Intelligence in the Second World War	Michael Howard
A History of the County of Middlesex Vol V	University of London
Hendon Electricity Supply Company	Roy Bourne
A Nature Conservation Strategy for London	GLC
Laing	Roy Coad
Barnet: A Picture of Health	Dr Fiona Sim
Annals of Westminster Abbey	E T Bradley
The Story of Westminster Abbey	Violet Brooke-Hart

GENERAL INDEX